SENSE OF ORIGINS

SUNY SERIES IN ITALIAN/AMERICAN CULTURE
Edited by Fred L. Gardaphe

SENSE OF ORIGINS

A STUDY OF NEW YORK'S YOUNG ITALIAN AMERICANS

ROSEMARY SERRA

Translated by Scott R. Kapuscinski

Cover art: *Mid-Manhattan Winter Night* by artist William Papaleo, oil on canvas, 20 by 28 Inches. Courtesy William Papaleo.

Published by State University of New York Press, Albany

© 2020 State University of New York Press
All rights reserved

No part of this book may be used or reproduced in any manner whatsoever without written permission. No part of this book may be stored in a retrieval system or transmitted in any form or by any means including electronic, electrostatic, magnetic tape, mechanical, photocopying, recording, or otherwise without the prior permission in writing of the publisher.

For information, contact State University of New York Press, Albany, NY
www.sunypress.edu

LIBRARY OF CONGRESS CATALOGING-IN-PUBLICATION DATA

Names: Serra, Rosemary, author. | Kapuscinski, Scott R., 1987- translator.
Title: Sense of origins : a study of New York's young Italian Americans / Rosemary Serra ; Scott R. Kapuscinski, translator.
Other titles: Senso delle origini. English
Description: Albany : State University of New York Press, 2020. | Series: Suny series in Italian/American culture | Includes bibliographical references and index.
Identifiers: LCCN 2020000960 (print) | LCCN 2020000961 (ebook) | ISBN 9781438479194 (hardcover) | ISBN 9781438479200 (ebook) | ISBN 9781438479187 (paperback)
Subjects: LCSH: Italian Americans—New York (State)—New York—Ethnic identity. | Italian Americans—New York (State)—New York—Social conditions—21st century. | Italian Americans—New York (State)—New York—Attitudes. | Youth—New York (State)—New York—Social conditions—21st century. | Youth—New York (State)—New York—Attitudes. | Ethnicity—New York (State)—New York. | New York (N.Y.)—Ethnic relations.
Classification: LCC F128.9.I8 S4713 2020 (print) | LCC F128.9.I8 (ebook) | DDC 305.8009747—dc23
LC record available at https://lccn.loc.gov/2020000960
LC ebook record available at https://lccn.loc.gov/2020000961

10 9 8 7 6 5 4 3 2 1

Dejen tranquilos a los que nacen.
Dejen sitio para que vivan.
No les tengan todo pensado,
no les lean el mismo libro,
dejen los descubrir la aurora,
y poner le nombre a sus besos.

Leave the newborn in peace
Leave room for them to live
Don't think for them
Don't read them the same books
Let them discover the sunrise
And name their own kisses

—PABLO NERUDA, *Estravagario*

CONTENTS

ix FOREWORD *Jerome Krase, Professor Emeritus*
xiii ACKNOWLEDGMENTS
1 INTRODUCTION

PART I: FIELD RESEARCH

11 CHAPTER ONE
Theoretical Structure, Methodological Path, Description of the Sample

23 CHAPTER TWO
Values, Family, and Primary Socialization

43 CHAPTER THREE
Ethnic Identification

77 CHAPTER FOUR
Different Identity Models of Young Italian Americans: The Significance of Being Italian American Today

109 CHAPTER FIVE
The Image of Italian Americans

125 CHAPTER SIX
Italy and the Italians

149 CHAPTER SEVEN
The Stereotypical Images of Italian Americans

187 CHAPTER EIGHT
Attitudes and Affiliations

217 CHAPTER NINE
The Future

237 CHAPTER TEN
Knowledge of and Attachment to the Italian and Italian American Cultures

PART II: IDENTITY PROFILES

247 CHAPTER ELEVEN
The American Identity in Generational Flux

279 CHAPTER TWELVE
Profiles of Young Italian Americans: Sketches in Chiaroscuro

311 CONCLUDING REFLECTIONS
331 NOTES
341 BIBLIOGRAPHY
355 INDEX

FOREWORD

Like Rosemary Serra, my own interest and even more so my involvement as an activist-scholar, in Americans of various generations of Italian descent has grown over a very long period of time. As opposed to her natural and deeply-felt personal Italian roots that connect her to the subject of her research, I did not discover my own shallow half-Italian (rather Sicilian) roots until I was about twenty years old. This is not a random reflection on my putative ethnic origins. My distinguished old friend Rudolph Vecoli, (1927–2008) would consider that Dr. Serra was one of the millions of firmly rooted (racinated), although hyphenated, Americans. On the other hand, I would clearly fit the bill of being one of the uprooted (deracinated) by the premier scholar of turn of the twentieth century American immigration, and fellow Brooklyn-born, Oscar Handlin. Handlin's *The Uprooted: The Epic Story of the Great Migrations That Made the American People* (1951) is considered by many in the field of immigration as the father of modern immigration studies. Vecoli passionately criticized Handlin's thesis, which overemphasized the willingness of America's immigrants, especially those of the Italian kind, to assimilate in his *Contadini in Chicago: A Critique of The Uprooted* (Mississippi Valley Historical Association, 1964). He went even further in his criticism of this widely accepted misinterpretation in an essay with the provocative title "Are Italian Americans Just White Folks?" (1995). Dr. Serra's *Sense of Origins*, without directly wrapping it around Vecoli's thesis, is a major confirmation that, in fact, Italian Americans are not "just" anything.

My pioneering studies of Italian American students at Brooklyn College (1975, 1978, 1986) came about because of my commitment, not to my yet unrecognized co-ethnics, as I did not yet see them in that light, but because, like other minorities in the CUNY system, they were not understood and therefore suffered academically because their needs were neglected. Had Dr. Serra conducted this research at that time (1975), I am sure their needs would have been better met than was the response to my limited study. My limited survey research, introduced by Vincent J. Fuccillo, who at the time was director of the Center for Italian American Studies at Brooklyn College, led, not coincidentally, to the establishment of the Institute to Foster Higher Education that was the precursor of the John D. Calandra Italian American Institute, which greatly facilitated Dr. Serra's later, more expansive work. The major finding of my work was that Italian American students of all immigrant generations did not feel at home at Brooklyn College.

Given the guaranteed praise that Dr. Serra will receive for her work, I am more than pleased that she included my own, more limited discussions of Italian Americana as to changes in the community leading to the obsolescence of simple notions of "Italian-ness" (Krase, 2004, p. 136). One might have simply assumed this, since, as she notes:

> Between 1870 and 1970, approximately twenty-six million people left their ancestral home to work abroad; many of them ultimately returned to Italy. From 1876 to 1914, one-third of the fourteen million Italian migrants reached North America (primarily the United States) and another one-fourth arrived in South America (especially Argentina and Brazil). (Gabaccia, 2003)

Today there are sixty million descendants of Italian ancestry living outside Italy, and two-thirds of this diaspora live in the Americas.

Dr. Serra honors me as well with reference to my argument as to the powerful impact of real and imagined Little Italies on the simple and often damaging representations of Italians in American society. Over the years of her research I have had the pleasure to meet and intensely discuss her work at various stages of development. I know I learned a great deal from her and was always impressed by her intelligence, and exceptional diligence, during her difficult labor of love as well as scholarship. Dr. Serra was also far better prepared than most scholars, including myself, for this extremely detailed, in-depth, almost exhaustive multimethod study of a segment of Italian Americans. As to research design, I am sure she will be lauded for a project that includes an excellent review of the multidisciplinary literature on Italian Americans and the careful employment of a wide variety of qualitative as well as quantitative methods. In my opinion, multi-methodology is an approach that is required in order to see the multifaceted phenomenon of adjustment of immigrants as they variously struggle, for example, to "make it" in America, or simply to tolerate or fit into it. As an urban ethnographer, the most impressive feature of the study for me were her fifty-one in-depth interviews. Such probing is the only way to get at the core, the heart of ethnic identity. The details provided in *Sense of Origins* of the questionnaire she used, should be used as a guide for others. Most importantly, this exceptional work provides a solid platform from which to do much-needed comparative research within and between ethnic groups and cohorts. As a visual sociologist, I also have a special interest in the image and stereotype of the members of the Italian American community as they have a reciprocal relations to both still and moving images as well as their portrayal in literature. Dr. Serra's book clearly demonstrates that there is no easy "one image fits all" for her—and may I now say "my"—community. As will what I hope shall be many other readers of *Sense of Origins*, I look forward to the many scholarly fruits of her labor, and especially await to learn of the future prospects for Italian American culture.

JEROME KRASE, PHD
Emeritus and Murray Koppelman Professor
Brooklyn College of The City University of New York

REFERENCES

Handlin, O. (1951). *The uprooted: The epic story of the great migrations that made the American people*. Boston, MA: Little Brown.

Krase, J. (1978). Italian American female college students: A new generation connected to the old. Reprinted in *N. L. Ziehler (Ed.), Italian-American students in New York City, 1975–2000: A research anthology*. New York, NY: John D. Calandra Italian American Institute, 2011.

———. (1986). Educational attainment and educational values of Italian Ameri-can generations. Reprinted in *N. L. Ziehler (Ed.), Italian-American students in New York City, 1975–2000: A research anthology*. New York, NY: John D. Calandra Italian American Institute, 2011.

———, & Fuccillo, V. J. (1975). Italian Americans and college life: A survey of student experiences at Brook-lyn College. Reprinted in *N. L. Ziehler (Ed.), Italian-American students in New York City, 1975–2000: A research anthology*. New York, NY: John D. Calandra Italian American Institute, 2011.

Vecoli, R. J. (1964). Contadini in Chicago: A critique of *The Uprooted*. Mississippi Valley Historical Association.

———. (1995). Are Italian Americans just white folks? *Italian Americana*, 13, 2.

ACKNOWLEDGMENTS

There are numerous participants who contributed to this study. I have to thank the very many people who helped me along the way, most notably the young Italian Americans who took interest in my work and volunteered to take part in the survey. Their invaluable input made this study possible.

I thank all of them here for their time and the great generosity of detailed, precise, and attentive sharing of personal information. The long responses to open-ended questions attest to the seriousness and importance with which the participants treated the research. Participants were offered an outlet, a chance to express their reflections, interpretations, and feelings that would have been shrouded within personal experience, and overshadowed by the daily routines of life. For their generosity of time and willingness to share, I thank them for being Italian, a group that loves to talk a lot and at great length.

Beside these individuals, there is a long list of people who contributed to the materialization of this project.

I'm grateful above all to Professor Anthony J. Tamburri, Dean of the John D. Calandra Italian American Institute (Queens College—CUNY) and to Professor Fred L. Gardaphé for the faith and sustainment which—in the name of the Institute—they offered for my study, allowing me to conduct it while I was the Institute's Visiting Research Scholar.

I'm also indebted to Joan Migliori, Joseph Sciorra, Rosangela Briscese, Siân Gibby, Rosaria Musco, Vincenzo Milione, Carmine Pizzirusso, Itala Pellizzoli, Lucia Grillo, Joseph Grosso, and Dominic Carielli as members of the John D. Calandra Institute who helped me during various phases of the work.

A special thanks goes out to Judy Frost, Valentina Fratti, Anne Berlin, Dorothy Szorc, Lorenzina Laera who all offered so much help and support over the course of my New York stays. From Italy, I am deeply grateful to professors Anna

Maria Boileau, Bernardo Cattarinussi, and Alberto Marradi, friends and teachers all, whom I encountered throughout every phase of the research. Acknowledgment also goes out to Franco Masarin for the impassioned and lively discussions on the themes of my study.

Thanks also to Professor Giuseppe Sciortino, director of the Sociology and Social Research Department at the University of Trento, who introduced me to Dr. Enzo Loner, who offered incomparable help with the multivariate analysis phase of the data.

Moreover, I'm grateful to the entire Italian American community of New York, to the associations, cultural centers, and the research institutes that sustained, prompted, and divulged the information related to my study via member mailing lists, Web pages, bulletins, and newsletters; these enabled me to connect with young people interested in taking the survey. I wish to thank the following organizations in particular: NIAF (*The National Italian American Foundation*), *Order Sons of Italy in America—Grand Lodge of New York*, NOIAW (*The National Organization of Italian American Women*), *UNICO National, UNICO Brookhaven Chapter, the Westchester Italian Cultural Center*, the Zerilli Marimò Italian House, *New York Italians,* Young People's Commission of New York, *the Center for Italian Studies (Stony Brook University), Garibaldi-Meucci Museum, Italian Cultural Foundation* at the Belvedere House, *United Pugliesi Federation, Federation of Campania Organizations USA*, and *Arba Sicula*.

Specifically, I thank Lisa Capezzuoli (*New York Youth Commission*) and Pasquale Maio (*New York Italians*) who assisted me in disseminating information.

I am grateful to Claudia Harris, Angela Manzolillo, Silvia Schneider, and Cinzia Lipera who helped immensely with the transcription of interviews.

Throughout the research process, I was also fortunate enough to be a guest at various events and meetings, during which I was able to talk about my work with the people around me.

Thanks to Sam Patti, who met and hosted me in Pittsburgh and gave me the opportunity to present my study-in-progress during a gathering at the Santa Maria Goretti Parish in August 2013.

Thanks also to Steve Bonventre, then president of the Brookhaven Chapter of *UNICO National Italian American Service Organization* for having invited me to the *Monthly Member Meeting at Port Jefferson in October 2014*, allowing me to showcase the initial results of my work.

Then there's a list of fifty-one people interviewed by me who hold distinguished positions—association presidents, artists, scholars, academics, politicians—in the Italian American community of New York who supported and encouraged me and believed in the importance of my project.

I would like to include their names here as a sign of my heartfelt thanks for their interest and the time they dedicated: Mary Jo Bona, Claudio Bozzo, Louis Calvelli, John Calvelli, Dominic Carielli, Michael Cetera, Maria A. Conelli, Thomas DeGenaro, John De Santis, Constance Del Vecchio Maltese, Thomas DiNapoli, Joseph DiTrapani, Angelina Fiordellisi, Cristina Fontanelli, Mario Fratti, Valentina Fratti, Frank G. Fusaro, RoseMarie Gallina-Santangelo, Fred L. Gardaphé, Florence Gatto, Daniela Gioseffi, Joseph Guagliardo, Jerry Krase, Kenneth P. LaValle, Richard Laurenzi, Joseph R. Lentol, Nancy Macina, Serphine Maltese, Vincenzo R. Marra, Dominic R. Massaro, Joan Migliori, Mario B. Mignone, Aniello Musella, John Mustaro, Richard Nasti, William Papaleo, James J. Periconi, Stanislao G. Pugliese, Joseph Sciame, Mary Ann Re, Aileen Riotto-Sirey, Diane Savino, Joseph Sciorra, Jack Spatola, Anthony J. Tamburri, Maria Tamburri, William A. Tramontano, Joseph Tusiani, Richard Vetere, Catherine Vignale, Robert Viscusi.

There are another twenty interviewees that I would like to recognize and thank for the time they dedicated to me sharing their own experience and their lives: there are ten young Italian American professionals and ten young Italians who came all the way to New York in order to complete their university studies in recent years.

Specifically, my thanks go out to Sophia Antonelli, Carmine Berardi, Alessandro Bernini, Alberto Calabrò, Lisa Capezzuoli, Clarissa Caprio, Martina Casagrande, Alessandro J. Chiaro, Salvatore Fabbri, Paolo Magnani, Lydia Miner, Megan Minutillo, Roberta Navone, Andrea Occhi, Nicole Pandolfo, Rino Pietanza, Mario Piccioli, Francesca Scalettaris, Fabrizio Verga, Michelina Zambella Lasalle.

The project had the financial support of the Bianco & Fusaro Foundation, via the research grant of the Paolina Bianco and Isabella Fusaro Memorial Fellowship. Furthermore, the following individuals contributed financial support, through voluntary donations under their own names: Mario Fratti, Angelina Fiordellisi, Maria Tamburri, Joseph Sciame, Richard Laurenzi, William A. Tramontano, Stanislao G. Pugliese, James J. Periconi, Daniela Gioseffi, Catherine Vignale, Serphine Maltese, Constance Del Vecchio Maltese, Sam Patti, Joseph Lentol.

To all of these people, my deepest and most heartfelt thanks.

Their support allowed for the proper transcribing of the interviews as well as the use of the Qualtrics platform for recording data collection from the questionnaire online.

Lastly, thanks to my parents for having instilled in me the desire for discovery and the intellectual curiosity that steered me toward this study.

INTRODUCTION

There are many reasons that might guide one's interest toward a subject of study. Certain events and encounters, which, as one conducts research in course of a career, provide opportunities for thematic study; or perhaps there are motivations tied to one's own history, which lead to questions and the search for answers that affect us directly, an intellectual curiosity linked to subjects held dear for sentimental reasons driving us to deepen our own understanding.

My interest in the Italian Americans is deep rooted and has developed over time; its winding course began a long time ago. On a personal level, that interest relates to the histories of migration that have marked my family for generations, within and beyond the national confines, in search of fortunes to be made and life-opportunities to be achieved; it is connected to my own personal migrant story from southern to northern Italy, a south that I've always loved—despite being so young when I left—and which I rediscovered unexpectedly in the ensuing years, in different parts of the world, following traces of an identity which I'd imagined to be so far from my own. It's connected also to expanding my studies on emigration, which started with my graduate thesis that examined the transformations of the Italian families that had emigrated to Argentina.

Subsequently, I was able to spend long periods of time in the United States and to meet the Italians of America. I had encountered them in Italy, even before visiting the United States, through their writing, music, the wonderful films that moved me deeply and sparked my imagination. Then I met them in New York, where I first set foot in December 2001, three months after the mournful events of September 11.

And so my interest and study of them developed and matured over the years, an interest that drove me to search for how these people still felt connected to Italy and to the legacy inherited from their forebears; although we no longer shared a native language, what meaning could I attribute to the familiarity that I recognized in their ways of thinking and speaking?

In March 2012, I began to develop my research project with the patronage of the John D. Calandra Institute of Italian American Studies in New York, under the aegis of Queens College (CUNY). The objective I set for myself was to study the transformations that occurred, across the generations of the Italian Americans, related to their connection with cultural and historic Italian heritage and the representations and interpretations of it within the perspective of the present day.

To accomplish my cognitive goal, I constructed a research project composed of two working phases: the first is based on a qualitative approach and utilizes an in-depth interview as the technique for collecting information; the second phase focused on a quantitative approach, using a standardized questionnaire as a surveying tool. The project started in March 2012 and concluded in October 2013.

I was introduced to numerous Italian Americans in the course of my work. Some of them contributed to the history of a great city—New York City—which is where they live and work, often holding positions of great importance in the Italian American community and American society in general. They were predominantly third-generation immigrants, descended from Italians who had arrived in the United States during the period of large-scale migration. Their contribution profoundly affected the social, economic, political, and cultural achievements and the recognition of Italian Americans living in the United States and abroad; they provided a level of visibility, acquiring power and prestige, which had a major impact on the public at large, and enabled them to attain institutional positions at multiple levels. Their hard work facilitated the creation of bridges that connected to Italy, thus resuming a dialog which had been suspended in time. The fifty-one in-depth interviews provided me with an understanding, through their accounts of personal and family histories and the descriptions of their perception of the Italian American community, of how they depict and interpret their sense of belonging and their sense of identity connected to *italianità*. I also listened to the stories of some Italian emigrants who came to New York in recent years—some already adults and others still children or adolescents—who occupy key positions in the economic, political, cultural, and artistic fields and consider themselves Italian Americans, despite being born in Italy. Their vision is accompanied by those of the previous groups and helps compose the complex framework of how these representatives of the third generation perceive and represent their own sense of Italian Americanism.

Within the first research phase, I also interviewed twenty—mostly professional—young people, including ten Italian Americans. Their testimony shed light on a double bond with Italian tradition and current culture, each bearing its own nuances of meaning.

The other ten young people interviewed are recent arrivals, having come from Italy after the completion of their university studies, driven by inner strength and fierce determination, comparable to what spurred the first Italian emigrant to leave Italy, bearing the spirit of all those who want to "make it in America." Within twenty years, many of these young Italians, arriving in New York both culturally and educationally well equipped, acquired professional status and obtained respectable positions and recognitions in various fields. Beyond my interview work, I would occasionally meet other Italians of America who at times, despite possessing an Italian surname or some Italian blood in their family tree, don't attribute any significance or relevance to those remnants: they lacked any trace of knowledge about an ethnic past that has faded, vanished, perhaps lost or just buried; all that remains for some is a quick flash of a look in the dark eyes of the southern people.

Throughout the in-depth interviews—which will be the focus of a separate and forthcoming analytical work—I was able to collect the most significant themes pertaining to the perception and representations of identity of Italian heritage, on the individual and on the collective level. Using these points of reference and based on these assumptions, I then constructed the research design, which brought me to the realization of the second quantitative phase, in the form of the survey taken by 277 young Italian Americans. The following pages contain the results and analyses through the interpretation and critical reflections that emerge from processing that data. Today we are faced with the valuation and rediscovery of ethnicity, with numerous ethnic and racial minorities reaffirming a connection with the "culture of the past."

The Italian Americans may also stake their claim, which makes it very important to understand the significance that the youth attribute to that cultural heritage.

Does a connection still exist with this cultural baggage, and if yes, what kind? In the future, will this connection weaken and ultimately disappear, or will it be preserved by future generations? How does one transmit such a cultural legacy? Are the new generations interested in safeguarding it? What are the points of concern for this future? What are the strategies for promoting the preservation and revival of a dynamic perspective of this legacy?

Trying to understand self-representation as it relates to the cultural inheritance of young Italian Americans, its intersection with their sense of personal identity, and how these young people imagine they are perceived by other Americans are all of strategic importance for the future of the Italian American community.

The main reason for studying young Italian Americans rests in the importance of envisioning the future of the Italian American culture; to do so we must understand the position of those who would pass on this cultural heritage to the next generation.

Speaking more generally, recalling Pasqualini (2012), to study the youth primarily implies an analysis of the sociocultural changes of which the youth are a driving force.

Regarding the past, there are traces of both continuity and disruption in the passage of generations, and the objective of study is to find possible models for describing the more significant changes and fluctuations that occur.

The research thus aims to delineate and comprehend—via sociological reading—the actions, representations, and orientations of a group of young people who live in the greater New York area, as related to their descent from Italian ancestry.

By studying the value systems, attitudes, and behaviors, as well as lifestyle and life practices, we will seek to understand how these elements potentially intersect with ethnic identity, by breaking up and analyzing the various components thereof.

The data interpretation aims to highlight the behaviors and demeanors as new, renewed, or in absolute continuity with regard to the preceding generations. The three most important cognitive questions connected to the motivations for studying young Italian Americans correspond to three types of needs:

— heuristic: namely, to understand who are the "new" Italian Americans;
— predictive: that is, to understand what changes within the Italian American youth denote anticipation and expression;
— strategic/practical: in the sense of analyzing the process that can facilitate the transmission of Italian heritage to future generations.

The perspective chosen for this consists of a vision of the group "from the inside." It's composed, indeed, of young people who self-identify as Italian Americans. Therefore, the study seeks to understand how these individuals define themselves in reference to the Italian legacy, specifically analyzing how the youths: (1) represent themselves; (2) view the Italian American community as a whole; (3) perceive the Italian American community to be viewed "from the outside," namely, by other Americans.

The volume consists of two parts. The first part examines the results of the survey respondents, young Italian Americans living in the greater New York area, while the second part presents further analytical deepening based on the research data, which includes some constructed identity profiles of the youth in relation to Italian heritage. This part describes, analyzes, and interprets the results of the survey.

The description of the theoretical structure, methodological path, and the sample construction constitute the objective of the first chapter.

The second chapter concerns the reference values of the youths; beginning with the general framework of the research, the analysis delves into greater depth on the family, through the profile of the mothers and fathers with references to the process of primary socialization for the interviewed young people.

The third chapter discusses ethnic identification. The argumentation begins with a description of the ethnicity of the respondents and of their partners and delves into the deepening of the knowledge of the historical memory linked to their ancestors' immigration to America.

A thorough analysis of the sense of belonging for those who define themselves as Italian Americans was effected by establishing a series of justifications that could support this self-representation. This led to the individuation of two dimensions that characterize such an identification: one of these, the "gaze" toward Italy—knowing the language, an attachment to family origins, feeling connected to an international network of people who share Italian values and culture—and, for the second dimension: the privileging, instead, of belonging above all to America, and more specifically to the Italian American culture and community.

Within the study there was a focus on the comprehension of the level of understanding of the Italian American community, the degree of importance the interviewees placed on ethnic background, and the motivating factors underpinning their choices. It thus becomes necessary to understand which members of the family—in the process of the transmitting ethnic identity—had drawn the interviewees toward Italian culture.

The emotional-affective aspect of identity becomes a significant area of inquiry, as potentially opposing sentiments converge within this space, including the pride or the shame of being/feeling Italian American, which can also lead to real identity crises, characterized by instances of malaise and distress.

The fourth chapter continues to seek insight into the identification with Italian heritage, including an investigation of its significance for today's Italian American youth on the ways that influence the perception of reality in everyday interactions, the values, and symbolic references. The significance of this area was such that the interviewees were asked to express their own definitions, interpretations, and experiences connected to that significance in great detail.

The next two chapters connect the image of the Italian Americans with that of the Italians and Italy.

Specifically, the fifth chapter considers the image of the Italian Americans, studying it from various angles, at the individual and collective level, in exacting detail. The indication, according to the interviewees, of distinctive traits and characteristics that typify this image has led to a meaningful portrayal within contemporary society.

For comparative purposes, it appeared relevant to establish an image of the "typical" Italian and Italian American; furthermore, in searching for similarities and differences in the perception of the image of Italian Americans with respect to Italians as well as other Americans, there was also study of characteristics related to work, family, cooking, television preferences, etc. with the goal of finding parallelisms and divergences of perception among the three groups.

Once the image of the Italian American as an individual subject was analyzed, the scope was expanded to the collective image and, specifically, to the group structure of the Italian Americans; in this perspective, the group's composition, organization, and integration were examined.

The sixth chapter covers the images of Italy and the Italians. There were multiple facets studied: from the level of knowledge of Italian culture to the opinions held by the youth regarding Italian society and Italians, along with the emotional aspects, as they connect to life experiences within Italian society, moving toward an understanding of the profounder dimensions, which constitute the foundational aspects contributing to this image.

A significant part of the study is dedicated to the direct, personal relationship with Italy and the Italians. This appears to be a very relevant aspect, as an indicator of the vitality of the connections with the land of origin and the places one's parents came from; the relationship is shown through the contact maintained with relatives, friends, and acquaintances, by means of the visits made over the course of time. Personal knowledge of Italy also connects to other aspects that affect one's identification; for example, there is a linguistic facet, tied to one's familiarity with the Italian language and the dialects, which is positively affected by direct contact.

The seventh chapter reflects on the stereotypes and prejudices surrounding the Italian American image, envisioned by the interviewees as it exists today. It does so from historical premises that go back to an earlier time, to the history of the Italians in the mother nation, particularly those from the South in the time before the great migrations to the Americas Notably, the reflection is focused on the image of the Italian Americans as presented by the media, with specific references to the Guido subculture.

The eighth chapter studies some of the youth's attitudes and behaviors in multiple spheres of action; it examines their relationship with religion, politics, food, mass media, and territorial attachments to significant places.

A considerable part of the reflection is dedicated to the role of associations. The objective was to understand the frequency and methods of participation in Italian American associations and organizations, and in results showing a lack thereof, what caused the young people to distance themselves. Close attention was paid to the level of satisfaction/dissatisfaction regarding the activities promoted by the associations, argued by the motivations that would lead to one opinion or the other. The promotional aspect wasn't overlooked; there was a concerted effort to determine which kinds of activities should be promoted by the associations to facilitate and encourage youth participation.

The ninth chapter discusses the future prospects of Italian American culture. Here it seemed interesting to compare the position of the scholars in Italian American studies with those of the young people interviewed. The proactive dimension was also under consideration here, expressed through the youth proposals and suggestions for keeping Italian American culture alive.

The first part of the volume concludes with the examination of two interpretive categories considered meaningful in the construction of some explicative models of identification with an Italian cultural legacy: on one hand, level of understanding of Italian and Italian American culture and on the other, the attachment, connection, and effective bond with them.

The second part of the volume is further subdivided into two sections. The first contains the analysis of the data cross-referenced with the generations of immigration for the young people interviewed. Relating the various significant aspects of the study—namely, structural data, socialization and values-systems, ethnic self-identification, the Italian and the Italian American image, stereotypes, affiliations and belonging, and the future—with the generations of immigrations it became possible to create several interpretive models that could be used to delineate the physiognomy and the characteristics of every generation.

The second section of the second part contains the description, analysis, and interpretation of four identity profiles, representing four models of how the youth relate to Italian heritage. As with the generations of immigration, these identity profiles are also positioned in relation to structural data, socialization, value-systems, ethnic self-identification, the image of the Italians and the Italian Americans, stereotypes, affiliations, belonging, and the future. What emerges is a descriptive and interpretive framework of the presented typology, which sheds light on what today appears to be the ways, the forms, and the tendencies related to how Italian heritage is perceived, experienced, and represented by the Italian American youth.

PART I

FIELD RESEARCH

1

Theoretical Structure, Methodological Path, Description of the Sample

THE RESEARCH TARGET POPULATION

As noted by Vecoli (2002), the Italian Americans of today are descended—predominantly—from the roughly six million immigrants that arrived in the United States over the course of 150 years (1850–2000).

Historically, the Italians have been among the most mobile European populations, characterized by waves of migration both within and beyond the continent (Sowell, 1996).

Between 1870 and 1970, approximately 26 million people left their ancestral home to work abroad; many of them ultimately returned to Italy. From 1876 to 1914, one-third of the 14 million Italian migrants reached North America (primarily the United States) and another one-fourth arrived in South America (especially Argentina and Brazil) (Gabaccia, 2003).

Today there are sixty million descendants of Italian ancestry living outside Italy, and two-thirds of this diaspora live in the Americas (ibid.).

Over time, various sources have produced data that have enabled a demographic, social, and economic mapping of the Italian American profile.

In the 2000 Census, American citizens of Italian origin occupied the sixth place (15.6 million equal to 5.6%) of the fifteen indicated ancestral ethnic groups; in first place was German (42.8 million equal to 15.2%), second place Irish (30.5 million equal to 10.8%), followed by African Americans (24.9 million equal to 8.8%).

In reference to the regions of the United States, the population of Italian descent occupies the second-highest place in the Northeast, at 14.1% indicated, while among the five most represented groups at the state level, Italians represent the first place in Connecticut, New Jersey, New York, and Rhode Island.

Conducted in 2016, the ACS (American Community Survey) estimated the Italian American community included 16,896,518 individuals.

Interesting to note is that since 1990 the Italian origin component is trending upward in the United States. The population variation of Italian Americans is approximately equal to 26% of the incremental change of the entire United States population. Since family size and immigration statistics haven't experienced any significant incremental change, the growing number of Italian Americans is likely due to an escalating awareness of one's own Italian American identity, which translates to an explicit self-identification through the chosen responses to questions regarding ethnicity within the Census.

In reference to the Census 2000 data, Gardaphé (2008) observes that the significant increase in the number of people identifying themselves as Italians doesn't correspond to a comparable growth in immigration from Italy during the preceding decade. The interpretation presented by the scholar refers to the Italian American component of identity, which is defined here as "fluid, constantly changing in form, transformable."

Information on the number of individuals identifying as Italians also comes from the 2010 American Community Survey (1-Year Estimates) and from the 2008–2010 (3-Year Estimates) of the American Community Survey.

The 2010 Census indicates the total United States population is equal to 308.7 million people, which is an increase of 9.7% over the number reported in the previous Census 2000 that indicated a total of 281.4 million people.

Of these, 17,235,941 claimed to have Italian origins, equal to 5.6% of the population. That number increases further when considering the calculations for the 2008–2010 triennial period, where the indication reaches 17,486,056, equal to 5.7% of the total. In the 2015 Census, there were roughly 18 million Italian Americans recorded, or 6% of the United States population. However, the findings of the National Italian American Foundation (NIAF) estimate that more than twenty million individuals possess some Italian lineage within their family. Among these individuals, there are over 200,000 (233,429 according to the survey from the end of 2012) registered in the *Anagrafe degli italiani residenti all'estero* [Registry of the Italian residents abroad] (AIRE), which documents people who possess Italian citizenship or dual citizenship, Italian and U.S.

Composition according to gender exhibits a slight prevalence of the female component; yet there is no significant difference in the proportion between males and females, except in the elderly population, where there is a decisive female majority (55.3%).

Distribution across age groups reveals that young people between eighteen and thirty-four years old comprise 23.6% of the total community.

The 2010 American Community Survey claims that the total number of Italian Americans living in New York State is equal to 2,633,293, of which 589,803 live in New York City. Dividing by gender indicates a slightly higher percentage of women (51%), further accentuated within New York City (51.6%). The adult groups represent slightly more than one-half of the reference population, both in the state (52.6%) and in the city of New York (56.3%). The young adult group between twenty-five and thirty-four years old is notably large in New York City (17%). Regarding the age group from eighteen to thirty-four, the evidence shows this group reaching 22.6% of the total in New York State, while the percentage increases to 25.5% in New York City.

According to estimates of the population with Italian origins by the 2010 American Community Survey, a more numerous concentration of Italian Americans is projected in Nassau and Suffolk counties.

Table 1.1 The New York State Population with Italian Origins Divided by County

	TOTAL
Erie County	150,888
Kings County	140,565
Monroe County	138,787
Nassau County	289,030
New York County	98,093
Queens County	149,084
Suffolk County	416,724
Westchester County	173,811
TOTAL	1,556,982

Source: U.S. Census Bureau, 2010 American Community Survey

Subdivision of the population by age group within eight counties shows an elderly population (sixty-five and older) concentrated primarily in Kings (25.6), Queens (22.7), and Westchester (18.3) counties. The under-eighteen population is more numerous especially in Suffolk (26.9), Erie (24.8), Monroe (24.5), and Nassau (23.7) counties.

Throughout the country, Italian Americans are increasingly improving their level of education. The majority of today's Italian Americans age twenty-five or older possess a high school diploma, a three-year university degree, or a graduate degree.

THE SAMPLE

The study examines a sample of young residents in New York City and the greater NYC area, who self-identified as Italian Americans.

The wide acceptance of the label "Italian American" has resulted in the opportunity for those descended from Italians to take part in the survey—even people who claimed solely the paternal or the maternal line. This identification encompasses the second and subsequent generations of emigration (thus excluding those who did themselves emigrate from Italy to the United States). In sociological terms, the "first generation" is made up of immigrants from a foreign country.[1] In cases where generational profiles of paternal and maternal ancestors were different, regarding the time of initial arrival on American soil, the oldest generation of settlement was connected to the interviewee.

The field research phase was preceded by participation in the basic training course *HSR for Social & Behavioral Faculty, Graduate Students & Postdoctoral Scholars* to be able to acquire the ability to perform *Human Subjects Research (HSR)*. Participation in the course and successful completion of the exam were essential, subsequently submitting the research project for the approval of the Queens College (CUNY) *HRPP Office (Human Research Protections Program)*. The project "Italian American Identity: A Study of New York's Italian American Youth Population" was approved in June 2013 and research was conducted between March and October 2013.

Young people between the ages of eighteen and thirty-four comprise the target group for the study. The cases studied—born between 1978 and 1994—belonged to the "tail end" of Generation X and part of the Millennial generation, meaning subjects with an age in the first half that divides the generation in two.[2]

Reaching the population of interest entailed publishing information relative to the study in newspapers, periodicals, Italian American websites, and at institutions actively dedicated to research and study in the fields of Italian and Italian American culture.[3]

News of the study was also available on webpages for associations and organizations dedicated to promoting and expanding Italian and Italian American culture.[4]

The student body of the institutions that make up the City University of New York (CUNY) was approached in various ways: meetings were conducted at the end of classes; flyers and notices were posted around the campuses; news was delivered via the student mailing list which was provided by several universities (Queens College, Brooklyn College, College of Staten Island); meetings were conducted with some Italian American student associations at certain campuses (Queens College); news was sent out through university e-bulletin (for example, via Brooklyn College News & Events).

The following universities participated: *Queens College, Brooklyn College, Borough of Manhattan Community College, College of Staten Island, Hunter College, John Jay College of Criminal Justice, Kingsborough Community College,* and *Queensborough Community College.*

Considering that the sampling method does not reflect the standards of probability, and because the total number of questionnaires received is 277, this is a study of an exploratory nature; the results cannot be generalized—given the potential for sampling errors—for the entire reference population. Thus, the study should be interpreted in terms of developing trends.

COGNITIVE OBJECTIVES

This research seeks to address a basic question; namely "What changes have affected the ways in which the youth may or may not identify with an Italian cultural legacy and overall background?"
The primary focus of the study is to formulate an outline of the opinions, attitudes, behaviors, and perceptions of the youth regarding the heritage they all share in their familial past.

One hypothesis is these opinions, attitudes, behaviors, and perceptions vary in relation to age, gender, generational belonging with respect to immigration, and self-assessment of social class.

Questions were raised regarding what connotation the youth attributed to the broad label of "Italian American" and how this influences one's own sense of identity: Does the label affect the individual's daily life or is it merely a concept of a background lacking relevance that had lost its performative power on identity? Who are the young Italian Americans of today? Does being or feeling Italian American have an influence on values, behaviors, beliefs, and notions of Italy and the Italians? Where does "feeling Italian" come from, in terms of an emotional framework? Is there a sense of "uniqueness" in being Italian American, with respect to Americans in general? What are the recognizable differences among the Italian forms of American-ness, differences in perception and in reality? What is their viewpoint on Italy and the Italians? What does the future hold for this part of "Italian history," that has migrated to the other side of the ocean? What aspects remain, are reborn, reimagined, or have disappeared in the succeeding generations—children, grandchildren, and great-grandchildren of Italians—who were born and lived in the United States, but who feel a sense of belonging to this culture and history? What sort of contacts are created—if any—with the "new" and "very new" young Italian immigrants?

Thus, the study focuses primarily on the analysis of dimensions and characteristics of the images and self-representations among the youth with respect to Italian heritage.

THE QUESTIONNAIRE

The tool implemented to acquire information is a self-completed questionnaire presented online via the Qualtrics platform for data collection.

Structuring the information collection tool focused on five principal dimensions, which combined the elements and symbols of ethnicity. Mitrano (1999) identified four of these, namely the dimensions pertaining to physique, personality, culture, and psychology; this study adds the emotional/affective dimension to these four.

The *physical dimension* analyzes the image of the Italian American related to physical traits and other physical characteristics.

The *personality dimension* was studied through various characteristics that aim to describe an ideal Italian and Italian American personality type.

The *cultural dimension* was thoroughly studied by analyzing the knowledge of history, Italian and Italian American traditions and practices, modern

Italy—including comprehension and use of the Italian language and dialects, and the consumption of Italian and Italian American food.

The *psychological dimension* is expressed as the level of attachment and sense of belonging to ethnic heritage and the Italian American community.

The *emotional/affective dimension* concerns the emotions and sentiments that are connected to ethnic identification and self-representation.

The questionnaire is comprised of eight sections delineated as follows:

1 *sociographic data*: refers to information concerning the personal characteristics of the interviewees (gender; age; marital status; birthplace; city, state, and neighborhood of residence) education level, occupation, composition of the family, self-identification of social class, citizenship, ethnic self-identification, generation of immigration). Information was also requested regarding the ethnicity of the interviewee's partner. Furthermore, data were collected regarding the parents' ethnicity, generation of immigration, religion, education level, and employment/occupation.
2 *socialization and values*
3 *immigration and memory*: includes questions related to the migratory experience of the family leaving Italy (which ancestors, regions of emigration, year of arrival in the United States) and any applicable personal migratory experience;
4 *ethnic self-identification*: questions in this section pertain to the two dimensions of self-identification, namely as an individual and as a group.

The first part of the fourth section is dedicated to understanding how young Italian Americans view and represent themselves in relation to their Italian background: if they consider themselves Italian American or not, and how they may otherwise identify; how much do they know about Italian American culture; what motivates them to identify with this ethnic heritage; who transmitted their ethnic legacy within their family; what level of importance is placed on a sense of belonging to an ethnic background and why; what sentiments are connected to this identification (pride, shame, conflicting).

The second dimension of self-identification concerns the perception of the interviewees regarding the Italian American community as whole: how it is viewed not only "from the inside," meaning from those who form a part of it (self-representation), but also "from the outside," namely perceived hetero-representation (projected image), that is, how the interviewees imagine the Italian American community is viewed by other Americans and by Italians.

The self-image of the group was studied by means of two sub-dimensions:

a *the object of the image*: the group or the "typical" individual of the group;
b *the content of the image*: the image may refer to various aspects of the individual (features) or the group (dimensions), located along a physico-cultural continuum (Boileau, Sussi, 1981).

Physical features, personality (temperament and character), and sociocultural traits are distinguishable for the individual; for the group, ecological (relationship between the group and the physical environment), social (social relations), and cultural (norms and group values) dimensions can be examined (ibid.).

The image of the typical "Italian American" has been studied using a list of seventeen contrasting adjectives, utilizing Osgood's semantic differential technique.[5] Conversely, the structure of the Italian American community was analyzed according to three dimensions: the overall relationship of position or "composition," "organization," and "integration" (Boileau, 1981).

The study does not intend to reveal the objective structure of the group; rather, the images of the group held by the interviewed subjects, namely the "perceived" structure. The structural image of the Italian American community was analyzed via the perception based on the following properties:

a *composition level*: comprehensiveness of the group;
b *organization level*: group potential for unity or division, relative power of the group, relative social importance of the group, expected duration of the group;
c *integration level*: measure of social interaction within the group, nature of social relationships in the group, level of group visibility, level of component involvement in the group;

5 *image of Italy and the Italians*: this section of the questionnaire aims to analyze the image of Italy and of the Italians according the perceptions of the interviewees. The semantic differential was used for both profiles to delineate the "typical Italian" and to obtain a speculative image of the "typical Italian American" for comparison;
6 *stereotypes, prejudices, and discrimination*: the sixth part of the questionnaire examines these three aspects surrounding the representation of the Italian Americans, specifically through the media;
7 *attitudes, behaviors, and affiliations*: the seventh area of the questionnaire explores behaviors, attitudes, and opinions regarding the use of the Italian

language and dialects, religious affiliation, political involvement, eating habits, sense of spatial belonging, civic and ethnic participation, free time dedicated to reading books and/or periodicals, and watching television;
8 *future of the Italian American community*: the eighth and final section of the questionnaire assesses the future of the Italian American community, providing respondents with space to suggest ideas and personal interpretations.

SOCIOGRAPHIC DATA

GENDER, MARITAL STATUS, PLACE OF BIRTH AND OF RESIDENCE

In total, there are 277 questionnaires deemed valid for analysis. The age range for the sample is eighteen to thirty-four years and the female component—equal to 72.6% of the sample—is predominant compared to the male component. Age-based data were classified according to three age categories.

Table 1.2 Age Categories

	NO.	%
18–23 years	95	34.3
24–29 years	100	36.1
30–34 years	82	29.6

Regarding marital status, most respondents were single (73.3%) (justified by the young age of the sample), followed by married (16.6%), 7.9% cohabitate with a partner and 1.8% are already divorced.

Almost all of the interviewees were born in the United States; only two of the subjects were born abroad.

Regarding the area of birth, the most numerous group includes those born in Brooklyn (19.1%).

Compiling the data according to birth state, New York is the largest group (72.9%). More than one-tenth of them were born in New Jersey and another one-tenth were born in other American states. Only 2.5% were born in Connecticut.

In terms of birth by county, the young people interviewed were born predominantly in Kings County (19.1%) and Nassau County (10.8%).

Considering residence at present, those living in Manhattan comprise the most numerous group (17%), followed by Queens residents (14.8%), then Brooklyn (13%). Beyond the five New York boroughs, a considerable number of people, equal to 13%, live in the rest of New York State.

Synthesized according to state of residence, New York State is where the majority of the interviewees reside (79.4%).

EDUCATION LEVEL, OCCUPATION, SOCIAL CLASS

Regarding education level, more than 70% of the interviewees hold a university degree, and more than 10% possess a graduate degree. Furthermore, 5% of the young people have attained a PhD.

The sample is composed primarily of people working full time (48.7%) or part time (7.9%), while more than 20% work and study simultaneously. Full-time students represent 17.3% of the sample, whereas a marginal portion of the subjects don't fall under any occupational category.

Regarding the types of occupations held, the number of young professionals (17.7%) is most prevalent in the sample, almost equal to the number of students (17.3%). Managers, business people, and entrepreneurs (14.1%) are followed by those employed in the service industry (11.9%), and teachers (11.2%). Other occupations represent a marginal portion of the total.

More than one-tenth of the respondents engaged in studies attend Queens College. The other students who participated in the survey are scattered over other campuses—falling under the CUNY system—within New York City and the surrounding area.

With respect to their chosen major, these students tend to enroll in courses in the social sciences (38.7%), natural sciences (27.9%), and the arts and humanities (12.6%).

In terms of social class self-identification, the young people positioned themselves primarily in the middle class (48.4%) and in the upper-middle class (24.9%). Over 13% claim to belong to the lower-middle class, while 7.2% identify as working class. At the ends of the spectrum are the people claiming to belong to the lower class (1.8%) and those who identify as upper class (2.5%).

Synthesizing this, 22.7% of the young people feel they fall into the lower class, 48.4% in the middle class, and 27.4% in the upper class.

FAMILIAL SITUATION

More than one-third of the respondents live with their parents, and 5% live in a single parent household. Fourteen percent live alone, more than 15% live with a husband or wife, around 10% cohabitate with a boyfriend or girlfriend, and over 12% share a living space with roommates.

The family composition shows a prevalence of the two people (27.8%) and three people (21.7%). Almost one-fifth of those interviewed are part of a family made up of four people.

More than half of the respondents have no children (56%), while the percentage of respondents having one child and two children are both equal to 4.3%. Only two of the interviewees indicated a progeny comprised of three children.

2

Values, Family, and Primary Socialization

VALUES

Values[1]—considered by sociologists to be an expression of fundamental orientations and collective beliefs of a society (Galland and Lemel, 2006)—are "conceptions of what is desirable, felt to be obligatory and not to be inferred by one's behaviors" (Sciolla, 2008, p. 93). Over the last thirty years, values have been studied comparatively via research programs conducted by international observatories; notable among these are the European Values Study (EVS) and the World Values Study (WVS).[2] The resulting analysis from the data produced in the latest survey by Inglehart and Welzel maintains that there are two principal dimensions of cross-cultural variation in the world: traditional values versus secular/rational values *and* the values of survival versus the values of free expression. Traditional values emphasize the importance of religion; connections between parents and children; respect for authority and traditional family values; and national pride—as well as opposition to divorce, abortion, euthanasia, and suicide. Secular/rational values tend to support opposing preferences and put less emphasis on religion and on traditional family and authoritative values. Values of survival favor economic and physical security over freedom, abstinence from political activism, distrust of foreigners, and a low emphasis on happiness. Values of free expression place a higher priority on environmental protection, increasing tolerance toward foreigners, gender equality, and a growing demand for participation in the decision-making process in economic and political arenas.

The United States is within the societal group that places a higher points value on traditional values and personal freedom. Specifically, the value of the family has retained a consistent and high percentage of adhesion in the United States throughout every age group.

There is an observably high percentage of importance placed on family when analyzing—also in this case—specifically the youth component of the American population (Table 2.1).

Table 2.1 Percentage values of the importance attributed to the value of the family

	1995–1999			2000–2004		
	TOTAL	AGE		TOTAL	AGE	
		18–25	26–36		up to 29	30–49
Very Important	95.2	92.2	95.8	95.3	93.7	95.1
Somewhat important	4	7.8	3.6	3.8	5.9	3.5
A little important	0.6	0	0.6	0.4	0.3	0.6
Not important	0.1	0	0	0.4	0	0.6
N/A	0	0	0	0.1	0	0.3
N	1.542	225	369	1.2	316	516
	2005–2009			2010–2014		
	TOTAL	AGE		TOTAL	AGE	
		up to 29	30–49		up to 29	30–49
Very Important	94.2	94.6	94.1	90.9	85.5	92.4
Somewhat important	4.9	5.2	4.8	7.3	10.6	6.5
A little important	0.5	0.3	0.6	0.8	1.6	0.4
Not important	0	0	0	0.6	1.7	0.3
N/A	0.4	0	0.4	0.4	0.7	0.4
N	1.249	272	456	2.232	488	746

Source: World Values Survey, 1995–2014 time series

In the research of young Italian Americans, values were studied according to their placement on a list comprised of twenty-seven values. Respondents were asked to provide a valuation for each one of these, rating it from 1 to 5.

The value of the family holds an especially relevant position in the lives of the respondents—thus reflecting national tendencies—considering that 95.5 % of those interviewed assigned this component a score between 4 and 5.

Using synthetic parameters of the distributions, it is possible to construct a table where the values are sorted according to increasing values of the mean, which indicates an increasing degree of importance of the listed values.

As evidenced by Table 2.2, the value of the family occupies the highest position, followed by love and health, while power is generally considered to be not very important.

Religious faith, matrimony, competition, concern for the environment and for power are values that display a higher disparity among the young people interviewed; indeed, the highest recorded standard deviations are in reference to these values.

In particular, results for the value of the family—possessing the highest percentage on the list determining the importance of values—conform to the national trends expressed by the *World Values Survey* [3].

The scorings of importance attributed to values were subjected to factorial analysis to obtain some summary factors, which could provide insight to better understand the propensities and the personality of the subjects who assigned different levels of importance to each value.

The analysis has resulted in the derivation of six synthetic factors—independent of each other—that represent different orientation types regarding values.

The first factor is associated with the dimension of *individualism*, which focuses on the responses related to independence, individualism, self-actualization, affirmation of one's rights, and albeit in a more nuanced way, to the value of responsibility. This factor embodies the essence of the American "self-made man."

The second factor represents the component of *emotional support*; this expresses the convergence of homogeneous responses to items regarding love, family, health, and education.

The third factor reflects the dimension of *materialism*. Here homogeneous responses are recorded regarding items including power, wealth, possession of material goods, physical appearance, and—in a less marked way—competitiveness.

The fourth factor represents the dimension of *religiosity*. Homogeneous responses are recorded here relating to the value of religious faith and matrimony.

Table 2.2 In your personal life, how important are the following values?

	NO.	MEDIA	STANDARD DEVIATION
Family	268	4.79	.660
Love	268	4.67	.738
Health	268	4.66	.710
A stable job	267	4.63	.785
Education	268	4.59	.781
Directness/Openness/Honesty	268	4.57	.686
Friendship	268	4.53	.757
Ambition (future orientation)	268	4.49	.757
Self-reliance	268	4.48	.757
To be helpful to people	268	4.48	.771
Independence	268	4.45	.755
Responsibility	268	4.41	.791
Success	268	4.38	.791
Culture	268	4.32	.863
Self-realization	267	4.31	.820
Equality/fairness	268	4.28	.896
Individualism	268	4.21	.819
Cooperation	268	4.18	.848
To assert your rights	268	4.13	.899
Marriage	268	4.00	1.207
Physical appearance	268	3.73	.893
Wealth	267	3.42	.928
Environmental issues	268	3.22	1.083
Competitiveness	267	3.17	1.207
Religious faith	267	3.11	1.387
To have material possessions	268	2.81	.974
Power	268	2.72	1.039

The dimension of *cultural and social sharing* represents the fifth factor. It includes collected responses to friendship, culture, and stable employment.

The sixth factor illuminates the *environmentalist* dimension. The responses related to environmental concerns are collected here.

Subsequently, scores are calculated within the six factors for every subject and the relationship among them is analyzed along with other variables.

The first factor connected to "individualism" scores especially high among the interviewees, from 4 to 5 (85.4%) as well as the cultural and social sharing factor (84.8% also between 4 and 5). For the "emotional support" factor, the score of 5 was marked by 70% of the interviewees; while for "materialism," there is a bell-shaped distribution concentrated especially between 2.50 and 4. Finally, the "religiosity" and "environmentalism" factors present a more variegated distribution with respect to points values, though there is a notable accentuation of 3 and above for the first. Studying the six factors through the analysis of their relation connected to other variables, it is notable that gender influences the average point value of the "individualism" factor. In fact, there appears to be a connection trend—though not statistically significant—between them.

Scores between 3 and 3.5 are especially predominant among males, while the more elevated point values—namely, 4.5 and 5—are selected prevalently by the women in the sample.

On the report with other variables, there is a significant differentiation recorded (sig. = .002) of "the emotional support" factor in relation to gender. Particularly, there appears to be a female emphasis, especially if one considers that the feminine component is prevalent in the 4 to 5 point range. However, it is also observed that males are predominant between the two genders in the intermediate point values.

Analysis of the same factor with respect to generation illuminates a connective trend, though the statistical significance is not elevated. It's especially the second and third generations that attribute a higher level of importance, considering that 78.6% of the second generation and 74.8% of the third generation assign a value of 5 for this factor. It's also worth noting that the fourth generation—albeit less markedly—attributes a great importance to this factor.

Age categories also appear to influence the points values in this case (sig. = .052). Young people especially between twenty-four and twenty-nine assign a value of 4 and 4.5, while it's the youngest of the sample—those between eighteen and twenty-three—who assign the maximum value of 5 to this dimension.

Regarding the relationship to other variables, there is an observably significant differentiation (sig. = .002) of the "materialism" factor with self-identification of class. The emerging tendency of intersecting points on this factor sheds light on how individuals who self-identify as middle and upper-middle class assign to it higher value, while the value is decisively lower for young people who claim to belong to the lower class, lower-middle class, and working class.

Gender represents a significant differentiation for this factor (sig. = .001). In fact, higher points with respect to average reference values are observed in points comprised between 4 and 5 especially among the male interviewees.

The generation of immigration is a determinant for points assigned in the "religiosity factor" (sig. = .008). The intersection of scores with the variable connected to generation of immigration demonstrates how those especially from the second generation assign the greatest importance to this factor (between 4 and 5 points). The age of the interviewee also affects the scoring for this factor (sig. = .055). The score of 4 is especially prevalent in the youngest age group, while 4.5 is predominant among the thirty-year-olds. A score of 5, however, is assigned primarily by those in the youngest group.

Gender is relatively significant (sig. = .078) for the "social and cultural sharing" factor. Specifically, point values 4 and 4.50 are favored by males, while the score rises to 5 with respect to the average value, especially among females.

In the case of the "environmentalism" factor, a trending connection is observable connected to the generation of immigration, though not statistically significant. Specifically, this connection is most noticeable among those belonging to the third and second generation, which assigned a point value of 4 in many cases (29.9% and 29.1% respectively). But it is especially the fourth generation that attributes a great relevance in this case, considering that 17% reach a score of 5 on this factor.

THE ITALIAN AMERICAN FAMILY: SOME REFLECTIONS FROM THE RESEARCH

The family has been a very important part in the experience of the Italians of America. As Cinotto (2001) points out, "[T]he ideal of centrality of the family is often presented as the true essence of the group's ethnicity" (p. 29). This represents a sociohistorical construct with a double value: on one hand it's a social entity and, on the other, it's a moral ideal together with its objectification (ibid.). The Italian American family has been described—for a large part of historiography—in terms of both a "particularly inclusive delimitation" and a "moral substance" that implies loyalty, reciprocal aid, sacrifice of individual interests for the collective well-being, marked gender roles, and a pronounced closure toward the external world.

Toward the end of the fifties, Banfield (1958), based on his study conducted in Basilicata, coined the expression "amoral familism" to describe a presumed "defect" fundamental to Italian society connected to the fact that the individual would only pursue interests pertaining to their nuclear family and never those of the community, which would require cooperation among people lacking a blood relation. The amorality doesn't refer to the internal behaviors of the family, but the absence of a community ethos or moral social relation between families and between individuals outside the family, from which a chronic deficiency of civic sense could be derived.[4]

Southern Italians immigrating to the Americas brought with them a "system of unwritten but deep-rooted laws, the *ordine della famiglia*, which prescribed internal relations, responsibilities toward one's family, and the appropriate conduct to maintain regarding those outside of the family" (Belliotti, 1995, p. 2). The *ordine della famiglia* divided the world into four morally significant spheres of social relations. The social group of primary value was the family, composed not only of nearby components (nuclear family) but also relatives, often extending to reach the third and fourth degree of separation. The second sphere of relations covered the system of *comparaggio* or "godparentage," the third involved *amici di cappello* or "hat friends" (those who would be greeted by a tip of the hat), and, finally, the largest group, which was composed of strangers. Belliotti recalls that "the *ordine della famiglia* was at once simple and complex, protective yet marginalizing, humanitarian yet also distrustful" (p. 3).

Gambino (1974) describes the primary categories of Sicilian relations in those years as family (or "blood of my blood"), godparents (godfather and godmother) and friends, those who would be greeted. The others are "strangers," though this could include people seen every day.

There have been various studies that attempted to discern how the families of Italian immigrants provided emotional, practical, and financial support during the immigrant crisis and subsequent period. Moreover, it appears that the extended family, viewed as a unit of functional importance, was developed as an adaptive solution to the circumstances of immigration (Johnson, 1985).

A picture of the continuity and stability of the familial organization within families immigrating from South Italy to the United States emerged from the historic study conducted by Yans-McLaughlin (1982) on a group of Italian immigrant families in Buffalo between 1880 and 1930 and observed over that period of fifty years. Furthermore, it appeared evident that there were specifications that characterized the first generation of immigrants, so much as to differentiate them from other ethnic groups within the working class: these differences were derived from the Italian traditions and were connected to "male superiority" and to "familism," which tended to appear more strongly with respect to their expression in other ethnic groups. Occupational models also distinguished them from the other groups of the working class. The ethnic community played an important role in this process as well, in the sense that it represented a stable point of reference when confronted with the shock of immigration: this became helpful for components of immigrant families in the transition from agricultural workers to urban laborers (Fried, 1967).

Even though the structure remained firm during the transitional phase from the old to the new world, it didn't prevent conflicts and tensions. Yans-McLaughlin notes that the relationship between modernity and tradition was neither dichotomous nor linear; rather, it was dialectic. From this perspective, the family represented "a flexible organization that, while adapting to new social conditions, could still rely on traditional forms and modes for relating" (1982, p. 23).

In this dialectical movement, the family had experienced a shift, but it had also transformed itself, adapting some of the ways characteristic of the old world to the new one, while others tended to disappear: this had the possibility of obstructing, rebutting, or adapting to social pressure. Different family systems showed a varying capacity to sustain themselves when confronted with situations of stress and urbanization; immigration and industrialization impacted people differently depending on their places of immigration.

In fact, it was the "urban villages" and not the society as whole that absorbed the Italians and other national groups: networks of relations and friendships were created in this environment that demonstrated the need for preserving familiar traditions. It was there that the Italians learned to adapt and find new ways of living. These close connections between relatives and friends cemented the social network and enduring duration of these relations helped to explain the persistence of values and inherited behaviors (Yans-McLaughlin, 1982, p. 23).

Covello's research (1967) in Brooklyn during the 1930s highlighted how the social exclusivity of the family and relatives submerged the individual within the family and removed emphasis from his/her personal interests.

Gans's study (1962) examined second- and third-generation Italian Americans in a Boston suburb where a prevalent number of individuals belonged to the working class. He presented an overview based on observations of the family during the 1950s. His findings indicated that the family structure orientation was halfway between the nuclear and extended compositions. Despite numerous observed characteristics that seemed to indicate a model continuing from the Southern Italian culture, Gans made the connection with the subculture of the working class, which transcended ethnic boundaries.

A study of the Italian American community of Roseto in Northampton County, Pennsylvania[5]—lasting from 1961 to 1966—brought forth a positive correlation between health and the nature of human relationships in the community (Bruhn, Wolf, 1979). The same tendencies of support from family, relatives, and friends for resolving problems and personal or familial crises were clearly discernible in this ethnic enclave, established at the beginning of the twentieth century. Familial relations were close-knit and mutually supportive there; this cohesive quality was extended to neighbors and the community as a whole. These observations coalesce in the theory that lifestyle defining Roseto—its social model—had a substantial effect on the level of health and well-being in the community.

It is significant to note that as traditional values were abandoned by the younger generations, the number of deaths caused by heart attack appeared to rise in Roseto until the number reached the average American value.

Johnson (1985) conducted a study at Easton, in the northeastern United States in 1970 by interviewing around four hundred middle-aged people who belonged to three groups: families of Italians married to Italians, families of Italians married to a partner of a different background, and white protestant families. In the research, middle-aged and older Italian subjects provided a description of family life, both of its traditional form connected to the immigrant model primarily originating from Southern Italy, and of its organization during those years. The control group, composed of Italian families based on mixed marriages and on white protestant families, agreed to perform a comparison highlighting the changes that occurred in the families formed by Italian Americans. Specifically, the majority of studied families were in the intermediate stage of the family cycle, when the middle-aged couple is forced to confront the changes affecting the relationship of commitment with their own parents—as they become elderly, their health declines, and their financial resources tend to diminish—and also with their children, who are themselves going through the adolescent or early-adulthood phase, and are in search of their own independence.

The perspective of study that characterized the research was based on the fusion of two approaches to ethnicity, that is, the combination of the perspective emphasizing structural variables in the reading of phenomena with one that instead favors cultural variables. The significance of ethnicity is based—according to the scholar—on how much belonging to the ethnic group acts as a determinant on one's overall status, as well as on the rules and composition of the social network. In other words, if belonging to the ethnic group is used as the basis for social organization, it can be assumed that such a process is associated with cultural aspects expressed through standards, values, feelings, and significances transmitted across generations. These factors intermingle with structural variables, including matrimony models and social/geographical mobility (Johnson, 1985). The study of ethnic families offers a privileged observatory of these phenomena. Thus, if ethnicity continues to be relevant to members of ethnic groups, it will be expressed through value systems and more specifically through the norms governing interactions, models of familial rules, socialization of young people, relationships among generations, and ethnic characteristics in social interaction networks. These dimensions were studied in the research to better understand how the family of Italian origin constructed its internal support system and if this was different than the dominant American model.

The scholar observed that there were differences among Catholic families of European origin with respect to the model of the American middle class; this difference is summarized as "traditionalism," but a traditionalism that is subject to many changes. The factors studied were the ones associated with this concept. The traditional family being referenced was characterized as a hierarchical family system, with a segregation of gender-based roles, child-rearing practices in conformity and in the dependency of the family, a strong sense of filial obligation, and an elevated level of family involvement. The structural factors, including social class, generation of immigration, and mixed marriages were also analyzed in combination with preceding characteristics. From this, the following series of generalizations can be summarized: (1) where the family was composed of both husband and wife of Italian origin, the social class by itself did not appear to influence significant changes in the family; (2) mixed marriages exerted a great influence with respect to social class, particularly on the decrease of the influence of the extended family; (3) the generation of immigration did not result in being an important source of familial changes; (4) relationships of a matrimonial nature, in the absence of extended family, take on a more central role in the family.

Another historic study conducted in Providence, Rhode Island, also highlighted familial cohesion (Smith, 1977). The comparative study of documentary material, dating from 1880 to 1930, demonstrated how the children of Italian immigrants had a higher probability than those from Jewish families of continuing to live in the city: among the married children in 1930, 60% lived at the same address as their parents.

From a study conducted in a Chicago neighborhood, Suttles (1968) described the Italians as individuals leading a double life: "During the day, they live in the neighborhood and go about their work without considering their ethnicity. When they go back home at night, however, they're obliged to reassume their Old World identity" (p. 105).

Another essential element in the description of the Italian American family is the manner in which emotions and feelings are expressed in everyday life. Vecoli (1974) identified this area as one of the principal distinguishing characteristics of the Italian American family. Johnson (1985) described the family atmosphere as follows: "A fluctuating emotional atmosphere exists wherein expressions of love can rapidly erupt into rage and hostility; at the end of the conflict, there is minimal observable resentment. Consequently, conflict is a common characteristic of familial life, but it is usually confined to periodic outbreaks and rarely results in permanent, open wounds" (pp. 84–85). Neutral emotionality in the family is considered an American characteristic that is in contrast with the Italian way of relating to one another. While the expressions of emotion, of affection, of love, and of self-confidence are highly valued, these also possess a negative aspect, yet the weight of the positive aspect ultimately prevails over the other.

Another study was conducted by Maglione Chiacchio (1985) during the 1980s in Hewittown, an Italian enclave of New Jersey City predominantly comprised of immigrants from Casandrino, in the province of Naples. The research, of a qualitative type, analyzed the models of socialization and adaptation over the course of time, through 150 in-depth interviews within twenty families and other interviewees belonging to various community institutions.

The analysis highlighted how ethnicity was dynamic, yet persistent: in Hewittown the traditional institutions and values remained relatively stable and intact throughout the generations.

Residents of the community had shed light on the central role of the family and on the concept of the neighborhood as an extension thereof. Despite institutional changes, certain traditions were maintained. The boundaries of the neighborhood continued to erode as many non-Italians and other ethnic groups arrived; this could lead to the presumption that the future would hold the end of the Italian American ethnic community. At the same time, however, there was a renewal of interest and trends that presented the hypothesis of a stabilization of the group's ethnic identity. The residents, the community leaders, and the city administrators expressed this shift in terms of a renaissance. The emotional connections, the values, and the traditional institutions remained relevant not only for the residents, but also for those who left the community; the latter "have taken Hewittown with them" (Maglione Chiacchio, 1985, p. 282). The future of the Italian American ethnic community has been left in the hands of the younger generations and, at the time of the study's implementation, the community was in the midst of a "dynamic balance of transformation and persistence" (ibid).

The importance of the family for the Italian Americans has deep roots, grounded in Italian history (Riotto Sirey et al., 1985). For the Southern Italian farmers, historically, the family represented "the center of life, the support network, the measure of all things" (p. 7). Those who emigrated to America during the early years of the twentieth century brought with them a deep and established conviction that one could only trust the family.

The family—particularly the Italian American family from the years between the two world wars—was not viewed historically as the context within which the ethnic group had been able to preserve its own traditions at the cost of interference of social institutions and attraction to mass consumption, but rather it was viewed as the place where ethnic traditions—especially regarding diet—were created, by selectively drawing from the old values and characteristics and reformulating them in response to new tensions and contradictions, new needs and social pressures. The concept of the separateness of the family as a source of preservation and the transmission of ethnic traditions was also taken into consideration from the observation that

> the family (is a) subject producing ideology and traditions, (which) conditioned and were conditioned by the multiplicity of relations established over time by the Italian American community with other ethnic groups.... The family ideal influenced not only the "private" organization of relationships, roles, and generational and gender identities, but it has also shaped the negotiation of a collective positioning as "Italian Americans" in the public dimension—insofar as concerns social comportments and relationships with institutions, in the marketplace, within a social system organized by racial castes. In other words, the processes of Americanization, construction of a familial ideology, formation of an ethnic identity and a distinct dietary culture are interwoven in a complex manner. (Cinotto, 2001, p. 32).

PROFILE OF THE MOTHERS

Moving to the results from the study, it emerges that the mothers of the interviewees are most prevalently second generation of immigration (39%). More than one-quarter of the mothers had themselves emigrated and thus belong to the first generation, while slightly less than a quarter fall into the third generation. Altogether, the quota of mothers who are part of the fourth and fifth generations is equal to 8.6%.

More than 88% of the mothers belong to the Catholic faith, while only 4% profess a protestant religion.

Maternal education level results are primarily senior high school (38.6%), though the percentage of college graduates at the undergraduate and graduate level is collectively equal to 33.9%, to which can be added 2.5% who completed a PhD.

Within the occupational profile, the mothers of the interviewees primarily carry out clerical work (16.2%), teach (15.5%), or are housewives (16.2%). Over one-tenth respectively work in managerial departments and activities. Independent professionals are equal to 7.6%. Five percent are retired.

From the indications provided by the young people interviewed regarding maternal ethnicity, it emerges that the prevalent component is Italian (62.5%), which exceeds the indication of belonging to the generic "white ethnicity" by more than ten percentage points. Over 36% of the sample connects maternal affinity to the Italian American grouping, while slightly more than 12% have a mother of Irish origin (Figure 2.1).

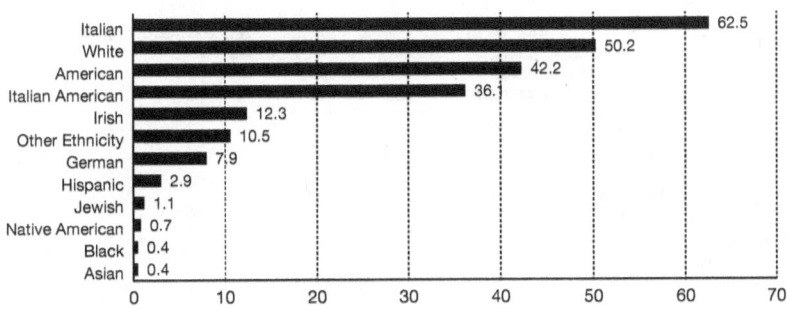

Figure 2.1 Ethnicity of the Mother

PROFILE OF THE FATHERS

The fathers of the interviewed young people belong, analogous with the mothers, especially to the second generation of immigration (37.5%). There is also a very elevated percentage for those arriving in the United States as immigrants (30.3%). More than one-fifth of the reference group indicates the fathers belong to the third generation, and altogether 6.8% of the quota fall within the fourth and fifth generation

Of the fathers, 84.5% are Catholic, while the number of fathers professing a protestant faith is lower (3.2%), compared to the mothers.

Regarding education, one-third of the fathers obtained a high school diploma; another third completed a university degree, including both undergraduate and graduate levels, to which can be added another 4% who obtained the title of PhD.

The prevalent paternal occupations include the managerial and entrepreneurial sector (19.9%) and independent professionals (17%). One-tenth of fathers are businessmen and the same quota work in the service sector. More than one-fifth of the fathers are not active participants in the job market.

Regarding the ethnicity of the fathers, as it was observed for the mothers, the young people indicate primarily the Italian component, reaching a superior percentage—though only slightly—with respect to the mothers. The same tendency is recorded for the indication of belonging to the generic "white ethnicity," which is indicated at a decrease of ten points compared to Italian-ness (53.4%). More than 39% of the fathers have Italian American origins, and the same amount claim American origins (Figure 2.2).

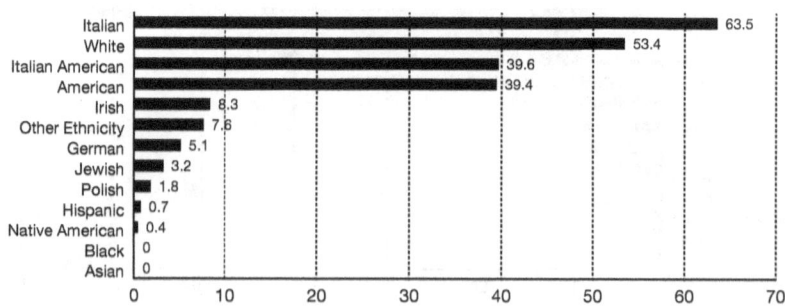

Figure 2.2 Ethnicity of the Father

SOCIALIZATION IN FAMILY AND PEER GROUPS

Before beginning to analyze the data, it's necessary to specify which socialization model is being referenced.

The first way to define socialization is to consider it a "transmission" of the cultural patrimony and, specifically, of its values. This concerns a top-down, unidirectional transmission, namely, from one generation to the next. Emphasis on this interpretation was much stronger with respect to the perspective of horizontal transmission or bottom-up transmission (which was described, in a certain period of social unrest, as "reverse socialization") (Torrioni, Albano, 2008). In contrast to this vision is the idea of socialization as a local and contingent "construct," wherein those socially affected are seen as autonomous, reflective, and proactive subjects. A third hypothesis for the study of the socialization of values in a familial atmosphere is defined as a process of "joint regulation" and aids in the comprehension of the reciprocal relationship as it currently exists between parents and children living together. The two authors intend regulation to mean "the manner of producing and developing an action process" and, as befalls every social process including socialization in the family, these "sets of decisions and actions reciprocally oriented, necessarily ordered through rules of varied origins" (p. 68) come into play. In the process of joint regulation, the concrete processes are derived from the meeting of values and institutionalized rules with rules produced locally, in the family. Moreover, the regulation is derived from the meeting of rules defined by the parents and rules autonomously produced by the children; thus, the regulation in the family setting is inspired by the principle of reciprocity (ibid.).

This process is described as follows:

> From the first days of life, parents regulate—even unconsciously—their children's activity based on practices and values that they themselves had absorbed, discovering that regulation as such is not an entirely unilateral act. As time passes, the children's regulatory autonomy with respect to the parents grows and the process of regulation becomes even less unilateral. In joint regulation, social values are selected, adopted, and continually redefined in a reciprocal exchange among family members and between the family and its significant surroundings.

One question in the survey was aimed at investigating the continuity between the parents' generation and the children's generation, according to the perceptions of the latter, in relation to various aspects including the system of values, ways of thinking and acting, habits, gestures and behaviors, physical appearance, and way of speaking (Table 2.3).

What emerges from the results emphasizes a notable continuity on the ethical level between parents and children. More controversial is the translation of reference values in the ways of thinking and dealing with life. Almost 20% of the young people have, in fact, indicated feeling little or not at all like their father in ways of thinking and 26% declared having little or no similarity to his way of dealing with life. The same percentage of indications apply regarding the mother, in the sense that over 20% share little or nothing with her in the way of thinking and over 26% of the young people don't recognize any resemblance in the way of dealing with life.

Table 2.3 Resemblances of the interviewed young people with their parents (value percent).

	WITH THE FATHER			
	Very much	Some	Little	Not at all
Values	52.7	33.2	6.9	4.0
Way of thinking	34.3	43.0	13.4	6.5
Ways to deal with life	31.8	37.2	19.1	7.9
Habits	28.2	42.6	16.6	8.3
Gestures and behavior	39.0	41.2	11.2	5.4
Physical appearance	33.6	44.8	13.4	5.1
Way of speaking	27.8	42.2	18.8	7.9
	WITH THE MOTHER			
	Very much	Some	Little	Not at all
Values	54.9	31.8	4.7	1.4
Way of thinking	29.2	43.0	15.5	5.4
Ways to deal with life	27.4	39.0	18.4	8.7
Habits	26.7	47.3	14.1	5.1
Gestures and behavior	38.3	38.6	12.6	3.2
Physical appearance	36.8	40.1	12.3	4.7
Way of speaking	31.4	39.0	18.4	4.7

*The missing responses are calculated by subtraction in the respective items

More then 24% of the interviewees do not possess similar habits to their father and 19% recognized little or no connection with maternal ones.

The percentage of the individuals that demonstrate little inclination to adopt parental behaviors and gestures is limited to 16% for the father and 15% for the mother.

The results of the research appear to be in keeping with the products of other comparative surveys and studies internationally, that is to say, the values for the children do not substantially differ from those of the parents, and, more generally, from widespread societal views; this indicates a substantial uniformity throughout various social strata (Torrioni, Albano, 2008). Thus, within socialization, elements of continuity are recognizable, especially in explicit values that connote the dialog between parents and children; observing the aspects of regulation wherein the values do not cease to be effective, yet are predominantly implicit and translated into actual practices and behaviors, there are notable elements of discontinuity with respect to the past (ibid.).

The family is thus confirmed, as it were, in its "work of socialization for the values of the new generations, both as a point of reflection and as of a moral discussion more in general: the family contributes to the reproduction of values in a group, in a community, in a society" (ibid, p. 84).

However, the rules of cohabitation for parents and children change, owing to both the growing importance of other agents of socialization and the significant transformations that occur in the course of life.

Returning to the results of the study, the continuity between generations appears more marked regarding physical appearance; only 18% claim to have no physical resemblance with the father and 17% with the mother.

In the way of speaking, instead, differences are accentuated: in fact, more than 26% of the interviewees record only a slight or no similarity within this aspect with the father and 23% with the mother.

In summary, the major continuity between parents and children is observable on the ethical level, in gestures, in behaviors, and in exterior physical appearance. A major discontinuity is noted in comparisons of inclinations concerning actions, that is to say, in ways of thinking, dealing with life, and in verbal mannerisms.

This would indicate that, although reference values are often shared with their parents, a different significance is attributed to them when translated to the level of daily life.

Furthermore, it is interesting to note how contacts of friendship are configured during the various phases of socialization, particularly as it relates to different ethnic groups, including the Italian Americans.

Table 2.4 Ethnic belonging of friends over the course of life (percentage values)

PERIODS OF LIFE	ONLY ITALIAN AMERICANS	DIVERSE ETHNIC BACKGROUNDS INCLUDING ITALIAN AMERICANS	DIVERSE ETHNIC BACKGROUNDS BUT NOT INCLUDING ITALIAN AMERICANS
During primary school	15.5	72.9	9.4
During secondary school	6.5	80.5	10.5
At the present time	5.1	80.1	12.3

As observable from Table 2.4, more than 15% of the interviewees' formative years, when they entered school, were in a setting that included only Italian American children. The number of those whose period of secondary school was within a uniform ethnic environment is notably reduced by over half, and, has further decreased within the present moment. Those that claim to have been raised since infancy in a mixed setting from an ethnic standpoint are equal to 73% of the respondents. Over the course of secondary school and at the present moment, the percentage of those with friends of differing ethnic compositions including Italian Americans increases further, encompassing over 80% of the total.

One-tenth of the young people interviewed declared having had friends of diverse ethnic backgrounds, other than Italian Americans, during primary school. The percentage of those who experienced this trend in friendship attendance increases in the course of secondary school (10.5%) and further still at the present moment (12.3%). This signifies that currently—apart from the majority of people having friends with diverse ethnic backgrounds—there is, on one side, a group of young people that only consort with Italian Americans (equal to 5%) and another more numerous group (12.3%) that has friends with diverse ethnic backgrounds, but not including Italian Americans.

Undoubtedly, among those who grew up with and also currently have friendly relationships in a mixed context in terms of ethnic profile—including the

Italian Americans—the group belonging to the fourth generation stand out noticeably. The second generation was most prevalent among those who instead had, in the course of primary and secondary school, only spent time with other Italian Americans. Analyzing the friendly consorting at the present time, one notes that it's now, again, especially the young people belonging to the second generation whose friendships are exclusively within Italian American groups; but also, vice versa, among this group there are also young people having friend groups in which Italian Americans are not present.

3

Ethnic Identification

ETHNICITY OF THE RESPONDENTS

The section of the questionnaire dedicated to ethnicity begins with a question referring to citizenship. Of the interviewees, 84.8% possesses American citizenship. In addition, the group that also possesses Italian citizenship is equal to 13.4%.

Among the ways of understanding the phases of change that accompany the ethnic processes, there is that which is connected to the generations (Alba, 1985). Generation, in this context, is defined as the "distance from the point of immigration": the immigrants themselves count as the first generation, their children—the first indigenous generation—are counted as the second generation and so on. Every generation of an ethnic group potentially represents another step of accommodation within the host society. As this applies to American ethnic groups, Alba notes that every new generation is more accultured than the one preceding it, at least for the first four generations. Consequently, the description of ethnic changes is often observed through generational differences.

The position of the interviewee with respect to their Italian background places them primarily in the third (39.7%) and in the second (39%) generation, while one-fifth of the sample are part of the fourth and fifth generations (20.6%).

To analyze the self-identification in terms of ethnicity and race, a list was proposed containing twelve non-auto-exclusive categories, from which the subjects were able to choose without a number limitation of selections.

As noted by Figure 3.1, feeling "white" was indicated by 71.5% of the interviewees.

Subsequently, in the list of nationalities that break down ethnic self--identification, we find feeling Italian (63.5%), followed by an equal indication for feeling Italian American and American (59.6%). More than one-tenth of the respondents mention having Irish ancestors and 6.5% show ancestors of German origin in their ethnic background.

Waters (1990) noted that the tension between being American and having a specific ethnic origin is especially complex. The relationship between being American and belonging to an ethnic group can be represented as a series of—more or less inclusive—concentric circles of identity; the individuals picture themselves as American and within this as Irish, Italian, or Polish. In many cases, the two identities are complementary, even if there is a large variation with respect to the weight that people assign to the various components of their identification.

From the study conducted by Waters during the eighties, it emerged that the interviewed subjects indicated giving priority to being American in the relationship between the two identities; this identity was taken for granted on a daily basis and was only brought to light when the people traveled outside the United States. Feeling Italian American or Irish American was, instead, a modality that they used to differentiate themselves from those groups with whom they interacted every day.

A large number of people emphasized the fact that the identity as American was the primary one and there had never been a situation where this had presented an opposing position to another identification.

Being "American" is a political and national category rather than a cultural or ethnic one; as such, the identification as American takes on a political value in the sense that it is intended in terms of loyalty and patriotism, something in which to feel pride and connectedness.

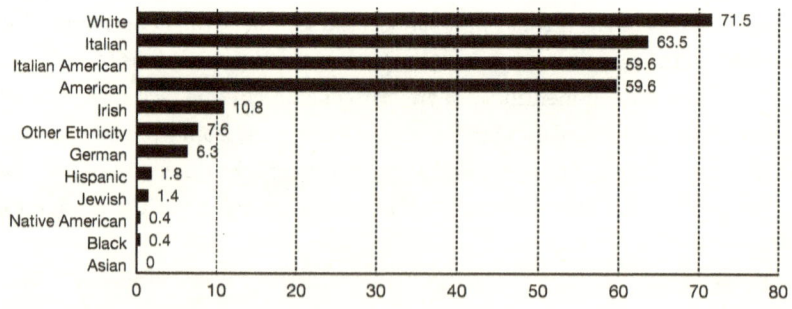

Figure 3.1 Ethnicity of the Interviewees

A successive question requested that the interviewees subdivide by percentage points—for a total of 100%—the diverse components of their ethnic background. From the indications provided, it is noted that 37.5% of the sample considers themselves "100% Italian descent," more than 24.9% feels "Italian together with another identification with a different ethnic group," while almost 10% describe their ethnicity as composed of "Italian parts together with belonging to two other ethnic groups." One group equal to 7.6% described itself as Italian and American while more than 5% of those interviewed believed themselves to be 100% Italian American.

Subsequently, from the indications that break down the ethnicity of the interviewees, the percentage of declared Italian-ness was "extracted." The variable constructed as such aimed to "quantitatively" understand the weight of the Italian component in the interviewee's overall ethnic identification. The reaggregation according to percentage intervals is presented in Table 3.1.

The group that expressed feeling 25% Italian equals 3.6%, while over a quarter of the sample felt half Italian. Those declaring to have a totally Italian descent are equal to 37.5% of the interviewees and those claiming three-quarters are equal to 13.4%.

Table 3.1 How Italian are you?

	NO.	%
0	1	0.4
25%	10	3.6
From 26% to 49%	9	3.3
50% Italian	72	26.0
From 51% to 74%	6	2.2
75%	37	13.4
From 76% to 99%	11	4.2
100% Italian	104	37.5
25% Italian + 50% Italian American	1	0.4
From 15% to 50% Italian American	6	2.2
100% Italian American	14	5.1
N/A	6	2.2
TOTAL	277	100.0

ETHNICITY OF THE PARTNER

Of the interviewees, 65.3%, equal to 181 subjects, have a partner/husband/wife. In order to analyze the ethnicity of the partner, the young people were asked to indicate the racial and ethnic categories to which their partner could be connected. The categories indicated are especially "white" (47%) and American (40.3%) (Fig. 3.2).

Subsequently, the category "Italian" was marked by 30% of the sample, while over a quarter of the respondents have an "Italian American" partner. One-fifth of the interviewees indicated having a partner of Irish origin, the most mentioned ethnic group after Italian and Italian American, 14.4% of them have a Hispanic origin, over one-tenth indicate German ethnicity for their own partner, while 11.6% make reference to origins from different European states than those explicitly proposed in the question (Greece, Denmark, Switzerland, Albania, Ukraine, etc.).

Other racial and ethnic lineages—including Hebrew, Scots, English, Polish, Asian, black, and Native American—receive residual indications.

As previously observed, the indications of those people who have a partner of Italian or Italian American origin are, respectively, equal to 30% and 25%, while the other indications of the ethnicity of the partner illuminates a jagged universe of lineages.

While there is still a certain endogamous tendency in the choice of partner, this is counterbalanced by an analogous tendency to select a partner outside of the Italian American community.

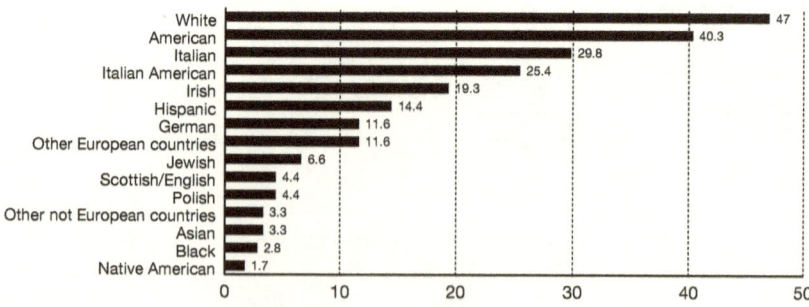

Figure 3.2 Ethnicity of the Partner

ETHNICITY: WAYS OF INTERPRETING IT

An alternative way to gain insight into the elucidation of their ethnicity from the young Italian Americans was the objective of a battery of questions, constructed according to the procedure of the Likert scale, which inquires the level of agreement/disagreement of the young people.

Figure 3.3 synthesizes what emerged from the collected responses of "very much and somewhat agree" and that of "slightly and not all agree" for the various items proposed.

More than 82% of those interviewed claim that the majority of people in America continue in the present day to demonstrate a large attachment to their own ethnic group. This opinion stands alongside the perception of 60% of the young people who claim that the permanence of diverse ethnic groups in America has also led to a homogenization of ethnic differences.

Conversely, over 62%—respectively—express little agreement with the idea that coming from diverse ethnic backgrounds is no longer important and that the interviewee him/herself doesn't for the most part feel this sense of belonging.

PATHWAYS OF ETHNIC IDENTIFICATION

Mary Waters (1990) observes that there are four factors that influence the choice of one's own ethnic identification among the various ancestors of European

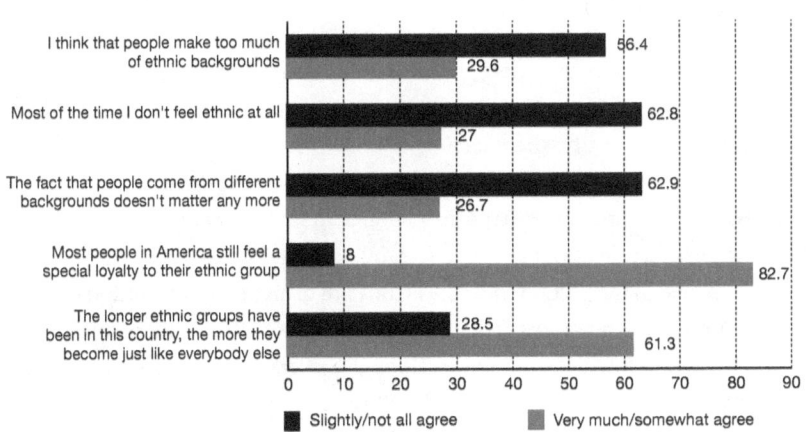

Figure 3.3 Ideas About the Ethnic Background

descent; included among these is the knowledge the individual possesses regarding their own ancestors, namely, which options are available to choose from within one's family tree. In turn, the knowledge and the interest for this identification are influenced by socioeconomic factors of the family status, especially the schooling, the family structure (divorce, geographic mobility, ways of living together and the effect this has on the level of intensity and contact among the components of the family), as well as the number of generations that have made up the historic frame of reference of the family since their arrival in the United States.

Different factors, however, interfere with the intergenerational transfer of information regarding the ethnic background. For the first and second generation, the transfer of information regarding the ethnic origin is not an intentional process but the result of socialization. For the third and subsequent generations, this becomes a more conscious process. The transfer of information tends to also become more complicated across the generations with the increase of mixed marriages.

The passage of information regarding ethnic background is also connected to the level of education of the family. According to what Lieberson (1985) observed, the families that attained a high level of education and an optimal social position have greater prospects of successfully transmitting to their own descendants the information connected to their ethnic heritage than those less educated and who occupy lower social positions.

Regarding the family structure, Waters (1990) observes that the passage of information across the generations is facilitated in the families that remain close over the course of the individuals' life cycles; these people have more time and opportunities to collect complex information about their predecessors. Families split by divorce, losses, or geographic mobility may lose access to official documents and key informants (grandparents, aunts, uncles, and other family members). These observations direct the focus of attention to another fundamental aspect of identity: the question of continuity.

How, then, can ethnic identity keep itself alive across the generations? History assumes a certain importance in the formation of the ethnic identity. Epstein (1978) thus describes its role as not so much to provide "an authentic recording of what really happened in the past nor by tracing the path of an historic evolution to show how the present has developed from the past, but rather offering individuals a perception of their past that enables them, through a selective accentuation of certain values, to carry out clear and explicit identifications with their ancestors" (p. 14).

Among the dimensions that structure the collective identity there is—as it has been observed—the semantic space within which it falls (Ashmore et al., 2004).

Included among the contents and significances associated with such a collective identity are the narrative representations that the individuals construct about themselves and the categories to which they belong (Mancini, 2006). There are two important aspects that define the types of narration and are fundamental for the conceptualization of the collective identity: one's own history as a member of a particular group, as well as the history of the group (Ashmore et al., 2004).

The story of these individuals as members of a group is composed of thoughts, feelings, images of the past, of the present, and of the future; the level of elaboration of this personal story can vary as well. The history of the group to which they belong takes into consideration the origins of the group, its history, and the relationships with the context. This dimension includes the mental images and the emotions that concern the group's past, the myth of its origins, past victories and defeats, the group's present status, and its anticipated future conditions. Thus, the narration of the group's history is not limited to the current state of the life of the group, but can also refer to mythical constructions of the past and hypothetical projections in the future (Mancini, 2006).

IMMIGRATION AND THE MEMORY THEREOF

As noted by Teti (2013), for the Italians leaving their own country/region, "[E]migration was a hope, but first it was a loss, a prolonged sorrow.... One world was coming to an end in the search for land and for bread, to escape hunger and bullying.... In spite of so much instrumental rhetoric and sterile, inauthentic nostalgias, life was not beautiful for people in that old world" (pp. 10–11).

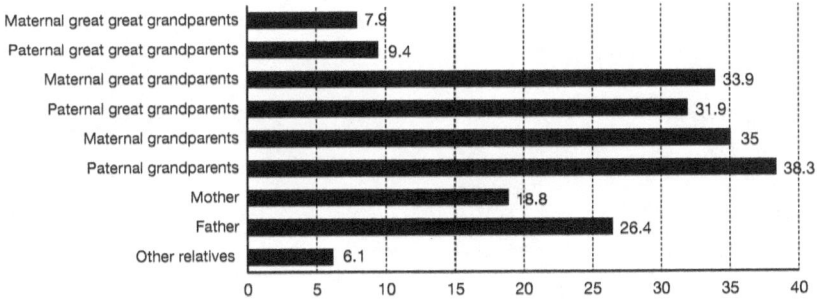

Figure 3.4 Ancestors who Emigrated to the United States

In Southern Italy, emigration was a "silent revolution" of thousands of farmers and laborers, a great catastrophe, a cause of abandonment and ruin. The exodus to America emptied regions that already in their own past had had to overcome the trials of an environment marked by continuous natural disasters, by quarrels, murders, and constant baronial oppression (Teti, 2013, p. 64).

From the survey, the memory of the ancestors who emigrated to the United States still appears vivid and present. Only three interviewees, in fact, claimed they did not know who their ancestors were that emigrated to the United States.

The places of their families' origins were also known by the majority of the respondents. Only eight of the sample, in fact, did not know from which region their ancestors had departed. Specifically, the regions of origin are compiled in Table 3.2, in which Campania, Sicily, and Calabria are notable as the points of

Table 3.2 Regions of Emigration

	NO.	%
Campania	136	30.5
Sicily	121	27.1
Calabria	52	11.7
Apulia	36	8.1
Abruzzo	23	5.2
Lazio	18	4.0
Basilicata	15	3.4
Tuscany	9	2.0
Emilia Romagna	7	1.6
Lombardy	6	1.3
North Italy	5	1.1
Piedmont	4	0.9
Molise	4	0.9
Veneto	4	0.9
Trentino Alto Adige	2	0.4
Central Italy	1	0.2
Umbria	1	0.2
Marche	1	0.2
Outside Italy	1	0.2
TOTAL	446	100.0

departure for a large part of the ancestors or the parents of the interviewees. Altogether, four-fifths of the sample come from Southern Italy.

Regarding the year of arrival, knowledge is limited: over 40% declared they did not know the year/s of their Italian ancestors' arrival.

Almost one-fifth of the ancestors arrived on American soil during the years of the great migration between the end of the nineteenth and the first twenty years of the twentieth century.[1] The predecessors of almost 15% of the interviewees arrived during both the postwar period—from 1946 to 1964—and the period that followed—beginning from the 1965 approval of the Hart-Celler Act[2] up to 1980. Arrivals after 1980 are very scarce.

THE ITALIAN AMERICAN IDENTIFICATION

A central part of the questionnaire was dedicated to analyzing the subjects' self-identification as Italian Americans. The analysis comes from a series of questions designed to study the level of knowledge of the Italian American culture, its history, its customs and traditions, its artistic and literary production, its music, the fairy tales, the prayers and the ways of speaking, the traditional festivals and, finally, use of recipes in the kitchen.

Figure 3.5—which aggregates the answers "much and some"—highlights how familiar the interviewees are with the popular traditions and customs (92.4%) and furthermore discloses that 90% use much or some the traditional recipes for cooking.

Analyzing this question in relation to the different generations of immigration among the interviewees, it emerges that the most comprehensive level of

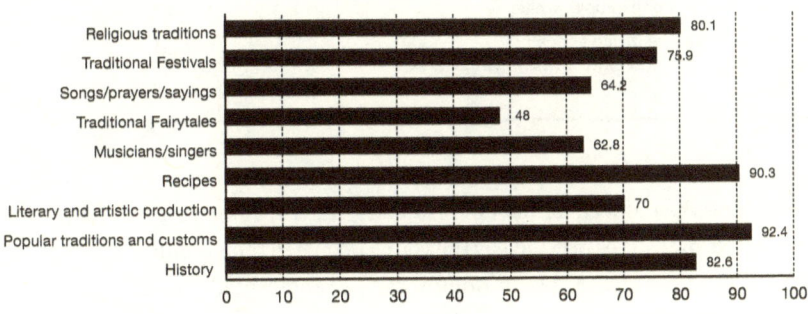

Figure 3.5 Knowledge of Italian American Culture (much/some)

knowledge of Italian American culture is held by the young people belonging to the second generation. Only in the fields of culinary recipes and music does the third generation attain the primary place for highest level of knowledge.

A question asked the interviewees to specify whether they considered themselves Italian American or, as an alternative to this, how they would describe themselves in terms of ethnic profile. From the studies conducted we find that young Italian Americans tend to position themselves and other Italian Americans along an ethnic continuum (Mitrano, 1999) that would represent different "grades and levels of Italian-ness," within which an individual could be more or less Italian on the basis of the number and quality of cultural, physical, and of personality elements that she/he possesses along this continuum. In the context of the present study, 85.6% claimed they identified as Italian American, while 11.6% expressed opposition to this self-definition.

The following synthetic categories, presented in Table 3.3, were created from a re-aggregation of the answers of the people who chose not to identify themselves with this label.

Table 3.3 If you do not consider yourself Italian American, how do you self-identify?

	FREQUENCY	PERCENTAGE
Italian and American	6	18.8
Italian, Italian born abroad	10	31.3
American with an Italian background	4	12.5
American	4	12.5
American Italian	2	6.3
In another way (for example, white)	5	16.7
Removed from the Italian ancestors	1	3.1
TOTAL	32	100.0

Beyond the reduced number of responses, it's very interesting to analyze the alternative modalities provided by the young people in their ethnic identification, inasmuch as the idea of the continuum can be represented across these various identifications. If we imagine a continuum that connects two opposing poles, where on one side we find "feeling Italian" and on the other "feeling American," there is a noticeable intermediate gradient that accentuates or lessens the sense of belonging to one nationality or the other.

Thus, while several modalities—such as "Italian," "Italian born abroad," and "far from the Italian ancestors"—are expressed as being located at the pole of most-expressed Italian-ness, others express an intermediate position, balanced between the two poles—as in the case of "Italian and American"—and, finally, there are modalities that reveal a leaning toward the American pole, expressed by "American with an Italian background," "American Italian," and "American."

To analyze more deeply the sense of belonging among people who identified themselves as Italian Americans, a series of reasons that could support this identification were specified (Table 3.4). Included among the elements that count the most in one's identification are having at least one parent of Italian origin (97.4%), followed by feeling connected to the Italian origins (95.4%); less often indicated are belonging to the Italian American community (70%), and feeling part of the Italian American culture (89%).

In the ranking of the responses that refer to identification, the choice of the Italian language is connected to the sixth postion in descending order, preferred with an intensity of "very much" and "somewhat" by 58% of the young people.

Table 3.4 How much is your consideration of yourself as Italian American affected by: (Very much/somewhat) (percentage values)

Having at least one parent of Italian descent	97.4
Feeling a connection to your Italian origins	95.4
Feeling a part of the Italian American culture	89.0
Belonging to the Italian American community	70.1
Belonging to an international network of people who share the Italian culture	58.3
Speaking Italian	57.8
Having a partner of Italian descent	28.3

The importance of the Italian language as a part of "being Italian," as a source of cultural wealth and value to be transmitted in the raising of one's own children for the cognitive benefit derived from bilingualism, has been confirmed by a study conducted by Fellin (2014) between 1994 and 2005 (which is referred to as a source of insight) on forty Italian immigrants between the ages of thirty-six and fifty, residing in North Carolina and belonging to a new wave of immigrants from Italy that have arrived over the last thirty years.

The battery of questions regarding the motivations that support feeling Italian American were subjected to a factorial analysis, to determine the dimensions that characterize this belonging. Observing the communality, the decision was made to include only five items in the factorial analysis, out of the seven proposed.

The analysis highlighted the gathering of variables around two dimensions that characterize the subjects' identification as Italian American: on one hand, the "gaze" toward Italy—through knowing the language, the attachment to family origins, feeling part of an international network of people who share a culture and its values—and on the other hand, giving priority, instead, to a primarily American belonging, more specifically to the Italian American culture and community.

Subsequently, the points values between 0 and 1 were calculated for each subject, within the two dimensions. Then, with the aim of creating a typology of four dimensions that would permit the understanding of the connection of the interviewees with respect to the specified areas, (nearness/distance from Italy, nearness/distance from America), the points values were split between the two values: 0 = the lowest level on the dimension and 1 = the highest.

The typology produced from the intersecting of the two dimensions can be represented as follows:

Table 3.5 Typology on nearness/distance from America and from Italy

	NO.	%	% CUMULATIVE
Yes nearness to Italy—Yes nearness to America	94	33.9	33.9
No nearness to Italy—No nearness to America	59	21.3	55.2
Yes nearness to Italy—No nearness to America	42	15.2	70.4
No nearness to Italy—Yes nearness to America	37	13.4	83.8
N/A (missing response to one or more of the items)	45	16.2	100.0
TOTAL	277	100.0	

The distribution of frequency in the typology categories highlights the prevalence of young people (equal to 34% of the interviewees) who feel a closeness to both the United States and Italy within their ethnic identification. There is also a quota of people—equal to over 20%—who don't seem to feel close to one or the other of the two nations. The intermediate situations—which collectively represent roughly 15% of the sample—highlight that there are young people who feel closer to Italy than the United States or vice versa.

THE TRANSMISSION OF ETHNIC IDENTITY

A relevant question addresses the continuity of ethnic identity, where the modalities through which the sense of identity is transmitted come into play. On one hand, there are explicit and institutionalized forms of transmission, including the teaching of history, which, together with other modalities, consciously augment the sense of ethnic identity. On the other, it should also be considered how a sense of ethnic identity awakens and grows in an individual. Such a process begins with the start of infancy: "It is within the experience of childhood that the roots of ethnic identity are firmly planted, and in the process acquire the emotional charge that can be such a powerful force in the subsequent course of life" (Epstein, 1978, p. 14). Moreover, the development of the sense of ethnic identity becomes intimately connected with subconscious identifications with the earliest figures of attachment; specifically, within this context, the grandparents play a very important role.

Flügel (1948) noted that "the tendency to imitate the grandfather can constitute an important factor in the modelling of beliefs, attachments, desires, and activities of the child" (p. 163, ref. in Epstein, 1978).

Epstein's hypothesis highlights the importance assumed by the nature of the relationship with the grandparents connected to ethnicity. The author maintains that when within the family structure the authority is embodied by the parents—especially the father—tensions are created that gradually increase as the child nears adolescence and approaches adulthood. This produces, moreover, conflict between the contiguous generations; such oppositions are offset by the identification developed between alternating generations: "It is in this process of identification with the grandparents that the child comes to attach itself to some values that they share and it is in such a way that the grandparents come to exhibit the function of a symbol of continuity that anchors the sense of ethnic identity" (Epstein, 1978, p. 254). Obviously, such observations must be contextualized in the diverse circumstances and in the structure of the social relations within which the relationship between grandchildren and grandparents is molded.

Furthermore, in order to guarantee the maintenance of one's own cultural origins, the level of involvement in the cultural practices of the same group of origin, together with the contact and the social support received from the community, are of crucial importance. Altogether, these aspects, which can be independent of each other and even in opposition, contribute to the psychosocial well-being of the people involved (Ashmore et al., 2004).

In light of the conducted research, there was no marked conflict observed between parents and children. The fact remains that between grandchildren and grandparents a significant relationship very frequently develops wherein the grandparents play an important identification role and contribute to the development of the individual in the sense of ethnic identity. One question in the survey, then, was focused on understanding which people in the family had contributed to bringing the interviewees to the Italian culture.

Table 3.6 exhibits to what extent the grandmother was the most important and significant reference of attachment with the Italian cultural heritage, since it was especially she—for more than three-fourths of the sample—who transmitted this legacy to the grandchildren; her influence is followed by that of other relatives (73.6%) and by the active role conducted by the interested person himself (69%). From the intersection of this question with the interviewee's generation within the immigrant family, it emerges that primarily the second generation is the one most connected—through family influence—to their Italian cultural heritage. Only in cases with referral connected to the influence of

Table 3.6 Within your family who put you in contact with the Italian culture? (percentage values)

	%
The grandmother	75.1
Other relatives	73.6
Yourself	69.0
The father	65.7
The mother	62.5
The grandfather	62.1
Everyone	48.0
No one	1.1

the grandmother does the number of interviewees indicating this belong prevalently to the third generation.

THE IMPORTANCE OF ETHNIC IDENTIFICATION

Another important query referring to the respondents' ethnic identification regards, more generally, the significance of this identification. The overwhelming majority of the interviewees indicated such heritage as very (71.1%) or somewhat (24.5%) important. Among those who selected the indication "very important," young people of the second generation after immigration were most prevalent, while those considering this factor "somewhat important" were especially of the fourth and fifth generations.

The maximum importance attributed to the ethnic heritage is positively correlated to the frequency of visits to Italy by the interviewee; among those people that are taken to Italy many times there is an elevated percentage that attribute great importance to their Italian heritage. Among those who attribute a less marked importance to their Italian background, the majority of interviewees have never visited Italy.

Observing the correlation level between the attribution of relevance to ethnic heritage and the presence of relatives in Italy, it is noted that among those attributing a higher importance to heritage there is a prevalence of young people who have relatives in Italy. Among those who, instead, assign less importance to this identification there is a particular majority of those who claim to have no relatives in Italy. Also marked among those who attribute great importance to their ethnic heritage are the young people having many or some friends in Italy, while notable among the interviewees who assign it a low importance are those who claim to have few or no friends there.

The majority of the young people who assign great importance to ethnicity were in the group of people who claimed to have among their friends "new" immigrants from Italy who are of a similar age to the interviewees and also those who have been in contact with that group, even if they don't count them among their friends. Among the interviewees who, instead, attribute a reduced level of importance to their ethnic heritage a majority have had only work-related contact with the young Italians recently emigrated from Italy, who haven't had any contact with them, or who have encountered them only sporadically.

There is also a positive correlation which connects the highest level of importance attributed to ethnicity with a high frequency of research of information and news related to Italy on the part of the young people. Among the interviewees who claim to give "some" importance to ethnicity, notable are those who never receive news from Italy and those who receive it only annually.

The indications that have emerged up to this point direct the focus onto how the importance attributed to ethnicity is corroborated and reinforced, especially among people who have a connection with Italy and the Italians of today; this reflects both their having visited Italy themselves and also having relatives and friends with whom they are in contact, as well as knowing and maintaining relations with young Italian immigrants of recent arrival in the United States, and of keeping informed on life in Italy; all of these serve to reinforce the sense and the importance of this belonging. It is the present that ties one to the past, revitalizing and reinforcing it, projecting it toward the future.

REASONS FOR THE SIGNIFICANCE OF ETHNIC IDENTIFICATION

The reasons for the significance attributed to the ethnic identification were considered extremely relevant and as such the views of the interviewees regarding these were collected using the open-ended question: "How important is your ethnic background to you and why?"

In fact, to some the attribution of its relevance is connected to reasons based in the past, others find relevance in the present or the future. Next to the response categories are the indications for the temporal dimension to which these can be ascribed. These circumstances can exist concurrently within the motivational orientations of interviewees.

The responses provided were classified according to fifteen analytical categories:

1. part of the respondent's identity (present);
2. psychological security (present);
3. resemblance, sense of belonging (present);
4. difference (present);
5. respect, sense of duty, appreciation, continuity, connection (present);
6. interpersonal aspects (present);
7. emotional and sentimental aspects (present);

8   desire to know one's personal history (past);
9   desire to know the history of the group (past);
10 values learned during infancy and childhood (past);
11 part of daily life (present);
12 connection with present-day Italy (present);
13 desire to transmit one's ethnic cultural background to one's own children (future);
14 marginalization of the ethnic identity (present);
15 physical characteristics (present).

The analytical categories that emerged from the reclassification of the open responses may be illustrated in the observations presented by the interviewees themselves.

1 *Part of the identity:* ethnic belonging defines the person, it models a part of the identity, it explains certain behaviors and personality traits; it offers an interpretation of the kind of education one received.

> My ethnic background as an Italian American is very important to me because it is a part of my identity—it is part of who I am as a person. Accordingly, much of my individual character, family customs and traditions, and religious beliefs have been shaped by my ethnic background.
>
> I am who I am because I am an Italian American. Everything about me reflects my ethnicity. How I talk, act, dress, what I believe in, values, et cetera are all characteristics instilled in me from growing up around my family. I take great pride in my ancestry and background.
>
> It really is who I am, it is with whom I associate and feel "at home," it defines me and I am all the better for it!
>
> My ethnic background is one of the ways I am defined in American culture.

2 *Source of psychological security:* ethnic heritage is a source of pride and trust, of a sense of honor, of privilege, of belonging, and of accomplishment.

> Another reason I'm proud to be an Italian American is because of the community's countless contributions it has made to America. Italian Americans have greatly impacted the arts, theatre, entertainment, music, and cuisine in America. They have bought their passion and flair for

life, making America, and especially New York City, the beautiful place it is today.

Being Italian is a privilege and the Italian culture is immense and of extreme value to me. Being Italian is a sense of pride, it flows in my veins and my heart swells at the thought of my country. Despite being born in the United States, my childhood was in Italy and Italy has never left me. Every time I land in Italy I breathe a breath of relief because I know I am home.

3 *Resemblance, sense of belonging to a group:* Epstein (1978) made a note that within a group of people that share the same ethnic identity, the individual "finds a refuge that offers comfort and security: among relatives and friends there aren't just 'shared values and knowledge,' there is also trust and understanding" (p. 15).

Give me [sic] a sense of solidarity with fellow Italian Americans. Camaraderie among all of us.

Ethnic background is important to me because it offers a sense of belonging to a larger community.

4 *Difference:* in this case, the difference is viewed not so much as a synonym for feeling "less than the others" or as a feeling connected to low self-esteem, but rather it is seen as a richness that differentiates in a positive sense.

I knew I was different than some of my peers, but, didn't know how to appreciate it until I was older and spent a year studying abroad in Italy.

Give [sic] the sense to be part of a culture instead to be considered just "white." Difference versus "Other Whites."

The diversity is beautiful, and I enjoy most of the diverse things in my ethnic background, that can be intimate, personal, artistic, brilliant, and complex.

5 *Respect, sense of duty, appreciation, connectivity, gratitude, continuity with the "fathers" (grandparents, parents. . .):* some young people perceive a continuity with the generations that preceded them, accompanied by a deep sense of respect and gratitude toward the ancestors.

My ancestors left their countries [sic] to create better lives for themselves and future generations. I am one of those future generations, and I am thankful for all the opportunities I've been given that I may not have had in another country.

Sign of respect toward who came in this country before us. Wish to know their lives, their fights, their goals. Homage to them.

6 *Interpersonal aspects:* for some, the ethnic identification is reflected through expressive and interpersonal modalities that characterize it and influence the relationships that are established with other Italian Americans, but also with Americans of different ethnic backgrounds.

Additionally, I enjoy the unique common experience shared by total strangers who happen to have come from a similar background and maintained its traditions. There is a sense of communality that occurs from that, in a city that has lost much that old connectedness I grew up with. I rely a great deal on my ethnic identity while in NYC, the same way while out of NYC I rely a great deal on my New Yorker identity.

To marry someone else with the same background.

Influence on the relationships with colleagues and friends not only of Italian origins.

Knowing your ethnic background inherently plays a role in how others perceive and treat you.

7 *Sentimental and emotional aspects (love, nostalgia, happiness...):* the emotional valence of identification is expressed through feelings of love toward the culture and the traditions, at times intermixed with nostalgia.

It is a part of me that is embedded in my soul and it has literally made me who I am at this time.

Love, nostalgia, embedded in my soul.

Emotional ties that link people and continue in the future.

8 *Desire to know one's own personal story:* at times, the identification translates

into the desire to explore one's personal story, to better understand one's own roots and family origins. One interviewee observed, "We are who we were."

> I identify strongly with Italian culture and people of Italian descent. I have a strong connection to the history of where my family originates from and how it has shaped our lives in America.

> I have always lived by the famous words of John Adams, "We are who we were," and that is how we have been raised. It's where my family come from.

> I am particularly interested in documenting my family tree so that my future children will have a "road map" and know what their heritage is too. Also, if you think of the saying "History repeats itself," you may see value in knowing your own personal history.

9 *Desire to know the history of the group:* even the knowledge of the history of Italy and of the Italians, as well as that of the Italian Americans, represents an important step for better understanding the significance of this identification.

> Wish to study your own origins, the history of Italians, Italian and Italian American culture, the past, the heritage.

10 *Values learned during infancy and childhood:* the reference value connected to the ethnic identification also emerges in a marked way. Specifically, for some young people, these values constitute the connective tissue of their own development since childhood.

> Since I was younger, I've had an interest in learning Italian. I took an Italian class in high school and more classes in college, and a personal goal of mine is to try to speak the language fluently. I've always been fascinated with Italian and Italian American culture; I have taken a couple of Italian and Italian American culture classes in college. The second course made me even more interested in the topic than I already was. I also made close relationships with people in college who are Italian American and also love and appreciate the culture and history like I do.

> Values (passion and flair for life, sense of family, togetherness, self-respect, work hard, dignity), sharing of meals, religious belief, faith, cuisine, history, all of those I grow up with. It's part of growing up.

I recently married, and I feel like the way I think and perceive things all stem from being brought up in an Italian household. I married someone of that same descent and I cannot image [sic] being with someone of any other culture. All the recipes and music and traditions bring me back to the time I was growing up and I get very nostalgic about it.

11 *Part of daily life:* the identification with Italian heritage finds expression in daily life and family activities.

It marks my daily life, my family life (way of thinking, acting, cooking).

It affects a lot of my parts of my life, from the way I think to the holidays I celebrate, the foods I eat, songs I enjoy and values I hold close to my heart.

12 *Connection with present-day Italy:* for some interviewees, it appeared fundamental to revitalize this identification through direct contact with present-day Italy.

We still maintain and pass down our Sicilian traditions, and I have been lucky to have had the opportunity to regularly visit my extended family in Sicily.

I also feel it's very important to keep in touch with the culture as much as I can by keeping my language skills sharp and visiting often. Even though that has become more difficult because of my schedule, I make every effort to keep up with current events, music, and sports in order to keep the connection with my culture strong.

13 *Desire to transmit one's ethnic cultural background to one's own children:* the recognition of the importance of one's own ethnic identification is affirmed through the desire to transmit it as a gift to one's children and to future generations.

I want to pass family recipes and stories to my children one day.

It is my connection with my living grandparents. I want to be able to share their culture with the children one day.

14 *Marginalization of the ethnic identity:* for some of the interviewees, their ethnic background does not influence life in a significant way. Ethnic identity is

instead seen as marginal and not as something that defines the person. The young people feel American above all, or in some cases, American Italian. One of the young people remarked that the Italian ethnic cultural background has now been lost, another noted that keeping this heritage alive would entail going against the desires of his own predecessors; others maintain that their personal identity has nothing to do with the stereotypes connected to the Italian American culture, while other people thought of themselves primarily and above all as American.

> I don't try to place too much emphasis on it, because I find it only shapes my personality at the margins.

> It's somewhat important to me because I feel it's been deliberately lost over the generations, starting with my great-great-grandparents that refused to teach their children Italian; so the knowledge I have has been censored and watered down. Sometimes I feel like it's important to look into it and other times I feel like my ancestors sacrificed so much to assimilate that it does them a disservice to backtrack onto it.

> I'm proud of my family's history. We're the American Experience. But part of immigration is a transformation. I'm the product of that transformation. I know where my family came from, but in the present moment I'm who I am. And that is very important to me. My personal identity is very important. I had a friend who tried to tell me since my part of my family had an Italian background then I was culturally Catholic. It really pissed me off. I hate the Catholic Church. But to her, that was what Italian American meant. I feel like for most people in the United States if you say, "I'm American" they understand that means a lot of different things. People are familiar enough with the different states and regions of our country. But if you say "I'm Italian American" suddenly I'm a character on *The Sopranos*. I'd rather let people figure out who I am first before they know my background.

> My country is who I am. It disturbs me how many Americans who have family that were born in Italy consider themselves Italian American instead of American Italian. This is our country, if we were born in Italy then that would be our country. I celebrate my ancestors and the culture I was brought up in but my place of birth and citizenship is in America.

I often emphasize that my family, being from Western New York, do not [sic] the New York City-centric stereotypes of Italian American, which I find somewhat offensive to all American Italians.

I am first of all American: American Italian. My allegiance is to the United States. Appreciation for the United States.

15 *Physical characteristics:* even physical characteristics can represent a symbol of ethnic identification.

Physically I look very Northern Italian. I love my family and they're Northern Italian.

Once the responses were interpreted, highlighting the constitutive elements that comprise them and arriving at the synthetic typology encompassing them and presented above, it became subsequently possible to analyze the distribution of frequency of the indications in the emergent categories.

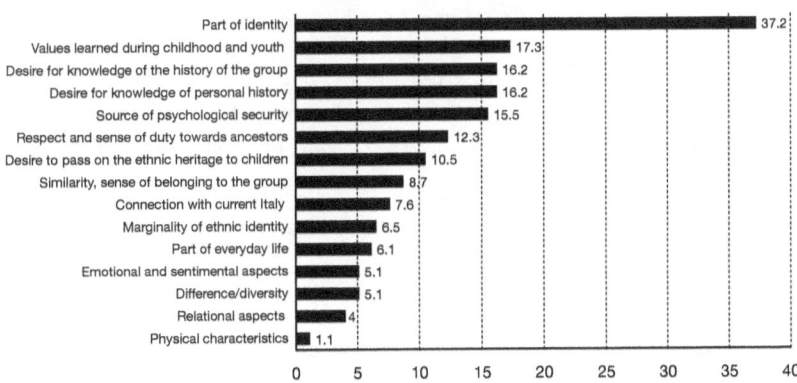

Figure 3.6 Why Is Ethnic Background Important?

Figure 3.6 synthesizes how it was expressed by the interviewees, shedding light especially on the foundational identity aspect occupied by ethnicity.

This component would highlight the deeper nature of the roots of this part of the identity, attributing to them a more substantive value than what was presented within the scope of Waters's research (1990), from which—for the respondents—it emerged that "these roots represent sources of pleasure, of a feeling a community, of a special status that makes the individual interesting and unique. This symbolically defined ethnicity does not place requests or demands on the individual, and they are not required to come together in any significant sense (unless the Saint Patrick's Day parade is defined as a meeting)" (p. 92).

In the case of this study, the sample attributed—in the majority of instances—a higher level of importance to ethnic heritage. This identification appears very strong and profoundly felt; and the reasons for the attributed importance are composed—as can be seen—of a variety of elements, which sometimes contradict each other, and which, for some, are deeply rooted in the structure of their identity.

The interviewees do not represent a uniform category in relation to their ethnic background and their identification with these identity components is often a choice, a personal and individual interpretation, which configures an overall picture full of meanings that are interconnected in a large fresco depicting the Italian heritage.

THE EMOTIONAL COMPONENT OF ETHNIC IDENTIFICATION

Epstein (1978) notes that identity touches the heart of individual personality and it is held together by a strongly emotional component. One of its aspects is certainly cognitive, but identity is also fed by roots that are based in the unconscious: "Thus the more that identity is clearly defined in its confines, so much so are its unconscious roots deepened and potentially more intense in emotional charge" (p. 182).

Ashmore and colleagues (2004) observed how attachment is that dimension of ethnic identity that implies the emotion a person feels regarding a category of belonging or the perception that the destiny of his/her own group overlaps their own personal destiny. What emerged from the conducted studies highlights how the emotional dimension connected to membership in a group is independent both in categorization and in its valuations and represents a predictor of important consequences of group belonging.

In literature, beginning in the sixties a theory arose—accepted by sociologists and psychologists—according to which some ethnic groups remained particularly vulnerable to feelings of low self-esteem and even self-loathing (Erikson, 1963, 1968; Klein, 1980; Shibutani, Kwan, 1965, ref, in Riotto Sirey et al., 1985).

Some studies also demonstrated that a clear sense of connection to one's own ethnic group was tied to greater self-esteem, a sense of well-being, and a positive concept of oneself[3] (Klein, 1980).

In 1983, a project was developed, financed by the Italian-American Institute to Foster Higher Education, which sought to understand—through three ethnotherapy groups—the psychological impact of the sense of belonging to one's ethnic group on the self-esteem of individuals.[4] The goal of the project was to explore the influence of ethnic identity on the development of personality as well as on self-esteem. The hypothesis guiding the project was that participation in the process of ethnotherapy would enhance ethnic pride and the sense of belonging[5]. The positive outcome of this path would be an increase in self-esteem. Moreover, the individuals of the group would have attained greater control over their own lives.

The study—in which twenty-seven subjects participated, comprising sixteen women and eleven men—provided a significant profile of the second and third generations of Italian Americans through their answers to questions connected to their ethnic identity and its role. The expected results were produced: as a result of participating in the study, their level of Italian American self-identification and their sense of ethnic affiliation increased, and their sense of self-esteem and of control were also enhanced.

It often happens that the Italian American identification is associated with a sense of pride or, vice versa, of shame or even the presence of internal conflict within the psyche of the individual owing to the influence of the ethnic background. Riotto Sirey et al. (1985) noted that the feeling of pride in one's own ethnic group was positively connected to feeling comfortable with oneself. From the present research it emerges that the sense of pride was always felt by more than 62% of the interviewees and most of the time by 19% of them; over one-fifth, however, claimed to feel embarrassed to be Italian American in some circumstances.

This pride of belonging especially characterizes the young people of the third generation of immigration, while those indicating feeling pride most of the time belong predominantly to the second and the fourth generation. Among the few who claimed to feel proud of being Italian American only sometimes there is a prevalence of interviewees of the second generation. The feeling of embarrassment associated with this identification is felt in some circumstances especially by young people of the second generation.

INTERNAL CONFLICT STEMMING FROM THE ETHNIC BACKGROUND

Slightly more than one-fourth of the respondents confessed to feeling an internal conflict owing to their ethnic heritage. This interior conflict is expressed particularly by the interviewees of the fourth and second generations. These individuals were asked to explain the underlying question, which were expressed through an open question.

The obtained responses were subsequently classified within nine explanatory categories:

1. general negative stereotypes (religious, political, etc);
2. disconnection and difference from Italians and from the Italian American community;
3. stagnant, fixed identity;
4. internal conflict with the Italian American culture;
5. desire to understand Italy, the language;
6. image suggested by others (aspect, appearance);
7. distortion in the portrayal of Italian Americans presented by the media;
8. division within the self (conflict between cultures);
9. generic nature and homogenization of the "Italian American label."

Now an attempt will be made to gain insight into the significance of these categories through the words of the interviewed young people.

> 1. *General negative stereotypes (religious, political, etc.)*: these stereotypes can result in a sense of shame owing to feeling victimized by them, but also connected to not accepting them. Specifically, a negative stereotype that most affects the interviewees is the association of Italian Americans with the Mafia.
>
>> I am ashamed by some of the negative stereotypes. Growing up in an area (in New Jersey) where Italians were prevalent, I wasn't aware of the stereotypes. Upon going to college in Main Line Philadelphia with students from other states and around the world, I learned more about how we were perceived. The television and film stereotypes are perhaps the most damaging."
>
> 2. *Disconnection and difference from the Italians and from the Italian American community*: some allege a sense of disconnection and diversity that gives them the perception of being removed from both the Italians and the Italian Americans.

I feel a conflict within myself, because there is an immense disconnect with Italians and the Italian American community. The Italian American community of the twenty-first century, and its leaders still construe this identity, individual and group, through the lens of Cold War anticommunism intertwined with a deep xenophobic sense of assimilation, and American Nationalism that has constantly come at odds with the way I view things politically, and historically.

Not to say this is all of Italy, or this isn't most people in different places but where my parents are from (Mola di Bari) I am not particularly fond of a lot of people there and the things they believe. The teens there all seem to have the unanimous ambition to get married and have children. In the first case, and it is in low number, that seems to be it for them, which is fine. However, this is an issue because the only things they seem to pay attention to is relationships and sex. It isn't official between couples until they have had sex there. I dated a boy in Italy and this pressure didn't make me feel comfortable. It also feels like the teens there are very hedonistic, they don't seem to have a lot of ambition besides finding pleasures in life. They don't have different ideas, they are all concerned about following the usual way of thinking that they don't know how to be open to different ideas. They are very materialistic. The adults can be very rude and narrow minded. I've had personal family issues with family taking advantage of the fact that my family is American and apparently they think we are loaded with money. This obviously isn't all of Italy but when I have to talk about my town, there are a lot of issues I'm not pleased about.

3 *Stagnant, fixed identity:* some wonder what the point is of holding on to the past, others still don't recognize themselves in this static and outdated vision of Italian-ness.

I have also found that Italian Americans have a hard time grasping and trying to answer a good many questions that need to be asked about our collective experience, they have thus produced a culture of self-denial and self-loathing, that produces an idea of solidarity based upon race or ethnicity and a paranoid sense that anyone who strays from that narrative is "attacking" the community. I also have a hard time as an *oriundo* (native), who can read, write, and speak Italian, being constantly told what the "real" Italy is, or for that matter who "real" Italians are from a set of individuals that perceive Italy as a backward nation, yet feel the need to bring about this idea of high class, style, and fashion, that strays from a more popular working-class narrative.

> My families' cultures are very family-oriented cultures. I like school. I like technology. I like new things. I am not about to move back to Italy to take up farming or having a huge family. That is not my priority. I cannot say if that is because of Italian culture or more so the culture of having a working-class formally rural background. Most immigrants to America at the beginning of the last century came from the rural areas in the South of Italy. I think when they came here, they brought the sensibilities of poor and rural life with them. My grandmother's house for a long time had a chicken coop in the backyard until the city told us we had to knock it down. We still eat dinner on Sundays even though my grandparents have passed on in the past few years. We still fry zucchini blossoms and make struffoli even though I can't think of a single relative who likes it. We keep these things. And, yes, I feel conflict for it because I can't always see the sense in keeping these things.

4 *Internal conflict with the Italian American culture*: generational and value-based clash. In some cases, one's own interior conflict can be traced back to a larger context that involves the Italian American culture in its entirety, covering a variety of spheres, from moral to religious and political. This conflict is sometimes expressed as an opposition between the generations, ultimately leading to a veritable intergenerational clash.

> Sometimes the conflict I feel comes from the family traditions and closeness that have been passed down despite our family's time spent in the United States. There are still expectations of living at home until married that have to be overcome, as well as other elements of being a free individual. Every new step in a young Italian American's life can be seen as a battle at times—to go away to college, to live with a significant other, to travel, even to eat somewhere else on Sunday.

> Growing up I often felt conflicted between my own desires to be with friends and my parents' expectations of being with the family. It was normal to live in the same house with my parents, grandparents, and another

relative. This was also true for my cousins and their families. My aunts and uncles would also send their children to live with different relatives for the summer. When I went to college and was exposed to people of other ethnic backgrounds, particularly, Irish, German, English Americans, I discovered they weren't familiar with these traditions.

Some of the conflict growing up surrounded my morals. I valued and followed certain guidelines in regard to being an Italian Catholic that others didn't. Whether it was in regard to premarital sex or living with my family until I was married as opposed to getting an apartment with my friends, it was difficult to find others who related the same way as I did. I was taught to always save and look at the bigger picture, which I did; however, my friends were constantly inviting me on trips and vacations which I usually declined due to family time.

My grandma immigrated to this country when she was sixteen, and through her I have learned many traditions not only of being Italian, but other things too. I sometimes feel a little conflicted because one part of me wants to put my family above everything else and spend my day working and baking and crocheting and learning. However, the other part of me is far more modern and wants to be ambitious, and pursue a degree in computer engineering, and leave my home for whatever job I am offered. I love my family and have a very traditional viewpoint most of the time, but I cannot let that hold me back from pursuing a modern job, moving away from home, and becoming a workaholic. (Not that my family is holding me back—they support me whole-heartedly—but I am the one that does not want to leave my family.)

For two main reasons—one, assumed association with organized crime and "Guido" characteristics amplified by the media; two, some "Italian Americans" exhibit racist tendencies and overt racism to other ethnicities and races.

When I was a teenager, I'd often feel embarrassed of my Italian American identity because my family's values often clashed with those of my friends. I'd have a hard time decided how to act or who to please—my family or my friends. Today I find that I still struggle with this dilemma as my parents' expectations may conflict with what I want to do.

5 *Desire for knowledge of the Italian language:* the use of the Italian language was mentioned at times as a basis for conflict since it was an object of derision. Speaking the language is recognized as an essential part of the identity.

> I can understand Italian quite well, but I can hardly speak it. I was mocked for this for many years of my life and because of this, I have avoided learning Italian many years. Speaking Italian is a very integral aspect of identity for me.

> I wish I learned the language when I was young or lived in Italy for a short period of time to truly be emerged in the culture.

6 *Image suggested by others (aspect, appearance, other characterizations):* from the words of the young people there emerges the projection of a negative image reflected from external sources, which has the effect of creating confusion or a backlash to the identification. It does not appear, however, that this reflection has reached a level that undermines the identity in a way that might create the basis for a negative identity, which happens when one's image of oneself rests primarily on the evaluations of others and the individual adopts it as his own, and when, coherent with this self-image, a large part of a person's behavior is conditioned by the desire to avoid "other people's expected reproaches or blames" (Epstein, 1978, p. 185). This typology of subjects doesn't appear in the present research, inasmuch as those who responded to the questionnaire expressed, by great majority, a positive identification with this belonging.

> When people tell me that I'm American and not Italian American, I feel confused. I am both, I think.

> I wish I had a stronger connection to my Italian heritage. I was never taught the language and I do not have the physical appearance of someone who has Italian roots. I feel left out because people do not see me as an Italian American.

> My real last name is Bologna, and I've had to use a different name professionally, because it's really annoying when people call me "baloney."

> My name sounds very Italian, and especially when I'm abroad everyone expects me to be "more Italian." But I'm blonde and blue-eyed and speak Russian, not Italian. I'm very close with my mother's non-Italian, Russian side.

My fiancé is from Rome and also all my friends are from Italy. I feel uncomfortable at times when I say, "Yes, I am Italian," because they consider me Italian Canadian or American. But for me being born as a child of Italians makes me feel just as Italian as them. When I am in Italy I'm considered the American Canadian girl but when I am here in North America everyone considers me Italian. This is complexing for us second generation children.

7 *Distortion of the portrayal of Italian Americans as presented by the media:* the media, as has been noted, plays an important role in the distortion of images and the transmission of negative stereotypes, which can produce various forms of embarrassment.

> The negative portrayal of Italian Americans in the media embarrass me. Current reality television programs such as *The Housewives of New Jersey* and *Mob Wives* focuses [sic] on a segment of Italian American culture that values materialism and aggression. I would like to see Italian Americans represented as educated ambitious people who came from humble origins. Many of my Italian American peers are professionals and are the first people in their family to be educated, this part of our culture should be celebrated.

> I never feel ashamed to be Italian American—but when I see shows on TV that portray Italian Americans in a negative light (for example *The Sopranos* and *Jersey Shore*), I feel as if I have to defend my culture, and I worry that people across the U.S. who do not have much exposure to Italian Americans will then have the wrong image of our culture and of what it means to be an Italian American in the United States.

> With the popularity of shows like the *Jersey Shore* and *Growing up Gotti* some years back, the tacky, gaudy, chauvinistic stereotypes were somewhat revived as well.

> Mafia in the media, Italian Americans being portrayed as dumb, arrogant, aggressive on television.

> I think Italian Americans get portrayed poorly in the media. It bothers me that people jump to the conclusion that I must be like the people on *Jersey Shore* or that my life is like a *Godfather* movie because I am an Italian American.

8 *Division within the self, namely conflict between cultures:* the difference between the two cultures, Italian and American, have been highlighted (values, morality). In some cases, the attachment to Italy places subjects in an uncomfortable position, as if this would correspond to a weaker connection felt toward America. Some consider themselves "white" or "Euro-American."

> There seems to be an outward conflict of identity. Americans see it as a threat if you outwardly identify and define yourself as another ethnicity. There is a belief of being "unpatriotic."

> I feel bad sometimes that I'm not actually an immigrant but yet I feel an attachment to another country besides the U.S.A.

> I am of Italian American descent. I do not consider myself to be white, yet I have adopted modalities of other Euro-American cultural phenomena.

> I was born in America. I consider myself Italian AND American, but sometimes I feel more Italian than American.

> People consider me 'white' because of my appearance but I don't—I consider myself to be Italian American, NOT White.

> Living in the U.S. Southwest, an area completely devoid of Italian influence, I feel very out of place and find it difficult to navigate social situations. I'm used to the very direct, open, and forward manner of speaking that characterizes New York (and specifically Italian Americans in New York), and here the prevalent culture is one of passive-aggressive repression. I expect a certain quality of life regarding food (for example the Rochester public market—a direct result of Italian immigration—or the numerous local family restaurants), art, music, and culture that people do not value out here.

9 *Generic nature and homogenization of the Italian American label:* the label does not describe the diversity of subjectivities in an accurate way. There are those who have observed that within the collective identity of the group there is no expressive space for personal identity.

> Sometimes I feel conflicted in describing myself by the term "Italian American," because I sometimes do not feel it accurately describes me. I do use it because of the basic definition (I am an American, since I grew up in

the United States and much of my life has been influenced by American culture; I am also Italian because it was my first language. Italian culture has influenced my life probably just as much as American culture since the majority of my family is Italian and many summers throughout childhood were spent in Italy). However, I feel the term "Italian American" takes on a connotation which I myself am hesitant to subscribe to. In my opinion, the majority of Italian American culture is very far removed from Italian culture itself. Many who identify as Italian Americans in the Tri-state area do not know to speak the language or expresses any interest in the culture of Italy today. My Italian language and literature classes taken at Seton Hall University were filled with many students who were not of Italian origin, yet many of the Italian Americans I knew who attended were not very interested in learning about the country's beautiful history and culture. Personally, I identify much more with authentic Italian culture, and not necessarily with Italian American culture, which is heavily permeated by stereotypes of Italians and of Italy which often times are archaic. Italian American culture is something which is stubbornly fixated on food and images of Italians as "tough guys" and mobsters. If I attend a typical Italian Feast, such as St. Gennaro's in Little Italy, I find little that reminds me of what it means to be an Italian. For this reason, I often find myself conflicted when describing myself as an Italian American because of what that term has come to mean in today's society.

I don't feel like the label Italian American allows for enough room when people are trying to picture you as a unique individual. Most Americans can't comprehend beyond the TV stereotype. But if I say "I'm American," that's it. Then they pay attention to my hobbies, my interests, my mannerisms.

I think a lot of times Italian Americans, especially Southern Italians, are depicted in popular culture a way that is unfavorable. But beyond the negative stereotypes, I feel like there isn't an understanding of the diversity within Italian and Italian American cultures. We don't all like the same thing. We don't all believe the same things. It feels good to know that there is a shared experience, but very often, you don't see a lot of room for individuality within that collective identity. Also—and this is a little thing—but I feel in conflict with my Italian American heritage on Columbus Day. Many historians decry Columbus as a brutal conqueror, while

Italian Americans use the day as a means of celebrating our heritage. There is so much more to Italian and Italian American heritage than Columbus.

Calculating the frequency distribution of the interpretative categories used, it emerges that a sense of disassociation produced by the double belonging to two cultures is the prevalent component of the interior conflict (Table 3.7).

Table 3.7 What are the reasons for the internal conflict? (absolute values)

Division within the self	20
Images suggested by the media	14
Stereotypes	14
Internal conflict with the Italian American culture	13
Impressions suggested by "others"	9
Static identity	7
Disconnection	7
The "Italian American" label	4
Desire to understand Italy and the Italian language	3

4

Different Identity Models of Young Italian Americans: The Significance of Being Italian American Today

INTERPRETATIONS OF ITALIAN AMERICAN IDENTITY
IN THE 1970S AND 1980S

There is no doubt that Italian American identity has been the focal point of interest and attention within numerous studies of diverse disciplines that have sought to identify the characteristics of the Italian American population. Since the beginning of the 1970s, Italian American identity has been, in fact, interpreted through various theoretical models.

Ethnicity was defined by Gambino (1975) as "a revitalization of the Italian American traditions and the contribution of new forms to American culture" (p. 327). It can assume either of two meanings, which represent different possibilities for America. The first is ethnocentric and chauvinistic and it distinguishes "us" from "them," producing a strong sense of identity and security, even if it is a blocked identity and a false certainty. The second is creative ethnicity, indicating a condition in which an individual learns to live not only based on the fact that he/she possesses roots but that he/she also goes beyond these and manages to fashion a synthesis that incorporates the prevalent contributions of different ethnic groups (p. 362). The creative ethnic utilizes "the ethnic background as a point of departure for his growth, rather than as proof of his value" and also "to better understand himself, thus presenting a significant and realistic sense of self-control to his own life" (ibid.). Identity is constructed based upon inherited ethnic characteristics considered to be of merit. One's ethnicity translates, thus, into an "educated ethnic consciousness which provides the creative ethnic identity with an energy and guidance" (ibid.).

In the mid-eighties, Alba observed that ethnicity among white ethnic groups was disappearing. This tendency—summarized by him as the "twilight of ethnicity"—would not manifest itself in an imminent way or in the near future, and the twilight would perhaps never "turn into the night" (p. 162). Alba maintained, as it were, that numerous factors would preserve the ethnicity of European origins as visible characteristics of the American panorama for the immediate future. He writes: "Some members of any ethnic group... will maintain a strong affiliation with the group and from this they will draw an unconditional identity. Among the Italians, the number of adherents in such a faithfully stable way undoubtedly represents a minority in the component of the young people of the third and fourth generation" (ibid.).

Nevertheless, the ethnic traces of European origins are still visible in the façade of American society, and after World War II an enormous reduction of ethnicity as a social force among white groups was observable. Ethnic groups, in fact, no longer represented the confines within which many white Americans would spend a considerable amount of time during their lives.

The demographic impact of the growing number of mixed marriages among those belonging to the third and successive generations in the Italian American group was, Alba attests, markedly influencing the attenuation of ethnicity and the reduction in intensity of a sense of ethnic identity. The members of those generations were born during the period in which overt discrimination toward Italians had ceased and differences with the WASP group were diminishing and even disappearing.

Mixed marriages not only demonstrated the extent of the existing cultural differences, but ultimately would have the power to modify them. Assimilation, both cultural and structural, would have thus penetrated the Italian American ethnicity. Specifically, the family ethos derived from the Italian background of the Southern immigrants at the end of the previous century would have undergone profound transformations, to the point that the attachments among Italian Americans would not have been, in perspective, very different from those among WASPs.

Thus, even the ethnic revival of the sixties and the apparent ethnic rebirth were interpreted by Alba as the result of "elusive ethnicity":

It is not that ethnicity suddenly became more vibrant after 1960... but rather... that ethnicity was previously much less visible. In the preceding period, ethnicity could be described as models of daily life carried on in relative isolation within ethnic communities; at the time that ethnics were becoming ever more the working class or lower middle class, the ethnicity lacked public figures to provide visibility of the group. But with the acceleration that followed the Second World War, the prevalent changes toward assimilation brought many ethnic people into positions of eminence within American life... raising awareness of the ethnicity among the American middle and upper classes, which had previously dismissed it as a transitional phenomenon with few consequences on its own world. (p. 171)

Furthermore, the supposed renaissance of ethnicity was more present in the eyes of the observers than in the actual strengthening of ethnic feelings, ethnic communities, or ethnic cultures. In reality, according to Alba, the great contribution produced by the renewed interest in ethnicity was the expansion of what it meant to be American as well as changing the interpretation of the melting pot, in which space was provided to allow for ethnic identity. Ethnic identity was described as intermittent and undemanding, focused on the symbols of ethnic cultures rather than on the cultures themselves, and it tended to be expressed through free time activities rather than in the fabric of daily life. In this interpretation, Alba's thoughts reflect those of Gans, summarized in the concept of "symbolic ethnicity," described as:

> This can take the form of curiosity surrounding the experience of emigration, often viewed in the nostalgic sense as bittersweet authenticity, which the third and fourth generations of ethnic Americans—themselves very assimilated—cannot share; or which can be expressed as participation in a political movement based on ethnic themes.... Or it can be recognized in little details, like objects in the home which have an ethnic significance, in the occasional participation in rituals, in the love for an ethnic cuisine. (Gans, 1979, ref. in Alba, 1985)

In 1980, James Crispino conducted a survey in Bridgeport, Connecticut, through which he analyzed the seven dimensions of assimilation proposed by Milton Gordon (1964). The results confirm how Italian Americans of the third and fourth generation were continuing to assimilate themselves. The portrait of the third generation highlights that this group had reached prominent socioeconomic positions and had abandoned many of the models learned by the second generation.

According to Gans's observations in the preface to Crispino's work, the third generation was choosing its own groups and friends prevalently based on the connotation of class, of personal interests rather than national origins. These individuals tended to marry non-Italians, although it was rare for them to marry non-Catholics.

Gans notes that the ethnicity of the first and second generation remained alive, but the study conducted by Crispino demonstrated that this had become a phenomenon tied to the working class. In other words, the third generation of blue-collar workers were as ethnic in their behavior and attitudes as the second generation of blue-collar workers. The ethnicity of blue-collar workers was a phenomenon connected to class in much the same way that assimilation was connected to white-collar workers. Ethnicity was also kept alive among the middle class of the third generation and was expressed primarily as acknowledgment and pride in the Italian American identity. A new form of ethnicity was emerging, characterized as voluntary and nonobligatory; it was expressive rather than instrumental, namely, what Gans refers to as symbolic ethnicity because it expressed itself through symbols, rather than through cultural practices or group belonging. Moreover, he affirmed that this new ethnicity, or symbolic ethnicity, could represent the subsequent phase of the assimilation process: specifically because it was easy and agreeable to express and would not obstruct upward mobility, this would be able to persist at least through the fourth and fifth generations.

Also in the mid-eighties, the interpretation of Fischer (1986), expressed through the concept of reinvented ethnicity, recalled the temporal connection between the past, present, and especially the future, which had already been highlighted by Gambino. This ethnicity was defined through retrospection and memory, enabling the signs of Italian-ness to be retraced in the past, and was ultimately aimed at identifying the cultural elements necessary for developing a complete identity. As a result, ethnic memory could be oriented toward the future and not toward the past.

In her research conducted in those years, Waters (1990) recalled Gans's symbolic ethnicity, and she noted that—despite this idea being in a certain sense superficial, intermittent, and unincorporated within the individual's daily life—it simultaneously represented a source of pleasure and significance for many people who invested considerable energy maintaining and perpetuating it. Waters observed that, even though ethnic identification was an increasingly voluntary choice, this did not indicate a lack of significance or that it would necessarily disappear over the course of time. In fact, it assumed an attribute of useful value, appreciated in people's daily lives (Waters, 1990).

Vecoli (1985) referred to the impossibility of giving an unambiguous definition to the Italian American identity, due to the complexity that characterized the population of Italian origins spanning over a century of immigration along with the differentiation between generations, social classes, and regions of origin and of destination: it was thus more appropriate to speak in terms of a multiplicity of identities (p. 89).

For Mitrano (1999), Italian American identity was facing a crossroads at the end of the twentieth century. Some maintained that within the assimilation process it would join the inclusive "European American" label (Alba, 1990); others, instead, felt that the identity would persist and would prosper in the future if it was cultivated attentively (Vecoli, 1996).

MORE RECENT INTERPRETATIONS

The current themes of debate on Italian American identity orbit around concepts including *italianità*, Italic culture, *italicità*, which are more generally part of the way that Italian heritage is interpreted and represented in today's America. Over time, Italian America "has continued to change and is struggling with its connection to what is now an obsolete notion of Italian-ness" (Krase, 2004, p. 136). Consequently, the significance of what is Italian and Italian American is up for debate, while recognizing a logic of important ethnic identification in all generations of immigration.

Italianità, that is "a taste for Italian things," would, according to Bona, escape any uniform definition and would itself comprise a series of significances (Bona, 2015, p. 186). Recalling the words of Tamburri, Giordano, and Gardaphé (1991), we note that the concept itself incorporates "images, both real and mythical, of the land of origin, the lifestyle, the values, and the cultural symbols of the [writers'] ancestors" (p. 6). Furthermore, it contains "the language, the food, its own way of determining fundamental values of life, a family-based structure, and a sense of religion" (p. 9). Thus, *italianità* is a polysemic term that eludes—as noted by Tamburri (1991)—any precise definition. It is a concept that expresses multiple notions, ideas, feelings, and sensations. *Italianità* and all the elements that it comprises can be interpreted as a continuum along two poles contrasting an elevated level of acceptance and recognition of the Italian background with marked feelings of disavowal and avoidance of this background in favor of an Anglo-American identity (Bona, 2000).

This continuum of *italianità* also emerged from the results of a study conducted by Mitrano in 1996, through in-depth interviews with twenty-five young Italian Americans under thirty years old. Many young Italian Americans identified a series of characteristics (eye color, skin, physical dimensions and build, hair styles and quantity of hair) that contributed to a distinct image of the typical Italian American, viewed in general as nice-looking, a characteristic that was extended to the entire group. Under the personality profile, many of the interviewees were convinced that there was a uniquely Italian personality, characterized by instability, aggressiveness, hard-headedness, noisiness; as well as being expressive, affectionate, protective, respectful, self-confident, and intelligent.

The results of the study confirmed the fact that the ethnic construct among the interviewed young people was fluid and malleable; any given Italian American would be located somewhere on this continuum based on their possession and exhibition of various elements in the dimensions referenced. Moreover, the study offers a response to the question regarding the process of ethnic identification, namely, the distinction characterizing it in reference to the passive or active selection of elements of definition and differentiation with respect to other ethnic groups. Was this choice actively exercised by those who make up the group, or did the group recognize that there were others making this choice for them without their consent or consideration?

Mitrano (1999) observed that the interviewed young people were rather passive in the formation process of their ethnic identity. These individuals were expressing the desire to actively create an ethnic identity, but in the process of doing so, "they continue to desperately attach themselves to cultural, physiological, psychological, and personality elements that essentially maintain the Italian American identity reactively." The process of formation of ethnic identity was obtained by taking the elements of what Mitrano called "the ethnicity's garbage can" (p. 87). Following from a theory proposed in the context of the study of the decision-making process within organizations, he supported the idea that the young Italian Americans were basing aspects of their identities on familial symbols of ethnicity that had been used in the past and were created for them both by the older Italian American members of the group of insiders (friends, relatives), as well as by ethnic outsiders, many of whom had produced and disseminated these symbols through the media, advertisements, and the market. The study revealed that the interviewed young people had not actively produced new symbols of ethnic identification; rather, they had simply recycled the ones derived from the past and that "they had been languishing in the 'ethnic garbage can' of the Italian Americans for years" (p. 94). The social construction of their ethnic identity often involved a reactive process rather than an active one, made in reaction to others. The endeavor to actively create an ethnic identity composed of new elements remained, according to the author, a question without a response, at the moment.

In the complex attempt to deconstruct the notion of *italianità* in Italy, in America, and elsewhere, Krase (1987, 1996, 2004, 2007) offers for the reader's attention a thesis wherein the representation of spaces and places is an important component of *italianità*. For many of those active in the humanities and the arts, Little Italy—besides being a product and source of social and cultural capital and representing the idea of the Italian American community—becomes a symbol of its inhabitants: "The enclave ultimately symbolizes its imaginary inhabitants and represents them independently of the fact that they may reside there or not" (Krase, 1996, p. 124).

D'Alfonso (2004), in his questioning of the future of the Italian culture in America, proposes to label this as italic culture, that is, "a higher level of culture with regard to Italy... something found both within and beyond the country's borders." But if one begins to question what the mental image might be, the common denominator that could unite individuals who share a common inheritance but live in different parts of the world, the author's answer is given by the "absence of a response," a response that may never be offered: "Perhaps it is precisely the lack of any reason to want to unite that makes the Italians what they are.... Their culture is a dream which never comes true" (p. 112).

Another proposal comes from Bassetti (see Accolla, d'Aquino, 2008; Bassetti, d'Aquino, 2010) and refers to the concept of *italicità*—a construct that goes beyond *italianità*—and of the *italico*: "The italico is a member of a vast network, a global aggregation, based on the moral values shared by a civilization... a post-Italian, a citizen of the world with a new identity. An identity that, based more on regional than national origins, leads to the encounter between the culture and a renewed interest in regional and ethnic characters" (Bassetti, in Accolla, d'Aquino, 2008, p. 63). *Italicità*, which is the development of *italianità*, is consequently akin to a global community, "a network of people, of interests, of lifestyles that are giving rise to a new aggregation. The italic aggregation, that is. This includes the inhabitants of Italy, both passport citizens and immigrants and their children... the natives, the Italian speakers.... In addition... to this network of people are the Italophiles: professionals and/or lovers of the Italian lifestyle who... out of passion or for economic and professional interest have embraced the Italian way of life" (ibid., p. 68). Therefore, *Italicità* tends to overcome national identity and is configured as a metanational and multibelonging identity. This vision fits with a concept of Italian and/or Italic identity that—as Tamburri (2010) points out—is not based on a monolithic notion of what it means to be Italian; the notion of *Italicità* cannot be built on "an internally consistent object of theoretical knowledge" and identity (p. x).

Ferraro (2005), in his book *Feeling Italian*, examines the evolution and persistence of Italian Americaness in the American nation, which he defines as postethnic, transnational, and a site where the genders are liberated. He questions how this "belonging/feeling" has developed through the growing contact between different ethnic groups and mobility phenomena, how it has influenced the country, and why this real *and* imagined culture continues to be a source of great interest. "Feeling Italian" means feeling the way that Italians feel, having Italian kinds of feeling, recognized or not; it is expressing the perception that their identity is Italian or similar to Italian, whoever their ancestors are.

There is a continuity that goes beyond distance and time and is not based on blood credentials (you do not have to be "one of them" to feel like "that"); feeling Italian is not so much a birthright as a choice, a "map for a polite, educated desire." Today, feeling Italian in America depends on how individual and personal experiences, negative and positive images, including impressions linked to the media's and other representations of Italy, are combined and interpreted: therefore, "there is no uniformity in the 'idea of Italoamericanità,' no place of ethnic convergence like a community with an identity and shared goals. Individuals select and choose which aspects to incorporate into their personal narratives insofar as these images collide with all other dimensions that contribute to the formation of identity" (Chirico, 2014, p. 68).

Krase (2003), with the intention of defining Italian Americans in today's society, maintains that although they are well integrated into the American social structure, they are still distinct. He adds that "despite the concrete disunity of Italian Americans, they are united by images shared in people's minds about who they are" (p. 14). These representations of Italian Americans can be contradictory because, despite the stereotypes, the individuals are very different from each other. In fact, as with other large groups of ethnic Americans, "Italian Americans do not comprise a monolithic and cohesive group, but they are instead members of the most disparate communities" (ibid.). Thus, it is possible to arrive at the paradox that "in many cases, Italian Americans have more in common with non–Italian Americans than they do with others in their own group" (ibid.).

AREAS OF MEANING ON BEING ITALIAN AMERICAN TODAY

In light of the considerations proposed so far, what significance does being Italian American today assume for the younger generations? How and how much does this aspect of identity affect the perception of reality, in everyday interactions, in the symbolic and value-based references of the young people? In order to delve more deeply into the attribution of meanings to this identification, an open question was posed, to which the respondents could respond by freely expressing the definition, the interpretation, and the experience connected to the question, "In your opinion, what does it mean today to be Italian American?"

The picture of the answers—220 in all—is rich in ideas of reflection and meanings that reveal a large fresco—complex and fragmented—that depicts how young Italian Americans represent today their Italian cultural heritage and their connection with the land of origin. Diversity, as one of the interviewees points out, characterizes the descriptions provided: *"It's different for everyone. Perhaps the diversity is a characteristic."*

The answers were assigned to thirteen interpretative categories, illustrated below.

1 *Descendant or nondescendant?* The two concepts referenced are connected to the two main interpretive currents in the debate on ethnic identity, namely, to essentialism and constructivism. Although the first approach has been widely criticized and the second is the dominant one in the current debate on ethnicity, the primordialist interpretation of ethnicity is prevalent from the perspective of "common sense."

   For some young people, this identification is defined by having descended from Italian immigrants:

   To me, an Italian American is any individual that was born in America, but, is a direct descendant of a relative born in Italy.

   Being Italian American is when both your parents are of Italian descent with a bloodline that can be traced back to Italy.

That your relatives originated in Italy and that you still carry-on some things from home, but that you also have a new home and new traditions and embrace what your ancestors fought so hard to provide to you.

For others it is enough to have only one parent of Italian origin:

Having at least one parent that has immigrated to this country that holds the values, traditions, and culture of Italy while embracing the traditions, and culture of America.

Today being "Italian American" means having fifty percent or more Italian blood. Generally residing in the New York/New Jersey region, having a large group of family or friends that follow Italian American traditions.

For others, it comprises those born in Italy who came to America and embraced American culture:

Any person born in Italy that has come to America and adopted American culture, while holding on to their native Italian identity and traditions.

Being an Italian American is that one was either born in Italy but lives in the U.S. or was born in the U.S. with Italian ancestry. It usually implies that some of the Italian culture (food, music, arts, religious observations and customs) are still practiced and there is an identification (the percentage of which is diluted with time) with Italian culture and customs.

Some young people think that being Italian American is connected to having been born in America but feeling strongly Italian:

In my opinion, being Italian American is when you are born in America but have a strong connection to being Italian, whether it be through upholding traditions or learning from those who personally lived there.

It means being someone with a foundation in Italy living as an American. Culture, customs, beliefs, lifestyles are all impacted having had Italian ancestors.

It means being born and raised as an American but having roots in Italy.

Others believe that anyone who wants to embrace and honor Italian culture can be considered Italian American:

Anyone that wants to embrace and honor Italian culture should be considered Italian American.

Still others think that being Italian American primarily means knowing the cultural heritage:

I feel that being Italian American doesn't just mean that you are of Italian descent, but that you have an understanding of your cultural heritage, or at least of the values, customs, and traditions of your ancestors.

For others, being Italian American is just a label that is not linked to a real knowledge of Italian culture and heritage, although—in spite of this—one feels pride and a sense of belonging to them.

I believe now, more than ever, it is harder to define what it is to be Italian American because those children who are fourth or fifth generation, like myself, are losing the family members or have lost the family members that originally immigrated to the U.S. These stories unfortunately are lost generation to generation. You may have some memories, but families no longer adhere to the traditions like Sunday dinner, or value family time as much as they used to. Now Italian American for this upcoming generation is simply a label, less a culture.

I don't know. Mostly I have seen it being used as an excuse for a lot of bad emotional behavior. Lawrence Ferlinghetti has this poem "The Old Italians Are Dying" that is what modern Italian American culture feels like. We have only the memory of the memory. My grandparents lived long long lives though, so I knew them well even though they were in their late seventies when I was born. I guess being Italian American means keeping the memory of their sacrifices and efforts for a better life. Also, that we have really excellent food at family parties. And still more family parties than most other people we know. So, maybe at this point it just means good food!

2 *Choice or non-choice: conscious and unconscious elements of ethnic identity.* Whether or not a subject had acquired a sense of ethnic identity and the extent to which it was accepted implies some element of choice, which is, however, subject to a series of limitations. Some are of a social nature and linked

to certain characteristics of the social system. The greater the possibility of choice in this aspect, the greater the importance of another set of restrictions, composed of various elements, in particular the unconscious ones that come into play in the image of oneself (Epstein, 1978).

The creation of ethnic categories, as well as general social categories, is a bidirectional process, whereby in defining the distinctive features of others, one defines one's own. Thus, the ethnic categories have a dual aspect: they are both objective, that is, external and independent from the actor, and subjective, or internal to the actor as a constituent part of the perception of the self.

There are both conscious and unconscious mental processes involved in these perceptions: "In fact"—notes Epstein—"just as certain behavioral traits... are often rooted in childhood identifications, the individual may not be fully conscious of the means by which one's sense of self can be modeled. From this perspective, then, the sense of ethnic identity appears as a function of the iteration of both internal and external perceptions and reactions" (Epstein, 1978, p. 41).

The conscious and unconscious dimensions of the Italian American identity are represented in the context of the critical history of Italian American literature. In the works of third-generation Italian American authors, Gardaphé (1992) sees the potential for being able to represent—explicitly or otherwise—their own ethnicity, a postmodern prerogative not accessible to previous Italian American writers. On the basis of this choice, he divides contemporary Italian American writers into two categories: the "visible" and the "invisible" in relation to their Italian American cultural "awareness." These two extremes represent how they can relate to their ethnicity in their work.

The first ones—including Giose Rimanelli—confront the Italian American experience by representing Italian American themes in their writing and openly expressing their Italian American identity, while the latter—of which Don DeLillo is an example—choose to avoid Italian American themes in their works; they create works that are implicitly Italian American. In the works of "visible" writers, Italian Americanness is more explicit, while in the words of the other authors it is more implicit, more subtle, more submerged. For "invisible" writers, Gardaphé employs the metaphorical expression "twilight of ethnicity," as described by Alba: however, he notes, "twilight tends only to shade signs that are visible during other hours of the day;... nobody... completely transcends ethnic origin to blend invisibly into American culture.... Their writings contain signs of Italianness that can be linked to an underlying philosophy, rooted in their ethnicity" (Gardaphé, 1992, pp. 212–13). Self-reflective ethnicity is absent in their works. Therefore, even the "invisible" authors might belong to the Old World more than they think. This may be the case for some young people who are scarcely aware of how much their heritage affects their lives.

This is how the interviewees describe the consciously chosen and the unconscious elements of being Italian American:

> To me Italian American doesn't just mean that you have blood lines running back to Italy, you have no choice over where your blood line runs. Practicing values that the Italians place on things such as food, family, and faith are big components and it shows that being of Italian culture lives through you instead of just being in your families' past.

> The problem now is that the Italian culture and traditions are slowly fading away because of the lack of knowledge and appreciation of the culture by the younger generations. As the generations increase, if parents don't preserve and celebrate the Italian customs and traditions, most likely, their children won't pick up on it and the Italian culture and language will become of the past. However, if the children are aware of the history and traditions, then it is up to them whether to carry it on to their children; but because of a lot of young people being absorbed in other things and not caring as much about their family history and genealogy, as well as the Italian language, this is where it all comes to an end.

> To be Italian American means that you are an American citizen, or you are an Italian who has lived in America long enough to truly understand and absorb its culture. While being an American living a largely American lifestyle, there are still elements of the Italian culture that you encounter DAILY. That, to me, is my definition of being TRULY Italian American, as opposed to being Italian American by blood or by association.

> Because it informed the values I still hold—consciously or not. Keep tradition.

3 *Knowledge of the Italian language and the dialects.* For some, language represents a discriminant in terms of belonging and recognition, while for others this is not so.

It means submerging yourself in the culture, practices, and values of your Italian heritage as much as possible, you do not need to be able to speak Italian to be considered Italian American.

It is very important to maintain one's Italian American identity as the generations who emigrated from Italy are lost over time and it's crucial to maintain our culture and identity. For example, many third, fourth, fifth, etc. generations do not speak Italian. It should be a priority to keep the Italian language alive on this side of the Atlantic.

In my opinion it means they can speak both languages. Share same customs and the same background. Share common factors together.

4 *Values and strong feelings.* For many, the value connotation is the determining characteristic of being Italian American. The greatest emphasis is placed on the family. For an interviewee, passing time with one's own family denotes them as "retrogenerationally" Italian American (this term was coined by the interviewee, and can be interpreted as an Italian cultural inheritance felt within oneself that is transmitted through contact with one's own family environment). The connection with values is associated and reinforced, quite often, by feelings connected to the Italian identification.

Spending time with my family. I am retrogenerationally Italian American.

Being an Italian American means family first always. It also means working hard, making an honest living, being generous, and living up to values put in place by your ancestors. It means I get to make the sauce at the end of every August, make the *pupa di Pasqua* during Easter time, basically getting to participate in these great traditions with my family.

Being Italian American means having a strong relationship with your family, and extended family. It means having Sunday dinner every week, and, making sauce with your mother. Being Italian means yelling to everyone to express every emotion, even positive emotions. It means having very strong feelings of protectiveness, strength, and suspicious. Being Italian means having a connection to the motherland, Italy, and knowing that no matter where you live, that is the amazing and beautiful place that your family originated from years and years ago.

It means that you are close with your family, you have family dinners together, you celebrate the holidays together, there are big family weddings and funerals which is the time where you get to catch up with one another. You have a sense of being that comes from the values and beliefs you were raised with.

In the U.S., when you are in high school and college, being Italian American is considered to be "cool." You are looked highly upon if you are Italian, developing meaningful relationships with your family that are based on loyalty and trust. Taking an interest in your grandparents' stories, struggles, hopes for their families' lives, and how you can honour them. Bringing honour to your family name by being a high achiever. Always honouring, caring for, and spending time with your parents.

Italian Americans have a strong work ethic and strive to become not necessarily powerful in terms of money, but rather content and happy, even with modest means.

Today it means being part of an ethnic group that has significantly influenced American culture. Despite the negative stereotypes, many positive contributions have also been made, especially in the culinary industry. Being Italian American today also means being part of a culture that values family and love. Despite the negative representations of Italian Americans on popular television, I do notice some elements that are positive when it comes to showing how devoted Italians are to their relatives, especially the image of the quintessential overbearing Italian mother.... For many Americans seeing a young man spend so much time with his relatives is quite foreign. Many Americans ridicule how Italian Americans live with their parents until they are thirty years old, but behind that I think many Americans admire the closeness of the Italian family.

5 *Food: a value in itself.* As is well known, the collective image of the group presents as one of its distinctive features a marked attachment and interest in cooking and the centrality of food to the ethnic experience and the convivial moments of community life (Cinotto, 2001). The kitchen reflects a metaphor of the cultural background that immigrants brought with them to

America, and food plays a significant symbolic role in defining subjective and collective identities (ibid.). "Family meals—understood as a set of sensory experiences, tastes and smells—and ethnic food, with its traditions, typically represent the symbols... [of] the wealth of family life... [which constitute] an essential and distinctive part of the Italian American experience" (p. 2). A study conducted by Mitrano (1999) has also demonstrated the persistence of family cooking as a symbol of ethnic cultural identity among young third and fourth generation Italian Americans.

> Remembering the food your family carried over from their specific region I think is the most important part. And also seeing ourselves in history books because most Italians came over a long time ago.

> It is taking pride in the culture, food, music, and traditions. Food is the BIG one for me.

> To be honest, I don't think most Italian Americans today are nearly as in touch with the actual culture of Italy as they are with the set of prevailing mafioso stereotypes and television caricatures. I taught Italian at the high school level for two years and was very disappointed to find that most students of Italian descent weren't even interested in pronouncing their own last name correctly. Still, the one area that seems to unite us is food—the traditional recipes that we have in common.

6 *Tradition and relationship with the ancestors.* The feeling of pride in their ancestors is an element that arises transversely across many reflections offered by the interviewees, accompanied by the descendant's regard for the older group as a "generation of survivors." Being Italian American also means achieving the American dream, as demonstrated by the predecessors.

> It means belonging to a group of people who share a rich history, who believe in strong, close-knit families, who possess a strong work ethic and desire to succeed, and most of all, coming from generations of survivors.

> Being an Italian American means achieving the American dream. Like my great grandparents did.

> Being descendants of a group of people who risked their lives to come to this country and give their families a better life, with a unique set of

principles and culture that is different than other Americans and also different than Italians in Italy.

… and listening to stories of how our ancestors arrived and how they lived the American dream for us today. To always keep traditions as well as wake up every Sunday to the smell of sauce and meatballs being made.

Living the values of family, education, loyalty, and beauty. Understanding why Italians came here, what they met when they arrived, and I [sic] they have been able to integrate themselves into society (both the good and the bad). Understanding the circumstances in Italy that led to immigration.

Today, being an Italian American means what I like to call "patriotism through heritage." By understanding where we came from, the sacrifices that were made, and the values we hold dear, we can see how our people helped build this country into the what it is today. We have to remember that our ancestors came to America for opportunity, and even though it wasn't always easy, I'd say we made it.

To be an Italian American is knowing the sacrifices your ancestors made to have the courage to voyage to America, with the intention of making a better life for their descendants. There is a will and drive in us to become more "successful" in life to honor and respect our grandparents. "Successful" not necessarily meaning making a ton of money and wealth, but, having the opportunity to be educated and be free to choose a career path that makes us happy in life.

Today being Italian American is continuing many of the values and traditions passed down from our parents and grandparents. Remembering our roots and incorporating them into American culture and values. I also believe that remembering our roots is a way of honouring our ancestors who came to this country, many with almost nothing except hopes and dreams for a better life.

Being Italian American means that not only your ethnicity is Italian or that you speak Italian but that you practice our cultural traditions. This includes everything from food preparation, to attending religious street *festas*, participating in cultural beliefs (such as *malocchio*) cultural stories

(*Befana, Strega Nonna*), cultural dances, etcetera. All or some of these make up an Italian American.

7 *The difference between the Italians and the Italian Americans.* Some young people highlight the cultural difference with respect to Italy and the Italians. It happens quite often, in fact, that people who have not deeply elaborated on the contents of Italian American culture confuse it with Italian culture. In the expression of Italian values and traditions, some interviewees claim to feel closer to these with respect to the Italians themselves, namely, they feel almost "more Italian than the Italians."

This last consideration brings to mind a long-standing question that has permeated the way each new wave of immigrants from Italy is characterized. The most recent arrivals were labeled as "real Italians" to distinguish them from the Italians who had preceded them in this movement to America. As noted by Ruberto and Sciorra (2016), the expressions "real Italians" and "Italian Italians" and their corresponding Italian translations, i.e., *italiano vero* and *italiano italiano*, have been commonly used to distinguish immigrants who arrived in the first decades after World War II from the Italian Americans who were the descendants of Italians who had arrived in the United States during the period of great migration. What lies beneath the term *real Italian* is "the presupposition of an authentic, recognizable cultural identity, fused to a solid association with Italy" (p. 9).

This perception connected to feeling like a "real Italian" resonates in the words of some interviewees.

> When I visit my family in Italy I often come to the realization that we, Italian Americans are a separate culture from Italians, in many ways we have retained more of the values and traditions of Italy than the Italians in Italy now do.
>
> Often, I feel, people (Italians and Italian Americans) confuse Italian culture and customs, with Italian American culture and customs (both are interrelated but unique in their own respects).
>
> To be of a direct and connected Italian descent. Connected, as to the cultural products—food, music, etc. And also to understand and appreciate the distance Italian Americans (as opposed to Italians) have to that culture.

It means being passionate about life and enjoying our friends and family as much as we can. I feel many Italian Americans have lost touch with their roots or falsely claim to be Italian when they know nothing of our culture, history, and Italy. We are constantly attacked and ridiculed in the media and portrayed as something we're not. I'm always proud and know the true meanings of being Italian.

In America it is a continually fragmenting community because there are very few Italian immigrants coming over to live anymore, and if they are, they are living in all different parts of the country. There are some exaggerated stereotypes of Italian Americans, like the ones on reality TV like the *Jersey Shore*, and although this is one kind of Italian American, it doesn't have much left in common with Italy or present Italian life. Italian and Italian American are two very different things, and they are growing further apart with the passage of time.

Not knowing the language, eating the food or cooking the food that we all know Italian American cuisine to be (lasagna, pizza, etcetera). Living separately in Italian or white only communities. It's a pride thing but it's hollow because people do not know themselves. And of course, people assume certain things with pop culture the way it is (Sopranos and Corleones). And being Italian American doesn't mean to actually go to Italy—it's a transplanted culture that severed most ties to the homeland, but still is happy to wave the flag here—if only to differentiate themselves in America from others, which is what most people like to do (any ethnicity will wave their flag but may not know what that represents).

8 *The relationship with Italy.* Italy is represented through an image, sometimes real, which is connected to the fact that some of the young participants in the survey have visited the country and have had experiences there; for others it is "an imagined Italy" on the basis of what they have learned of it culturally and emotionally, even if they have never visited personally; still, for others, it is a reinvented image, reinterpreted and reread, sometimes mythologized.

In my opinion, being Italian American is having a relationship with the Italian culture and people. I consider myself Italian American because I have friends and family in Italy. My parents always cook Italian meals and we always watch Italian television and we follow the Italian tradition. I would consider myself American if I did not have any ties in Italy or keep up to date with what's going on in Italy. Especially, the food!

For me, being Italian American means that I have strong connections to Italy the way it was one hundred years ago when my grandparents left it. Having lived in Italy, I know that the culture we have preserved is not really similar to current Italian culture, but, is rather very antiquated. I do however, obnoxiously believe that I am the heir of a culture that greatly shaped, through both the Romans and the Renaissance, the way the entire world is today.

9 *Past, present, and...* Another approach presents the meaning of being Italian American from a diachronic perspective: in some cases, it is based in the past, while others recognize the defining elements in the present. Some also accentuate the importance of the transmission of the cultural patrimony to future generations and to their own children. These three dimensions can be coexistent in the definition of what it means to be Italian American.

There are two types of Italian American. The older, more traditional, definition is descendants of Italian immigrants who were born here before the eighties or nineties and grew up in their family's "idea" of Italian living. Most of the time this was not "generally Italian" but rather specific to a town or regional idea that they left with when they left Italy. These descendants grew up in Italian American communities which held on to some Old World traditions but also created new ones native only to their own local communities in America. The other, newer definition is young professionals who are highly educated and intermingle with many people of other ethnicities who create a new life in America. However, due to higher education levels, coming over as adults, and with easier and cheaper traveling (back home) possibilities, as well as internet and globalization, these future parents can show their children a more "true," "real" Italian culture instead of an American made Italian American culture of years ago.

There are two groups of Italian Americans in my mind—I know that in reality there are many! I draw the distinction between Americans whose parents and grandparents were also born in America and do not know much about Italian culture and Americans with a rich understanding of their Italian culture, whether because their parents or grandparents are Italian-born or because they have educated themselves about their background. Italian Americans tend to have a shared sense of emphasis on the family, but other than that, are very diverse.

In 2013, being an Italian American doesn't mean what it did back when my family came to America. Even in my town of Bensonhurst which was once entirely Italian populated now houses more Asians, Russians, and Middle Easters than ever before. Although I have kept in strong contact with roots, many of my Italian American friends have not. Most can't even understand the language. We have all been Americanized in some way or the other. Living in a place as diverse as today's New York, it's hard to stick to your native culture. To many of my generation, being Italian American simply means having Italian blood. My personal view goes far beyond that.

10 .... *future*. As with the other characteristics examined up this point, the image of the future connected to Italian American culture presents contradictions and discordant aspects. There are forces at work that compete with each other when these young people attempt to form a concrete description of the future through their choices, personal beliefs, and the goals they are able to pursue.

Unfortunately I can't even think of any Italian American friends I have. Growing up it seemed like those were all I was surrounded with and by going to college and into the world I realized that unless I joined Italian groups I had a hard time finding others in the same culture background. I feel like today people who consider themselves Italian are those who have a small percentage of heritage in them. Whether it be solely great grandparents who were born in Italy or just grandparents. I think people now married outside of their cultures so much it's hard to find anyone of actual Italian descent.

I think that being Italian American is when you are born in America but follow Italian traditions and customs learned from your parents and relatives. By following these Italian traditions, you insure that these traditions will be passed on to future generations.

11 *Socialization and the transmission of the ethnic identity: inheritance and acquisition.* The senses of belonging and maintaining ethnic identification are

transmitted through socialization by significant family figures—among whom parents occupy a predominant position—through contact and growth within a community whose members share the same ethnic background, and on the basis of one's own will and personal choice of learning and in-depth study.

> *I think family history, genealogy, and trying to learn the language play a big part in it too. In some cases, young people can become interested in the culture themselves, but most of the time, it is the parents' role to introduce the Italian culture and language to their children.*

> *Being Italian American means having one's own unique blend of characteristics and traditions—both learned and inherited—in a sea of other Italian Americans, whose experiences are not always the same. Much of Italian American identity has to do with where one grew up in the U.S. This is perhaps how Italian Americans first find commonalities with one another—through geographic location. Then we reach out to other Italian Americans through common knowledge of traditions.*

12 *The negative aspects of identification: stereotypical images.* Being Italian American, for some, has a connotation linked especially to unfavorable aspects. The problematic aspects are often connected to the negative stereotypes that are proposed and reinforced through the media. The need to fight against them through various, externally visible behavior models is also presented.

> The media has done a very good job of screwing up people's perceptions of Italian American culture. In the late twentieth century, we were all mobsters and now we're arrogant, vain party animals who only care about dancing, drinking, having sex, and shopping. It's unfortunate that many Italian Americans in the younger generations have actually found appeal to and created this type of life for themselves and this is what challenges my pride in my Italian American culture. However, I feel as if through myself, I can help change this perception (and growing reality) by maintaining the values and beliefs that my ancestors had when they came to America: being hard-working and responsible will lead to success and a better life for you and your family. Being Italian American also means coming from a culture and group of people who were victims of discrimination and racism but were strong enough to overcome these obstacles and gain equality in the perception of a major part of other Americans.

In very general terms, it means someone born and raised in America has an ancestor who emigrated from Italy at some point. But there is a whole culture around being Italian American, especially since that horrible show *Jersey Shore* aired. There is certainly a pride that comes with having an Italian background, but there also remains a negative stereotype of the *Guido*. My father, as a member of the *Order Sons of Italy*, works closely with Italian men and women who battled stereotypes in America their whole lives. There used to be intense discrimination against people of Italian descent, and even though the discrimination is mostly gone some of it still exists in the form of stereotypes and also in other parts of the country that are less tolerant of diversity. Personally I have encountered some of these stereotypes, especially having both a German and Italian heritage—people make jokes about my family being part of the Mafia or Nazi party. But I am never ashamed to let people know what my heritage is. I think I wear it very proud, and I will never let a negative stereotype get in my way of success.

Italian Americans are stereotyped as *Guidos*, *Jersey Shore*, *Gotti Boys*, movies like *Goodfellas*; these are the examples we have of young Italian Americans. I do not feel there is enough true Italian culture in New York City. It is limited to the inside of a few authentic Italian families owned restaurants.

In my age range, being Italian American means nothing but stereotypes. My age range does not speak the language, does not care to speak the language. Being Italian American is more than just street festivals, "Sunday dinners," the Italian national team, etcetera.

To have much passion for your life... in good ways and bad... people tend to love us for how much we care and communicate but also label us too aggressive and ignorant at times... so many of us are educated leaders but we get stained by Mafia lifestyle and *Jersey Shore*... every culture has its up and downs though as a whole... as an individual it can hinder you since we never seem to mind being labeled or fight back hard enough against stereotypes... I almost always hear negative comments about being Italian American by non-Italian Americans and feel it can hold us back from a social perspective... it's sad but the media does play a huge part in how people are viewed.

Today's definition of being Italian American has been somewhat besmirched by negative portrayal in the media with TV shows like *Jersey Shore* or movies like *The Godfather*. There exists this dangerous, romanticized idea of what it is to be Italian American—the truth is that most Italian Americans are not involved in organized crime nor do not consider themselves *Guidos*. Yet this image of the loud, gaudy, uneducated, immoral is what I think comes to mind when most people hear the words Italian American.

I think the role of an "Italian American" has shifted greatly over the generations. There are many less one hundred percent Italian Americans in my demographic, but yet, it seems that many more people (of maybe partial Italian descent) are claiming the roles of "Italian Americans." These people do not know the true culture and traditions of the heritage, they just want to be like what they see on TV.

Unfortunately, I think that a person is placed into this category relative to the products they consume, and how their behavior reinforces certain stereotypes.

Being Italian American ultimately is not based on a knowledge of the Italian language and history, it has based itself more on consumerism and pageantry.

13 *Membership in the group: which community(s)?* The extension of the relational aspect to the broader context leads many to refer to the concept of community. Here again, the interpretations are discordant, based on the personal perceptions that the individuals have. Thus, for some the community exists and it is a place of recognition and cohesion, while for others this community—though still existent—appears fragmented, divided, and scarcely cohesive. The sense of membership in a culture or group is perceived—in many cases—as a reason to be proud.

It is a way of life, it is something ingrained into our DNA. However, here in America it has been forgotten and it is evident from the fact that we do not have a strong community feeling. Is our presence still strong in the major areas of America? Yes, as in politics, industry, business, and so on. But are we a unified people who speak the language, keep in contact with what is going on back in the motherland, know the current status of life and culture there? No and by a long shot. I envy other hyphenated Americans who stay true to who they are. Yet we Italians who have so much more to boast about and be proud about do very little. I envy seeing other hyphenated Americans speak their native tongues and here I am, not able to find one person I can speak to. Language is the main carrier of culture in my opinion and we have lost it.

I am first and foremost an American. But, I was raised with strong Catholic values and Italian cuisine. Professionally, as a lawyer, I lean on other Italian American lawyers as a subset community within the larger NYC legal community. This is wonderful as it allows me to connect with people immediately based on a common trait and builds trust and understanding while seeking advice and mentorship. It also means I have very big, dark hair and other Italian physical traits and a wonderful Italian last name.

Italian American means to have Italian roots and ancestry (relatives, i.e., parents, grandparents, etcetera) that immigrated from Italy to the U.S. But beyond that, it's become a culture of people who enjoy similar things (festivals, beliefs, upbringing) and the like that they can connect and understand each other and their history. It's a sense of pride in your community.

This is a difficult question to answer. I would say that most Italian Americans today are "getting the short end of the stick," so to speak. The major issue is, since we are considered white, statistics do not accurately show just how much of a minority we are. I could see it as I grew up—the Italian American community was slowly dwindling away. Finding fellow Italian Americans seems to be a struggle, which is why I feel that we have such a strong feeling of camaraderie. Also, I feel that we have never really been portrayed in the media as a positive ethnic group. In many cases, non–Italian Americans associate us with either *Jersey Shore* or the Mafia culture, and they assume that we don't have a brain in our heads. This is just not true, but we will never be able to overcome the stereotypes, and even if we could, we don't really have the numbers anymore, so it would probably make little impact. I feel that to be Italian American today is to continuously make a conscious effort to overcome the stereotypes associated with us. I feel that to be Italian

American today is to continuously make a conscious effort to overcome the stereotypes associated with us.

To be an Italian American means to be immersed in American culture and society (speaking the language and engaging with the cultural norms) but also having a strong connection to family, and Italian culture. I live in Howard Beach which is a very Italian American neighborhood and it is nice to see Italian flags hanging and the close community that has been built on top of these values and traditions that are still so important to Italian culture.

THE PLURALITY OF ITALIAN AMERICAN IDENTITIES

The relationship between honoring one's Italian background and being American exists in a delicate balance. Where the meeting of these two identity components occurs, balancing assumes different forms of equilibrium that are expressed in differentiated and multiple forms of identification. The first is that of dual ethnicity. The young people express—in the majority of cases—their condition as an integrated identity composed of two ethnicities, a double cultural membership that represents a dynamic union of the two worlds, Italian and American, simultaneously present and perceived as advantageous. This confirms what Phinney (1996, cited in Chirico, 2014) and others argue, namely that a strong ethnic identity along with a strong national identity is the road to successful adaptation for the immigrant. Therefore, a "hyphenated" identity is required for the achievement of scholastic and economic success (Chirico, 2014).

It also happens that the coexistence of the two cultures experiences a division in the areas of influence wherein Italian heritage is expressed privately in the family sphere (private ethnicity) while outside the home the codes of American society prevail.

To be an Italian American means to live both an American and an Italian lifestyle equally. Whether it be doing Italian things at home and living an American life outside of the home. I also think being Italian American means that you live a better life than if you lived an Italian lifestyle because you still have the freedom of being an American and the culture of Italy.

For me, being Italian American is all I have known. Coming from my family experience, being Italian American is the instillation of the best of Italian and American culture. They have embraced their new homeland and are as patriotic as any other Americans. While at the same time, have retained the best aspects of Italian culture, and have taught their children not to forget where they came from.

It means getting the best of both worlds. The beauty of being part of different places is that you get to see different perspectives and you get to decide what you think is most helpful and useful for your own personal growth or way of living. I enjoy the culture and morality in my Italian culture but being an American especially from New York allows me to be very open to different people and ideas. It allows me to enjoy and appreciate different parts of the world since New York is so diverse.

Today, I have found that as an Italian American, there are a lot of misconceived notions about our culture especially within the younger generations in which such misunderstandings have been passed down upon. Young Italian American adults will often reference words in dialect, but don't truly understand what they're saying or where it comes from. There is a large population of young Italian Americans who don't actually know why we celebrate Columbus, or why eating only fish is a tradition on Christmas Eve. Most identify strongly as Italian Americans, but very, very few have a wider knowledge about where their Italian traditions come from, and what actually goes on in Italy today. Still, there is a population of professional men and women who keep the true spirit of Italian tradition respectably aligned with their American values. To be Italian American for me, personally, means to continuously grow my knowledge about Italian culture traditions and language, in the past and currently, yet take advantage of the opportunities only available to someone as an American.

In my opinion to say you are an Italian American means you feel attachment to being both Italian and American and that you cannot separate the two. I am not purely Italian, I was born in the United States, and enjoy a lot of American customs, however, my parents are both Italian, and I appreciate the culture that filled my house. I love both and enjoy both, I consider myself neither more or less one or the other.

Being an Italian American today means really being a regular American citizen. I believe the two now are inseparable. I feel that much of my family's culture is shared by friends and family who are not Italian American. I feel that the Italian American identity has crossed many boundaries and is deeply seeped into all American culture.

It is bringing parts of the Italian culture and traditions to America with some changes and adaptations to American society. It is a merging of ideas, traditions, and values.

While in most cases the two cultures are mixed in an integrated formula that for each subject acquires a different nuance of meaning, there appear to be some cases where a conflict exists between the two cultures and an ambivalence that can generate identity confusion. This situation can also produce a sense of marginality, of exclusion, of diversity perceived as an inferiority, a "double non-belonging." Some feel they are "neither fish nor fowl."[1]

Sometimes I feel that I am not quite Italian and I am not quite American; I don't fit into either group.

It mostly became apparent when I lived in Italy (Perugia) for six months. The feeling is hard to characterize. It was a mixture wanting to be completely immersed in the "Italian" way of being in the world but always being aware of a disconnect that existed between myself and native Italians. A lot of times it was a sad feeling of nostalgia for something I could have been had circumstances been different. Other times, or simultaneously, it was a firm realization of my Americanness.

I feel split between Italian and American (partly because I have dual citizenship and I grew up between the two places). Whenever I'm in one country, I miss the other one. I don't know where I will choose to settle when I grow up, because either way I worry that I will be missing certain places, people and customs.

I am here and feel like I am not part of a community anymore... not that I ever really was... but the sense I get is that my parents and grandparents had more of that feeling... it seems as if it is being lost and so I want to go to Italy perhaps.

In some cases, the Italian culture and heritage have been rejected or stay in the background, and the young people have embraced American culture either exclusively or prevalently. On this point, Viscusi (1990, 2006, 2015a) observed that a hidden problem for the Italian Americans is Italy. The author specifies this affirmation, claiming that this problem is hidden in two ways, one is that "many Italian Americans have forgotten everything about Italy. These people assume that the old country has nothing to do with them, even in the cases where the individuals keep their Italian names. They are Americans, pure and simple, and happy to be that way" (Viscusi, 2015a, p. 116). For the scholar, this is seen as "an enormous act of negation... *Italian* is what emphasizes the difference in the expression *Italian/American*, and for a long list of reasons Italy continues to play an important role in giving meaning to the expression as a social and historical fact" (ibid., p. 117).

I just don't like being labeled as "the other." I'm an individual person. And I feel like "I'm American" encompasses that individuality much better than the label Italian American.

Growing up in North Carolina I would often get, "Where are you from?" before I even opened my mouth. Even after I had lived there for over twenty years. I would say, "I'm from here." And they would persist. "No, where is your family from?" And I'd say, "Well, we moved when I was seven from New York." And still they would persist, "No, but where is your family from?" And at that point, I'd get it. Because I had olive hued skin and very dark hair I was considered foreign to the people originally from the rural South. And I'd say, "Well, my dad's side is Italian." And they'd say, "Oh so you're Italian." And I'm definitely not Italian. I've never even been to Italy.

I'm not really sure what it means. But I definitely feel like non–Italian Americans see a stereotype in their head. And my dad doesn't really talk to his side of the family that is Italian American. I'm not really sure what they are like. People my age with relatives further back (great-grandparents) who immigrated don't usually think of themselves Italian American before just American.

Italian American to me means someone who has come from Italy, and lives as a citizen of the United States. Being third generation, it is hard to feel like I can claim "Italian American" status. It almost feels like I'm not "Italian" enough to use that term, even though I identify with Italian culture and heritage. I'm the only person in my family who speaks Italian, who has lived in Italy, and yet, I still see myself as plainly "American." It is difficult to know what gives you that identity... much like being a "New Yorker." Five years? Ten years? Who knows?

On the other hand, other young people feel more Italian than Italian American or American.

> Today it is very different. Honestly, I call myself "Italian" and not "Italian American" because I have never felt very American anywhere or doing anything. I may carry a U.S. passport, but I am working on obtaining my dual citizenship with Italy.

> In my opinion, the majority of Italian American culture is very far removed from Italian culture itself. Many who identify as Italian Americans in the tri-state area do not know to speak the language, or expresses any interest in the culture of Italy today. Personally, I identify much more with authentic Italian culture, and not necessarily with Italian American culture, which is heavily permeated by stereotypes of Italians and of Italy which often times are archaic.

The perspective of the "new second generation" is different from that of earlier generations, which is worth consideration. These are children of parents most of whom immigrated to the United States between the 1960s and 1980s; for these young people, identification with their Italian heritage is mainly the result of family socialization—which has transmitted knowledge of Italian culture in a direct and felt way, considering that one or both parents are Italians—and of personal interest, which leads to the deepening of cultural knowledge also by using the Italian language understood by most—and of feelings of emotional attachment that have been grafted onto the different personality structures of the interviewees. For the new second generations, Italy is not a transmitted memory, nor an imagined or reinvented land, but a known place—often visited many times—to which they are connected through very close contacts.[2] These individuals very often tend to mark their difference from previous generations of young Italian Americans, based especially on the direct knowledge of Italy and the Italian language; frequently, they see other Italian Americans as having only a superficial knowledge of their Italian-ness, disconnected from any real vision of Italy and Italians, and accompanied by a lack of mastery of the mother tongue.

> It's hard to define Italian American because I believe there are two kinds. The first kind, is the Italian American like me. I've been traveling to Italy since I was born. I spent months there before I started going to school. Once I started school, my family and I would travel to Italy every summer and spend at least three months there. We all have dual citizenship. My siblings and I grew up

bilingual. We only speak Italian at home. I travel to Italy several times a year. I lived in Milan, studying and working, for almost six years. I know there's more to the Italian culture than just pizza, pasta, and bocce ball. The second kind of Italian Americans are more of the third and fourth generation Italian Americans, who perhaps have never been to Italy. Or they've been only once. Their idea of "Italian" is pasta, pizza, and bocce ball. They think wearing the *corno* means that they're Italian. And they certainly don't speak the language.

I think there is a difference between second generation Italian Americans and third generation. Second generation still hold the same values as their immigrant parents and know the culture and how to speak the language.

5

The Image of Italian Americans

THE IDENTIFYING CHARACTERISTICS OF ITALIAN AMERICANS

In order to identify the distinctive features of Italian Americans in today's society, the interviewees were asked to indicate to what extent they believed certain characteristics might model and distinguish Italian Americans. The percentages given in Table 5.1 are obtained by reaggregating the data according to the responses "very much" and "somewhat." It is observable that family values and characteristics are in first place for the reports of the individuals who believe these traits are specifically distinctive of Italian Americans, together with cooking, which is well known to represent a reason for strong identification by the Italian American group in general.

THE IMAGE OF THE TYPICAL INDIVIDUAL: COMPARING THE ITALIAN AMERICAN AND THE ITALIAN

In order to determine the "typical" image of the Italian American and the Italian, a list of seventeen pairs of opposing adjectives was prepared, using Osgood's semantic differential technique (Table 5.2). The two lists—identical in the composition of adjectives utilized—were first used in reference to the "typical" Italian American and subsequently for the "typical" Italian.

The self-image of the Italian American bears the connotation of an individual who tends to be rigid, short-tempered, loud, somewhat individualist, open,

Table 5.1 How much do the following traits identify Italian Americans? (very much/somewhat) (percentage values)

	%
Family characteristics and values	88.8
Cuisine	88.1
Tradition	87.3
Cultural interests	84.5
Temperament and personality	82.7
Mentality	80.5
Physical traits and appearance	79.8
History	71.6
Music	54.2

honest, tough, somewhat deep, traditionalist, creative, confident, tenacious, energetic, bossy, conceited, free-willed, and generous.

The profile linked to the Italian image presents parallel results to that of the Italian American, so much so that in all the adjectives that describe them, the differences from the statistical average are minimal with respect to those that characterize the image of the Italian American, and the trend of average value is almost identical.

Specifically, the Italian is perceived by the young Italian Americans as rigid, short-tempered, loud (though to a lesser degree than the Italian American connotation for these three characteristics), to the same degree individualistic, more reserved than the Italian American, equally honest, slightly less tough, more deep and less traditionalist, slightly more creative, confident in the same way, less tenacious, less energetic and less bossy, equally conceited and free-willed in their choices, and less generous than the Italian American.

Figure 5.1 presents the trend patterns from which it is observable that the two profiles assume a parallel trajectory. The results are not surprising and reinforce what Viscusi (2015a) pointed out, according to which "today, many Italians/Americans not only continue to identify with the nation that rejected them, but also maintain many of the fundamental themes of Italian culture" (p. 111).

Looking back at the history of Italian immigrants who arrived in America during the great migration, it is observed that many of them surrendered in the face of racial and class hostilities that they encountered in America and returned

Table 5.2 Mean values and standard deviation of the semantic differentials in reference to the typical Italian American and Italian

	TYPICAL ITALIAN AMERICAN					TYPICAL ITALIAN				
	N	Min.	Max	Means	Standard Deviation	N	Min.	Max	Means	Standard Deviation
Rigid-Flexible	253	1	7	2.91	1.292	237	1	7	3.16	1.753
Calm-Shorttempered	254	1	7	5.34	1.137	236	1	7	5.06	1.498
Loud-Quiet	254	1	6	2.22	1.238	237	1	7	2.47	1.355
Individualistic-Altruistic	252	1	7	3.84	1.419	236	1	7	3.86	1.495
Reserved-Open	254	1	7	5.07	1.518	236	1	7	4.86	1.594
Deceitful-Honest	254	1	7	5.27	1.273	237	1	7	5.17	1.320
Weak-Tough	254	1	7	5.78	1.112	237	2	7	5.57	1.204
Deep-Superficial	253	1	7	3.44	1.470	237	1	7	3.35	1.384
Traditionalist-Modern	254	1	7	2.56	1.302	237	1	7	2.82	1.558
Creative-Unimaginative	254	1	7	2.93	1.366	237	1	6	2.72	1.242
Insecure-Confident	254	2	7	5.43	1.129	237	2	7	5.43	1.105
Tenacious-Discouraged	254	1	6	2.68	1.127	237	1	7	3.05	1.322
Lazy-Energetic	255	1	7	5.20	1.288	237	1	7	4.79	1.439
Bossy-Docile	254	1	6	2.87	995	237	1	7	3.08	1.199
Conceited-Unassuming	253	1	7	3.48	1.049	236	1	7	3.53	1.077
Fatalistic-Freewilled	252	1	7	4.15	1.133	236	1	7	4.08	1.279
Generous-Tight with money	254	1	7	3.19	1.550	237	1	7	3.35	1.608
VALID (LISTWISE)	247					234				

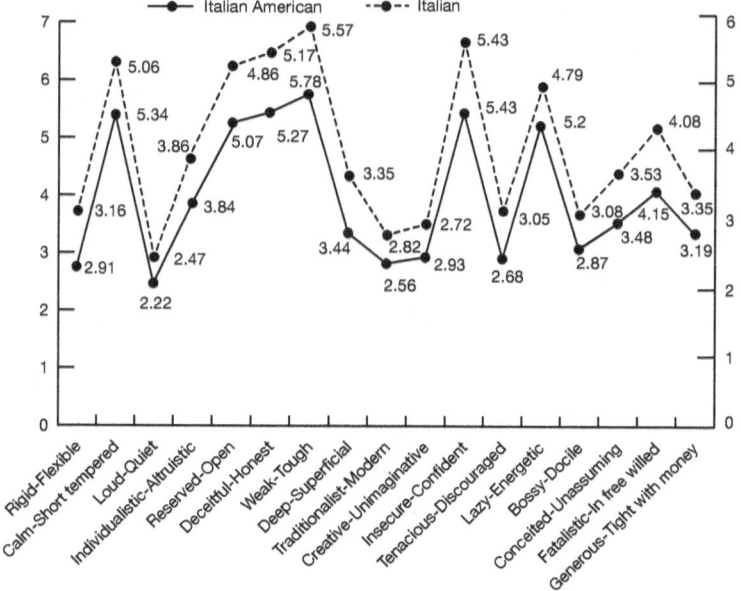

Figure 5.1 Comparison Between the Italian American and the Italian (mean values)

to Italy.[1] Millions of them, however, did not resign themselves to returning and instead tried to find a way to enter into the city community and American politics: "The secret was in accepting, even glorifying their national origins, in a way that was completely new to them. America pushed these immigrants from Italy to think of themselves as Italians... (but) Great Italy had not existed for long enough to make the national collective image become second nature for many of its people.... Immigrants recognized that the other Americans saw them as Italians and sought ways to make sense of this aspect of their being. The paradox of their existence was such that they could not become American without first finding a way of knowing what it meant to be Italian" (Viscusi, 2015a, pp. 139–140). Even today, as the results of the study show, young Italian Americans identify strongly with their homeland and "feel Italian."

Subsequently, the two semantic differentials were subjected to factorial analysis to obtain synthetic factors that allowed for a more in-depth interpretation of the results. This analysis permitted the specification of ten synthetic factors, which represent the dimensions—independent of each other—through which the self-perceived image of the typical Italian American and typical Italian are configured.

The first factor represents the component of "determination," which includes features that are common to Italians and Italian Americans and can be summarized in the following adjectives: energetic, confident, tenacious. This dimension is the dominant one in the image of the two groups; in order of importance, this is the first factor that emerged from the analysis.

The second factor brings out the dimension of "adaptivity" in reference to the image of Italians. It collects the homogeneous indications concerning the adjectives: calm, flexible, modern and reserved.

The third factor expresses the component of "submission" in reference to the image of Italian Americans. The attributes included in it are: calm, quiet, docile.

The fourth factor is connoted as the dimension of "superficiality" which characterizes the image of both the Italians and the Italian Americans. References are made here to superficial and unimaginative adjectives.

The fifth factor characterizes the dimension of "commitment," which applies to both Italian Americans and Italians. The characteristics included here can be summarized with the following adjectives: honest, tough, tenacious, confident.

The sixth factor is connoted as the dimension of "modesty" referring to Italians. Included are the attributes: unassuming and docile.

The seventh factor characterizes the dimension of openness concerning both Italians and Italian Americans and includes the adjective *open* in reference to both groups.

The eighth factor is characterized as the dimension of "parsimony" that describes both Italians and Italian Americans and includes the characterization "tight with money."

The ninth factor expresses the dimension of "altruism," which characterizes both Italians and Italian Americans. The adjective that falls within it is, in fact, altruistic.

The tenth and final factor refers to the condition "being free-willed," linked both to the image of Italians and to that of Italian Americans, and which can be defined as the dimension of "self-determination."

After identifying the factors described above, the score for each of the factors was calculated on a seven-value scale for each interviewee.

Since no interviewee scored below 3 and more than half of them registered high scores (greater than 5) in the first factor, it emerges that the dimension of "determination" is very strong in the self-perceived image of both the Italian American and the Italian.

A significant relationship of this dimension is found with age (sig. = .003) The two youngest classes in the sample have the higher scores in this dimension: in particular, the scores 5.50 and 6 are reached by respondents between twenty-four and twenty-nine years, while the maximum scores of 6.50 and 7 are a prerogative of especially the younger respondents.

The dimension of "adaptivity" that characterizes the image of Italians includes scores that do not exceed 4 in 87.7% of cases. Furthermore, the maximum score reached does not exceed 5.50. It seems, therefore, that this dimension connotes the image of Italians with relatively little weight, as perceived by the Italian Americans interviewed.

Regarding the dimension of "submission" referring to Italian Americans, the same trend of the previous factor is observed. The score does not exceed 5.50 and 96% of the respondents assign a maximum of 4 on this factor. In this case as in the previous one, it is observed that this dimension is less marked in the self-representation of young Italian Americans.

As for the dimension of *"superficiality"* that unites Italians and Italian Americans, the maximum value reached by the distribution of the scores is 6 and in 88% of the cases it does not exceed 4.

The age of the respondents discriminates the scores in this factor (sig. =, 004): the minimum scores are mainly present in the group of young people in intermediate age, while the highest ones are found among those who fall in the age group between thirty and thirty-four years. This indicates how this dimension especially connotes the image of the "oldest" of the sample.

The scores achieved by the distribution referring to the dimension of *"commitment"* that connects Italians and Italian Americans are decidedly more varied. The higher frequencies are found for the scores included between 4 (which is also the mode) and 6, lower on the score 6.50 and then rise to almost 12% with reference to the score of 7.

Here again, as in the previous case, age influences this dimension (sig = .001). Those who assign a score between 4 and 4.50 are mainly those in their thirties, while the highest scores on this dimension (6.50 and 7) are achieved mainly by the youngest of the sample.

Contrary to the previous dimension, it is the youngest who perceive "commitment" as a decisive aspect of the image of Italians and Italian Americans.

The distribution of the interviewees' scores on "modesty" records mostly low scores. The largest concentrations in the distribution are, in fact, between the scores 1 and 4.

"Openness" in reference to both the images of Italians and Italian Americans seems to be a dimension particularly felt by the interviewed young people. The frequencies of the scores are higher, in fact, starting from 4 and up to 7.

The "parsimony" factor mostly records low scores, considering that 60% of respondents do not exceed 3.50 in the ranking.

Regarding the relationship with the other variables, a significant differentiation is noted according to age (sig = .038). What emerges from the intersection of the scores with the age classes shows that it is primarily the youngest respondents who connect themselves to the minimum scores of the factor (up to 2.50), while among the thirty-year-olds the score of 4 prevails.

The scores related to the "altruism" dimension in the image of Italians and Italian Americans have a bell-shaped distribution, with scarce tails in scores between 6 and 7 and 1 and 2.

Concerning the component of "self-determination," there is a notably strong concentration of respondents on the value 4 which alone accounts for more than 38% in the distribution.

THE DIFFERENCES AND RESEMBLANCES AMONG THE ITALIAN AMERICANS, THE ITALIANS, AND THE OTHER AMERICANS

With the goal of analyzing the perceived self-image of Italian Americans compared to that of Italians and other Americans, respondents were asked to indicate how much they considered the three different groups representative of some selected characteristics.

As can be seen from Table 5.3, more than 35% of young people indicated a greater diversity in the diet of Italian Americans compared to that of Italians. More than half—respectively—believe that Italian Americans differ somewhat from Italians in terms of somatic traits, education, and cooking. Morality—for over 30% of the sample—does not present differences between the two groups.

With regard to the other Americans in general, the two aspects that show a greater differentiation between the two groups, for more than 44% and 42.6% of the interviewees, are, respectively, cooking and cultural background. Less

Table 5.3 How different are Italian Americans from Italians and other Americans with respect to the following aspects? (percentage values)

	FROM ITALIANS			FROM OTHER AMERICANS		
	Very different	Somewhat different	Not different	Very different	Somewhat different	Not different
Work	23.8	49.1	16.6	15.2	42.6	26.4
Family	18.8	31.0	39.0	37.9	37.9	8.7
Cuisine	22.4	50.9	15.2	44.0	35.4	5.4
Music	33.2	44.0	11.9	20.6	36.1	28.2
Education	20.6	50.9	17.3	11.9	37.5	34.7
Dress	30.7	43.0	14.4	13.0	39.4	30.7
Diet	35.7	45.1	7.6	27.8	41.9	14.4
Cultural background	29.2	45.5	13.7	42.6	37.2	4.7
Morality	11.9	45.5	31.8	18.1	51.3	15.2
Physical characteristics	10.1	52.3	26.4	20.2	53.8	10.5
Patriotism	23.1	44.4	21.7	16.6	40.4	27.8
Television preferences	23.1	43.0	23.1	7.2	36.1	40.4

obvious differences, though strongly felt by more than half of the interviewees, can be found in terms of somatic characteristics (53.8%) and morality (51.3%). Television preferences would appear to homologate the tastes according to the opinion of over 40% of young people.

What emerges from the data highlights how the alimentary aspect (both as a diet and as a way of cooking food), as well as the somatic features, represent very differentiated characteristics of Italian Americans compared to the other two groups.

Obviously, the research does not permit speculative vision, either of how Italians see Italian Americans, or how Italian Americans are seen by other Americans.

In particular, considering this last aspect, Viscusi (2015b) argues that Italian Americans play the "role of the Shadow of US imperial culture" (p. 145). More specifically, he believes that "Italoamerica is a colony where Americans can see their own faults in caricatured form, accompanied by good meals and beautiful songs" (ibid.).

THE IMAGE OF THE GROUP STRUCTURE

The image of the perceived structure of the Italian American community has been studied on three levels: the relational set of positions or "composition," "organization," and "integration" (Table 5.4).

Table 5.4 Indicators and structural level perceived by the group.

Perceived structure of the Italian American community	Level of composition	Completeness of the group	Individuals who claim not to belong to the group
	Level of organization	Expected duration of the group	Existence or future disappearance of the group
		Division or potential unity of the group	Presence of associations and organizations and community cohesion
		Relative social importance of the group	Esteem enjoyed by the group within American society
		Relative power of the group	Power of the group in American society
	Level of integration	Level of commitment of the group's components	Intensity of the feeling of belonging to the group
		Measure of the social interaction of the group	Friendly relationships in the group
		Character of the social relationships of the group	Agreement or disagreement among the members of the group
		Level of group visibility	Distinguishable at first sight

Source: author's revision from Merton (1966), cit. in Boileau, Sussi (1981).

The composition of the group was analyzed using the degree of completeness inferred through the respondents' answers to the question of whether there were individuals who, although having Italian origins, did not admit to being Italian. The hypothesis is that the more numerous these individuals are, the less complete the group is.

According to half of those interviewed, there is no one who, despite being of Italian origin, does not admit they are. Furthermore, 22% say that the number of people who do not recognize these origins are very few. Conversely, almost 5% of the sample highlights that there are many people who do not want to be associated with Italian Americans, while 16% believe that there are not many. Those expressing the belief that there are not many or very few people who do not admit having Italian origins belong especially to the fourth generation of immigration. On the other hand, among those who believe that there is no one hiding this lineage, second-generation youth prevail.

Questioning why people choose to dissociate themselves from being considered Italian American, Chirico (2011b) points out that, generally, a person who expresses hatred for some aspect of his/her personal identity experiences an external coercion. She argues that a possible explanation for self-hatred in the Italian American community derives from the profound conviction that being Italian American is similar to being nonwhite and that a greater barrier to assimilation is presented by this.

Farther on, she points out that the controversy over the definition of white/nonwhite has not been resolved by the Italian American community in general, and emphasizes the importance of establishing a "sense of group identity before it can have a fully represented voice in the general American culture that goes beyond the superficial" (p. 194).

Overall, though the motivations that push toward one opinion or another have not been investigated here, the Italian American group appears relatively "complete" at the self-perceptive level according to the definition that was given previously. Although unrelated to the perceived completeness of the group, it is interesting to note that the interviewees believed that there were people who identify with the characteristics and peculiarities of Italian Americans, even though they are not of Italian origin. More than 35% of young people are convinced there are many, while more than 26% believe there are not many. Therefore, according to more than one-third of the sample, there are many people of different backgrounds who try to emulate Italian Americans and identify themselves with the characteristics that distinguish them. Among those who indicate their belief that many people identify with this characterization, fourth-generation respondents stand out.

ORGANIZATION

The first indicator used to reveal the perception of the group's level of organization was the expected duration of the group. The question that referred to this dimension was formulated as follows: "Do you think that the characteristics that differentiate Italian Americans from the other ethnic groups present in American society will tend to expand and strengthen, will remain the same as they are today, will not disappear but will be less evident, will tend to disappear, or have they already disappeared?"

Sixty-five percent of respondents believe that the differentiation factors that characterize Italian Americans as compared to other ethnic groups will not disappear, but these will be less and less evident (Table 5.5). This prevailing idea is felt by the young people of all four generations of immigration, though slightly less among those belonging to the third.

Table 5.5 Factors that differentiate Italian Americans from other groups (percentage values)

	%
Will not totally disappear but will be increasingly less evident	65.0
Will remain the same as it is today	17.7
Will disappear	5.1
Will expand and grow stronger	2.2
Has already disappeared	1.8
N/A	7.9

The second indicator used to analyze the level of organization of the group is the division or unity of the group. This was analyzed through a question that combined the presence of Italian American associations with membership and community organization (Table 5.6).

The two dimensions studied—of associations and the sense of community belonging—intersect, presenting conflicting situations. Over 45% of respondents say that Italian Americans have associations but are not organized as a cohesive community. Conversely, there are those who believe that associations are present and that the group is compact and forms a united community (28.5%). Some maintain that there are no associations of Italian Americans, but that the feeling of community is shared (12.3%). Finally, 5.8% assume that Italian Americans belong to a community only in name and that nobody thinks they are really part of this community. The lack of a sense of community, therefore, is perceived as such by more than half of the respondents. In fact, as noted by Riotto Sirey and other colleagues (1985), "While American culture is inclined to consider Italians

Table 5.6 Presence of associations and community organization (percentage values)

	%
They have their associations, but they are not organized as a cohesive community	45.1
They have their associations and they are well organized as a cohesive community	28.5
They do not have associations, but they feel a sense of belonging to the same community	12.3
N/A	8.3
They are only a community in name; no one or almost no one thinks he or she is a part of a community	5.8

as a homogeneous group, Italians themselves have never had a strong sense of belonging to a united group" (p. 7).

The third indicator selected to analyze the level of organization of the Italian American group is linked to the social importance of the group. This is deduced from the respondents' opinion of the esteem enjoyed by Italian Americans in American society. More than half of those surveyed believe that Italian Americans are fairly respected and over a fifth that they are highly esteemed. It should not be overlooked, however, that more than 16% of the young people in the sample think that the group is esteemed very little.

The fourth indicator used to analyze the group's level of organization relates to the group's power in American society. According to more than one-half of the respondents, Italian Americans as a group enjoy a certain power and for almost 6% it has a lot of power. However, it should be noted that for more than 28% of the sample, the group has little power.

INTEGRATION

The level of Italian American integration in American society was studied using four indicators: the degree of commitment of the group members, the measure of social interaction, the character of social relationships, and the degree of visibility.

The degree of commitment of the members of the group was revealed through their self-evaluation of the intensity of their feelings of belonging.

The question regarding the importance attributed to the ethnic background, already commented on above, shows that for over 70% of respondents this aspect is considered very relevant. Furthermore, pride in being Italian American is felt all the time by more than 60% of young people, and it is felt more often than not for 20% of them. Feelings of shame connected to this belonging—only in some circumstances—have been indicated by more than one-fifth of the sample.

In order to analyze the extent of the social interactions of the group, the relationships of friendship within the group were considered. The level of social interaction with members of their own ethnic group appears high, in consideration of the fact that more than 85% count these among their friendships, albeit mixed with others of different ethnic backgrounds. The self-perceptions of the group's internal cohesion achieve the level of satisfactory, reflecting the fact that overall almost 90% of young people say that Italian Americans get along with each other, even if they detect different levels of intensity in this regard.

In reference to identification at first sight among members of the Italian American group, the majority of respondents—almost 80%—believe that they are easily identifiable on the basis of physical characteristics and appearance.

DIMENSIONS OF THE IMAGE OF ITALIAN AMERICANS

To understand the dimensions around which young people construct their image of Italian Americans, twenty-three questions were selected that elicited, from different angles, the characteristics that compose this image, which were then subjected to factorial analysis. The data processing resulted in eight factors that synthetically represent the components of this image.

The first factor can be called "culture and values" and collects the homogeneous answers to the questions regarding how much the traditions, the history, the cultural interests, and the family identify Italian Americans today.

In the second factor, called "physical and personality traits," the answers to the questions regarding how much temperament and personality, physical characteristics and appearance, cooking and mentality identify Italian Americans have been assembled.

The third factor expresses the "sense of belonging to the community." Here the answers to the questions regarding getting along or not within the group converge, reflecting the feeling of being or not being part of a community that brings the group together and, moreover, the presence of more or less organized associations, always within a community that may seem more or less united.

The fourth factor can be denoted as "prestige and power" and contains the answers concerning opinions on the power that Italian Americans have in the United States, on the presence of discrimination against them, on the esteem in which they are held by other ethnic groups and, finally, their agreement or not with the proposition that the mass media projects a distorted and often negative image of Italian Americans.

The fifth factor has been labeled "reaction to stereotypes." This factor brings together the answers to questions concerning the reaction of Italian Americans when the *Guido* or the *Guidette* is mentioned by non–Italian Americans, the reaction when Italian Americans themselves use these terms, and lastly how the majority of Italian Americans react—according to the young peoples' opinions—to the stereotypes that represent them in the media.

The sixth factor is called "sharing of stereotypes" and collects the homogeneous answers to the two questions that solicit opinions on being a stereotype of *Guido* and *Guidette* or not, and, having encountered these and similar Italian American stereotypes, considering them authentic or not.

The seventh factor expresses "representation through the media." This factor includes the answers to a single question that asked if the representation of Italian Americans by the media appeared realistic.

The eighth and final factor is called "recognition of group membership." It concerns the responses to two questions that asked, first, if there were Italian Americans who did not admit to being part of the group, and then to what extent music is an identifier of Italian Americans nowadays.

After specifying the factors described above, the score for each interviewee was calculated in all of the factors.

The first factor, which is also the most important for describing the image of Italian Americans, is denoted as "culture and values." The weight attributed to this dimension in the composition of the image varies between 1, or the maximum presence of this aspect in the image, and 0, the minimum. This identification appears very strong considering that 67% of the interviewees assigned a points value equal to 1 and 0.8 and, if the points value 0.6 is added to this, the cumulative total reaches 85.4%.

The second factor, "physical and personality traits," represents a very important connotation in the image of the interviewed young people if one considers that more than 70% assigned a points value comprised between 0.8 and 1.

In the case of the factor denoted "sense of belonging to the community," an increase in points value also augments the intensity of the sense of belonging. The scores achieved by the interviewees demonstrate that these individuals are concentrated especially in the middle of the distribution, namely between 0.50 and 0.83, thus indicating a widespread conviction that the sense of belonging to the community represents a significant dimension in the composition of the image that directly refers to them.

The fourth factor is connected to the dimension of "prestige and power" as linked to the image of the Italian Americans. The scores proceed such that an increase refers to a growing intensity that a dimension takes on in this representation. Twenty percent of the interviewees position themselves within the low points (comprised between 0 and 0.33), while the more elevated percentages are recorded on the intermediate points values—located between 0.50 and 0.67—which is where more than half of the interviewees are located. There is a significant relationship between this factor and gender (sig. = .038). In particular, the more elevated points are an especially female characteristic, demonstrating that the women in the sample attribute more importance to this dimension than the men do.

The factor that represents the dimension "reaction to the stereotypes" was measured through a points scale from 0 to 1, which proceeds in an increasing way beginning from a total sense of recognition of the stereotype (specifically the *Guido* subculture) and arriving at feeling offended by this representation (point 1). A portion equal to 18% of the interviewees achieve a point value between 0 and 0.33, which would indicate a mild reaction toward the subculture that represents them in a stereotyped way. The points values comprised between 0.67 and 1 comprehensively represent a percentage equal to over 70% of the interviewees, denoting that this appreciable portion of the sample takes offense regarding this representation.

The points on the sixth factor, which identifies the "sharing of the stereotypes," proceed from 1 point—indicating the maximum level of identification by the interviewees with the stereotypes connected to the image of Italian Americans—while 0 expresses a low level of sharing regarding the influence of these stereotypes on the Italian American image. What emerges from the points distribution is that the more elevated percentage values are situated around the points comprised between 0.50 and 1 (comprehensively 76.5% of the sample), indicating an elevated level of identification with the stereotypes; a portion of the interviewees equal to 22.8% assigns a points value between 0 and 0.25.

Regarding the relationship with other variables, this factor demonstrates a significant differentiation in relation to the age of the interviewees (sig. = .000): the more elevated points values are predominantly selected by the "elders" of the sample, while the lower points values characterize especially the younger age range of the sample. This indicates that among the respondents it would be the thirty-year-olds who are most likely to believe that stereotypes are part of the image and are based in truth, while younger people in the age group eighteen to twenty-three consider the stereotypes far removed from the real image of Italian Americans.

The factor that expresses the "representation of Italian Americans in the media" records almost total positioning of the interviewees' selection at the scores 0.5 (52.9%) and 1 (46.6%), scores that express a partial or total disagreement with the notion that media representations express a realistic image of who Italian Americans are today. With reference to the variables, we note that this factor bears a significant relationship with age (sig. = .007). The 0.5 score mainly connotes the younger and the intermediate age group, while the score 1 mainly characterizes the thirty-year-olds.

The relationship with the immigration generations also appears to be significant (sig. = .034). The score 0.5 shows an increasing trend from the second to the fifth generation, while the score 1 tends, inversely, to decrease from the second to the fifth generation. This indicates that a total disagreement with this representation of Italian Americans prevails especially among second-generation youths and decreases in subsequent ones.

The last factor, linked to the dimension of "recognition of group membership" highlights through the scores of 0.66 and 1—achieved by 23.9% and 53.7% of respondents, respectively—the greatest disagreement, that there were Italian Americans who did not admit to being part of the group. Age and gender represent discriminators in the points assigned to this factor. The notion that Italian Americans feel they belong to this group characterizes especially the thirty-year-olds and the youngest of the sample, while the highest scores associated with this belief especially characterize women's responses.

6

Italy and the Italians

ORIGIN MYTHS

The ideal and metaphorical aspect plays a very important role in the Italian migratory experience in America. Gardaphé (2004) points out that Italian America was an invention that began with America first: this was "an idea long before becoming a place and, as an idea, it contained all the hopes of complete freedom, real equality, lack of persecution, and unlimited potential to live life in all its fullness" (p. 13). Furthermore, Gardaphé claims that America represented a goal that contained a promise within itself for the Italian immigrant: "going west across the ocean where work was available." The American experience became mythologized in the stories told by the emigrants who returned to the homeland: "The myth of America was created through the stories and the myth was communicated through the metaphor" (p. 14). This way of seeing the encounter produced a dichotomy between dream and reality, and through this myth America became a metaphor and something to fight for.

The myth[1]—as noted by Roland Barthes (1974)—is a message, a communication system, a means of signification, a shape. He claims that "the myth is not defined by the object of the message, but in the way it is told" (p. 191). Moreover, he reminds us that "regarding myth, people are not in a relationship with truth, but with use" (p. 224). But myths are not eternal, "because it is human history that passes the real to the state of speech, and this history alone regulates the life and death of the mythical language... the myth is a word chosen by history" (p. 192).

Thus, Italian immigrants—in response to the cultural and social dynamics of the United States that were passed along to the generations succeeding the first one—lost sight of the original idea of America, along with the metaphorical connotations that accompanied it; this loss necessitated the replacement of the myth with another ideal: "It was then that the notion of 'old country' came into being" (Gardaphé, 2004, p. 18). Italy became a metaphor for post-immigrant generations and its image came to be built through the stories told by immigrants' relatives: "With that image in mind, we went to find the place called 'bella Italia.' But such a place did not exist anywhere. Italy had changed: the metaphors of the past could no longer be found in the present reality" (ibid.). The mythologized version of Italy persisted in the minds of young Italian Americans. This narrative is found especially in the words of those who have no personal experience of Italy but have only heard stories about the country.

Barthes (1974) emphasizes the fact that "the relationship that unites the mythical concept to meaning is essentially a relationship of deformation" (p. 203). As in Freudian psychoanalysis, where the latent meaning of behavior distorts its revealed meaning, so in myth the concept deforms meaning. Such deformation is possible insofar as the form of the myth is already established by a linguistic meaning. Thus, the characteristic of the myth denotes transforming a meaning into a form. Barthes goes on to say: "The myth hides nothing and declares nothing; the myth deforms; it is neither a lie nor a confession: it is an inflection... reduced to revealing or dismissing the concept, the myth resolves to naturalize it. We are faced with the very principle of myth: the myth transforms history into nature" (p. 210).

Returning to the experience of Italian immigrants in America, Viscusi (2015a) points out that one of the false and harmful stereotypes surrounding the world of Italian Americans depicts Italoamerica as an "underground criminal empire where gangsters reign" (p. 103). It is also—in this case—a myth that produces another: that Italoamerica is an underworld, an iceberg, hiding a large part of its mass beneath the surface. Very often, Italian Americans do not realize that they act on the basis of "tacit assumptions," namely, "old extracts of Italian propaganda deeply rooted in Italian/American culture"[2] (p. 104). Many shared beliefs were handed down through the generations and continue to survive in the unconscious and dark meanderings of the psyche, exerting a strong power: these are what Viscusi calls the "buried Caesars." One of the most famous signals of their reemergence is the myth of organized crime. From this myth of a huge "underground conspiracy" comes the widespread belief that Italian Americans cannot be trusted beyond a certain point (p. 111). This "foundational dimension of illegality" also serves as a constant limit on the social and political ambitions of Italian Americans (ibid.).

"LA BELLA ITALIA"

Viscusi (2015b) claims that "the Italian/Americans are unable to forget Italy, even if they would like to" (p. 120). The meanings attributed to Italy by Italian Americans are "many and not always easy to classify—or even to discover" and "the Italy of the mind is large and complex" (p. 121).

Chirico (2014) observes in the immigrants who arrived in the United States before World War II an extraordinary disconnection from Italy; often, these immigrants have cut ties with Italy both on purpose and as a reaction to circumstances such as the war itself. Unless there are relatives still living in Italy, the descendants of the earlier immigrants have no idea or knowledge of the nature of the country after World War II. In reality, today's Italy is very different from what the immigrants' children imagined was the country left behind by their ancestors, but many Italian Americans are not aware of this profound disjunction. For some, the result is an idealized image of Italy derived from family memories handed down through the generations; for those who do not have direct experience of Italy it is a "collage of phantasmagoria created by the media" (p. 68).

H.W. Haller (1993), in a survey of Italianisms[3] in the English and Anglo-American languages, observes that Anglo-American society has a dual image of Italy. On one hand, "the un-adapted Italianism" that has established itself in music and art evokes the characteristics of a highly prestigious civilization; on the other hand, there is the expression of regional culture bearing peasant origins—associated with the community of Italian emigrants in the United States—which is particularly expressed in the gastronomic discourse. The Italy of art, architecture, music, and painting is also perceived, he observes, as "the country of *la dolce vita*, of neo-Latin exoticism" (p. 111), as if to say that one's love for and interest in Italy and its civilization are both "folkloristic and nostalgic" (the 'garden of Europe,' the 'promised land')" (p. 116).

Returning to our study, the section of the questionnaire dedicated to the image of Italy was introduced by an open question asking respondents to indicate what thinking about Italy evoked in them.

Five levels of perception can be distinguished from the resulting answers:

1. the idealized, mythologized Italy: the idyllic place, the country of "la dolce vita";
2. the real, experienced Italy;
3. the imagined Italy;
4. the absent Italy;
5. the past, nostalgic Italy.

The first category seems to highlight those who—in the words of Viscusi (2015b)—think of Italy as a source of pride: "We painted the *Monna Lisa [sic]*. We discovered America. We invented the opera" (p. 116). This representation portrays sometimes mythologized images that recall an "ideal homeland," an "idyllic place." Schepis (2006) defines this image that Italian Americans have created of Italy as "tourist-aesthetic," or in Bertellini's formulation, a "contemplative and de-historicized conception, reified around the notions of art, poetic inspiration and scenic beauty, in sharp contrast, though often cohabiting with the 'intrusive' concept of the dirty and illiterate immigrant" (1999, p. 240).

For those in the second category, their image of Italy is based on direct experience or on travel and on the relationships that keep them connected to it.

The third category echoes what Viscusi (2015b) has defined—delving into the representation of Italy proposed through Italian American writing—"the homeland of desire." It is an image wherein a vision prevails based above all on the emotions associated with this connection. Recalling the words of Calvino (1990), cited by Schepis (1999), "Often the country discovered is only a land of utopia, a social allegory that in reality shares only some characteristics with the existing country; but this does not take away from its significance; on the contrary, the elements emphasized are precisely those needed by the situation" (p. 6). Schepis also claims that over time America and Italy have exchanged roles: the fanciful image was previously represented by America, an uncertain future and a mythical land to be discovered. Today, this collective image envelops Italy, the land of ancestors, a place of the past just as mythical and uncertain, to be rediscovered.

Italy can sometimes appear faraway and absent. Viscusi (2015b) maintains that the place is "Slow and reluctant to accept Italian/Americans on a cultural level" (p. 119). It expects a relationship of "colonial" subjection with the rich Italo-America colony, and, "Whenever Italian Americans dedicate their time, their money, their energy, and their will to promote Italy, they strengthen an order of colonial prestige that places them at the bottom of a very large, ancient, and heavy pyramid.... The message between the lines is that Italian/Americans can not achieve cultural equality. These individuals belong to Little Italy and they will never be able to escape it" (p. 120).

Nostalgia as a theme is particularly connected to the history of the Italian Americans.[4] It resonates especially when Italy is the object of what Viscusi (1996) defines as "reminiscence of splendor that no longer exists": this nostalgic vision expresses itself more precisely as an object of political desire, namely "the glory" (p. 70). Moreover, Viscusi highlights how the concept of nostalgia in literary history is often associated with that of Little Italy; it entails two preferred themes: "its own nostalgia and its own death" (p. 65). These two themes inspired, among others, the poet Lawrence Ferlinghetti, who wrote the nostalgic poem "The Old Italians Dying," which is considered both the swan song of the old Italian neighborhood in San Francisco's North Beach and a testament to the dying immigrant culture:

> For years the old Italians have been dying
> All over America
> For years the old Italians in faded felt hats
> Have been sunning themselves and dying
> You have seen them on the benches
> In the park in Washington Square
> The old Italians in their black high button shoes
> The old men in their old felt fedoras
> With stained hatbands
> Have been dying and dying
> Day by day...." (Ferlinghetti, 1979)

Returning to the interviewees' answers to the open question that evoked the image of Italy, these were reaggregated according to the following twelve interpretative categories:

1 *direct, personal experience:* the journey, memories;
2 *the past, history, traditions:* historic sites, folk festivals, birth of Western civilization, Europe, the cradle of civilization, the flag;
3 *values:* the family and its strong ties, friendship, religion, the church, being tireless workers, the sense of community and altruism, being connected to one another;

4 *the negative aspects*: the lack of rules, corruption, scarce opportunities, political instability, unemployment in general and among youth in particular, the bureaucracy, Berlusconi, faulty services (the dirty streets, buses never on time), the antagonism between North and South, the conflict between Italy in the past and the current one, the corrupt morality, the bad economic situation, the strong disputes and the territorial and regional rivalries;
5 *places, architecture, the countryside, the cities, the weather:* the beauty of the historic and architectural landscapes, the churches, the sea;
6 *food and wine, the cuisine;*
7 *family's place of origin:* ancestors, roots, the places where the relatives live, the extended family, family of the grandparents;
8 *art and culture*: cinema, writers, music, song, literature, language, sports, various dialects;
9 *relationships and lifestyle*: the relaxed lifestyle, the way of life that distinguishes it, sociability, patience, the high quality of life, appreciation of quality and not of quantity, the attention to details, the very open and direct way of speaking, distinct and noisy mannerisms;
10 *feelings*: love, passion, romance, pride, fun, freedom, kindness, friendship, the "smile," authenticity, thoughtfulness;
11 *aesthetics and creativity*: beauty, style, design, fashion, craftsmanship, artistic creations, experiences, "the Vespa";
12 *the sense of diversity*: feeling different from Italians ("we are Americans").

The five perceptive levels in reference to Italy and described above transversely intersect the twelve categories; taken from the specifications that the respondents have proposed, these represent a meta-analytical level of reading, aimed at capturing the perception and representation of Italy in a synthetic form. Once the interpretative categories were defined, their distribution frequencies were calculated.

As Table 6.1 highlights, food and cooking appear markedly in the image that respondents have of Italy, as do the presence of places, art, and culture, which appear in the conceived image of more than a third of the interviewees. One-quarter of the young people interviewed view Italy in reference to its past, its history, and its traditions.

It should be emphasized that cooking for Italian Americans is an important symbol of ethnic identification; this great symbolic strength is due to food's value

Table 6.1 Elements connected to the image of Italy (percentage values)

	%
Food and cooking	49.8
Places	33.6
Art and culture	30.7
The past, history, and the traditions	24.9
Aesthetics and creativity	19.1
Family	18.8
Relationships and lifestyle	18.1
Values	15.9
Feelings and emotions	13.4
Direct experience	9.0
Negative aspects	8.3
Differences from the United States	5.1

as a "tradition" for the members of the group while also being perceived in terms of a "tradition" within their collective image (Cinotto, 2001). Tamburri (2015b) also points out that food and the family are two great themes ubiquitous within Italian American cultural productions. Recalling the words of Barolini, he emphasizes the fact that the writer claims her "first memory (of Italy) is gastronomic," a "sort of transcendental exaltation," comparable to the "solemn moment of the First Communion" (Barolini, 1988, cited in Tamburri, 2015b).

KNOWLEDGE OF ITALIAN CULTURE

The level of knowledge of Italian culture exhibited by the interviewees was analyzed by applying the same battery of questions that were utilized to delve into Italian American culture. The answers to this question also highlight the overwhelming extent to which cooking and food dominate the respondents' cultural knowledge of Italy. Table 6.2 highlights, in fact, how widely the Italian culinary recipes are known by almost all the young Italian Americans; the same goes for the traditions and popular customs. More than 85% of the sample claim to have either some or a lot of knowledge of Italian history.

If these responses are compared with previously cited data regarding the level of knowledge of Italian American culture (chapter 3, Figure 3.5, p. 51), a deep

Table 6.2 Level of knowledge of the Italian culture (%) (percentage values)

	VERY MUCH/ SOMEWHAT
Culinary recipes	94.2
Folk traditions and customs	91.8
History	85.2
Religious traditions	82.4
Traditional festivals	78.3
Artistic and literary productions	70.4
Songs/ prayers/ ways of speaking	66.4
Musicians, singers	66.0
Traditional fairy tales	52.7

parallel seems to appear between the two: this is, in fact, confirmed by the frequency distribution trend of the various items.

Another area considered to be very important is that of feelings and experiences regarding Italy. Over 73% of respondents feel a sense of admiration toward Italy and more than 65% feel an identification with it; at the same time, more than half warn that it is very different from American society.

To explore the opinions of young Italian Americans with regard to Italy and the Italians, a set of questions was created, which included a Likert scale as a response modality. Aggregating the responses "very much" and "somewhat agree," it emerges that over 80% of the young people believe honor, respect,

Table 6.3 Feelings and perceptions regarding Italian society (percentage values)

	YES	NO
Admiration	73.3	11.9
Disdain	6.1	78.7
Identification	65.3	19.9
Disappointment	12.3	72.2
Indifference	15.9	68.2
Difference (very different from my own society)	50.9	34.3
Resemblance (very similar to my own society)	33.9	50.5

and honesty are among the greatest Italian virtues (see Figure 6.1). Equally apparent is the feeling that Italians have a great sense of solidarity, combined with kindness and generosity. Aesthetic sense and good taste in clothing and furniture are also characteristics that are attributed to Italians by a large number of respondents (73.7%). On the other hand, more than 66% of the opinions registered do not support the notion that superficiality, cunning, and negligence are among the vices of Italians. Over 60%, moreover, do not share the opinion that Italian Americans have a negative image of Italy due to corruption and/or organized crime in the country.

More than half of the sample does not agree that Italians have a low propensity to accept rules and obligations, just as there is no agreement regarding the

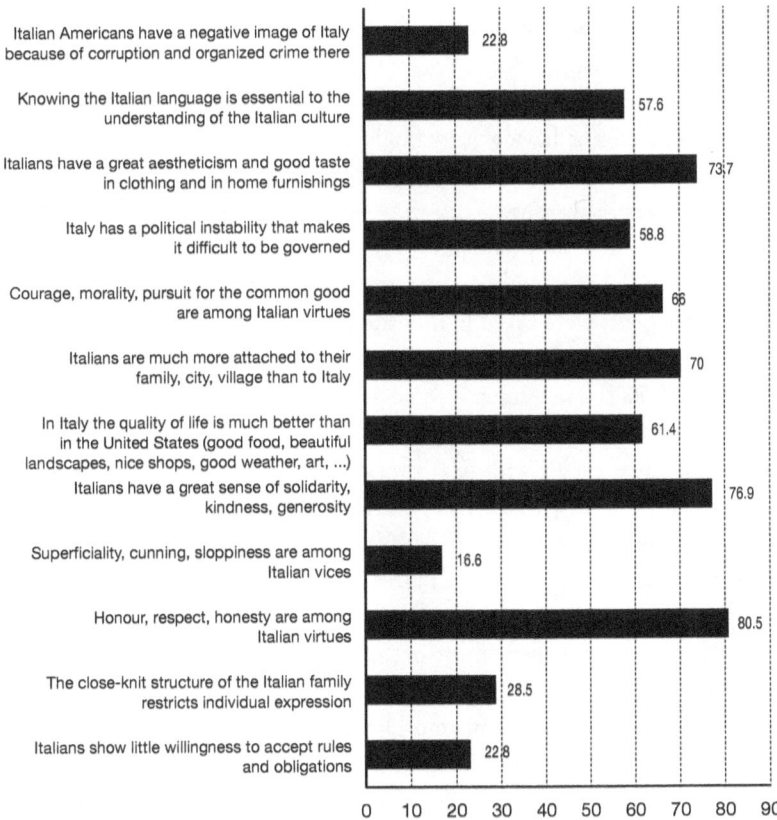

Figure 6.1 Opinions on Italy and Italians (very much/somewhat agree)

fact that strong family ties, typical of the Italian family, represent grounds for restriction of individual expressiveness (56%).

PERSONAL RELATIONSHIP WITH ITALY

Then the interviewees were asked if they had personally visited Italy. One-fifth of the sample declared they had never been (58 subjects), while more than two-thirds of the respondents had traveled there, either many times (29.2%) or a few times (37.9%). Those who had been to Italy were asked to indicate how old they were during their first visit. Twenty-nine percent of the young people visited Italy during their childhood years, while more than half went during adolescence and young adulthood; about one-fifth made the trip during their adult years.

Those who went to Italy were also asked if they had visited their family's places of origin. More than 55% had gone, either often or sometimes, while a quarter never had. More than 60% of those interviewed are aware of having relatives in Italy, while just over a quarter say they do not know whether they have any. The relationship between having visited Italy and the presence of relatives there is direct: prevalent among those who say they have relatives in Italy are the people who went there many times, while the majority of respondents who say they do not have relatives in Italy have never visited the country.

To analyze the frequency of contacts between young people and relatives in Italy, respondents were asked to indicate how often they were in contact with their relatives and how often they went to visit them. The frequency of contact is quite varied. The largest group—equal to one-quarter of the sample—are those who communicate with relatives monthly (25.9%). Equally, many respondents do not have any contact with relatives (24.1%). Seventeen percent connect on a weekly or even daily basis. The percentage of young people who visit their Italian relatives annually or more is equal to 14.2%, while those who go to visit them once every five years or less (34.7%) are much more numerous; the latter group is equal to half of those who indicated they had relatives in Italy. However, there is a sizeable percentage of the people surveyed—34.7%—who never visit their Italian relatives.

In addition to the familial relationships in Italy, it seemed important to understand whether there were any friendship ties that keep young people connected to Italy. Just over one-tenth of the interviewees claimed to have many friends in Italy, while about 14% have some and almost as many have fewer. Almost half of the respondents, however, have no friends in Italy with whom they are in contact. To calculate whether having visited Italy reflected the influence of the number of Italian friends with whom young people are in contact, the two questions related to this information were intersected. What emerges highlights a direct relationship between the frequency of visits to Italy and the number of friends that young people claimed to have there. In fact, among those who indicated that they have many friends in Italy, those who visit most often take the lead, while among those who have only "some" friends are mostly young people who have been to Italy only a few times. Prevalent among those who have few friends in Italy are the young people who have visited only a few times; and among those who have no Italian friends, the majority are those who have never visited the country.

Another extremely significant area of relationships is the one related to young Italians who recently immigrated to the United States—more specifically, to the greater New York area—who are more or less the same age as the young Italian Americans in the sample. Respondents were asked if they had contacts with these young Italian immigrants and, if so, what was the type of relationship. Half of the interviewees admitted to having no relationship with the new arrivals. One-fifth declared they had had only occasional contacts and only one-tenth of the sample numbered the recent immigrants among their own friends.

On the presence and on the modalities of this relationship it is again important whether the respondent has had the opportunity or not to visit Italy. In fact, among those who are friends with young Italians of recent immigration, among those who have contacts with them but do not consider them real friends, and among those who have met them but only occasionally there is a prevalence of young people who have visited Italy many times. On the contrary, among those who said they only have business contacts or no contact, there is a prevalence of young people who have never been to Italy. The opportunity to visit Italy unquestionably not only represents a real opportunity to engage with the country's culture, but also defines the fabric of the relationships that connect the two sides of the ocean.

Regarding information about Italy, only one-tenth of the young people interviewed receive news of this nature daily. Twenty-seven percent are interested in the Italian situation on a weekly basis, while 28% are updated on a monthly basis. Six percent of the sample have no interest in what happens in Italy.

In order to determine the information sources that were used by young people to get news about Italy, a list was proposed that includes both Italian and American outlets.

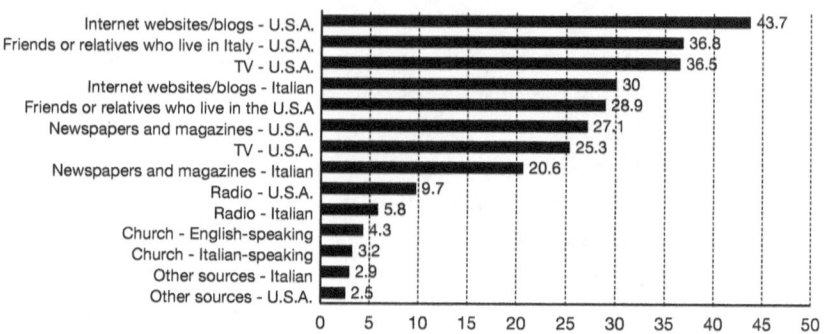

Figure 6.2 Sources of Information about Italy

Figure 6.2 shows that the information sources most accessed by young Italian Americans are American blogs and websites. More than 36%, however, make reference to Italian friends and relatives, while a similar percentage rely information about Italy from what they perceive from American television.

USE OF THE ITALIAN LANGUAGE AND VARIOUS DIALECTS

Language represents a powerful and reassuring identity bond, which every human being needs. As Maalouf (1998) observed, "Nothing is more dangerous than trying to break the umbilical cord that unites a man to his language. When it is broken, or severely damaged, there are disastrous repercussions on the whole of the personality" (p. 123).

The Italian language has undergone many changes since the first immigrants introduced it to the United States.[5] Until recently, dialects represented the true mother tongue of Italian emigrants. Haller (1993) noted that "it is essentially a non-standard variety, impoverished and hybridized, handed down from one generation to another" (p. 37). As for Italian, the language remains "a vital symbol of group solidarity among emigrants" (ibid.). In order to understand whether there was any knowledge of and/or interest in the language of their ancestors among the young people, a section of the questionnaire was dedicated to the knowledge and use of the Italian language and dialects.

Before analyzing the answers in this section of the questionnaire it is necessary to make some clarifications concerning the meaning of the terms *dialect* and *language*. In fact, both terms are accompanied by a variety of different, perhaps contradictory, meanings, depending on whether linguists or the Italian

Americans themselves define them, that create interpretative ambiguity. In the case of many descendants of second and third-generation Italian immigrants of the early twentieth century, what has been left by their forebears is only a handful of words and fragments that are interpreted as if they were a dialect in its entirety (Tortora, 2014). As Tortora argues, for some Italian Americans "to speak dialects" means knowing only a few words but not the Italian dialectal linguistic system that accompanies them, leaving them, therefore, a fragment that is absolutely infinitesimal and without the structure of the dialect that was spoken by previous generations. Likewise, the word *Italian* referred to language that is generally, but not always, used, connecting it to the standard language. In fact, the term can also be used to mean "Italian dialect," as it is in the U.S. Census form, which shows Italian as the language of many households. In fact, the "Italian" language that an Italian American family cites in answering the census may not be the same as the Italian language taught in American classrooms. In summary, Tortora concludes that there was little awareness of what language was actually spoken by the first Italian immigrants and the word *dialect* was given a totally new and different meaning; the same happens for the word *Italian*, which is used in an ambiguous way, to define both "standard Italian" and Italian "dialects." If "Italian" were attributed to the latter, it would be correct to say that the Italian American ancestors spoke "Italian." Therefore, the analysis of the following data must be read with due interpretative attention and an awareness of this basic ambiguity.

The section was introduced by two questions that referred to the use of a language other than English within the family, during childhood and currently (see Figure 6.3).

What emerges highlights how the use of the Italian language and dialect were present during the childhoods of the interviewees (for more than 46% and 29% of the of the cases, respectively). Even today, the use of Italian in the family has not been abandoned, considering that over 38% of young people live in a family in which Italian is spoken. In one-fifth of the cases (22.4%), even dialect continues to be a vehicle for communication within the modern family. However, there is a decreasing trend in the use of the Italian language and dialects in the life of the interviewees and in the transition from childhood to adulthood.

Subsequently, the young people were asked if they spoke and understood Italian and one or more regional dialects. The answers to the two questions highlight a varied panorama in the use of the language and dialects. Overall, just under a tenth of the sample does not understand and does not speak Italian, while the

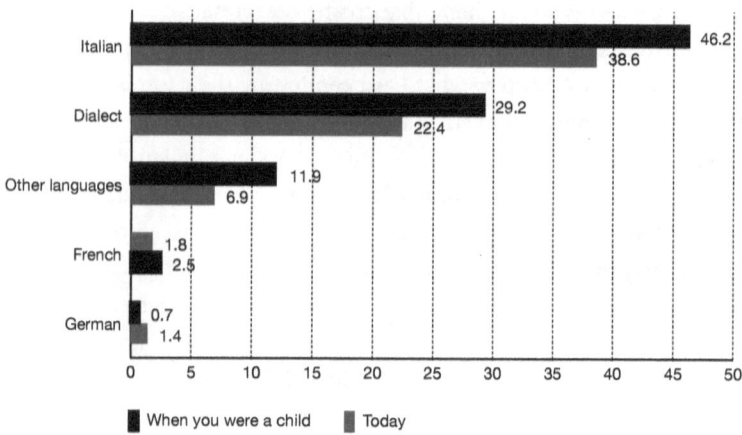

Figure 6.3 Language/Dialect Spoken in your Family

percentage of those who understand the language is over 77%. In particular, those who speak it regularly number only 14.4%, while 32.9% speak Italian occasionally. Still others understand Italian but never speak it (23.1%), while almost 7% understand the language quite well, but never speak it (see Table 6.4).

In summary, one-half of the sample speaks Italian, one-third understands it but does not speak it, and one-tenth does not understand Italian.

Intersecting this question with the age groups of the interviewees, it emerges that among those who do not speak or understand Italian, thirty-year-olds predominate; also, within this group are the higher percentages of those who understand Italian quite well but do not speak it. Among those who understand the language a little but never speak it, there is a higher percentage in the youngest and intermediate ages of the sample. These first two age groups also include the majority of those who understand Italian and occasionally speak it. Finally, among those who understand and usually speak Italian, the youngest members of the sample decidedly prevail (18–23 years).

A subsequent intersection of the same question with the immigration generations of the interviewees shows that it is primarily the second-generation young people who understand and usually speak Italian. This is foreseeable, considering that they are the children of parents who have recently immigrated from Italy. In fact, as noted by Fellin (2014),[6] the use of Italian is very strong and deep-rooted and for those who belong to the newest wave of immigration from Italy, the Italian language assumes great importance as a component of "being Italian."

It also emerges that the Italian language is considered an element of cultural wealth and of great value in the education of their children for the appreciable cognitive benefit derived from bilingualism. This type of attitude toward the Italian language expresses, more generally, a sort of "cultural fidelity" among the new Italian immigrants.

Even among the respondents who understand Italian but speak it only occasionally, those belonging to the second and third generation prevail. The interviewees who do not speak the language but understand it well are predominantly part of the third generation. It is also noted that as arrival on American soil recedes farther from the present day, understanding and use of the Italian language are more likely to have become lost for the generations that follow. In fact, among those who do not speak and do not understand the language, the young people belonging to the fifth and fourth generation definitely predominate. Moreover, within the group that understands Italian a little but never speaks it, there is a majority of fourth and third generation respondents.

Having visited Italy or not represents a variable that considerably affects the knowledge and use of language. Regarding the individuals who understand and usually speak the language, those who speak it occasionally, and those who understand Italian but do not speak it, there is a prevalence of respondents who have visited Italy, while most prevalent in the group that does not know the language are those who have never visited the *bel paese*. The percentage who do not understand any Italian dialects is much higher that the percentage of those who do not understand Italian at all (see Table 6.4). In fact, more than 27% of the interviewees do not understand any dialects and do not speak them, while the percentage of those who understand them in varying degrees is 58.5%. More specifically, a quarter of the respondents understand and speak one or more dialects. Then there are those who—although they understand dialects rather well—never speak them (8.3%) and, furthermore, those who understand them a little but never speak them (25.3%).

In summary, one-fourth of the interviewees speak dialects, a third understand them but do not speak them, and 27% do not understand them.

The comprehension and the use of dialects among the younger age groups of the sample highlight diversified modalities of experience with linguistic dialects. The intersection of this question with the age classes reveals, in fact, how the dialects are spoken—either habitually or occasionally—especially among the youngest and the thirty-year-old groups in the sample. Concerning the group with no comprehension or speaking ability of any dialect, there are especially

Table 6.4 Use and comprehension of Italian/dialects (percentage values)

	ITALIAN LANGUAGE	DIALECTS
Understands it/them and speaks it/them habitually	14.4	4.0
Understands it/them and speaks it/them occasionally	32.9	20.9
Does not speak it/them but understands it/them rather well	6.9	8.3
Understands it/them a little but does not ever speak it/them	23.1	25.3
Does not understand it/them and does not speak it/them	9.0	27.4
N/A	13.7	14.1

those who belong to the youngest part of the sample, while the interviewees belonging to the intermediate group—between twenty-four and twenty-nine—are distinct among those who understand a little but do not speak dialects. Also, it is still the youngest of the sample who prevail among those who do not speak dialects but understand them reasonably well.

Regarding the understanding and use of dialects there is confirmation, as previously observed, with regard to the Italian language, that is, the farther the generations evolve away from the first arrivals on American territory, the more the dialects that accompanied the first arrivals tend to get lost, both in understanding and in use. The fifth, fourth, and third generations predominate within the group that neither speak nor understand dialects, and also among those who understand them a little but do not speak them. The understanding of dialects—whether spoken habitually, occasionally, or only understood but not spoken—characterizes a majority of those subjects who are in the second generation of immigration.

The relation of these answers with those related to having visited Italy is decidedly positive. It emerges that among the interviewees who understand and speak a dialect usually and occasionally and among those who understand it but do not speak it there is a prevalence of young people who have traveled to Italy many times. The subjects who, instead, understand a dialect slightly but do not speak it are prevalent amid those who have visited Italy a few times. There is a majority of young people who have never visited Italy in the group that does not speak and does not understand any dialect. The use and understanding of the Italian language and dialects is an expression of a strong connection with modern-day Italy, a connotation that mainly characterizes the second generation.

Then the young people were asked to indicate the languages used for habitual communication with the significant others in their lives. As shown by Table 6.5, they speak Italian predominantly with their own children. Although the number of respondents with children is very small, it is interesting to note that there are several young people who consider it important to transmit this communication heritage to their descendants. Furthermore, Italian is the language for communicating with one's grandmother for almost one-fifth of the sample; for more than a quarter of the interviewees, dialect is the selected communication method. As revealed in other parts of the research, grandmothers seems to be the most active referents in the transmission of Italian cultural heritage to to the respondents.

More than 17% speak in dialect with the grandfather. The prevalent language with parents and siblings is English; 79.4% of respondents communicate with their mother in English, 75.8% do with their father, and over 71% with their siblings. Very high percentages indicate the choice of English as a language of communication with friends, children, partners, and other close relatives.

Table 6.5 Language/s of communication with:

	ITALIAN DIALECT	ITALIAN	ENGLISH	OTHER LANGUAGES
Mother	11.2	14.1	79.4	2.2
Father	11.9	13.4	75.8	0.4
Brothers/sisters	4.0	10.5	71.1	1.1
Grandmother	22.4	24.2	52.3	1.1
Grandfather	17.3	14.8	45.8	0.7
Boyfriend/girlfriend/spouse/partner	4.7	16.0	75.1	4.7
Other close relatives	11.6	20.6	75.1	2.5
Friends	3.2	15.5	79.1	2.2
One's own children	11.5	38.5	76.9	3.8
Neighbors	1.1	5.8	70.4	1.1
Other people	2.5	8.7	70.8	4.7

Going through the layers of the research and crossing these questions with ones relating to the respondents' generation, significant differences emerge. The second generation tends to speak with the mother, the father, the grandmother, the grandfather, other relatives, friends, neighbors, and with other acquaintances especially in dialect and in Italian. When communicating with siblings, a trilingualism of dialect, Italian, and English prevails, while with the own partner/spouse the language used most is Italian. Finally, to communicate with their children, members of the second generation mainly use both Italian and English.

The use of the languages by the third and subsequent generations is very different from the second; the profiles of these later generations within the context of communication in family of origin, however, are very similar to each other. Specifically, the third generation mainly uses English to communicate with the mother, father, siblings, grandmother, grandfather, other relatives, friends, and neighbors; on the other hand, with their spouses or partners, third generation respondents use mostly dialects and the English language. With their own children, these individuals primarily communicate in dialect.

Among the fourth and subsequent generations, it is observed that young people speak with their mother, father, siblings, grandmother, grandfather, and with other relatives and friends mostly in English, as also occurs in the third generation. However, the use of both Italian and English is prevalent when communicating with one's spouse/partner. Interviewees communicate primarily in English but also in Italian with their own neighbors and acquaintances.

SOME CONSIDERATIONS REGARDING THE USE AND THE FUTURE OF THE ITALIAN LANGUAGE AND ITS DIALECTS

In summary, the research data show that there is a tendency toward reduction in the use of Italian and dialects in the life of respondents during the transition from childhood to adulthood. Even if the use of Italian has been lost through the generations of Italian Americans, along with its position of communicative dominance in the most intimate affective relational contexts—particularly within the family—its use would seem take on a wider dimension, assuming the role of a language appreciated and studied by many Americans who do not come from an Italian background.

The survey shows that, despite the tendency toward contraction in the use of the Italian language and dialects among the interviewees during the phases of their life, the percentages of those who understand Italian—equal to 77%—and Italian dialects—58.5%—are quite high, indicating that the original linguistic component was not lost over time or, if this did happen, that it was subsequently recovered. Moreover, one can infer from the research data how the use of language is especially linked on one hand to a particular type of interaction context, and on the other to the generation within the family with which young people interact.

The prevalence of English dominates the conversation, especially in the context of friendships, while the use of dialects and Italian divides the sphere of family relationships in half. In particular, dialect is a communication channel widely used with the grandparent generation, while the use of "real" Italian projects young people toward the future, considering that some parents use it to address their children. This tendency is confirmed by the section of the questionnaire[7] that refers to the opinion of the interviewees regarding the future prospects of Italian and Italian American culture in the United States, wherein examining the level of agreement with the claim that children should learn to speak Italian discloses that half of the interviewees agree that this choice is "very," or at least "somewhat," important.

The intersection of the data related to questions on the use of the Italian language and dialects among the immigration generations highlights how, despite their use and their understanding having faded through the generations, it seems clear that the second generation plays a strategic role as a *link* between past, present, and future. Closer to modern-day Italy and its language, this generation shows a keen interest in affirming and reevaluating its culture of origin within the United States through multiple expressions and practices. Often trilingual, the second generation uses Italian and dialects as means of communication, both in the context of the family of origin and that of its own progeny; in the latter instance, members tend toward bilingual communication—in Italian and English—with their children.

As previously observed, personal contact with Italy contributes to the maintenance and development of language through more or less frequent visits. In addition to competence in the Italian language, exposure to Italian culture increases the sense of identification and belonging.[8] These data should serve to further strengthen the curriculum in Italy; for university and high school students there are many possibilities. To cite just one fact, in Italy there are eighty-one universities that have about eight hundred agreements with American colleges and universities, aimed at cooperation on high-level research projects, exchanges of teachers and students, and the implementation of joint degree programs (Cineca, International Agreements United States Italy, cited in Dolci, 2013).⁹ In general, although the number of American students who have studied abroad has more than tripled from 1990 to 2010—from 80,000 to 270,604—they represent less than 1% of university enrollment (Dolci, 2013). In 2010, Italy—in second place after Great Britain among the most selected European countries—was preferred as a destination by 27,940 American students, equal to 10.3% of the total (ibid).

The survey on our sample of young Italian Americans highlights how strongly they feel about the Italian language and the transmission of its value to future generations; likewise, the propensities manifested by the "new" second generations toward the Italian language and culture could have a domino effect among the other generations of young Italian Americans, strengthening and renewing interest in their cultural heritage on the other side of the Atlantic.

THE DIMENSIONS OF THE IMAGE OF ITALY AND THE ITALIANS

I have subjected the answers to twenty-five of the questions described above to factorial analysis by isolating nine independent factors that represent the whole of the relationships among the opinions expressed. The questions included in the analysis refer to (1) beliefs and attitudes toward Italy and Italians, (2) feelings regarding Italy, (3) the presence of friends and relatives in Italy, (4) contacts with recently arrived young Italian immigrants in the United States, (5) visits to Italy, (6) staying updated on the news in Italy, and, finally, (7) knowledge of the Italian language.

The first factor, the most important in describing the image of Italy and Italians, refers to the "evaluation of the value system attributed to Italians" and collects homogeneous opinions regarding the acceptance of rules and obligations by Italians; to their virtues linked to honor, respect, and honesty; to their sense of solidarity, kindness, and generosity; and finally to their values linked to courage, morality, and the pursuit of the common good.

The second factor can be called "personal involvement with Italy and Italians," as it collects homogeneous answers to questions about friends in Italy with whom the interviewees are in contact, their use of the Italian language, whether they have visited Italy, how they acquire news of Italy, and the extent of their contacts with the new generation of young Italian immigrants in the New York area.

The third factor expresses the respondents' "distance from Italian society" and includes the answers to the questions about the presence of relatives in Italy and the respondents' feeling of disdain toward Italian society.

The fourth factor focuses on the "affinity between American and Italian society." This factor brings out the perception of differences and similarities between the two societies.

The fifth factor comprises the dimension of the "evaluation of public/private shortcomings in Italians." The collected answers refer to the negative perception of Italy caused by images of corruption and organized crime, as well as the stereotyped shortcomings of Italians including superficiality, cunning, and sloppiness, and the political instability that makes Italy difficult to govern.

The sixth factor can be defined as "feelings of identification and admiration toward Italy." Collected responses here refer these sentiments regarding the nation.

The seventh factor brings out the dimension of "feelings of disillusion and disappointment toward Italy." This factor collects the only item related to expression of this sentiment.

The eighth factor represents the component "recognizing the refinement and taste of the Italian culture." Here responses are collected containing affirmations relative to Italian aesthetic sense and taste, as well as to the importance of knowing the Italian language in order to appreciate the Italian culture.

The ninth and final factor expresses the "evaluation of Italian localism and familism." Homogeneous answers are collected regarding the three items that highlight (1) how the compact and united structure of the Italian family can limit individual expression; (2) the fact that Italians are more attached to their family, their city, and their country than they are to Italy as a nation; and finally, (3) how the quality of life is much better in Italy than in the United States.

Once the nine factors had been identified, the scores were calculated.

The first factor—the most important in the definition of the image of Italians—concerns the "evaluation of the system of values attributed to Italians." Scores range from 0 to 1, with 1 identifying the strongest agreement regarding the notion that the distinctive features of Italians are honor, respect, honesty, solidarity, kindness, generosity, courage, morality, and the search for the common good; along with the idea that they show little regard for accepting rules and obligations. This level of agreement fades as the points value decreases to 0 regarding the possession of the aforementioned values by Italians.

The frequency distribution highlights the fact that over 80% of the respondents are placed, with respect to this factor, on scores between 0.75 and 1, which indicates a high presence of this component in the composition of the image of the Italians. The age variable is a discriminator of the points in the factor (sig. = .013). The score 1 is selected primarily by the youngest of the sample (18–23 years), while the score 0.88 mainly characterizes those who fall in the intermediate age class, namely between twenty-four and twenty-nine years. The points of 0.75 and below were selected especially by the thirty-year-olds. This leads one to reflect on the fact that the youngest people have the most positive vision of Italy and Italians, that is, an association of this image with the values and virtues of Italians. As the age of the interviewees increases, this positive perception fades.

The second factor—called "personal involvement with Italy and the Italians"—presents a distribution of the scores that focuses mainly on the central values and thins out on the extremities. The interpretation of the scores proceeds from 0 to 1, where 0 represents a low degree of involvement and 1 the maximum degree of personal involvement. There is a significant relationship between this factor and the length of time the immigration generations have been in America (sig. = .000). The lowest scores are recorded mainly for the third and fourth-generation respondents, while the highest scores—from 0.57 up—are mainly produced by the second generation. This indicates that it is especially the second generation that has the closest personal contacts with Italy and Italians.

Regarding the factor that expresses the feeling of "distance from Italian society," we observe that few respondents—equal to only 1.7%—attain the score 1 in their responses, indicating that there are few people who feel distant/detached from Italy. The respondents' generation of immigration is a discriminator in the points value of this factor (sig. = .000). In particular, young people belonging to the second generation feel closer to Italy, while the intermediate score mainly refers to the interviewees who belong to the other generations. Age is also a significant discriminator in the points values of this factor (sig. = .028). The youngest members of the sample feel particularly close to Italy, while the intermediate points are predominantly connected to thirty-year-olds.

The fourth factor represents the perception of "differences between Italian and American society." Forty-nine percent of respondents selected the score 1 on this factor, thus expressing the perception of a very marked difference between Italian and American societies. Conversely, fewer than one-third of the respondents are positioned on the score 0, indicating the prevalence of a less marked perception of difference toward Italian society. Twenty percent of the young

Italian Americans interviewed selected the intermediate value, which occupies a position of equidistance from the two extremes. Scores are discriminated by age (sig. = .007). The younger ones in the sample perceive the most difference between American and Italian society.

The fifth factor comprises—as stated—an "evaluation of the public and private shortcomings in Italians." The score 1 expresses a strong agreement with the hypothesis that the image of Italy is characterized by negative connotations due to its association with corruption and organized crime; that superficiality, cunning, and sloppiness represent some of the "vices" of Italians; and that political instability makes governance difficult in Italy. At the opposite extreme, the pole equal to 0 expresses total disagreement with the vision of Italy characterized by these traits. Observing the distribution frequency of the scores, it may be noted that the respondents who agree with this description of Italy and Italians in a very marked way represent 30% of the sample, namely, those who achieve scores between 0.63 and 0.88 (none has reached the score 1). The highest percentages are found on the scores between 0.13 and 0.38, where a total of over 58% of respondents are positioned, expressing a marked disagreement with this negative connotation of Italy. The variable of gender is a significant discriminator in points values (sig. = .031). In fact, the points values between 0.13 and 0.38 are recorded especially by women.

With regard to the scores that express the position of the interviewees on the dimension linked to the "sense of identification and admiration toward Italy," 18.9% of the interviewees scored 0, which expresses a low level of this perception. The rest are positioned on 1, which, conversely, expresses a shared sense of identification with and admiration for Italy.

The next factor, which expresses feeling "disillusionment and disappointment toward Italy," contrasts with the previous factor. The score 1—where 14% of young Italian Americans are placed—expresses this perception, while, on the contrary, those who reach the score 0 do not share in these negative sentiments regarding Italy. The points values are significantly linked to the generation of immigration (sig. = .039). Among the young people who have achieved the score 1, most prevalent are those who are part of the second generation, while on the score 0 are especially those who belong to other generations of immigration.

The factor that identifies the "recognition of Italian cultural refinement and tastes" may be analyzed by examining a score ranging from 1—which expresses the highest degree of agreement with the hypothetical notion that Italians have great aesthetic sense and good taste and also confirms that knowledge of the language is essential to understanding the culture—to 0—which connotes the positions of maximum disagreement with these statements. As is shown by the distribution frequency of the scores, those who record scores of 0.38 and lower comprise just over 13% of the sample. The others—positioned on scores between 0.5 and 1—express with different nuances of agreement how much they share these affirmations about Italy and Italians. Regarding the relation of this score with other variables, there is a significant relationship with the generation of immigration (sig. = .026). Among those who express the highest degree of recognition of these qualities in Italian culture, second and third-generation young people predominate, while the 0.75 and lower scores particularly characterize those of the third and fourth generation.

The score of 1 in the factor "Italian localism and familism" expresses the evocation of marked localism in Italian society, expressed through the entries that indicate the belief that the family structure constrains the possibilities for personal expression of individuals, that Italians are more attached to their family and to their place of origin than to the Italian nation, that the quality of life is much better in Italy than in the United States. The score 0 connotes, however, the maximum deviation of opinions from these positions. More than 36% of the interviewees reached the 0.25 mark and almost 28% ranked on the 0 score, which, as mentioned, expressed disagreement with the parochial viewpoint within Italian society. One-quarter of the interviewees reached the 0.75 points value, which indicates a high level of agreement with this affirmation. In relation to other variables, gender significantly differentiates the assigned points value (sig. = .098). The higher points values are especially a masculine prerogative, while the lower values are found more often among women, which indicates that especially males perceive a parochial mindset in Italy.

7

The Stereotypical Images of Italian Americans

THE STEREOTYPE

In the social sciences, the term *stereotype* defines a "belief articulated through a set of characteristics attributed to a category of persons and formulated according to 'unscientific' criteria" (Boileau, 1981, p. 17). In general, the stereotype is based on partial and fragmentary knowledge and is concentrated on some aspects of the real or imaginary behavior that are characteristic of the group under consideration. They become the basis for the identification of individuals belonging to this group, as well as the group as a whole (Epstein, 1978). They suggest, sometimes implicitly, a double definition: they serve to reinforce the perception that one has of others, but also underlie a definition of oneself.

Closely related to prejudice, the stereotype consists of "the cognitive nucleus, namely the collected elements of information and beliefs about a certain category of objects, reworked in a coherent and potentially stable image, capable of sustaining and reproducing the prejudice against them" (Mazzara, 1997, p. 16). From a terminological point of view, "stereotype" was coined in a typographic environment toward the end of the eighteenth century to indicate the reproduction of printed images by means of fixed forms (ibid.). The term then entered the psychiatric field and referred to pathological behaviors characterized by obsessive repetition of gestures and expressions. The journalist Walter Lippmann introduced the term into the social sciences in 1922 when his book on the training processes of public opinion was published. According to Lippman the cognitive relationship with external reality is mediated through the mental images that everyone forms of it; the press, which was then already connoted as mass communication, would strongly condition this process. He also argued that such mental images very often represent coarse and rigid simplifications—stereotypes—because the human mind is unable to understand and process the great complexity and infinite variety of nuances with which the world presents itself.

As Mazzara maintains, this process of simplifying reality does not take place accidentally, nor by an arbitrary individual choice, but by methods that are culturally established; stereotypes are part of the culture of the group and as such are acquired by individuals and used to effectively understand reality. These stereotypes, moreover, play a defensive role for the individual. Continuing with Lippmann's reflections, the most important effect of the stereotype is directing the research and evaluation of experience data; these are, in fact, altered according to current stereotypes. Stereotypes tend to reproduce without the possible contradictory information being taken into consideration, indeed this information tends to be ignored or neutralized (Mazzara, 1997).

The stereotype can also be defined as the use, or misuse, of categories: usually the stereotype is considered as implying a categorical response. Belonging to a category is sufficient to evoke the opinion that the person possesses all the attributes that characterize that particular category (Boileau, 1987b). The categories can be defined, in turn, as homogeneous sets that can be treated as a whole and which group elementary information. They derive from a process, defined indeed as categorization, which consists of "putting together similar things," based on the idea that the cognitive system needs to reduce and simplify the complexity of the world. Categorizations and classifications offer answers, both individual and social, in response to complexity, to introduce a certain measure of simplicity and order; in short, they constitute the main tool for achieving this simplification (Mazzara, 1996). This reduction of complexity through the categories is continuously applied to the physical and social world and represents a way of knowing, communicating, and relating to events in a natural and normal way. In the social world, categorization leads to seeing others based on criteria that allow them to be grouped, then giving individuals the attributes that define the whole category. Through stereotyping a generalization is carried out, which is always a simplification of reality; the stereotypes express, therefore, a sort of mental shortcut, that is, perceiving an individual as belonging to a particular category; by inference, we are led to attribute to the individual not only the general characteristics of the category but also to have certain expectations toward the person (Zanfrini, 2004).

Ehrlich (1973) emphasizes this statement by arguing that in the course of social interaction, when a social actor is placed within a category, the outcome will be determined more by the traits (image) of the category than by the individual's ones. The process of social categorization leads us to exaggerate elements of similarity within the groups and to emphasize, instead, the differences between the different groups, in particular between the group to which we decide to belong and the one(s) to which we address our negative prejudices (obviously, prejudices and stereotypes are also positive). Thus, our thinking becomes the victim of stereotyping, that is, of the tendency to cognitively represent a particular social group, associating some peculiarities and emotions to it: in this way the stereotype constitutes the cognitive nucleus of prejudice (ibid.).

What has been said so far highlights that much of the stereotype does not derive from direct interaction, but is the product of social learning. In general, the content of the categories to which people are assigned according to their social identity is produced within the culture over a long period of time; it is a type of social information that is transmitted to individuals in the process of socialization and social learning. Social prejudice, like any other element of culture, can be acquired "normally" through the internalization of norms concerning attitudes toward social groups. From here is derived the importance of primary and secondary socialization agents in maintaining, modifying, and transmitting the cultural models of prejudice, the definitions of the different social groups, of the reciprocal relationships and their positions (Boileau, 1987a).

Among the different meanings of the stereotype emerges a more socially connoted one that focuses on the images related to social groups, specifically to the negative ones. As Mazzara writes, "The concept of stereotype makes it possible to grasp all the negative characteristics attributed in certain contexts to certain social groups, almost always minorities who are somehow disadvantaged" (1997, p. 17). To understand the operational processes of the stereotype, there are three elements to consider: the degree of social sharing, the level of generalization, and the greater or lesser rigidity of the same (ibid.).

The first connotation refers to the negative image of the group under consideration and to how much this is shared by another social group and within a given culture, that is, the extent of sharing the image. The result is two interpretations that are based on this constitutive dimension of the stereotype: on one hand, it can be seen as a tendency of the individual who develops his own stereotypes and is influenced by them. On the other, the stereotypes would require a level of social sharing.

The level of generalization refers to the fact that the negative characteristics attributed to the group object of the stereotype are more or less homogeneously distributed in that group. This level of homogeneity would be essential—as evidenced by certain interpretive theories—to identify the perceived target group as, in fact, homogeneous.

The various levels of rigidity within the stereotypes represent the "measure" of their resistance to alteration. High rigidity means that they are difficult to transform because they would be "deeply anchored in culture or personality"; conversely, a less rigid vision of stereotypes leads to their being interpreted as contingent phenomena and, therefore, easily eliminated once the causes that produced them are identified and given the will to do so (Mazzara, 1977, p. 18).

In summary, despite the contentious positions in the debate, characteristics of the stereotype include a disconnect with reality, relative rigidity, and the indiscriminate manner by which the elements of the image are attributed to all the components of the category.

Stereotypical images remain relatively stable over time until they prove useful for adaptive behavioral regulation (Boileau, 1981). To understand the persistence of the stereotype over time we need to examine the institutionalized role relationships within the social system, which represents the most frequent context of interaction between groups, as well as mutual observation between them; in other words, the actors are sensitized to the group characteristics that are relevant in the relationship and thus become part of the group image. The elements that are developed from institutionalized role relationships have a certain social validity and tend to be generalized to extend to other contexts, introducing what Boileau defines as a "sort of socially structured distortion in mutual perceptions" (p. 19). The institutionalized relationships between the groups are the object of widespread and consensual knowledge in the social system and even the images of the groups are shared on the basis of this widespread knowledge. Role relationships constitute the most frequent opportunities for interaction, and in this context group images orient behavior in an adaptive and appropriate way. Institutionalized role relationships usually change over a long period of time, thus remaining relatively constant; in this way, the group images remain stable. Therefore, only a change in institutionalized relations can lead to the change of the image, of the stereotype.

It should also be added that repeated and frequent contacts between different groups often provide information that is inconsistent with the stereotype. As Zanfrini recalls (2004), the history of the countries of emigration is full of examples of strongly stigmatized groups that have gradually managed to free themselves from the heavy burden of prejudices, which they initially sustained. When many members of the group are able to construct social mobility paths and hold roles of prestige and power, there is a potential impact on the negative stereotypes that have shrouded the initial image of the group.

Obviously, people can choose, within certain limits, not to rely on stereotypes. However, a significant role is played by those who play a crucial part in shaping public opinion, especially people working in the media, who should be aware of the consequences that can be associated with stereotyping.

PREJUDICE

If the stereotype reflects the social image of the group, prejudice is linked to its social evaluation and, normally, is based on one or more stereotypes. Over time, the term *prejudice* has undergone a change of significance in its commonly used meaning. The original sense was of judgment based on previous experiences and decisions. Subsequently, it acquired the significance of a priori judgment, formulated prior to examination and without consideration of the facts. Ultimately, the latter meaning was also associated with the emotional connotation of favor or disfavor that accompanies a priori judgment (Boileau, 1987a). The social sciences generally refer to the latter meaning, although there is no agreement on the definition.

The explanation proposed by Mazzara (1997) highlights the negative emotional aspect that impacts the image of the group; it is about "the tendency to consider persons belonging to a particular social group in an unjustifiably unfavorable way" (p. 14). This interpretation also contains the idea that prejudice is not limited to evaluations with respect to the object but can also concretely direct the action toward it.

A notable definition of prejudice is the one proposed by Allport (1954), which describes it as follows: "An antipathy based on a false and inflexible generalization. It can be felt internally or outwardly expressed. It can be directed toward a group in its entirety or toward an individual insofar as he is a member of that group" (p. 9). This judgment is formulated prior to having direct knowledge and—while theoretically it might be positive, negative, or neutral—this psychosocial construct refers solely to a negative judgment.

Allport's explanatory proposal is still considered valid, even if it is limited in some respects. Prejudice is not only a feeling of "antipathy," but more broadly can involve judgments, evaluations, and even emotions and behaviors (Voci & Pagotto, 2010).

Voci and Pagotto (2010) propose the following definition: it is the "outcome of the process that leads to a negative judgment of an individual simply on the basis of her/his belonging to a social group" (p. 5). Prejudice is associated with stereotyping, which—as we have seen—refers to the characteristics and traits generally considered typical of a certain category and behavioral discrimination, that is, a negative behavior implemented on the basis of a stereotype or prejudice (ibid.).

The capacity of this concept—as well as that of the stereotype—derives from the joint action of three factors that act in an integrated way and which, if taken separately, are not able to account for the complexity of the phenomena examined (Voci & Pagotto, 2010). The first is connected to the characteristics and limits of the cognitive system, which has the need to simplify reality and to have expectations toward people and the development of events. The second is in reference to the need for belonging, which drives people to recognize themselves in like-minded groups and foster an aversion—perceived as apparently spontaneous and natural—toward those who do not share the same culture and memberships. The third recalls historical and social reasons that define the positions and functions of every minority group over time and, generally, the comprehensive array of relationships among the groups in a given society, and the state of interethnic and international relations.

Analyzing the causes of prejudice clearly conveys the interrelations between the factors of cognitive nature and motivational nature, which both contribute to the emergence of this phenomenon. The bases of cognitive nature are made up of the elementary processes of perception, processing, and coding of information and are difficult to erase. The motivational bases are, however, largely untouchable. Psychosocial approaches consider motivations as linked to the search for a definite and positive social identity, useful to protect oneself from the uncertainty and fear resulting from the transitory nature of the phenomena. This search leads to discrimination and prejudice when others are perceived as threatening or excessively different from oneself. The basic problem seems to be linked to the exaggerated perception of a psychological distance between self and others, between one's own group and the extraneous groups. Consequently, as Voci and Pagotto (2010) maintain, reduction of prejudices requires the diminution of this perceived distance. The strategies to limit this disparity all share the idea of the usefulness of approaching the other, feeling it to be less different from oneself and, consequently, less threatening.

The various psychological explanations of prejudice emphasize the conscious or unconscious processes of the individual, while sociological and psychosocial interpretations of prejudice derive from the dynamics of collective identity and the relationship among groups. There is another perspective that considers prejudices and stereotypes as a social construction; according to this interpretation, they would be an accumulation of knowledge and collective memory, "a sort of historical archive of the way in which a certain community conceives, describes and explains the relationship between groups, codifying it into a system of shared symbols and practices for interpreting group events" (Voci & Pagotto, 2010, p. 83) The explanation shifts from why to how they are realized, what are the modalities of their production and social reproduction; and it is through this knowledge that we come to identify the real cause of their diffusion (ibid.).

Hence the emphasis that is attached to communication practices—where stereotypes and prejudices take shape—and the context in which this occurs. Communication takes on a strong value, in the sense that it is not only the means through which prejudices and stereotypes spread, but it is their seat and their substance. There are two particularly crucial areas for the production and reproduction of prejudices: mass communication and daily interpersonal communication.

Recalling the distinctive characteristics of stereotypes and prejudices, Mazzara (1997) proposes some operational guidelines to counter them. He opposes the relative rigidity of the stereotypes with the importance of understanding the characteristics of mental processes as well as the dynamics of social communication—extremely useful mechanisms for planning interventions to contrast the self-reproduction process of these stereotypes.

Through the cognitive processes that allow us to relate to the world, individuals express expectations and hypotheses that lead to the visualization of a possible course of events. Very often these expectations are expressed by using social categories with related stereotypes, which should then be verified during the interaction. In reality, what happens is that the information confirming the hypotheses is more evident than what contradicts them, since they are inserted in an already present and active interpretive scheme. Therefore, information that disproves stereotypes is detected with greater difficulty and also more easily forgotten. This is why Mazzara deems it important—in the interventions aimed at modifying the stereotype—to provide an alternative interpretive scheme to the stereotype in advance.

He asserts, ultimately, that the human mind does not preserve stereotypes because of a "deplorable tendency to error"; rather, out of a necessity to maintain patterns and expectations. Thus, sometimes, to potentially obtain the reduction of false and discriminating stereotypes, "it is sufficient to provide timely, valid alternatives that perform the same cognitive and also... protective functions of the social identity" (Mazzara, 1997, p. 103).

Another important phenomenon, known in the literature as the "self-fulfilling prophecy,"[1] is often involved in the reproduction of stereotypes and prejudices. Interaction with others takes place on the basis of one's own expectations, and sometimes these others actually live up to these expectations. In the case of prejudices, we find ourselves faced with value judgments that highlight socially connoted differences in terms of skills, moral qualities, and correspondence to societal models. These expectations can also have an effect on the self-image of those who are the target of stereotypes, creating a consequent drop in self-esteem and the objectives that the concerned parties try to achieve. It is important to recognize the mechanisms that underlie these phenomena in order to design interventions to counter them.

This situation refers to another important study conducted by the Swedish economist Gunnar Myrdal regarding black people in America. The survey conducted on the black population sought to identify the obstacles that obstructed their integration into American society. Among the results achieved, it became clear that the discrimination enacted by the majority, or rather by the "dominant,"[2] which was considered superior to an inferior minority, had repercussions on the image of the world of the same black minority, which ended up believing themselves and behaving as inferior, further aggravating that inferiority in a process of "cumulative circular causation." According to Myrdal, it is truly a vicious cycle where discrimination and prejudice create a self-image of inferiority in the victims who then behave in ways that confirm and reinforce the prejudices that generated them (Myrdal, 1944).

More generally, we can see how prejudices and stereotypes can be internalized even unconsciously, altering the self-image. The identity and its representation would be, therefore, interrelated with prejudices and stereotypes and they would be nothing more than the cultural product of a social development.

Thus, it is necessary to be mindful of the risk that stereotypes and prejudices are reproduced via the self-fulfilling prophecy mechanism and seek to counteract their self-realization. A crucial element to this end is "the awareness of their possible effect on expectations, both from the point of view of those who feed them, and who is the object" (Mazzara, 1997, p. 107). For those who are the subject of stereotypes and prejudices, being aware of their own personal characteristics and thus the probable noncorrespondence of their traits with the stereotype is essential "in order to recognize and contrast the effects of self-fulfillment that should occur. Indeed, it can be said that self-consciousness, both as a person and as a group, is the most powerful factor of protection with respect to the self-realization of prejudices" (p. 108).

Though it is important to recall that the greater or lesser openness of those who act on the basis of stereotypes, as well as the greater or lesser awareness of who is the object, cannot be seen as purely individual variables, linked only to the characteristics of the people involved in the interaction. Instead, they have to do "with structural elements of interaction, that is to say with the context in which the stereotyping takes place, the aims that it proposes, and above all the relationship of power among the subjects involved" (Mazzara, 1997, p. 108).

So far, the cognitive aspects of the problem have been analyzed, that is, the mental mechanisms through which stereotypes reproduce and the potential means to counteract them. However, the social and cultural conditionings that define the framework of the relationships between the interested groups count in the analysis of these themes. Thus, historical, economic, and political factors—as well as ideological reasons—come into play; their analysis allows us to understand how the rooting of prejudices and stereotypes must also be studied in the dynamics of relations among groups.

It is therefore important to implement defense strategies that—even if they are not able to remove the social causes that produced them—can potentially reduce their negative impact on social dynamics. This can also be done by implementing programs engaging language, communication, and deconstruction of stereotypes in order to dispel the meanings and effects produced through stereotypical representations that devalue the social image, as is the case for Italian Americans.

To achieve the effects of a reduction in prejudice, another aspect to consider is also reinforcing the feeling of belonging to the group through the enhancement of the positive traits that constitute the cultural heritage of that group in its entirety. This will lead to visibility and maximum diffusion of the positive experience and, consequently, will have the effect of reduction of prejudice (Mazzara, 1997, p. 108).

ETHNIC PREJUDICE

Although there has been a tendency, shared by many, to attribute a sense of naturalness to the concepts of race and ethnicity, in reality these represent the outcome of complex processes of social construction, deeply linked to the ways that each social group defines their own identity (Zanfrini, 2004). Widely held among social scientists is the belief that boundaries between different ethnic groups are the result of self-definition and hetero-definition practices that aim to differentiate each group from others, based on criteria deemed beneficial (Barth, 1969).

Individuals derive a high level of self-esteem from group memberships; this motivation represents one of the major forces contributing to a perceptive and cognitive distortion in favor of one's own group (in-group) and to the of detriment groups other than one's own (out-group) (Tajfel et al., 1971). In the process of defining the boundaries between "us" and "others," racial and ethnic differences become the object of a social evaluation: a value, usually negative, is attributed to the difference. In almost all cultures, prejudice and discrimination toward other groups contrast the esteem and favor enjoyed by one's own group. As with any ascribed differences, there is also a tendency to associate peculiar characteristics of personality and behavior with ethnic differences, which are accompanied by different forms of access to opportunities and social rewards (stratification on ethnic basis).

Zanfrini (2004) observes that the processes of defining ethnic boundaries serve to "naturalize" the differences between dominant and minority groups, in turn legitimizing asymmetric social relations and transforming diversity into inequality. These differences produce inequalities in the distribution of social roles and, consequently, in access to social rewards. The main mechanisms conditioning the distribution processes of ethnic discrepancies are prejudice and discrimination. Ethnic prejudice is connected, therefore, to the dimension of aggravated diversity that can be read in terms of distance and inferiority "from us" (Colasanti, 1994). This distance takes the form of emphasizing the different origins, the peculiar visibility, the attribution of opportunistic behavior in the economic sphere, the diversity of traditions and customs, along with other traits of inferiority, aggressiveness, filthiness, and noise (Zanfrini, 2004).

In short, the ethnic group has a social value as a category of ascription of social actors, and the distinctive characteristics of its members are the object of social evaluation (Boileau, 1981). The stereotyped elements carry a potentially evaluative component. In the case of ethnic categories, the instrumental utility of the prejudice is closely linked to the selection of the symbols of identity, namely, the characteristics that facilitate categorical ascription. Invoking the ethnic categories and stereotypes that describe them means approaching a dimension of prejudice, which Boileau (1981) defines, more generally, as an "attitude with emotional connotation favoring or disparaging a whole group or category of people" (p. 21).

The social images of the categories of people are developed through interaction experiences that represent a reduced sample of the possible interactions; these images then contribute to giving meaning and structure to subsequent experiences. The evaluation that initially connects to a particular interaction becomes a global evaluation of the category; "It becomes the value attributed to a group of people designated by a symbolic name" (ibid., p. 22).

The emotional connotation of favor or disfavor depends on the evaluative beliefs inherent in the cognitive component (images and evaluations). Therefore, ethnic prejudice is an "attitude whose cognitive, affective, and active components have objectified an ethnic group as an ascribed category designated by a specific name.... And this applies to both the in-group and the out-group" (Boileau, 1981, p. 22).

It should be reiterated that the emotional component of the attitude depends on the evaluative beliefs that are included in the cognitive component and the social diffusion of the prejudice is closely linked to the social diffusion of the image that is the stereotype of the various ethnic groups.

STEREOTYPES ABOUT AND PREJUDICES AGAINST ITALIANS

The theme of the so-called national characteristics ranks among the expressions of ethnic prejudice (Mazzara, 1997). There have been many studies conducted in this context, based upon a common idea: "Various national groups would be characterized by a sufficient homogeneity from the perspective of sensitivity, habits, behavioral dispositions, and evaluation guidelines; this would enable a precise discussion of a specific character typical of that nation, resulting from both a common cultural matrix, and from the widespread diffusion of certain psychological traits" (pp. 34–35).

The descriptions of the single nationalities derived from this vision are examples of stereotyping—or sets of beliefs—often but not always negative, referring to the characteristics of the members of a certain group—in this case the one defined on the basis of the nation—with the capacity to orient expectations and the evaluative orientations toward this group. Social scientists and even writers and philosophers have addressed these national characteristics, as they have become the property of conventional wisdom, which has developed simplified and rough versions of the characteristics. Mazzara (1997) thus summarizes the contents of these stereotypes connected to the Italians: "Fanciful and amiable, oriented more toward a specific community (above all to the family) than to the social collective, inconstant and superficial, spontaneous and sincere, more concerned with appearances than with substance" (p. 35).

In reality, the contents of national stereotypes are not entirely arbitrary, nor artfully invented by adversaries and foreigners. They express tendencies that are to some extent real and the result of complex historical and cultural sedimentation (ibid.). The history of the negative typing of Italians goes back to the Middle Ages, when accusations of avarice, irreligiousness, and dishonesty spread throughout Europe, initially leveled against Florentine and Lombard bankers and merchants (Teti, 2013). With the advent of Humanism and the Renaissance, the elites within different areas of the peninsula assumed a privileged position, becoming the object of positive consideration linked to their being active, dynamic, and innovative. When Italy went through an economic and cultural decline at the end of the seventeenth and the beginning of the eighteenth century, within the polemic of Protestant countries against Catholic superstition, the negative images of Italians were based on the apathetic, indolent, and effeminate character typical of populations living in a Southern climate. The distinction between Northern (continental European nations) and Southern (including all the Italian regions and provinces) was mainly based on climatic factors, which explained the idle and indolent temperament of Italians and the economic, moral, and civil backwardness of many areas of the peninsula. Historical, geographic, and climatic differences began to morph into differences of an ethnic nature. The warm climate was making the Southerners (the Italians) vicious, lazy, superstitious, and apathetic. The Italian elites, faced with these negative judgments, sought to refute and attenuate the external stereotypes, but they sometimes participated in their elaboration, becoming creators of self-stereotypes with the intention of pushing the populations to abandon the old vices (Teti, 2013).

Both the Enlightenment thinkers, first, and, later, the patriots of the Risorgimento, on the one side refused the negative external representations and on the other reproduced and amplified them to criticize the dominant classes and their apathetic way of governing, believing that reviving Italy and stemming its decline was only possible through national unification. Subsequently, the bankers and merchants of central and northern Italy overturned the stereotypes which the continental Europeans had assigned to the Southern people. The South was no longer the whole of Italy, but was restricted to the Kingdom of the Two Sicilies. Among the stereotypical traits that characterized the Italians, idleness began to emerge as an ethnic trait of Southern populations, and the anti-Italian clichés were transformed into the ethnicization of the Southern people, seen only for their defects and vices. The South is a place of idleness and its inhabitants are considered unsuitable for the modern world: "The ethnicization of idleness becomes the sign of otherness within Italy and provides an alibi for decisions regarding internal colonialism" (Teti, 2013, p. 19). Recalling Teti's words, "Idleness is not a cause of backwardness and misery, but a consequence of hardship and suffering, of the destruction of economies and production models that followed national unification... the indolence and laziness assigned to the southerners were the fruits of the economic and political choices of the new state" (pp. 20–21). Nevertheless, the stereotype is affirmed: the stereotype of the idle Southerner becomes a curse that comes true. "The South is seen in a sort of ahistorical light; it is mythologized and relegated to a metaphysical framework that prevents the perception of contradictions, details, and nuances" (p. 24). The stereotype of Mediterranean idleness imposes itself with positive and oppositional connotations, and the slow rhythms of the South start to be reimagined with an antimodern function.

The racialization of the South becomes marked toward the end of the nineteenth century when—as T. A. Guglielmo (2003) points out—the Northern bourgeoisie tried to unify the different regions of the peninsula and the islands to form a single nation: "They attempted to tame the 'barbarian' south through a process of military occupation and mass arrests of those who opposed the new taxes, the self-employment of land ownership, and other impoverishment policies carried out by the government" (p. 9). Northern political leaders confronted Southern resistance movements against the state not only with martial law, but also with the stigmatization of peasants "as criminal members of a racially inferior people who preferred religious superstitions to Italian civilization" (Gabaccia, 2000, p. 52, cited in Guglielmo, 2003).

In the second half of the nineteenth century, the *positivist school* schematized the Southern stereotype in a metahistorical category, utilizing a naturalistic, anthropological foundation (Galasso, 1982). The conviction spread that the

Southerners were cursed and unable to change and progress; the evocation of a "cursed race" served to explain the moral, economic, and civil inferiority of Southern Italy (Teti, 2013). The positivist theory led to the blaming and criminalizing of populations; it pushed to create mistrust, dependence on external perceptions and judgment. This theory led to a sense of guilt, self-denigration, susceptibility, and fatalism. As Teti noted, "The theory of the curse and immutability of race have provided comfortable and simple explanations for every dramatic and painful event that occurs in the South" (p. 50).

Positivist anthropologists supported the racial disparity between the Southern Mediterranean peoples with dark skin and the light-skinned Northern Aryans, on the basis that the former possessed "inferior African blood" that showed they possessed "a moral and social structure that recalled the epoch of primitives and quasi-barbarians, a completely inferior civilization" that had been transmitted to the people of the South, inheritors of this racial inferiority (Guglielmo, 2003).

Alongside these negative stereotypes, a "mythology of brigandage" developed, which was substantiated by the Lombrosian vision that linked Calabrian "barbaric criminality" to racial components. The state of primitiveness and savagery was explained in ethnic-racial terms and the blood crime, typical of the inferior civilization present in the South, was used by Lombroso to explain delinquency through an external, somatic alteration. However, Teti (2013) points out there is no geographical, historical, social, or cultural continuity between brigandage and 'ndrangheta, which originated in the province of Reggio Calabria, an area where the phenomenon of banditry had been negligible, even compared to other parts of Calabria. The Mafia and the Camorra were traced back to archaic, barbaric crime by scholars of the late nineteenth century. The criminality of the South recalled the primitive populations and the Sicilian Mafia was seen as a survival of times now gone: "In reality Mafia, Camorra, 'Ndrangheta, far from being archaic survivors, were an expression of a desired, sought, and imposed modernity. The Mafias represent the exit from feudalism, but they do not establish an entry into modernity. A mixture of archaic and newly invented elements characterizes this increasingly disturbing and elusive phenomenon" (p. 75).

Alongside the negative depictions of the people of the South, the image of the good Southerners is shown through the narrations and the iconographies beginning from even the seventeenth century. Thus, for example, a Neapolitan is portrayed as a partier—restless, rash, and volcanic—which is expressed through the way he/she speaks and gesticulates and through the humorous, sonorous, and nuanced Neapolitan dialect. Often, these characteristics become a colorful, picturesque, fanciful stereotype, often assumed by the Neapolitans themselves who often tend to exaggerate their behaviors to show and represent themselves as others want. The frenzy and joy of the southerners seem the other side of their melancholy and sadness. But perhaps the two faces and the two "masks" coexist as the result of the same historical and anthropological affair.... [T]he Southerner seems to be condemned on one hand by his gloominess and on the other by his burlesque and fun-loving temperament. The feeling is that these external images, which do sometimes support reality, were accepted uncritically for the narration and representation of Neapolitan-ness, Sicilian-ness, Calabrian-ness, or Southernness; thus as opposed to grappling with a complex, controversial, and mobile identity, these images have satisfied the observer's need for the picturesque and exotic and have fostered notions of self-satisfaction and self-exaltation regarding the local people. (Teti, 2013, p. 97)

PREJUDICES, STEREOTYPES, AND REPRESENTATIONS OF ITALIAN AMERICANS

Before the great mass immigration, the American collective image associated Italy with its high culture in the arts, literature, and music; and the Italians, who demonstrated great assimilation skills at the time, reflected this noble and positive image of Italy. This judgment regarding the Italians shifted radically at the end of the century, when Southern immigration superseded that from the North. As bearers of a weak national identity, these immigrants found themselves doubly discriminated against. In the homeland, the anti-emigrationism that dominated a large part of the Italian ruling class and the creeping anti-Southern prejudice fed on the racial one that had developed within Italian positivism.

Based on this paradigm, Northerners were considered white and the dark-skinned Southerners were associated with the Africans through an intermingling of bloodlines. This prejudice was acknowledged by the American immigration offices that issued different visas depending on this status.

> The southerners were incorporated ex officio... into the Mediterranean and southern European immigration stocks who received *a priori* their worst suspicions regarding (scarce) industriousness and (innate) brazenness even before their actual behavior and certain life practices in "Little Italy" and elsewhere intervened; offering apparent yet cyclical confirmation in the eyes

of both the American authorities and public opinion, as well as a considerable part of their own countrymen... abroad, how these individuals were perhaps even more active in Italy in the journalistic and academic arenas. (Franzina, 2007, p. 28)

The Italians of the North and those of the South differed profoundly from each other and, as Niceforo and Sergi argued, this difference was evident in language, physicality, character, and geographical distribution (Guglielmo, 2003). The former were "calm, prudent, patient, practical, as well as capable of great progress in political and modern civilization associations; the latter were excitable, impulsive, impracticable and lacked adaptability to a highly organized society" (Jacobson, 1998, p. 56).

The interweaving of the racial issue with the ethnic-cultural one boldly marked the history of Italian emigration in the United States (Muscio, 2007a). Anti-emigrationism was strengthened through a widespread anti-Americanism around the nineteen eighties—not only in Italy, but in many areas of European departure—which was expressed through "a diffuse and almost generalized rejection of the bourgeois public opinion towards America as a destination for peasant and proletarian migrations" (Franzina, 2007, p. 23). This anti-emigrationism resulted in the demonization and condemnation of peasants and laborers, blamed for desertion from working the fields and accused of simplicity and gullibility (ibid.).

On the other side of the Atlantic, a climate of xenophobia arose, following the wave of immigration from Southern and Eastern Europe, accompanied by the fear of the foreigner, which led, in the case of Italians, to episodes of lynching—in New Orleans and elsewhere—and in the emblematic death sentence of Sacco and Vanzetti.[3] Muscio (2007a) thus describes the situation of the Southern emigrant in North America: "The condition of the southern emigrant in North America, and consequently his/her sense of identity, are made difficult by an intersection of negations and exclusions: disliked by the landowners in Italy who lose a superabundant (therefore cheap) labor force, and despised in the land of arrival, where dark skin and different customs alarm the WASP community. Questions of race... and virulent prejudices attack a weakly identified community" (p. 10).

The result of this "intersectional cultural veto" was a "resentful non-assimilation" that encroached upon a community that closed in on itself in the preservation of dialect, of food and religious traditions, of the centrality of the family. This lack of assimilation kept the culture inside the home: "Like the threatened faiths that are strengthened in the catacombs, every family has a secret recipe, a collective legend, a myth of origins" (ibid.).

Anti-European-immigrant prejudice as part of the American opinion focused mainly on two ethnic groups—Jews and Italians—because of their associated stereotypes (Alba, 1985). Richards (2004) noted that the structural injustice that supported political racism was enabled by two cultural processes: on the one hand, "the imposition of dehumanizing stereotypes as a measure of people and as an issue worth mentioning" and, on the other, "the reduction by racism of its victims to a private dimension. The withdrawal of Italian Americans from the public debate responded to both of these processes... the stereotypical images of the Mafia were the parameter of the public discussion on the life of Italian Americans" (p. 264).

The prejudice affecting the Southern immigrants was noted by the media (press, publishing, cinema) and thus expanded and emphasized. While on one hand this process is attributed to American xenophobia toward the immigration wave, on the other—Muscio notes—in Italy there have never been institutions or intellectuals ready to come to its defense.

The diversity and inferiority of the Italians compared to the Anglo-Saxons was sustained—as already mentioned—by anthropologists (Sergi, Pigorini), criminologists (Lombroso, Ferri), and sociologists (Niceforo) of the positivist persuasion who came to affirm that the Southerners were part of a less-developed Mediterranean lineage because of strong African influences (Luconi, 2007, 2010). The assumed African ancestry of the Southerners questioned the belonging of the Italians to the white race, particularly in the Southern states, where they were often equated to African Americans. In addition to this image, the most frequent and recurring stereotype toward the Italians was their alleged propensity to crime and violence, endorsed by popular culture, which helped to disseminate and enhance these representations (ibid.). In contrast to the perceived self-control and Anglo-Saxon balance, behavioral propensities such as impulsiveness, passion, lack of discipline, inclination to violence, and the inability to conceive collective interests outside the restricted sphere of the family were attributed to Italian immigrants.[4]

The association of Southern Italians with African ancestry had repercussions regarding the acceptance—at least until 1920—of the Southerners compared to Northerners, the former considered largely incompatible with American society; consequently, their presence was not desirable because it might have introduced disruptive elements in the long run and irreversibly altered the fundamental characteristics of society. Subsequently, the negative judgment was extended to all inhabitants of the peninsula. The disparaging term that connoted an individual halfway between the Caucasian and African race was *Dago*, and this designation applied to both Italians and Hispanics (Gardaphé, 1996a).

As Luconi (2007) recalls, besides their physical aspects, the religious faith of the Italian immigrants worked against them: "Predominantly Catholic, the Italians were considered potential agents for the insinuation of papism into otherwise protestant territory" (p. 37).

Moreover, prejudice further isolated the Italians even within the worker's movement. Italian immigrants, mostly agricultural laborers lacking prior experience in factories, could only offer handiwork as unskilled and at a reduced wage in the industrial context, making them part of the underclass. Although there was a strong demand for workers of this kind due to the transformation of the United States production system, the presence of Italians was seen as the cause of this change in the productive structure rather than its effect. As a result of this, the newcomers became the scapegoat of the growing tensions in the labor market and the charge of compressing wages was leveled against them, for accepting lower pay than their specialized comrades and maintaining anti-union behavior (a willingness to act as scabs) during strikes.

While Italians were accused of lacking class consciousness, they were also considered dangerous subversives and importers of European radical ideologies, such as anarchism and socialism, prepared to use to violence to overthrow bourgeois institutions (Luconi, 2010). Specifically, Alba (1985) points out that the stereotypes associated with Italians were those linked to a turbulent group of lower-class extraction.

Bryson (2014), in *L'estate in cui accadde tutto*, describes how Italians arriving in the America in the early twentieth century were excluded from occupational and educational opportunities as well as from certain neighborhoods:

> In some cases, Italians who moved to the American deep south were forced to attend schools for black children. At the beginning it was not entirely clear if they were allowed to use the water fountains and restrooms for whites. Other immigrant groups... obviously encountered similar prejudices.... Italians, however, were generally treated as a sort of special case, considered more fickle, unreliable, and troublesome than any other ethnic group. Wherever conflict arose, Italians seemed to be at the root of the problem. The

widespread perception was that if Italians were not fascists or Bolsheviks, they were anarchists or communists, and if they were not any of those, they were still involved in organized crime.[5] (Bryson, 2014, p. 308)

In those years, moreover, the new "science" of eugenics, which, to use Bryson's words again, "could be defined in simple terms as the breeding, on scientific bases, of higher beings" (2014, p. 391), infiltrated academic and societal discourse. In the United States, it took an unpleasant turn and led to restrictive rules on the granting of housing, forced deportations, the compulsory sterilization of many people, and the suspension of civil liberties. One result was the radical reduction of immigration in general and the almost total abolition of migratory flows from some parts of the world. In 1916, Madison Grant published *The Passing of the Great Race*, considered "the bible of the advocates of negative eugenics—as it was called in the United States" (ibid.). Grant believed the only healthy group of humans was constituted by what he called "the Nordic race," within which all Europeans with the exception of the Irish fell. As one proceeded south within Europe, there was a gradual degeneration. Faced with the historical protest that pointed out that "depraved" peoples had succeeded in producing the Roman Empire, the Renaissance, and other wonders of the past, he maintained that the ruling classes were Nordic Achaean—northern Europeans who had migrated south. Every one of the great Renaissance artists was also, according to Grant, of Nordic origin. Bryson observes that this author argues that "all the others, the true Italians, were dull, stunted, and shady—genetically condemned to remain so forever."

In the decades between the two world wars, stereotypes and prejudices affecting Italian Americans contributed to a sort of awareness of shared national origin among immigrants and their children (Luconi, 2007). During the twenties and thirties, however, the national identity developed among Italian Americans was accompanied by new prejudices related to their origin. During World War II, Italians who emigrated to America were victims of the "widespread suspicion of constituting a potential Fifth Column under Mussolini's orders," and Italian citizens who were not naturalized were considered enemy aliens (p. 41). These were also the years in which the process of inclusion of the second generation of Italian Americans, born and raised in the United States in the period between the two world wars, may be said to have started.

Gardaphé (2004) notes that "for too long, the American media was all too ready to give support to limit Italian assimilation attempts as white Americans."

He points out that "the majority of Italian Americans are law-abiding citizens, but this is not shown through television, radio, narrative, and non-fiction. Italian Americans have been brutally typecast through constant repetition of negative representations. These images have become fundamental elements of the American cultural image which has petrified the stereotype. This reproduction of endless negative stereotypes has so impoverished the minds such that everything Italian is immediately associated with gangsters and ignorance" (Gardaphé, 2004, pp. 125–26). To become Americans, Italians had to do everything possible to differentiate themselves from the images of gangsters and buffoons that had dominated the public representation of their culture.

After the first and second generations had achieved success, they were able to consolidate their energies for the defense of Italians against defamatory attacks. Currently, the image of Italian Americans is associated with a series of qualities linked to design, fashion, cinematography, and the cuisine of their homeland. This connotation has contributed both to rooting immigrants' descendants in the middle class, and also to the rise of Italian personalities in the fields of entrepreneurship, politics, and justice.

Although prominent figures (such as Chrysler president Lee Iacocca, U.S. Supreme Court Justice Antonio Scalia, and four mayors of New York: Fiorello La Guardia, Vincent Impellitteri, Rudolph Giuliani, and Bill De Blasio) have offered positive images of the generations following the period of mass immigration, the stereotypes of the past have not been completely erased, despite improvements in the reputation of Italian Americans in the American collective imagination, as a consequence of an increasingly positive regard for Italy. Except for small groups, "Italian Americans no longer seem willing to mobilize on... campaigns as they did in the past when, for example, the Italian American Civil Rights League managed to bring fifty thousand people to Columbus Circle in New York on June 29, 1970 to protest against the systematic use of terms such as 'Mafia' and 'Cosa Nostra' in reference to Italian Americans" (Luconi, 2007, p. 43). "The full integration achieved into US society and the stable insertion in the middle and upper classes have made Italian Americans immune from the negative consequences of prejudices and stereotypes about their individual and collective life" (p. 44).

Despite the fact that major discrimination toward Italian Americans is a thing of the past, it has not entirely disappeared today (Gardaphé, 2004, p. 129). In fact, Italian Americans are still tormented by a veiled manipulation of their image within American culture (Gardaphé, 2010). Young people are associated with different stereotypes and images, which are attributed to them by society and produce a distorted vision that—consciously or unconsciously—influences their identity: "They have to face the reality that the dominant culture's proposed representation of Italians casts them as semi-serious characters, caricatures that include the most distorted aspects of their culture.... If young people get the idea that being Italian means what the media claims... then they will avoid it if embarrasses them, or they will adopt it if it focuses on them" (Gardaphé, 2004, p. 129). This distorted image associated with Italians is "reassuring" for the dominant culture (Gardaphé, 2010).

RACIAL DISCRIMINATION AGAINST ITALIANS IN AMERICA AND THE PRIVILEGES OF BEING WHITE

Italians have been through contradictory and complex experiences in the United States regarding race. They have borne harsh racial discrimination as well as the recognition of many privileges linked to being white (Guglielmo, 2003). Many authors argue that upon their arrival in the United States, Italians were placed among the whites in the most critical of ways, yet also had to endure racial prejudice (ibid.). Their sense of identity as whites took more time to form. They were categorized from a racial point of view while simultaneously developing an awareness of the "color line,"[6] and in many cases they acted on the basis of this consciousness (ibid.). The historian Jacobson (1998) wrote that "the Italians did not seem white for some social observers, nor did they act as whites" (p. 57).

Racial discrimination and prejudice toward Southern Italians, Latinos, and the Mediterranean in general were violent, powerful, and pervasive in conjunction with the beginning of mass immigration from Italy during the late nineteenth and continued during the twentieth century (Guglielmo, 2003). These anti-Italian feelings and behaviors called their "whiteness" into question in various circumstances.

Thomas A. Guglielmo (2003) introduces a distinction between race and color as two different metrics used between the mid-nineteenth and twentieth centuries to categorize human beings based on presumed innate mental, physical, moral, emotional, and cultural characteristics. He specifies that color is a social category and not a physical description: for example, "white Italians" may be darker-skinned than many "black Americans" (p. 32). Race, on the other hand, can mean many things; large, medium-sized, and small groups can be part of it, as well as Italians of the North and South. The race/color distinction during this period was not absolute and changed over time, even though for some people and institutions the difference was very clear. In the case of Italians—Guglielmo claims—they suffered from their alleged racial undesirability as Italians, Southerners, and so on, but they nevertheless benefited in countless ways from their privileged status as whites.

The double system of stratification linked to race and the color line meant that the Italians never occupied the lowest social positions in America. This happened because, while the racial hierarchy denigrated and exploited them, in the order linked to color they were greatly privileged. This different positioning in the two hierarchies involved the fact that, although strongly discriminated against and subjected to racial prejudice in the first years of arrival, Italians were still accepted as whites and enjoyed many benefits linked to this status (Guglielmo, 2003). Realistically, the most contested status associated with color within Italian American history was connected specifically to the Southerners. As Thomas Guglielmo observes, the Italians found themselves in a precarious position with respect to their status tied to color, even though the controversial position regarding this aspect "never led to any substantial and systematic positioning of Italians as non-whites" (2003, p. 36).

Moreover, the Italians' whiteness was more visible in some communities in the country's interior. Guglielmo notes also that "in the workplace, Italians met with discrimination both from the unions and from the employers. However, they could always benefit from more opportunities and work options than 'colored races'" (p. 37) and "enjoyed numerous advantages over non-whites in housing, jobs, schools, politics, and practically any other significant area of life" (p. 43).

Despite this favorable position with respect to other ethnic groups, a distinct and pervasive color line existed separating Italians from other "whites" and, because of alleged inadequacies due to race, they were definitely placed among the lowest in this hierarchy.

In the years between the two wars and those following the postwar period, "whiteness" continued to profoundly influence the life of Italian Americans and this characterization was conferred in a more marked way by the federal government, as compared to other institutions.

According to Gardaphé (2010), the process of identifying as white for Italian Americans has led them to two consequences: invisibility and hiding the history of being a "colored" people. The fact that they have not always been white is inescapable: "Despite sharing experiences with other minorities, many of them have adopted the attitudes and positions of the dominant culture of racism, a culture that maintains control through division based on difference and unites through the illusion of resemblance. The extinction of their culture is the price they have paid for becoming white. The quasi-disappearance of Italian American culture allowed them to remain invisible" (p. 1).

Gardaphé later wonders about the reason that led many of those who were victims of racism to adopt its ideals. He notes that in reading Italian American history and literature, beyond the different shades of skin color, it emerges that Italian Americans have shared a lot with other minority cultures, commonalities that have been hidden through selective representations of American history and, in this way, did not lead to them becoming aware of it. For Italian Americans—he observes—"making it" was accompanied by a high price: "It cost them the language of their ancestors, the principle means through which their history and legacy passed through the generations. They had to barter or conceal any custom that portrayed them as picturesque, yet labeled as strangers (alien) in an effort to prove their equality to those above them on the scale of success. In this way, the Italian Americans became white, but a different genre of white from the whiteness of the dominant Anglo-Saxon culture. The Italian Americans became whites 'on a leash.' And as long as they behave well (act like whites), accept the images of themselves presented by the media (they do not protest against defamation), and as long as they stay within the social and cultural boundaries (they do not identify with other minorities), they will be allowed to remain white" (p. 4).

The interpretation provided by Orsi (1992, cited in Gardaphé, 2010), examining the relationship between African Americans and Italian Americans, is linked to a position of "in-betweenness" that characterizes immigrants. Within this position the immigrants seek "to decide the boundary between them and the 'dark skinned other.' This entailed an intimate battle, finding a context in which to place oneself when confronted with the initial uncertainty regarding which side of the racial dichotomy dark-skinned immigrants could fit in, and against the fact that history and geography had inscribed this ambiguity in the urban landscape" (Orsi, 1992, p. 316). According to Gardaphé, Orsi concludes that "Italian immigrants became Italian Americans as soon as they learned how to become white" (p. 6).

Richards (2004) argues that Italian American identity was formed in circumstances of injustice due to American racism, and Italian Americans were placed among the victims of this ideology, considering them non-visibly black. He highlights the capacity for resistance and the deep-rooted force of American racism, which has targeted groups of immigrants considered to be not visibly black, that is, "people worthy of the same disdain and of the same violence that the African American community was subjected to, despite the fact that they were not colored (i.e., visibly black), because they, like American blacks, did not have an English origin" (Richards, 2004, p. 11). At the same time, this form of racism has stifled or tried to suppress those multicultural traditions that could have challenged it.

Racism was present in America long before the great immigration from Southern and Eastern Europe between 1880 and 1920; and cultural racism had significantly shaped the identity of Americans of Irish descent. Richards argues that racial affiliation in America is culturally determined by the so-called one drop is enough rule, according to which being even remotely of African American descent is sufficient to be considered black, including those who effectively bear absolutely no belonging to the black community. He notes that

> those who are defined as black in this way could easily pass for white. Most of them, including some historically important leaders of the African American community, chose not to be white. Choosing to be considered white would have removed them from personal relationships of great intensity, with the family and with the community that nurture self-respect and personal integrity. The price of escaping racial prejudice would in fact be an unreasonable, unacceptable sacrifice of the basic resources constituted by one's personal and ethical identity. (Richards, 2004, p. 171)

Richards's thesis is that "American racism would not have had its characteristic strength and political power, both in the popular perception of American culture and in the corruption of constitutional ideals of universal human rights, if immigrants—often viewed as belonging to a lower race—were not led to accept and support a good part of its logic" (2004, p. 171). Later on, he argues that American racism could not have established such deep and unbroken political value if it had not extended its strength, not only to all Americans, but also to new immigrants, many of whom had been targeted by it themselves. Such an unjust logic has come to deeply distort and stifle the American multicultural identity by putting it at the service of this injustice; the Italian American experience is a clear example of this iniquity (ibid.).

Topp (2003), expressing his disagreement with the position of Richards, argues that the concept of "blackness," visible or not, is not an appropriate metaphor for the Italian American experience. According to Topp, during the peak years of their migration to the United States, Italian immigrants occupied a much more complex position in the national racial hierarchy. Historically, the racialization of Italian immigrants in the United States has been a complex process in which the immigrants themselves have taken part, building their sense of place in the racial hierarchy insofar as they have been able to do so.

Gabaccia's (2003) interpretation of how the concept of race has historically developed connects to the ideas of social Darwinism in its attempt—common in the British Empire—to define nations as groups of consenting citizens. Before Darwin, nationalists on both sides of the Atlantic used human differences rooted in biological lineage to define new nations. Both Italy and the United States recognized themselves as civilized and also acknowledged the barbarians within their borders. "In the Americas," Gabaccia argues, "those focused on statecraft were particularly conscious of color as a marker of descent, excluding Africans and natives from citizenship. But they also differentiated between a nation of citizens and the majority of the American people, represented by a great variety of descendants and cultures" (p. 51).

The 1859 publication of Darwin's *Origin of Species* sparked international debate among the "scientific racists," usually called in the English-speaking world "Social Darwinists," and elsewhere "positivists." Both linked a wide variety of physical traits, which they considered measurable and presumably inherited, to the human history of cultural, linguistic, and religious groups, reinforcing the equation between race and nation. "But while social Darwinists saw racial competition and domination based on the most suitable races as the engine of cultural evolution, the positivists often referred to the Lamarckian notions of racial evolution through the characteristics acquired via education, social relations and biological amalgamation... scientific racism significantly altered national self-understanding towards the end of the nineteenth century" (Gabaccia, 2003, p. 51).

In the United States, the simultaneous end of the Civil War and the spread of Darwinist ideas on human evolution created a new, explosive tension between a nation of consenting citizens and a pluralist American population.

> Following the Civil War, the United States abolished slavery and opened citizenship to former slaves and, more gradually, to Native Americans. At the same time, social Darwinism encouraged white Americans (who often called themselves "old stock") to embrace descendancy from their British ancestors. The Anglo-Saxonists argued emphatically that the same consensual citizenship had originated in the forests or blood of Northern and Aryan

Europe, raising new questions about which American people could join the nation.... From 1880 until 1965, local, state, and even federal laws based on the racial hypotheses of social Darwinism, restricted access to citizenship and full enjoyment of its rights to former slaves, Native Americans, and new immigrants arriving from Asia, Mexico, and Europe.... Beginning in 1899, the United States categorized newcomers, even Europeans, as components of 36 races, including both Northern and Southern Italians. (Gabaccia, 2003, p. 55)

In 1911, the *Dictionary of Races or Peoples* was published, which introduced a new term to define cultural differences between races—elsewhere considered as national—by calling them "ethnical." Gabaccia thus maintains that "the use of the term 'ethnic' in the United States emerges as part of the racial discourse linked to social Darwinism and was used for Italians in a context that justified limiting of their right to enter the country" (2003, p. 57). Gabaccia contends, however, it was not their color—in the case of the dark-skinned Jews and Italians—that created uncertainty about considering them citizens of the nation, but social Darwinism. Race was not intended as a difference in color, but rather as a product of heredity, descent, and biological amalgamation, just as the positivists perceived it. Therefore, ethnic identities in the United States represent the legacy of racial exclusion from a nation as the Americans themselves have defined it, and not "whiteness."

Ethnic identities—including the "hyphenated" ones of the Italian Americans—originated in the state policies that reinforced their exclusion. Beginning in 1964, the United States abandoned scientific racism as a state policy; this occurred only when "Jim Crow Laws"[7] and racially discriminatory immigration policies were rejected (Gabaccia, 2003, p. 57).

THE INTERVIEWED YOUNG PEOPLE'S PORTRAYAL OF STEREOTYPES AND PREJUDICES REGARDING ITALIAN AMERICANS

As noted by Viscusi (2015a), the history of Italian American stereotypes is closely linked to that of Italy. It is a story of a long subjection to other European powers, added to the conditions of life in the United States; this contributed to the subordinate condition of life for Italian Americans, "a colony inside a colony" (p. 118).

Moving from theoretical reflections to research results, the question that introduced the section dedicated to the stereotypes and prejudices surrounding the image of Italian Americans inquired whether the interviewees had come into contact with any of these. Eighty-three percent responded in the affirmative and only ten interviewees said they had not. Subsequently, the interviewees were asked if they believed that such stereotypes provided a reflection of reality. Affirmative responses would be asked to indicate which stereotypes were considered accurate.

Almost half of the interviewees maintained that stereotypes of Italian Americans were true. Such affirmation may refer to either positive or negative stereotypes, but the insinuated mechanism is that of the internalization of negative stereotypes. And, as noted by Riotto Sirey and colleagues (1985), unconscious identification with negative stereotypes leads to feelings of shame and low self-esteem.

Moving to an analysis of the answers to the open question asking the interviewees to indicate which stereotypes they thought were true, we can see that they can be traced to two major interpretative sides, one of which highlights microsocial features and the other includes macrosocial aspects. In the first ambit we can find (1) personality characteristics and (2) physical traits, and external aspects, while the other interpretative trend includes facets related to (3) cultural factors. Both sides influence each other, establishing mechanisms of self-identification and emphasizing the stereotype; it arises externally, in cultural contexts, but is often chosen and internalized at the individual level as a source of identification.

Let's look more closely at the most recurrent indicated stereotypes, classifying them according to the two areas cited. First, *personality traits* mentioned constitute a long list:

loudness
use gestures
using their hands when they speak
everyone gossip
not too bright
being cheap
procrastination
hot-headed
strict
uncouth

aggressive
warm
uncultured
ignorant
sexist
superficiality of youth
boisterous
closed minded
dumb
tough
free with money
tight with money
somewhat closed minded to other groups
we are excitable
always yelling
strong willed
chauvinistic
loving
effusive
welcoming
short tempered
vain
jealous
mannerism
bossy
show-offy
shallow
cunning
over the top
racist
cheaters/players
materialistic
superficial
everyone has a nickname, "tuttie," "gappy," "vince," and "pip," but no one knows their real names
we do all have at least one "cousin Vinnie"
some of the boys are conceited womanizers

Someone observed: "*lack of intellectualism. Even if Italian Americans are professionals, some are very provincial in their thinking.*"

Through this testimony it is possible to comprehend one of the given interpretations regarding the recurring characteristic of "loudness" often associated with Italian Americans: "*I think both Italians and Italian Americans are direct, overt, and open to the point of seeming loud or pushy to others.*"

The second listing itemizes *physical traits* and characteristics connected to *exterior appearance*:

some physical characteristics
sometimes people do have large noses
they like to dress well
the clothes we wear
being very interested in their appearance
too tanned
too into looks
many Italian Americans care much about their appearance
greasy or oily hair

For some, exterior appearances represent the manner through which they express their *italianità*: "*Tight shirts, spiky hair and jewelry. Some Italian Americans try to be Italian by dressing like this. Like Jersey Shore. Italian American dress flashier.*"

One interviewee highlights the Italian American's exaggeration of some Italian characteristics: "*They dramatize the small characteristics in genuine Italians. Ex: Italians like to take in sun, Jersey Shore are overly baked Italians.*"

Among the stereotypical Italian American *cultural aspects* and *values*, the young people mention primarily:

1 *Food:*

we like to eat
we eat a lot
love of good food
we eat a lot of pasta
food obsession
the Sunday dinner
many Italian Americans overeat
expression of love through food

Food represents a means of communication transmitting a loving feeling. It also serves as a means of uniting the family: "*I think that many Italian Americans do enjoy food and use it as the centerpiece of family life and celebrations.*"

2 *Family and Tradition:*

family oriented
close knit family
mama's boy
caring mother/strict father
value family and tradition
men being taken care of by their mothers for too long
men not being active in household chores
the treatment of sons, expectations of family
the need to protect your family
family structure (matriarchy)

One interviewee used this expression to define the special connection established within the families: "*Our families are as thick as thieves and we look out for one another.*" For another, the maternal figure is the focal point of the stereotypes: "*mothers being overprotective, not wanting to let go of their sons.*" At times the family can become constrictive and suffocating: "*The overbearing family that stifles individual expression can sometimes be true.*"

3 *Values:*

value highly on honor and respect
Italian business routinely runs on favours, not always by the "rules"
a strong identification and association with Catholic church
a lot of Italian Americans do not appear to value education

4 *Depictions in television and film:*

Some of parodies of the way Italian Americans speak and dress in parodies is pretty close.
Some of it comes from behavior that is overblown by the media.

5 *Criminality*:

that all are in the mob
the provincial, racist, homophobic, traditionalist, superficial, Mafioso
being affiliated with organized crime
Mafia
crime-related

One youth noted that the connection with the Mafia represents a positive identification for some people: "*Many Italian Americans think that Mafia-related things are cool rather than negative.*"

6 *The "Guido" subculture*:

I think there are those who promote the gangster or "*Guido*" style in real life, but it isn't a fact for all Italian Americans.

I've grown up with "*Guidos*," but I also know that they do not represent the majority of the Italian-American population.

The most common stereotype today is the "*Guido*," a bad representation in terms of look and attitude from "fake Italians" or Italian Americans who overexaggerate.

Where I live, many Italian American boys have the "blowout" haircut and a tan—it is true (unfortunately!)

Anyone from the Jersey Shore or Staten Island, they are not Italian Americans... or even Italian.

The analysis shows that the stereotypes describing Italian Americans on the level of personality are predominantly negative, while the positive characteristics are predominantly associated with values and family. It is also interesting to examine some observations made in the margin, regarding the way in which Italian American stereotypes are generally perceived. A portion of the interviewees pointed out that these stereotypes do not reflect the totality of Italian Americans, but that some individuals substantiate these qualities, while others may only use them.

One interviewee observes: "*Rather than pin-pointing 'true' stereotypes, I would say that there are Italian Americans who exemplify certain of the stereotypes.*"

Another claims: "*Well, they are true but they shouldn't be. Big hulking overemotional guys use their 'Italianness' as justification for abusive behaviors sometimes.*"

These words clearly express the opinion that while the stereotypes may be true, they are not uniformly applicable. "*They are all somewhat true in that there are some Italian American who fit the stereotypes, but that doesn't mean any of the stereotypes apply universally.*" Others maintain that many of these stereotypes are true, while others acknowledge only some of them. There is also the opinion that "*most of stereotypes are incorrect.*"

One respondent replied thus to the question of whether or not the stereotypes were true, emphasizing the voluntary choice of some people to perpetuate them: "*Yes and no. I think a lot of people purposely perpetuate the stereotypes they know of Italian American alla Jersey Shore.*"

Some of the interviewees claim that the stereotypes are somehow derived from reality: "*I believe all sterotypes are true to some extent as they had to be based on something.*" And again: "*All stereotypes stem from truth, they're just usually exaggerated. We are definitely loud!*" Two interviewees noted, while admitting the potential veracity of stereotypes, that these must not be applied to every individual claiming a certain lineage: "*All stereotypes are based on some kind of truth, but they are generalizations that don't have to apply to everyone of a specific heritage*"; "*I do think some things are true, that we are racist in some ways. People are obnoxious, yeah. But things like this are found in any race.*"

One respondent observed that stereotypes arise from what happens in reality: "*Every stereotype exists for a reason; there are in fact some Italian Americans involved in organized crime, who are hot-heated and loud.*"

There was one who pointed out that while true, the stereotypes were exaggerated: "*They are based on people who pepper our culture... they are true but perhaps amplified.*"

Others take up more critical positions: "*Italian Americans seem to embrace their stereotypes compared to other ethnicities.*"

Another found two of the more common stereotypes to be false: "*Some Italian Americans are superficial and some are fat—two major stereotypes. But an unbelievably small amount has Mafia ties, and many of us are quite intelligent, as opposed to these two false stereotypes.*"

STEREOTYPES OF ITALIAN AMERICANS IN THE MEDIA

Continuous media exposure to denigrated stereotypes is given as one of the reasons for the lack of pride in the Italian background. An analysis conducted between 1980 and 1981, and referenced by Riotto Sirey and colleagues (1985) observing television programs during peak hours, highlighted that the negative representations of Italian Americans were more numerous than positive ones by a ratio of about two to one (Lichter & Lichter, 1982).

Particularly, the study highlights that:

- one in six Italian Americans represented on television takes part in some criminal activity;
- the number of professional criminals exceeded the total number of qualified professionals and executives;
- the majority of Italian American personages had low-status occupations, only one in seven worked as an executive, manager, or freelance professional;
- the majority of Italian Americans did not speak English correctly and their anomalous use of the language frequently made them the target of jokes.

Returning to the results of the research, respondents were asked to indicate what their opinion was regarding the reactions of the majority of Italian Americans with reference to the stereotypes that represent them in the media. What emerges shows that half of the sample is divided in turn between those who believe that the majority of Italian Americans are entertained by this representation and those who, instead, believe that they feel offended. Over 12% claim that Italian Americans regard these representations with indifference and one-tenth feel that the group has in fact adopted and emphasized these stereotypes. According to the interviewees, practically no one has taken an active role to combat these stereotypes.

Subsequently, the survey inquired if the representation of Italian Americans through films, reality shows, and fiction demonstrated a realistic image of them today. Only one respondent replied that the image is accurate, while the sample is otherwise divided between those who believe that it correctly captures some aspects (45.5%) and others who, conversely, do not recognize it at all (40.1%).

The interviewees were then offered a list of famous television programs and reality shows with Italian American characters, and asked to express their level of satisfaction. Collecting the responses of high and medium satisfaction, the shows liked the most are ordered as follows: *Everybody loves Raymond* (50.5%), *Giada De Laurentiis (food network)* (46.5%), and *The Sopranos* (32.9%). The least liked shows are *Jersey Shore* (53.1%), *Mob Wives* (36.4%), and *Real Housewives of New Jersey* (32.8%). The least-viewed shows include *Big Ang*, *Mob Wives*, and *Real Housewives of New Jersey* (Table 7. 1).

Table 7.1 How much do you like it?

	VERY MUCH	SOMEWHAT	A LITTLE	NOT AT ALL	I DON'T WATCH IT	N/A
Jersey Shore	4.0	9.4	14.1	39.0	20.2	13.4
The Sopranos	18.1	14.8	18.1	10.1	25.6	13.4
Mob Wives	3.6	7.6	9.0	27.8	38.6	13.4
Big Ang	2.5	5.8	6.1	23.5	48.0	14.1
The Real Housewives of New Jersey	9.7	7.2	7.2	25.6	36.1	14.1
Everybody Loves Raymond	26.0	24.5	14.4	7.2	14.4	13.4
Cake Boss	13.0	17.3	14.1	8.7	33.2	13.7
Giada De Laurentis (food network)	27.4	19.1	7.9	4.0	27.8	13.7
Other TV shows	2.2	0.0	0.7	0.4	13.0	83.8

THE "*GUIDO*" SUBCULTURE

In autumn 2009, MTV launched a reality show called *Jersey Shore*, which was a great success that also aroused controversial opinions. The show followed the daily life of a group of young Italian Americans "self-defined as *guidos* and *guidettes* by their appearance and questionable behavior" (Cappelli, 2011). Even before the show appeared on American television, the leaders of some Italian American organizations launched anti-defamation campaigns demanding its cancellation. They alluded to the fact that the term *Guido* recalled profoundly offensive anti-Italian stereotypes: it was "originally a derogatory term referring to the urban, working-class Italian Americans. Since the '70s and '80s the term has referred to young Italian males who use heavy amounts of gel, are excessively muscular and poorly educated with an openly macho attitude, as well as their corresponding female cohort [*guidettes*]" (ibid., p. 14).

Despite this, the show became an unexpected media phenomenon and six consecutive seasons were produced, set in New Jersey, Miami, and Italy. After three years, the final *Jersey Shore* episode aired in the United States in December 2012.

The original *Guido* myth takes us back in time, to the seventies when the musical genre known as disco gained popularity and was identified with the 1977 film *Saturday Night Fever* and the iconic figure of Tony Manero, played by John Travolta (Tricarico, 2010). According to Chirico (2011a), *Guido* culture takes prevalent traits and applies them to a specific ethnic group: "This makes sense for a group that is so removed from its original ethnic identity, as is the case of the third, fourth and now fifth generation of Italian Americans; any attempt to recover that original sense of ethnicity today would include aspects common to all those who belong to a particular age group.... [T]he original culture is so distant that what is seen among the young members of a group are the stereotypes, caricatures, or idealized images of that culture that have been handed down alongside a beloved family recipe or a photograph" (p. 81).

For Tricarico, the show *Jersey Shore* demonstrates first of all, the power of the media to influence the discussion within popular culture. He maintains that global companies such as Nike and MTV "sell cool" to the young generations (2010, p. 106). More specifically, *"Guido"* is interpreted by scholars of the Italian American experience as a category of prejudice—a pejorative term—to the extent that it has become "the new ethnic insult reserved for Italian Americans" (Tricarico, 2010, p. 163).

Tricarico argues that the term does not indicate a "concept imposed from outside to defame Italian Americans, but a complex 'transaction' within and across ethnic borders... [and it must be relocated] in youth culture practices that are located in a wider experience of an ethnic group" (2010, p. 164). As a "youth grouping," *Guido* represents a particular position of the subject within the ethnic boundaries. In short, this is a "construction site" of ethnicity and "ethnic formation" within the popular youth culture (Tricarico, 2007).

"Guido" emerges from the urban experience of the Italian Americans of New York City and indicates, in particular, the moment when the American consumerist culture of youth, and by extension the mainstream American culture, became strategically linked to Italian ethnicity. Tricarico interprets *"Guido"* as "a collective challenge to the ethnic stigma" and claims that "the denigration of the *Guido* goes beyond local youth cultural practice, despite the distinction between *Guido* as a subcultural criterion and as an indistinct ethnic category. In

this scenario, *Guido* emerges as a category of ethnic prejudice" (Tricarico, 2010, pp. 164–165). He later claims that the *Guido* represents a youth subculture that designates a group of young people defined by a style; the characterization of the style is comprised of goods and leisure activities taken from the popular commercial culture. Furthermore, he adds that the "symbolic work of the style-based youth subcultures conveys a shared identity that is immediately eloquent in terms of the selection and composition of cultural elements" (p. 165). The style-based identification places the *Guidos* in a "youth category" that distinguishes them from other young people; this awareness is shared by those who feel they are part of it. These dynamics of collective identity and differentiation are produced within the peer group.

Tricarico also argues that youth ethnic subcultures take possession of ethnicity in order to "make it work for them," in the sense that ethnicity is evoked "to corroborate the authenticity of the components. This ethnicity gives coherence to a collective style profile that expresses a position within contemporary youth culture" (2010, p. 166). In spite of this subculture, it takes over the commercial modalities of markets and global media such as television and the internet, it is distinguished by a "typical subcultural arrogance" linked to the fact that the "*Guidos* have their own style." This expressive modality collects various cultural elements and is significant in building a youth group that is designated in relation to Italian ethnicity. In summary, the Italian American ethnicity is symbolically represented through the *Guido* by the style depicting a local youth category and *Guido* makes precise the relationship between Italian ethnicity and certain youth trends. The social ritual that expresses the quintessence of *Guido* is frequenting night clubs; this location becomes the stage for style performances and competition for sexual partners. Moreover, there are identity transactions that cross boundaries: *Guido*'s identity is confirmed by its perception among other young people, who are able to make subtle distinctions linked to this behavioral and expressive modality and to recognize its specificity.

The dance club culture, in turn, facilitates a shift toward a more inclusive identity regarding ethnicity and codified as "*Guido*," defining a specific Italian American position in this culture. Tricarico points out that the trend of dance club culture "has sublimated, if not replaced, the neighborhood as a frame of an Italian American urban ethnicity in the context of youth culture" (2010, p. 169).

Compared to the young people of the seventies, today's youth can choose from a wider range of goods, services, and consumer images; and the new urban nocturnal panorama of consumerism "offers abundant resources for experimentation and play" (Chatterton, Hollands, 2003, p. 11, cited in Tricarico, 2010). This Italian American youth subculture has also incorporated places such as tanning centers, gyms, pool halls, and beauty salons; moreover, money is a symbol of high social status, an extremely important means to meet all the needs arising from the attending these locales.

GUIDO SUBCULTURE AND YOUTH

Returning to the results of the survey conducted among young people, there was an attempt to understand how the young people perceived the representation of Italian Americans through the phenomenon of *Guidos* and *Guidettes*. To this end, they were asked to indicate their reaction when the *Guidos* and *Guidettes* were mentioned. The question was addressed twice using the same formulation but in the first case, the reaction was produced following the mention of the *Guidos* by Italian Americans, while the second question alluded to the fact that the *Guidos* were named by individuals with different ethnic backgrounds.

As can be seen from Table 7.2, if the connection to the *Guido* subculture comes from an Italian American, the prevalent reaction of young people is divided between those who are indifferent (29.6%) and those who are entertained (21.7%). Almost one-fifth of the young people expressed taking offense in this case.

Table 7.2 How do you react when an Italian American/nonItalian American mentions the Guido and Guidette? (Percentage values)

	MENTIONED BY ITALIAN AMERICANS	MENTIONED BY NON ITALIAN AMERICANS
Entertained	21.7	14.4
Somewhat offended	18.8	41.2
Accurate, truthful	5.4	2.2
Indifferent	29.6	19.9
I don't know who they are	0.7	1.4
Other reactions	10.8	7.2
N/A	13.0	13.7

The percentage value of those who feel offended by this reference doubles if the speaker is a non-Italian American individual (41.2%), while one-fifth of those interviewed remain indifferent.

Interviewees were then asked to indicate whether, in their opinion, the *Guidos* and *Guidette* could be considered Italian American. A third of the sample considers them part of the Italian American culture and another third, conversely, considers them outside this context. Seventeen percent abstain from a judgment in one way or another, affirming a position of non-knowledge. In general, interviewees highlight a predominantly negative connotation linked to this subculture.

Two questions referred to discrimination against Italian Americans. The first asked the young people whether there was discrimination against Italian Americans today, and the second referred to potential cases of discrimination experienced in the family because of the Italian American background.

Seventeen percent of the sample claims there is no discrimination against Italian Americans today, while the remaining opinions are divided between those who believe there is, at a slight level (32.9%), and in a more accentuated form (36.5%). Discrimination suffered by their family owing to their Italian background has affected more than one-quarter of the sample (25.6%). The remaining group declared there have been no such episodes (60.6%).

8

Attitudes and Affiliations

This chapter examines the attitudes and behaviors of young people regarding religiosity, politics, food, associations, as well as territorial attachment and use of the media.

RELIGIOSITY IN AMERICA

Religiosity is deeply ingrained in the life of the American people, to such an extent that the Swedish theologian Stendhal (1968) observed that "even atheists in America speak in religious tones." Americans are classified among the most religious populations of the world: in analyses of membership, behavior, and religious beliefs, the percentages of those who identify with and practice a religious creed are very high. However, the secularized population is growing. Putnam and Campbell (2010) point out that this polarization between religious and nonreligious individuals derives from important societal changes.

Religious polarization has consequences that go beyond the religious sphere, because identifying with one pole or another implies a strong correlation with a worldview, especially with attitudes regarding intimate aspects of people's lives, including sex and family. This religious confluence has had repercussions especially on political parties, creating rifts and coalitions with consequent voting implications.

Looking closely at how Americans with different religious backgrounds interact, we note that America peaceably combines a high degree of religious devotion with a vast diversity of religions, including growing levels of nonreligiosity (Alba et al., 2008). How can religious pluralism coexist with religious polarization? The answer to this query is connected to the fact that religion is highly fluid in America, it has a malleable nature, and it represents individual preference, rather than a fixed characteristic.

At the end of the last century, the vast majority of Americans declared that they followed a religious belief, while only 10% considered themselves atheists. In the early years of the 2000s, reports showed that about 60% of Americans declared having some religious practice.[1] According to data from the 2006 Faith Matter Surveys,[2] 83% of Americans indicate that they belong to a religion, 17% say they do not identify with a religion, 40% take part in religious services about once a week or more, while 15% do not attend them. Thus, one can deduce that the overwhelming majority of Americans identify with a religion, even if this does not often correspond to an active faith practice.

From the same source it emerges that women are more religious than men, African Americans are much more religious than whites or other ethnic or racial groups in America, older people are more religious than young people, as are those who live in rural communities compared to those living in the city. Ultimately, the Americans living in the South are more religious than those in the rest of the country.

As for Italian Americans, despite the decrease in percentage from 81% to 70% between the seventies and the nineties of the twentieth century, they still represent the second-highest percentage among all the groups affiliated with the Roman Catholic religion (Smith, 1992, quoted in Belliotti, 1995). However, the strength of their religious identification and church attendance is far below the national average. Smith observes the overall image suggests that Italian Americans are "certainly no more traditional, authoritarian, and patriarchal than other Americans in their religious convictions... [they] are not even especially strong, nor traditionalist in their faith" (p. 9). Italian American Catholics, compared to other Americans, are also a little more inclined to express what is called a "progressive and compassionate" image of the supreme being (ibid., p. 169).

RELIGIOUS FAITH OF YOUNG ITALIAN AMERICANS

Concerning their relationship with religion, it emerged from the study that one-fifth of the sample indicated they received a very religious education, while the same percentage—on the contrary—was educated without any link in this regard. Of this group, 28.2% claim to have grown up with some religious reference, while just over 16% of the respondents had little religious education.

Among those who declared having received a very religious education, there is a prevalence of young people with a Catholic mother and those who have a father who is Catholic or who belongs to a religion other than those mentioned in the list on the questionnaire. As for the religious beliefs of the interviewees, almost 60% of young people declared themselves to be of Catholic faith. However, 16.6% of the sample claim not to have a religious preference but trust in a personal inner belief. Those who do not refer to any kind of faith-based conviction make up 4.7% of the sample. Residual indications include the Protestant religion (2.9%) and other religions (2.9%). Just over half of the sample is part of a local church or another spiritual community.

Intersecting this question with those concerning the religious beliefs of the parents, we observe a very strict continuity between parents and children. In fact, among those who identify themselves as Protestant, there is a prevalence of those whose mother or father follows a Protestant religion. The same trend is observed for those who have declared themselves Catholics and also for those who have not expressed any religious and spiritual preference. In the latter case, higher percentages are observed among those who have an unbelieving mother or father. Among the young people who have mentioned that they do not believe in a religion but have a personal creed, there are higher percentages among those who indicated—both on the maternal and paternal side—belonging to other religions not expressed in the proposed list, or the absence of belief. As for attending religious services, more than one-fifth of those interviewed do not follow this type of practice, and 18.4% claimed they only go to church during ecclesiastical festivities. More than one-fifth (22.7%), moreover, attended a few times in a year and about one-tenth (10.8%) once a month. Overall, 12.2% say they regularly participate in religious rites.

More than 30% of the respondents stated that religious faith and spiritual life are very important and the same percentage of respondents always considers them somewhat significant. Those who attach no importance to religious faith or spirituality are equal to one-tenth of the sample, while just over 13% said that this component has little relevance in their lives.

ITALIAN AMERICANS AND POLITICS

The growing presence of Italians in politics, especially starting from the time of World War II, ranks among the signs that have indicated their growing integration in the United States (Pretelli, 2011). Indeed, the Italian origin community's entry into political life, specifically in New York, occurred more slowly than it did with any other significant ethnic minority in the metropolis; only at the end of the 1890s did the group leave the stage of extreme political marginality that had characterized its history up to that moment. That decade offered the first possibility to observe the inclusion of Italian American candidates on the electoral lists of the two major parties; "lists that had already been open to other new immigrants for some time, first among them being the organized, cohesive, and active Jewish minority" (Bugiardini, 2006, p. 125).

Luconi (2006) notes that analysis of the political behavior of Italian American communities has been overshadowed by other issues, and this propensity for historians to neglect researching the field derives from the fact that the involvement of Italian Americans in U.S. political events has been connected to specific characteristics of Italian immigration. In fact, the first generation of Italian Americans were notable in their indifference toward electoral participation: this propensity was influenced by their willful nonpermanence and their ignorance of the English language, conditions that influenced the acquisition of citizenship and, consequently, the right to vote (ibid.).

This sporadic attention to the role played by Italian Americans on the institutional front of U.S. policy has focused primarily on reconstructing the careers of certain successful personalities and collecting biographical material regarding mayors, governors, and members of Congress who are of Italian origin; themes addressing the subject of the political experience of Italian Americans expressed themselves, therefore, through the tendency to create profiles of the leadership rather than quantitative analysis of the electoral behavior of Italian American communities (Luconi, 2006).

Pretelli (2011) points out that in the thirties, some important U.S. cities had mayors of Italian descent: in the period between the two world wars, the best-known Italian politician in the country was Fiorello H. La Guardia, elected mayor of New York for three consecutive terms—from 1933 to 1945—with the support of the New York middle class. After World War II, Italian American political representation, both at the state and national levels, grew considerably. In 1948, eight Italian Americans were elected to the House of Representatives;

this number doubled at the end of the 1960s. In 1950, John Pastore—governor of Rhode Island—became the first U.S. senator of Italian origin, while, in the same year, the independent Vincent Impellitteri was elected mayor of New York. States including New Jersey, New York, and Connecticut have had governors of Italian descent, among whom both Mario Cuomo and his son Andrew, in New York, have achieved a certain notoriety. Between 1994 and 2001, Rudolph Giuliani was elected mayor of New York; he became famous for his campaign, called "zero tolerance," against urban crime and for managing the situation in the city following September 11, 2001.

In the Italian American political scenario, two women have attained some of the premier elected positions in the United States: in 1984, congresswoman Geraldine Ferraro would have become the American vice president if the Democratic candidate had won the election, although this did not happen. In 2007, Nancy Pelosi became the Speaker of the House of Representatives. From 2007 to 2009, the U.S. Congress included thirty politicians of Italian origin (six senators and twenty-four representatives).

Regarding electoral preferences, it bears mentioning that at the end of the 1920s through the mid-1930s, Italian Americans, who had been predominantly Republicans, began to shift their votes in favor of the Democrats. In 1932, the Italian American electorate played an important role in electing President Franklin D. Roosevelt, and also in the creation of the Democratic majority that dominated the U.S. political scene for two decades. In 1948, the Italian American electorate once again voted in support of the Democratic candidate, Harry Truman (Luconi, 2000), but subsequently in the fifties the Italian Americans partially shifted their vote to the right, as proven by the support they offered to Republican senator Joseph R. McCarthy and his "witch hunt," the campaign that he strenuously conducted in the U.S. sociopolitical world in search of infiltration by communists.

Relations between Italian Americans and Italy were also strongly characterized by anticommunism. During the 1948 general elections, Italian American communities mobilized in a campaign—whose main proponents were the *Il Progresso Italo-Americano*, a periodical run by Generoso Pope, and the *Order Sons of Italy in America*—through which they invited relatives and friends in Italy to vote in favor of the Christian Democrats and their moderate allies, thus in an anticommunist key.

In the 1960s, the Italian American vote once again turned toward the Democrats, thanks to the presence of John F. Kennedy, a Catholic, as the party's candidate in the presidential election (Luconi, 2002). After his murder in 1963, Italian Americans supported his successor, Lyndon B. Johnson, with a vote percentage of around 76%, even though many of them did not agree with his liberal policies in favor of the civil rights of African Americans. During the Vietnam War, Italian Americans distanced themselves from the movements opposing the war and were labeled as "conservatives, fascists and racists" for their behavior by liberal and radical groups (Pretelli, 2011, 110). In the 1960s, Italian American hostility toward African Americans was overt and, as studies conducted at that time showed, some Italian American communities implemented self-protection and surveillance practices against the presence of (nonwhite) "strangers" in their neighborhoods.

During the following decade, in opposition to the progressive policies of the Democrats, many ethnic groups of European origin switched their votes in favor of the Republicans. In the presidential election of 1968, the Republican candidate Richard Nixon obtained the greatest consensus among the Italian electorate in cities torn apart by racial tensions, such as Newark and Philadelphia. The Italian Americans' unfriendly attitude toward black Americans was perpetuated throughout the seventies and eighties, exemplified in the killing of Yusuf Hawkins, a sixteen-year-old African American, which occurred in August 1989 on Bay Ridge Avenue in Bensonhurst, an Italian American neighborhood in Brooklyn. The young man had gone there to buy a used car and was killed by a crowd wielding baseball bats and pistols. When questioned about the murder, many of the neighborhood residents felt that what had happened was attributable to the naiveté of the young black man, who had ventured into a predominantly white district. This episode contributed "to reinforcing the idea in the public opinion that Italian Americans were a racist ethnic group" (Pretelli, 2011, p. 111).

In the words of Joseph Sciorra (2003), who marched, four days after the assassination, in the streets of Bensonhurst protesting the incident, alongside another "100 protesters, 400 counter-demonstrators and 250 policemen," as a newspaper relates:

> The assassination of Yusuf represented a decisive turning point in the political history of the city, ultimately influencing the result of the mayoral election in those years; David Dinkins became the first African American mayor of New York City. This episode also had a dramatic impact on the Italian American community in New York, and also fueled the production of an enormous amount of critical reflection and activity by Italian American scholars and

artists, contributing to ultimately creating a broader, self-reflective, and socially engaged sense of identity. (p. 206)[3]

Sciorra adds that "the literature scholar and poet Robert Viscusi was deeply struck by the silence that hovered over Italian Americans following the assassination of Yusuf" (ibid). On this occasion Viscusi noted: "The problem wasn't that people ignored us. The problem was that we didn't say enough."[4]

In the years between 1970 and 1990, Italian Americans—as reported by the National Opinion Research Center, quoted by Belliotti (1995)—had moved to the right in terms of identification with a political party, presidential vote, and political ideology. Smith, in 1992, pointed out that "in the early seventies only 17% (of Italian Americans) were Republican. This percentage has since doubled and currently accounts for 35%.... In the early seventies 45% of Italian Americans were Democrats; this number has decreased to its current 32%. Similarly, identification as Independent has dropped slightly from 36% to 33%" (Smith, 1992, p. 17).

At the beginning of the seventies a study was carried out by Patrick J. Gallo (1974) who posed an extremely important question, namely whether the political system tended to exclude certain groups from the sharing of power.[5] Italian Americans were the target of his work, but the author developed a theoretical framework to study "political alienation"[6] among other ethnic groups as well. He—through the study of many dimensions of the individual perception of political life—tried to determine if the American political system would sharpen or neutralize an ethnic group's sense of exclusion from the rules, values, and dominant institutions, which might lead to types of behavior that differentiated that group from other white natives.

Among the study's results was the confirmation of a sense of impotence from the majority of Italian immigrants interviewed, especially of those who belonged to the first and second generation; and the shared idea that the government was managed by high-powered people and had no significant impact on their everyday life. There was a low level of political information amid the majority of Italian Americans interviewed; Gallo noted a positive correlation between this fact and political alienation. Although there was a consistency in voting behavior of the three groups studied, the individuals did not see their votes as capable of affecting the results of the elections; or they did not believe that their expression through voting would bring any change once the elections were over. Moreover, a majority of these individuals frequently discussed politics and were interested in political campaigns and specific elections. The lower strata of Italian Americans were more inclined to be influenced by the intersecting pressures of class and ethnic identification. They were also more likely to be politically alienated: a low position in the social structure was interpreted by them as inaccessibility to the means to achieve social, economic, and political goals; hence, this would imply exclusion from sharing in the dominant institutions, roles, and values of American society.

What emerged from the study highlighted the extent to which political alienation was associated with low levels of interest, political participation, and organizational adhesion. In general, the political activity of respondents gradually increased from the first to the third generation, even though this growth was not constant and tended to be irregular. On the other hand, an almost total absence of organizational membership was observed in the majority of the sample, from the first to the third generation of respondents.

In an attempt to determine the impact of a politically alienated ethnic group on the American political system, the study emphasized that the latter tended not to integrate some political groups and, indeed, systematically excluded some of them from sharing power. A structural separation excluded "politically alienated" people from participation and, despite their expressions of needs, they could not find answers through the American political system. Similarly, the American party system did not seem to act as a vehicle to encourage participation among the "alienated," who were not easily politically identifiable with either party. The study concluded by emphasizing "the need by the members of the dominant society to reinforce loyalty to something that their being in power permits them to think they are guaranteed" (Gallo, 1974, p. 207).

Considering the historical period in which the study was conducted, the conflict between ethnic groups is interpreted by the author as the result of an emptiness created by the withdrawal of WASPs from the centers of power and their inability to assist as mediators of an interethnic dialog. Gallo concluded by saying that "an alliance between whites and blacks, between white-collar and blue-collar workers is necessary, based on their common needs and interdependencies—an alliance of political participation. But before this can realistically happen, many ethnic groups must develop internal organizations, identity, and unity. Italian Americans can prove to be a vital ingredient not only in forging this alliance, but in serving as a cement that will hold our urban centers together" (1974, p. 209).

Returning to the general political framework, Italian Americans remained loyal to the Republican Party until the 1990s, when the majority of them voted Democrat, supporting Bill Clinton's bid for president. In 2000 and 2004 the Italian American vote shifted slightly in favor of the Republicans again, during the presidential election campaigns of George W. Bush. From 2009 onward, Pretelli (2011) believes, we can speak of a "postracial" phase that coincided with the presidency of Barack Obama and which also had repercussions among Italian Americans; although there is no specific data regarding their voting preferences, a survey conducted by *America Oggi* in 2008 showed that more than 70% of respondents declared their preference for the future president (Luconi, 2009).

Cappelli (2012a) pointed out recently that Italian American politicians do not act simplistically as a coherent, ethnic political bloc, comparable to the active electorate. On the whole, he observes, politicians could benefit from such an orientation, but they are not particularly focused on the Italian vote, nor are they necessarily willing to confront ethnic issues. Furthermore, while they are in government, we should not expect "Italian" political choices, in terms of representation of ethnic interest. Mignone (2006) notes that Italian American voters strongly support Italian American candidates and, as surveys show, there is a close connection between the two components; naturally, their votes also reflect political affiliation and ideological convictions.

POLITICAL PREFERENCES AND
CONCERNS OF THE INTERVIEWEES

The study of young Italian Americans' interest in the sphere of political life was introduced by a question concerning some aspects of the Italian and American situation.

The category that collects the highest number of reports that are very strongly felt is Italian culture, defined as food, entertainment, fashion, etc. (53.8%) (see Table 8.1). Almost 37% of the interviewees indicated American culture as an object of high interest, followed by U.S. policy and national affairs. The lowest levels of interest were reserved for Italian political life and its economy.

As for political preferences, over 31% of the sample declare their preference for the Democratic Party, while one-fifth of the respondents sympathize with the Republican Party. Over 13% claim they do not identify with any political party. Furthermore, the Independents are equal to one-tenth of the sample and

Table 8.1 Level of interest in some aspects of the American and Italian situation (percentage values)

	VERY MUCH	SOMEWHAT	A LITTLE	NOT AT ALL
The Italian economy	9.7	33.9	25.6	16.2
Italian politics	10.5	29.6	27.1	18.4
Italian culture	53.8	24.2	5.4	2.2
The American economy	31.4	34.3	15.2	3.6
American politics/domestic affairs	33.2	31.4	16.2	4.7
American culture	36.8	35.7	11.2	1.8
Other topics	2.5	1.4	2.2	9.7

almost 6% adhere to Libertarian ideals. Residual indications include other parties, among which is the "Occupy movement" (4.3%).

Several volunteer and community actions were included to analyze the commitment and political participation of the interviewees, who were asked whether they had participated or contributed during the previous year (Table 8.2). The resulting picture of political and community activism shows that one-fifth of the sample participated in political events and meetings, in campaigns and political organizations, and made economic contributions in support of the latter. Over one-tenth took part in public political demonstrations.[7]

The survey also asks if the government has done something significant for the Italian American population over the last ten years. The responses highlighted the youth's lack of information in this regard (48.7%), while more than 30% said that this did not happen. Only 5% of the interviewees expressed an affirmative answer.

Table 8.2 Have you expressed your political participation in one of the following ways over the last 12 months? (percentage values)

	%
I participated at least once in a community or political meeting/event	22.4
I participated at least once in a political or community public demonstration	11.6
I volunteered in a community or political organization/campaign	20.6
I contributed economically to a political or community campaign/organization	19.1

FOOD

As mentioned throughout the study, for young Italian Americans, food represents an important source of identification with their ethnic background. The close connection between food and familial life derives, as Gambino (1974) observes, from food's symbolic importance: he compares the family meal to "a daily communion" (p. 24). Gabaccia (1998) claims that for the Italian Americans, meals and cuisine are powerful expressions of links with the past and with their present identity. Both of these have always occupied a very significant place in their image. Italian Americans often feel insulted by the advertisements and pop culture images representing them as obsessed with food, much as Italians feel offended by too many negative stereotypes connecting them to food.

Ortoleva (1992) considers Helen Barolini's book *Festa: Recipes and Recollections* as the Italian American cuisine manifesto, presented as a symbol of identity and as an object of ethnic pride. Barolini's words define ethnic cuisine as a legacy, a wealth of knowledge and traditions, and as a means of recapturing that heritage: "Starting in her kitchen, my mother found her way back to her heritage, and this, I suspect, happened for many Italian American families who were rescued from lives of denials by the ethnic explosion of the sixties" (Barolini, 1988, p. 52). Farther on, Ortoleva observes that "in food the group rediscovers its identity" (Ortoleva, 1992, p. 34): for this reason, the cuisine presents itself, in general, as an object of recovery and memory, rather than creation; in general, every discourse about cooking is a gaze into the past.

Even Pretelli (2011) emphasizes how food and the rituals connected to its consumption prevail among the characteristics that define the identity of Italians in the world. Particularly in the United States, food represents a fundamental aspect of the life of Italian Americans and how they are perceived by other Americans (Gabaccia, 1997–98; Giunta & Patti, 1998; Cinotto, 2001, 2009). From a historical point of view, in a context in which the catering industry is largely irrelevant (see McDonaldization)[8] Italian Americans have always considered food consumption as an element of social conviviality with family members and also with friends and fellow countrymen (Pretelli, 2011). The aspect of sharing a table is a central element of Italian ethnicity and, as Luconi (2004) notes, food always plays a fundamental role in the migration story of families.

Moreover, the connection to food represented, in the migratory experience of the first generation of Italians, "a form of preservation of one's own identity that opposed the excesses of Americanization," as well as a generational clash, since the new generations saw the heritage of Italians as a legacy of the parental culture from which they wanted to distance themselves (Pretelli, 2011, p. 120).

There were traumatic aspects in the meeting between the Southern Italian and U.S. cuisines but also forms of compromise and mutual adaptation (Ortoleva, 1992). Over the course of two or three generations postimmigration, Italian American cooking developed into a parallel tradition, very different from that of the motherland, adapting forms of consumption and techniques of preparation for widespread customs in the United States. Americanization and tradition coexist and represent two complementary aspects of the Italian American culinary identity that is renewed from one generation to the next, but which is imagined as rooted in an immemorial past.

In the years of the ethnic revival, the Italian-ness of food and the importance of Italian-style eating have seen a resurgence between the third and fourth generations and, over time, there has been a hybridization and commercialization of cooking imported from Italian immigrants in America.

Sassatelli observed how the ethnic distinctions tend to be consolidated through cooking. This is especially the case when people encounter goods and contexts different from the obviously traditional ones. The phenomenon of ethnic cuisines emphasizes the dual nature of the path of hybridization between cultures: migrants undoubtedly use food to stay anchored to their traditions but, when these are reproduced in their destination, they often contain significant variations and become important agents of change for the host society (Cook & Crang, 1996). The gastronomic traditions have not simply been replaced by the development of the mass food industry; in fact, in the early years of the current century we are witnessing a real boom in ethnic cuisine (Belasco & Scranton, 2002). In the U.S. society of mass multiculturalism, the development of a national canned food industry did not require the denial of any ethnic reference; instead, ethnic traditions have been challenged and reinvented through a process of "creolization" (Gabaccia, 1998). The different ethnic or regional cuisines of the United States represent a code that helps consumers make their own meal choices from one time to the next. Moreover, these cuisines play an ambivalent role with respect to ethnic differences: on the one hand, they help to establish quite clear, though stereotyped, images of these differences; on the other, they provide an area in which the corresponding borders can be overcome without much risk (Sassatelli, 2004).

Since the eighties, the consumption of Italian food has become increasingly widespread among Americans of non-Italian origin, associated with the

Mediterranean diet and its healthy effects. This increased interest among the general public has been accompanied by the proliferation of culinary television programs that teach Italian recipes. The appreciation of Italian food is demonstrated by the fact that "for many people, dining in exclusive and expensive Italian restaurants has become a symbol of a high social status" (Pretelli, 2011, p. 121).

Returning to the research on young Italian Americans, interviewees were asked how often they ate Italian or Italian American dishes. As demonstrated by their answers, the strength of this link is supported by the consistency with which they choose Italian and Italian American food.

In fact, more than 28% of them eat Italian dishes every day and almost 45% enjoy them two or three times a week.

SENSE OF TERRITORIAL ATTACHMENT

The respondents' sense of territorial attachment was analyzed by proposing a list of places to which the respondents could express their sense of attachment, modulating it on a scale between "very much" and "not at all"" (Table 8.3).

More than 80% of the young people indicated a very close attachment to the United States, followed by the city where they currently live (68.9%), the State of New York (67.5%), and Italy (65.7%). More than 60% of the sample express a

Table 8.3 Level of attachment to (very much/somewhat) (little/not at all) (percentage values)

	VERY MUCH/ SOMEWHAT	LITTLE/ NOT AT ALL
United States	82.3	2.6
City where you currently reside	68.9	16.3
New York State	67.5	17.3
Italy	65.7	18.7
Italian region of ancestral origin	60.3	24.6
City where you were born	58.9	26.4
Neighborhood where you live now	58.8	26.0
Western world	53.4	30.3
Whole world	44.7	38.3
Europe	43.0	40.8
Other places	5.4	9.4

very strong and somewhat strong connection to their ancestors' region/s of origin. On the other hand, 40.8% express a mild or no adhesion to Europe, as well as a low level of affection toward the whole world in 38.3% of cases, and in the Western world for 30.3% of respondents.

The link to Italy and its regions is felt very strongly, especially among those who have visited the country many times, while among those who have declared themselves somewhat bound to it and its regions, young people who have visited it sometimes prevail. A minor or no attachment to the Italian nation and its regions is expressed primarily among those who have never gone there. Here again, it emerges that having visited Italy is the determining factor for the sense of attachment and for the bond established with that nation.

A question was posed whether or not with the passage of time the strength of the relationship had diminished, remained stable, or increased, to understand to what extent the emotional dedication to the place in which the respondent lives or has lived, to the United States, and to Italy has changed over time (see Figure 8.1).

The feeling of belonging to the United States has remained stable in the case of more than half of respondents, while more than one-fifth claim it has grown over time. Over one-tenth maintains that this sentiment has instead decreased over the course of time. Regarding Italy, the connection has remained stable for 44% of the young Italian Americans, while it has grown for 34.3% of them. Of the interviewees, 5.8% indicated a decline in this sentiment. As for the place

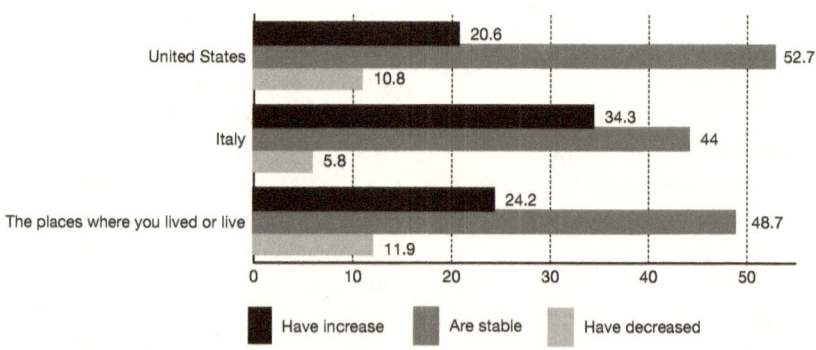

Figure 8.1 As Time Goes by, your Emotional Ties with...

where one lives or lived, just under half of the young people maintained a stable connection with it and a fourth increased their feeling of attachment. More than one-tenth of the interviewees noted a reduction over time.

To understand whether direct contact with Italy had affected the emotional perception of the three places mentioned, the three questions were crossed with one relating to having visited Italy or not. The emotional bond with the place where one lives has remained stable especially among those who have visited Italy many or a few times, but has decreased among those who have visited the country sometimes or never; finally, the strength of this bond has grown over time especially among those who have never been to Italy.

The emotional relationship with Italy has increased in intensity mainly among those who have visited it many times, while it has decreased especially among those who have never gone there. Those who have visited Italy several times primarily have a stable emotional connection with the country. The emotional union with the United States has remained stable mainly within the who have visited Italy many times, it has increased especially in individuals who have never visited Italy, while it has decreased for the interviewees who went to Italy several times. It seems clear that the link with Italy tends to grow in intensity or to remain stable in relation to the actual contact.

Regarding emotional relationships with the United States and the place where one lives, these tend to decrease or remain stable in their intensity among people who have visited Italy, while, conversely, they tend to grow among the

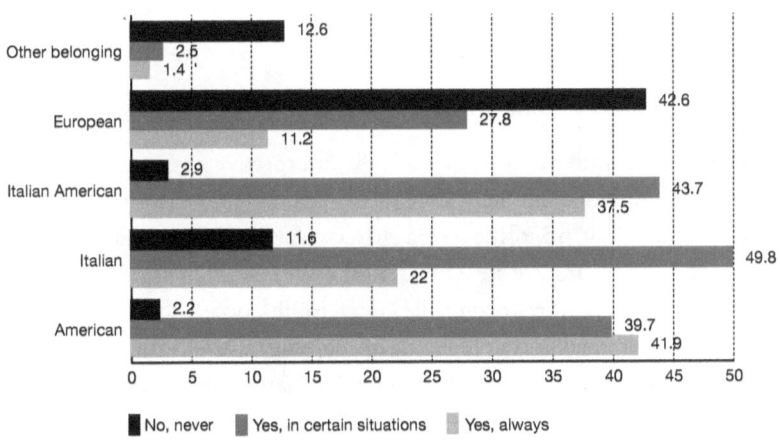

Figure 8.2 Are There Situations in Which You Feel Particularly . . .

interviewees who have never visited that country. This highlights the fact that a more "local" attachment to the context in which one lives primarily characterizes individuals who have never visited Italy. On the other hand, among those who have visited Italy there are predominantly attitudes of stable attachment to the place where one lives and to which one belongs, while the affection for one's ancestors' country of origin grows.

To understand if the feeling of being—respectively—American, Italian, Italian American, or European remained constant, was subject to fluctuation in relation to specific situations, or was never perceived by respondents, they were asked a question that linked this identification to the frequency with which they recognize this bond (see Figure 8.2). A number of respondents equal to 41.9% said they always consider themselves American, while this perception characterizes 22% of those who consider themselves Italian. Those who always identify themselves as Italian Americans are equal to 37.5% of the sample, while those who feel a constant sense of belonging as European falls to one-tenth (11.2%). A sporadic connection characterizes 39.7% of those who feel American and almost half of those who consider themselves Italian. Those who feel a connection with their own Italian American background, particularly in certain situations, amount to 43.7%; those who feel an affiliation to Europe in select situations is equal to 27.8%. Respondents who never feel American represent 2.2% of the sample, while those who never consider themselves Italian are little more than one-tenth of the sample. The percentage of those who never feel Italian American is also very low (2.9%), while the percentage of those who never feel European (42.6%) is growing considerably.

ITALIAN AMERICAN ASSOCIATIONS

The constitutive features that distinguish the interpretive framework of Italian associations in America highlight how these—much more than in the case of other American ethnic minorities—are characterized by fragmentation and the difficulty of creating unitary structures, in the context of an associative tradition already highlighted by Tocqueville (Bugiardini, 2002; Cipolla, 1978). It is also a reflection of the different methods of adapting to American society experienced by Italian immigrants based on their destination; therefore, fellowships that were formed in different parts of the United States during the same period but in diverse contexts—from urban to rural—are different from one another. This phenomenon—Bugiardini observes—is deeply connected to the dynamics of building the collective identity of Italians in America and how the evolution of the associative models punctuates the various stages of its formation.

Between 1821 and 1861 the first Italian associations emerged abroad, especially in the United States, formed by political exiles of the Risorgimento who were attempting to cope with the flow of sick and impoverished Italians pouring into the major metropolises of the host country. These associations were open to all Italian immigrants and focused mainly on welfare for political propaganda purposes of the Risorgimento, thus forming a "political identity character" while not addressing the social and recreational questions at all. In order to respond to these neglected needs, the first locally based associations developed in this period, created by the Italians in America utilizing the model of mutual experiences in Italy. Thus, the first mutual aid associations were initially denoted for their "closed" character, that is, based on a specific regional and interregional origin.

Initially promoted by Northern Italians, these associations were organized on regional or interregional bases; it was only later that these associations became more parochial, with the increase of Southern emigration, for the purpose of recreating the life of the country of origin and playing a role of psychological, social, and religious support (Bugiardini, 2002). Parochial societies developed as key institutions in Italian America and associations registered a great growth in all Italian communities between 1880 and 1915.

Parochial associations are an expression of different trends inherent in the Italian American community: they are, in some respects, related to the slow process of Italian integration into American society and Italians' late entry into trade unions. With the emergence of these associations, further divisions were created in the Italian American community, already lacking unity, but at the same time, they functioned much as the "ethnic quarter" did, serving as a cushion between the Old and the New World, making the impact of American society less severe.

Along with the associations of popular extraction, there were also those organized by the new postunification Italian American bourgeoisie, with the aim of offering services to immigrants, including placement in the U.S. labor market known as the "padrone system." Thus, the new Italian American bourgeoisie assumed—starting from the last decades of the nineteenth century—the role of community leadership and, in order to exercise a greater form of control over the labor market, the newly created associations were open to all immigrants.

From the perspective of religious associations, the U.S. ecclesiastical hierarchy, of predominantly Irish origin, opposed the parochial manifestation of Italian traditions in America and, in doing so, failed in the attempt to include

Italian Catholics in its organizational structure. For its part, the Italian Catholic Church in the United States played a unifying role, ensuring that exclusive associations were opened to the faithful coming from all parts of Italy and creating new national religious associations (Vecoli, 1983). Many Italian American associations dedicated themselves to honoring the patron saints of their hometowns, through annual festivals that included mass, procession, fireworks, games, and entertainment. These groups often acted autonomously with respect to the local churches. The most honored patron saints were San Rocco, San Giuseppe, Sant'Antonio, along with several Madonnas, especially Nostra Signora del Monte Carmelo (Andreozzi, 2000).

As for consular action, it developed primarily in the commercial field through the creation of Italian Chambers of Commerce abroad, which became important representatives for Italian American entrepreneurship in promoting exchanges between the two shores. Its fundamental objective, however, was promoting a sense of national identity. This was also achieved through the importation of associations such as *Dante Alighieri* and *Tiro a segno nazionale*, spreading overseas since 1888 with the declared purpose of nationalizing immigrants (Bugiardini, 2002). This promotional role was also developed by the protection of the "good Italian name" through supporting migrant associations working to contest the opinions of those who saw Italians as a threat to security and public order (Prencipe, 1976).

The beginning of the twentieth century saw the birth of the first antidefamatory associations among the Italian Americans and, at the turn of the century, a unified trend began to emerge, leading to the promotion of a series of initiatives for the development of Italian associations at the federal level. Despite the affirmation of this tendency, parochialism was still firmly rooted; war served as the primary reinforcement for unitary movements that had developed only with great difficulty. At the same time, migrant associations and trade union associations were moving toward the formation of a national collective identity of migrants, aimed at overcoming the often cloaked individualistic positions of parochialism and regionalism. The large Italian American working class became an active part of trade union organizations. The Italians created chapters of American fraternal organizations. In New York alone there were thirteen Italian Masonic Lodges.

During the Great War, the nationalism of Italian emigrants became more explicit and the war marked "the definitive discovery of so-called Italianness as the prevailing identity over all the others. The conflict actually strengthened the unitary processes already underway and promoted new ones" (Bugiardini, 2002, p. 573). Between 1915 and 1917, Italian associations mobilized throughout the country to support Italy's war effort, and from 1917 this mobilization continued on an even larger scale.[9] At the end of the war, the wave of nationalism did not diminish but, instead, grew stronger. The alliance between Italy and the United States had a significant impact on the future of commercial and political relations between the two countries, and nationalism—more effective than regionalism for the development of capitalism and finance—was promoted within Italian associations by Italian business contexts. These unitary tendencies continued to develop and can be interpreted as "the response to the widespread sense of unease that shook the Italian communities during that time. Attacked from the outside, they only found security through unifying on the most common ground possible (Italianness, in fact); this allowed them to overcome, at least momentarily, even some of the most deeply rooted internal divisions" (Bugiardini, 2002, p. 575).

Community leaders considered the advent of fascism more as an evolution of nationalism than as a true ideology. It proved capable of creating a mass collective identity and gathered a consensus among the Italian American ruling classes, insofar as it did not create problems with American society and the immigrant masses. However, this doctrine never managed "to truly control the community life of Italians in America. Nor would anti-fascism play an important role in it" (ibid., p. 576). In this frame of reference, social life appeared more and more guided by the rise of nationalism and the decline of local and traditional culture and coincided with the reduction of migratory flows due to restrictive immigration laws and in connection with the economic-financial crisis of 1929: these new conditions affected immigrant associations, reducing the number of participants and changing the physiognomy of the organizations.

The Order Sons of Italy in America (OSIA)—the largest Italian American association—was founded in 1905 in New York. It grew rapidly, incorporating the preexisting *Friendly Societies* and becoming the largest Italian American organization at the national level. Over the years, this association founded 2,746 lodges of adults and 366 lodges of young people in the United States and Canada (Andreozzi, 2000). Various groups broke away from the OSIA, and the "Independent Order of the Sons of Italy" was founded in New York in 1907. In 1925, other dissident groups were formed who established the "Sons of Italy Grand Lodge, Inc.," after a dispute concerning links with the Mussolini government. When Italy surrendered in 1943, this faction reunited with OSIA.

During the interwar period, numerous nationally oriented associations were formed. Among these, *UNICO clubs*[10] were created in Connecticut in 1922, while the *National Italian American Civic League* began its activity in 1934 and founded chapters especially in the Midwest. These two groups fused in 1947, becoming *UNICO National*. Over the years, more than 150 UNICO chapters have been locally formed. In 1975, the *National Italian American Foundation* was established with the goal of maintaining a continuous presence in Washington, D.C., to support an Italian American political agenda.

Many Italian American associations have focused, over time, on preserving their history and highlighting the achievement of prestigious positions. In 1966, the *American Italian Historical Association* was founded (now known as the Italian American Studies Association) to promote research and the conservation of documents by sponsoring an annual conference, assembling scholars from all over the United States and the rest of the world. Italian American women have created a number of societies, including the *National Organization of Italian American Women* (NOIAW).

In the space of 170 years, approximately twenty thousand associations have been created by Italians, and they—as Andreozzi notes (2000)—"represent a crucial aspect of community life and reflect the changes in identity and in needs of one of the largest ethnic groups of the United States. The history of Italian organizations reflects the variety and richness of experiences of Italian immigrants and their descendants in America" (p. 437). In the 1990s, however, Alba (1990) pointed out that the percentages of enrollment in ethnic organizations were low for all white ethnic groups, particularly for fourth-generation individuals and beyond. This kind of activity involves a very small fraction of the ethnic group and is typical, usually, of earlier generations. The current ethnic social affiliations of many whites seems far from what characterized the past.

FORMATION OF ASSOCIATIONS AND ITALIAN AMERICAN YOUTH

Today, as Bassetti noted (2010), the frame of reference, especially for young people, is the world. Adapting to this reality, various youth associations need to reorganize: "Their members first put the existing structures in crisis, asking that they be more flexible and find new aggregation dynamics. Otherwise, the risk is that young people would renounce their membership, no longer considering them able to adapt to their needs" (p. 94).

Let's now examine the results of the survey among young people regarding the dimension of associative life. In general, 40% of respondents are part of some group, association, or organization, while 45.5% have no affiliation. To connect to the Italian American community, 30.3% of respondents said they were using social media, while 55.6% did not take advantage of the possibilities offered by the Web. Facebook is the most utilized social medium of the respondents. Among those who use social media, the young people who have visited Italy many times prevail; and we see how its use decreases from those who have visited Italy many times to those who have never gone. In other words, the fact of having visited Italy affects the use of social media for this purpose, that is, of connecting to the Italian American community. A list of the best-known Italian American associations and organizations was then presented to the young people and they were asked to indicate whether they were associated with these, had occasionally visited them, had only heard about them, or whether they had never heard of them. As evidenced from the data shown in Table 8.4, the participation of young people in associations that promote Italian and Italian American

Table 8.4 Participation and frequency of activity in the following associations, organizations, centers for Italian American studies (percentage values)

	ASSOCIATED/ PART OF	VISITED OCCASIONALLY	ONLY HEARD THE NAME OF	NEVER HEARD OF THEM
NIAF (National Italian American Foundation)	10.8	11.6	23.5	37.2
Order Sons of Italy in America	6.1	13.7	33.2	28.9
NOIAW (National Organizations of Italian American Women)	6.9	6.5	18.4	50.9
Italian American Civic League	0.0	1.8	18.8	61.4
UNYTI (Uniting New York Italians)	0.4	1.8	15.2	64.3
John D. Calandra Italian American Institute	4.0	13.4	19.1	44.8
Columbus Citizens Foundation	5.4	7.2	23.5	45.5
UNICO National	1.8	6.1	27.1	46.9
Casa Italiana Zerilli Marimò	0.7	4.7	14.8	61.4
Westchester Italian Cultural Center	4.0	5.8	16.6	56.0
Casa Belvedere, the Italian Cultural Foundation	1.4	2.5	20.2	57.4
The Italian Academy for Advanced Studies in America—Columbia University	1.1	4.0	19.1	56.7
Center for Italian Studies—Stony Brook University	0.4	5.8	14.8	60.3
New York Italians	4.3	8.7	17.7	51.3
Other associations	1.8	0.7	2.9	18.1

culture is generally quite low. More than one-tenth of the sample claimed to be part of the NIAF, 6% of the Order Sons of Italy, and 7% are registered with the NOIAW. Occasional attendance at the Order Sons of Italy, the John D. Calandra Italian American Institute, and the NIAF characterized the contact—respectively—maintained by 13.7%, 13.4%, and 11.6% of the young people interviewed.

Continuing on the subject of Italian American associations, respondents were asked what the perception of the interviewees regarding the relationship between the various associations was. Here again, as with the answers given to other questions, a controversial vision emerges from young Italian Americans. Most believe that these relations take place in the name of cooperation (27.4%); for others they are limited to the exchange of information (24.9%); and for 9% there is a sense of competition. Finally, a notable portion of the subjects—equal to 18.8%—indicated that these relationships do not exist.

REASONS FOR THE LACK OF PARTICIPATION IN ASSOCIATIONS

Those who had never been members of or taken part in the activities of any Italian American association or organization were asked about the reasons for this lack of participation. The question, in open form, was subsequently reclassified according to the following interpretative categories:

1 *General lack of interest in participating in associations*:

> Sometimes I have reservations about meeting other Italian American [sic], that they might fall closer to the stereotypes than I consider myself to, or that they might not know much about the real Italy. Sometimes (and this is a broad generalization), I feel that these organizations are just "going through the motions" and not quite culturally accurate.

2 *Lack of motivation or desire to participate*:

> I have never heard of many; I didn't feel that I needed to be a part of a group in order to feel Italian, lack of time, lack of desire to commit to a group.

3 *Lack of knowledge of the existence of associations, their activities, and their location*:

> I don't know about them and I don't have time to go or haven't made time to go. I guess I don't find them that important to be a part of them.

Did not know they existed, also do not feel so strongly about the Italian American culture to get involved with others that are not family friends.

4 *Sphere of participation felt to be private*:

I don't really know about them, to be honest. I feel a spiritual connection to Italy that is more ephemeral and private than articulated and social.

The way I connected to the Italian American community is socially with my family, friends and community members, particularly through continuing cultural traditions. I don't feel a need to structure it within associations or address it from a political or educational perspective.

5 *Lack of family/friends involvement in the associations*:

I just don't participate in any associations, period. I guess it's because my friends/family don't.

6 *Lack of time*
7 *Associations primarily attended by elderly people; closed-mindedness of these associations to new ideas*:

They don't focus on issues I am interested in and are mostly older people who are unopen to new ideas.

They are very cliquey.

8 *Lack of associations in one's area of residence*
9 *Occasional participation*
10 *Associations do not reach out to young people*

Analyzing the frequency distributions of the explanatory categories referring to the contents from the open answers, it emerges that the primary reasons mentioned are the lack of knowledge of the existence of the associations, the lack of interest, and the lack of time (see Table 8.5).

LEVEL OF SATISFACTION/DISSATISFACTION REGARDING THE ACTIVITIES PROMISED BY THE ASSOCIATIONS, AND REASONS FOR THIS JUDGMENT

On the other hand, those who belong to Italian American associations have been asked whether or not they are satisfied with the initiatives and activities they

Table 8.5 Reasons for lack of participation in the associations (percentage values)

Does not know the associations exist	13.4
Lack of interest	10.5
Lack of time	8.3
Lack of motivation	4.0
Italian culture is a private aspect of one's life	2.9
Occasional participation	2.5
Does not reach out to youth	1.4
Mostly comprised of elderly people	1.4
Lack of associations in one's area of residence	1.1
Does not know anyone involved in these groups	1.1

promote. Comprehensively, more than 42% are considered to be very or somewhat satisfied; 14.5% of those interviewed, on the other hand, expressed a low or no satisfaction level.

The young people were then asked to provide a reason for their evaluation. The responses to the open question were regrouped into twelve explicative categories. The following emerge from listing the categories that express a mainly negative judgment:

1 *They do not coincide with the interests of young people*:

> The associations mostly reflect the interests of middle-aged people. There should be more communication with the youth.

> They are dusty and old for the most part. They care more about looking like they're doing something than actually really engaging the community in a meaningful way. The college youth clubs also seem to do nothing but eat pizza and go to San Gennaro. The things being done by people twenty-six or more years old in the city are encouraging. . . . Calandra is also a worthwhile organization. The writer's association needs to do far more outreach.

> I think they could do a better job grabbing the younger generation (my generation) into their events. I know they do some things; for example, they participate in the local parade and young woman gets crowned and participate in the float or car; no events geared for young men. Also, they do a lot of dinners and events for older people and for entire families but

are missing the boat with the young generation. If they don't change and get us involved, I think they may have membership decline when our parents' generation is gone.

It would also be good to bring young Italian Americans today for service-oriented activities.

2 *The activities do not meet expectations*:

The associations do not do enough and could do more. Furthermore, they could do better, in terms of promoting the "true culture" and not just promoting "heritage." They are disorganized and lack resources.

Just haven't been engaged. Not sure what the point is aside being "proud" of our Italian ancestry. I'd rather try to build relations. . .

3 *Focus on the wrong subjects*:

They are not connected to "real and current" Italy, but to "defunct traditions" and "not very sophisticated regional perspective."

4 *Aimed at Italian Americans who do not speak the language, who have never been to Italy, who do not have a connection with modern Italy*:

It's always the same thing. Vendors of food and loud music. I don't feel any of the Italian American activities are Italian.

5 *They are superficial; they do façade activities for the sole purpose of raising funds.*
6 *They are not inclusive A sense of estrangement arises from some of the interviewee's responses.*
7 *It is expensive to participate.*

Conversely, the following categories highlight a *predominantly positive judgment*:

8 *The events present topics for reflection based on everyday life, on the current news of Italian history and life and not nostalgic visions; they give a positive image of the Italian Americans. They teach the Italian language and cooking.*
9 *They preserve traditions, Italian culture in America, increase awareness, strengthen pride in belonging, play a role of advocacy, express and transmit the significance*

of being Italian American. They make you feel more connected. They are sources of information.
10 They organize events for meeting other Italian Americans. They provide support, entertainment, networking (festivals, events).
11 They offer scholarships, economic support.
12 They teach people things they never knew about Italian culture.

As evidenced from the responses, the most prevalent positive aspects include the promotion of culture and traditions and associated networking activities. Among the negative aspects reported above are the lack of communication with young people and the lack of closeness to their interests (Figure 8.3).

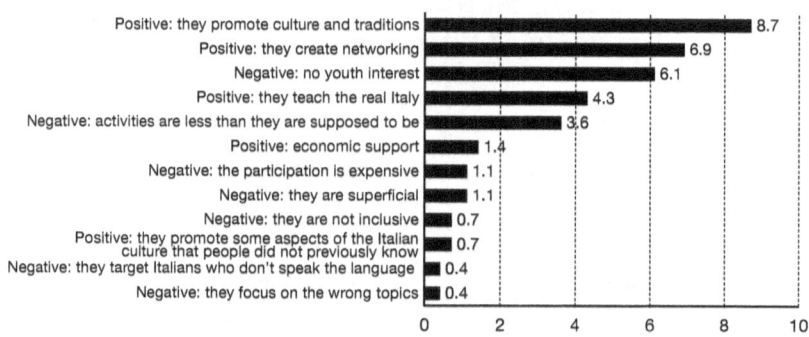

Figure 8.3 Why You Are Satisfied or not with the Activities They Promote?

ACTIVITIES THAT OUGHT TO
BE PROMOTED BY THE ASSOCIATIONS

Subsequently, interviewees were asked to indicate if there were any activities that young people would have liked to see promoted by the associations. The re-aggregation of the resulting contents led to eleven interpretive categories.

1 *recreational and cultural activities (games, social events) and cultural events in general (concerts, dance, cinema, bowls tournaments ...);*
2 *promotion of Italian American artists;*
3 *better understanding of modern-day Italy and Italian life;*
4 *broadening the scope of the initiatives to expand and promote the sense of community; networking activities; amplifying the activities of Italian American clubs and associations:*

> I would like to see the Italian club engage in more outreach. Many students are Italian American, but not many are members of the Italian Club. I think the importance of heritage needs to be reinstilled.

5. *knowledge of Italian artists (cinema, concerts)*;
6. *organization of events aimed at young people, young professionals, and also those who are part of the working class:*

> I would prefer that there be new events that cater to younger people and would attract working people, perhaps cultural nights at Starbucks or something, or movie nights.

7. *promoting culinary events*;
8. *organizing language courses:*

> Italian language acquisition. I would like to see more children learning Italian from a young age. Immersion is the most effective method, and I hope one day to send my children to Italian immersion schools. There are very few around the country and not sponsored by the Italian Ministry of Education. Whereas there are many French schools in the U.S. (as the French Ministry of Education and Consulates have worked hard to promote French culture), the options for families seeking Italian immersion programs are just not there.

9. *planning trips to Italy*;
10. *more career mentoring and scholarship program activities*;
11. *The residual category of "other activities" is comprised of the following:*

> Italian cultural education for people of other backgrounds;

> maintaining Italian traditions;

> promoting workshops and seminars;

> creating courses in various artistic, literary, and academic sectors, not specifically geared toward analyzing the significance of being Italian American;

> awareness raising and cultural promotion activities (e.g., breast cancer walks);

> activities aimed at strengthening the links between the two countries:

Ties between both countries and also bridging a gap between the new wave of Italian immigrants with the Italian Americans. Teach Italian Americans what really Italy is—different cuisines, culture, language, history throughout the different regions.

Ultimately, for some people there is no real interest in preserving the Italian cultural background:

> Italian AP bottom line, we do not see the excitement that other countries have in their cultural heritage.

The frequency distribution of the elements constituting the answers to the question conveys the prevalence of requests for cultural and recreational activities, language courses, community promotion initiatives, and events for young people (see Figure 8.4).

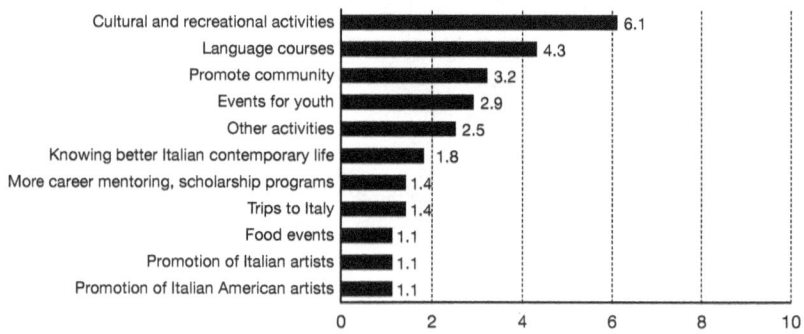

Figure 8.4 Which Activities Would You like Italian American Association to Promote?

USE OF THE MEDIA

Four questions on the survey were dedicated to analyzing the young people's relationship with the media. They were asked to indicate, in hours and minutes, the time they spent watching television, reading newspapers, using the internet, and reading books throughout the day.

According to the cultivation theory[11] developed by Gerbner (1986; Gerbner et al., 1998) in the seventies, referring to the effects of television on the U.S. population, the public is divided into three categories: the low users (those who watch television less than two hours a day), the normal users (who watch it from two to six hours a day), and the heavy users (who watch television for more than six hours a day). The young respondents' relationship to the use of the four media mentioned were classified according to these three categories. The frequency distributions result in the following picture:

Table 8.6 Time dedicated to watching television

	NO.	%
Low user	174	62.8
Normal user	43	15.5
Heavy user	2	0.7
N/A	58	20.9
Total	277	100.0

In regard to watching television, the young people predominantly fell into the first two categories, with a prevalence of those considered low users.

Table 8.7 Time dedicated to reading newspapers

	NO.	%
Low user	208	75.1
Normal user	11	4.0
N/A	58	20.9
TOTAL	277	100.0

The time that interviewees dedicated to reading newspapers also appears to be quite contained, considering that more than 75% devote less than two hours to this type of study.

The use of the Internet occupies the time of respondents in a more extensively than the two previous media types, and it is in this category that 13% of the sample rank among the heavy users. It is, however, taken into consideration that the internet could also be used to read books and newspapers.

Table 8.8 Time dedicated to using the internet

	NO.	%
Low user	80	28.9
Normal user	104	37.5
Heavy user	36	13.0
N/A	57	20.6
TOTAL	277	100.0

Table 8.9 Time dedicated to reading books

	NO.	%
Low user	183	66.1
Normal user	30	10.8
Heavy user	7	2.5
N/A	57	20.6
TOTAL	277	100.0

Reading books occupies a marginal portion in the "typical day" of the interviewees, considering that over 66% read books for less than two hours a day. One-tenth of the sample did claim to read books for between two and six hours daily.

9

The Future

PROSPECTS ACCORDING TO SCHOLARS

Analyzing the future prospects of Italoamerica and its culture means examining its strengths, the goals it has achieved, and the problematic aspects that still need to be addressed today. Over time, an Italian American political-economic elite has emerged and found its place within the American mainstream. Both on an individual and collective level, Italian Americans have achieved considerable political and economic success (Cappelli, 2015a). This social affirmation contrasts with "scarce cultural relevance," better defined as limited recognition of this subculture by the dominant culture (ibid.). The road to achieving cultural affirmation also leads to the need to "affect the cultural body of the group, bringing the consciousness of the self to maturity" (ibid., p. 20).

For Viscusi (2015b), Italoamerica exists in a state of cultural backwardness. The cause derives from the lack of what he calls "discursive power," which he defines as "the ability to confer authoritativeness in what one says. Those who possess it can use language to deal with their personal, social, and political problems," and this power presents a complex structure (pp. 65–66). Viscusi points out how important self-reflection is, specifically the "dialogic self-criticism" that the community must pursue in order to achieve a balanced comparison with others. Discursive power is comprised of three elements: (1) language: the primary characteristic of a people ("Italoamerica is very similar to a nation whose language has been stolen"); (2) the narrative: the description of the collective purpose of a people ("Italoamerica does not have its own history"); 3) dialectics: oppositional power to a position of weakness that makes one fall back on forms of self-closure and ethnic self-preservation. These three components can be read as "strategic imperatives" for Italian American culture and, at the same time, as three objectives to be achieved. Regarding language, Viscusi believes that Italoamerica should be bilingual: its language is neither English nor Italian, but a diglossia that freely alternates between the two. Even after several generations, there is a base of "linguistic desire" among Italian Americans to build upon.

Tamburri (2015a) believes that "the culture of the book" should be included among the shortcomings of the Italian American community (p. 51). He attributes a broad value to this concept, which includes all the arts. One of the major challenges facing the Italian American community is precisely the need to counter the insistence on its culture as being monolithic, or—as Tamburri specifies—the idea shared by many within the group of seeing Italian Americans as "born of a single mold" (Tamburri, 2010, p. X). This concept is also mentioned by Cappelli (2015a), who emphasizes the need to "break the unity of Italoamerica" on a political level. There is the notion of a fictitious political-cultural unity imposed by the "official Italoamerica" on the whole community, which monopolized public communications, referring to an imaginary "Italian American public opinion" (Cappelli, 2015a, p. 35). This unity—again according to Cappelli—is built on "a mixture of colonial myths (i.e. Columbus), of uncritical exaltation of traditional values (especially the family), and proud denial regarding the dark sides of its history (primarily the Mafia)" (p. 36).

Today, the Italian American community is different, a new community that wants to affirm a new identity; they are no longer the new immigrants or their descendants. Columbus Day, one of the great "ethnic" celebrations—along with Saint Patrick's Day—is now a festive occasion for everyone, not just Italian Americans (Bassetti, in Bassetti, d'Aquino, 2010). According to Bassetti, on Columbus Day, "We are no longer just celebrating what Italians have done for America, but rather what Italians—together with the Americans—have done for the world" (p. 111).

Canadé Sautman (2011) aims for a revitalization and a future of the identity, renewable by cultivating its "creolization," arguing that the creolization of Italian American identity can be built by taking inspiration from the cultural hybridization increasingly enacted within contemporary Italy as a response to racism, as well as on historical models based on racial/ethnic mixing and interfaces present in Italian American life. It would seem, therefore, that the desire of Italian Americans to articulate an identity through innovation and recreation finds much to emulate in the Italian practices of creolized cultural production.

Moreover, Canadé Sautman points out that Italian Americans have already experimented with cultural hybridization as well as the process of identity hybridization: "Linguistically and culturally, Italian Americans have incorporated a constantly evolving form of creolization. Upon their arrival, they spoke a mixture of Italian, Italian dialects, Italianized languages, dialectically conjugated with English, and English with local accents, or mixed with different languages, such as Albanian. On a cultural level, they have mixed, added, and invented, through the intersection of Italianized references and very American ways, tastes, and customs" (p. 135).

TRANSMISSION OF ITALIAN AMERICAN HERITAGE THROUGH THE FAMILY AND THE COMMUNITY

Chirico (2011b) observes that ethnic identity derives from the influence exerted by the family, rather than from the influences of society; it is also known that during the development of personal identity, when the expression of ethnicity is diminished in the family, young people will end up using other means—such as friends' families or media sources like films, TV shows, and music videos—to find ideas to affirm their ethnic identity. This is one of the reasons—Chirico adds—why Michael Corleone or Tony Soprano become role models.

Thus, in the young people's formation of identity, it is important to know which referents to emulate. Numerous studies have highlighted the fact that, in order to internalize parental values, children must perceive them as having been endorsed by their parents. Obviously, there is no guarantee that parental values will be preferred, but without any clearly defined ethnic or racial roles in the environment where adolescents live, they will be forced to find other sources and, "The media will be happy to provide [models] which are usually linked to consumption" (Chirico, 2011b, p. 195).

As Gardaphé notes (2004), the key to giving Italian American culture meaning that makes sense for today's youth is to ensure, first of all, that they have access to the stories of their families and their communities. In addition, young people also need to familiarize themselves with historical and contemporary models in the arts, business, and education—models that they can study, emulate, and overcome (Gardaphé, 2004, p. 19). He reminds us that "the Italian identity was formed both from history and from stories" (Gardaphé, 2008). To move beyond the experiences of immigration it is important for Italian Americans to know their personal history and that of the whole group. Without this, "they will remain tied to how others identify them: as gangsters, buffoons, obsessed with the production and consumption of food, as well as in the number of other ways in which society packages and consumes products inspired by Italian culture" (ibid., p. 10). Without this knowledge, Italian Americans, as well as other ethnic groups, will only react by incorporating what others produce, which will keep them from creating their own expressions: "Italian Americans have been defined by others, not by themselves" (ibid.).

According to Cappelli (2015a), identity construction is about acquiring a self-awareness that implies "a process of social and political self-categorization, in both an individual and group sense" (p. 15). He states that, more than "to distinguish the boundaries of their experience in America, Italian Americans need to acknowledge their allies (the other ethnic groups, immigrants or natives) as well as their opponents: namely the ethnic-racial prejudices of the dominant WASP culture, whose defeat would signify the success of multicultural integration in the country" (ibid.).

Life in traditional societies—in the Italian villages that the migrants had left— was based on daily contact, on the constant interaction between families and friends, and the shared knowledge background, and the ancestors' life stories handed down through oral tradition, passing through the generations to preserve the memory, so that "the past was always part of the present" (Gardaphé, 2004, p. 22). This also happened in the Italian immigrant neighborhoods, in the Little Italies, where the extended family and the villagers kept the oral tradition alive, relegating the use of reading and writing to sporadic occasions of an economic or social nature. The abandonment of the Little Italies, due in many cases to the need to live closer to the workplace, marked the growing diffusion of the Italian American presence in the outlying and multicultural areas and a consequent loss of access to the past handed down orally; the cause of this disappearance is attributed to the rarefaction of personal and direct relationships, since these were what characterized the components of traditional communities. The transition from urban ethnicity to suburban ethnicity also marked a social change from the working class to the middle class.

Lacking a written history and memory, personal stories were supplanted by a "public history that distorted the common representation of Italian Americans through the presentation and maintenance of stereotypes" (Gardaphé, 2004, p. 39). To counter the mass media's power that proposed and reiterated the stereotyped images of Italian Americans and to enable an evolution of Italian American culture, the need became clear—now in the fourth and fifth generation of immigration—to rely increasingly on the written word to document one's own story: "The evolution of Italian American culture is very dependent on the ability to produce a written history. Without these stories, the future Italian Americans will lose... the connection with their ancestral roots.... We say that tradition has been created only when the present will interact with the past" (ibid., pp. 22–23).

Tamburri (2015a) reiterates the importance of knowing one's own culture and history as one of the first steps for looking towards the future; this action also unites what he calls "a healthy dose of Italian/American self-love" (ibid, 52). He concludes that everything depends on "knowing how to recapture our own self-love, combining it with our ability (...) to document, maintain, transmit, and spread our Italian / American culture; doing any less than this is tantamount to failure" (ibid., 56).

Following Maalouf (1998), history is not synonymous with nostalgia or traditionalism: "It encompasses everything that has been built up over the centuries: memory, symbols, institutions, language, works of art, things to which we can be legitimately attached" (p. 43). The future will not be a mere extension of history, but must be built in a spirit of continuity, with profound transformations and significant external contributions. Perhaps it is worth reflecting on the fact that the future—in whatever context it is applied—"will be what we will do with it" (p. 95) and the notion of identity is interpreted as the "sum total of our memberships." Maalouf, recalling a quote from Marc Bloch, argues that "men are more sons of their own time than of their fathers" and emphasizes the fact that "young people often do not have the slightest idea what life could have been like for their grandparents, not to mention for previous generations" (p. 96). He adds: "In reality, we are all infinitely closer to our contemporaries than to our ancestors," not only in appearance, clothing, work, ways of living, but also in moral conceptions, ways of thinking, and beliefs.

Therefore, each of us—referring again to Maalouf—is the recipient of two legacies: "horizontal," which derives from one's own era and contemporaries, and "vertical," which comes from one's ancestors, from the traditions of one's people, from one's community in whatever form it takes. Between the two, the horizontal seems to be more crucial even if "this perception"—Maalouf observes—"is not reflected in our perception of ourselves. We do not empower ourselves through the 'horizontal' heritage, but the other" (1998, p. 97). Even the notion of identity—in the light of these considerations—is presented in two distinct aspects: "On one hand, there is what we are in reality... creatures who share their essential references, behavior, and beliefs with the vast community of their contemporaries. And on the other, there is what we think we are—what we claim to be—that is, members of one community and not of another. . . . It is above all. . . to highlight the fact that there is an abyss between what we are and what we believe we are" (ibid., pp. 97–98).

THE TRANSMISSION OF ITALIAN AMERICAN HERITAGE THROUGH INSTITUTIONS

Another important referent that operates in the transmission of cultural heritage is represented by institutions: artistic, cultural, economic, educational, political, and religious (Gardaphé, 2008). They complement the family in the passage of social and cultural values. Thus, cultural and educational institutions are tasked with passing on cultural background, not only inside, but also outside the Italian American community; for this to happen, the constituent intellectuals must work within and beyond these communities (Gardaphé, 2004, p. 42). According to Gardaphé, Italian American intellectuals have an essential guiding role capable of providing a fundamental impulse to the continuous affirmation of Italian American culture as well as indicating the path to strengthen that culture: without their contribution, "Italian Americans will choose to assimilate to the dominant American culture and lose contact with both the past and present of Italian culture" (Gardaphé, 2015, p. 153).

They are called to adapt their roles to the social and cultural dynamics that mark the changes in the United States and originate in the presence of different racial and ethnic groups that comprise the population. The task of the intellectual changes from "narrator of what happened"—a role that Tamburri (2015b) claims may tend more toward nostalgia than analysis—to "cultural examiner" and "cultural mediator" (p. 92).

Finally, if the transmission of one's cultural heritage takes place not only through the family but also, and increasingly, through the institutions, it is important to ensure that these institutions are receptive to the Italian cultural heritage and pay attention to the identity of Italian Americans (Gardaphé, 2010, p. 9). Academically, this step will be possible only when Italian American studies become a stable part of the program of American studies; this transition begins with their very creation (Gardaphé, 2008).

Projects developed in Italian American studies are not the result of direct, popular political action; indeed, political activity to support their development is a recent strategy. The formal constitution of Italian American studies began when scholars trained in the United States concentrated, in their disciplinary sphere, on the cultural output of Americans of Italian descent. This effort began as an individual action by American researchers. During the sixties it produced works by Italian American intellectuals that were based on the study of their own culture.

In 1967, the *American Italian Historical Association* was founded (which became the *Italian American Studies Association*), which became known for producing some of the best Italian American criticism. Over the years, many institutions have offered individual courses in Italian American studies: among these, the *Center for Italian American Studies*, which is based at Nassau Community College in Long Island; the *Brooklyn College Center for Italian American Studies, Center for Italian Studies* at Stony Brook University; and *the Joseph and Elda Coccia Institute for the Italian Experience in America* at Montclair State University in New Jersey. These institutions are accompanied by activities carried out at the national level by the *National Italian American Foundation* (NIAF), which was founded in 1975 and is based in Washington, D.C., and in the New York area by institutes and research centers that promote, disseminate, and preserve Italian and Italian American culture. Notable among these are the *John D. Calandra Italian American Institute, Casa Italiana Zerilli-Marimó, Casa Belvedere—The Italian Cultural Foundation*, and *Westchester Italian Cultural Center*. Amid the associations, organizations, and foundations committed to the promotion and enhancement of Italian American and Italian cultural heritage, there are *the Columbus Citizens Foundation, the National Organization of Italian American Women* (NOIAW), *the Order Sons of Italy in America* (OSIA), *UNICO* (the largest Italian American service organization in the United States), *New York Italians*, and many others.[1]

According to Tamburri (2015a), the past and present awareness of Italian American culture and its transmission to the younger generation passes through two channels: the first is linked to the presence of people who are involved in disseminating the information necessary to build this awareness, that is, teachers and lecturers at all levels; the second is through links to "cultural philanthropy." Tamburri argues that it is necessary to set up chairs of Italian/American culture and establish Italian/American study centers. Moreover, he emphasizes the importance of involving Italian American political representatives in the Italian/American discourse, which must be increasingly aimed at promoting and disseminating what has been achieved so far in a broader way.

Gardaphé (2010) argues that the battles of the first generations were fought and won on the economic and social front, while the battles of immigrants' grandchildren must be fought on the cultural front. It is therefore necessary to strengthen a positive cultural identity—created within the walls of the home—to maintain it and to demonstrate the continuity of this identification even outside of those walls (p. 7). To effectively change the image of Italian Americans in America, financial resources must be invested to promote a representation that Italian Americans can accept (Gardaphé, 2010). Not only that: it also means intervening to determine an appropriate perception of the Italian American cultural heritage. This is to suggest that people of various artistic talents come out of the shadows of their communities so that their art reaches the general public. He notes that the number of people taking part in events, conferences, exhibitions, and so on is minimal compared to those who see media representations such as *The Sopranos*, or *Goodfellas*.

THOUGHTS OF THE YOUNG PEOPLE INTERVIEWED ON THE FUTURE OF ITALIAN AMERICAN CULTURE

In the young people's world, two opposing tendencies seem to confront each other within the logic of "glocalism." Bassetti (Bassetti, d'Aquino, 2010) argues that "young people today are aiming for total cosmopolitanism but also, many times, for total localism. Their sense of borders is ever decreasing, but we often see them engaged in attitudes... defending 'small is beautiful,' for what they consider their territory" (p. 95). Later on, he notes the importance of not abandoning the search for identity and belonging by the young. *Italicità* offers a response in this direction:

> If (they) are convinced that the old national and nationalist memberships are outdated, then they must rediscover—not only local belonging... but also memberships that bring them closer to cosmopolitanism. *Italicità* is precisely the reply for this direction. It is not a new citizenship.... It does not require any eradication. Instead it requires adherence to a rich and complex system of meta-national values. It proposes, especially to young people, an additional membership that is neither exclusive nor exclusionary. It is a tool to find new belongings within the dialectic between global and local; to face the new challenges between value systems that different civilizations are bringing to the table (Bassetti & D'Aquino, 2010, pp. 96–97).

But is this the direction the interviewees are going?

In order to understand their opinions regarding the future of Italian American culture and their ideas for the maintenance and development of a sense of belonging to it by successive generations, two sets of questions were proposed, which provided a degree of agreement as a modality of response to the proposed statements. Two open questions were included at the end of the questionnaire, seeking to indicate predictions by young people regarding the future of Italian American culture and their personal suggestions for keeping it alive.

With regard to the first question battery, Table 9.1 highlights the responses provided by the young, re-aggregated according to the "very much/somewhat" and "little/not at all" degrees of agreement given to the items listed. As you can see, great emphasis is placed (74% of respondents) on the role of the family in transmitting their traditions to their children and on the importance of organizations in continuing to promote and enhance Italian culture (70%). Conversely, it is noted that almost 73% of young people agree only slightly or do not agree that knowledge of the history of the Italian people is not important. Furthermore, the percentage of those who are "little or not at all in agreement" with the possibility of offering money to preserve Italian traditions, as well as those who are

Table 9.1 How much do you agree (percentage values)

	VERY MUCH/ SOMEWHAT	LITTLE/ NOT AT ALL
It is important that the Italian traditions learned by the family are transmitted to the children	73.9	6.2
Organizations that promote Italian culture are important	69.0	10.1
It is too bad that Italian traditions are not carried on by many young people	63.9	15.5
The Italian American community should pay more attention to the needs of younger people	62.4	16.9
We need centers where young people can learn about Italian and Italian American culture	61.8	17.7
Mass media project a distorted, usually negative image of the Italian Americans	58.5	21.3
Public schools should teach more about the contributions of the Italian people to the U.S.	54.9	24.5
We should be willing to give money to preserve Italian traditions	50.9	28.5
Children should learn to speak Italian	50.6	28.5
We don't need to know the history of the Italian people	6.5	72.6

"little or not at all in agreement" that children learn to speak Italian, is equal to 28.5%. Yet almost a quarter of respondents indicate "little or not at all in agreement" with the proposition that public schools should supply more information about the contributions offered by Italians to American history.

The second battery of questions focused on some proposals to maintain and develop the feeling of belonging to Italian American culture by future generations. Table 9.2 is divided into two blocks with the degree of "very much/somewhat" agree with the statements listed on one side and, on the other "a little/not at all" agreement with them.

At the top of the list of indications of "very much" and "somewhat" agree, there are statements emphasizing the role and active involvement of young people: 68% of respondents believe it is very much/somewhat important that existing organizations become more relevant to young people and over 67% of respondents believe that it is very much/somewhat important to support the younger generations of Italian Americans in new cultural forms of creativity and expression. As you can see, the emphasis is placed on young people—that is, on the interviewees themselves—regarding the desire to feel involved and to take

Table 9.2 How much do you agree (percentage values)

	VERY MUCH/ SOMEWHAT	A LITTLE/ NOT AT ALL
Making the existing organizations more relevant to youth	67.9	8.7
Giving more support to the young Italian American generations to improve their cultural forms of expression and creativity	67.2	9.8
Being more active to promote a positive image of Italian Americans through the media	65.0	11.9
Creating long-term planning in terms of the exchange and collaboration between Italy and the U.S.	64.6	12.7
Using new forms of social media to reach young Italian Americans	64.2	13.0
Teaching the history and culture of the places of origin to the Italian immigrants to the U.S.	63.2	13.8
Reinforcing Italian American studies programs in the U.S. educational system	58.8	17.7
Promoting Italian American cultural initiatives in Italy	57.8	19.1
Reforming the existing organizations and associations	53.8	23.1
Other ideas	6.0	9.4

responsibility for passing on Italian American culture to the future. Sixty-five percent of the sample consider it important to be more active in promoting a positive image of Italian Americans through the media, and the same percentage of respondents claim they consider the long-term exchange and collaboration programs between Italy and the United States to be very important. Sixty-four percent of respondents emphasize the importance of using social media to reach young Italian Americans.

Conversely, the column that summarizes the responses aggregated based on "a little or not at all in agreement" reveals in the first place those who show a low agreement with the initiatives for reforming existing organizations and associations (23%). Moreover, almost 20% show little agreement on the possibility of promoting Italian American cultural initiatives in Italy and over 17% consider themselves unwilling to strengthen the programs of Italian American studies in the U.S. educational system.

The future of Italian American culture, according to the idea that the young interviewees have of it, was analyzed through an open question. Their answers were then re-aggregated into synthetic categories, and the percentage frequency distribution was calculated. Table 9.3 emphasizes how one-fifth, respectively, of the sample is placed in two opposing positions: on the one hand there are those who believe that the Italian American culture is declining, decreasing, and diluting. On the other hand, there are those who support the continuity of its existence. More than 12% of respondents believe that this culture will disappear, it will be lost, and will be assimilated, while 8% say it will change and evolve.

The last question in the questionnaire, in open form, asked young people to indicate their personal suggestions and proposals to keep the Italian American culture alive. The 165 responses obtained were analyzed and re-aggregated according to the twelve interpretative categories proposed below:

Table 9.3 The future of the Italian American culture (percentage values)

	%
It will continue to exist	19.9
It will disappear, be lost, die off, be assimilated	12.3
It will grow, evolve, change	7.9
It will decline, diminish, and be diluted	20.9
I don't know, N/A	39.0

1 *Spread the "real" culture, avoid using negative images and stereotypes; promote the positive aspects of Italian American culture and its contribution to American society:*

> Urge the media and TV programmers to show more realistic images and portrayals of Italian Americans. They [sic] are far more Italian Americans working in professional fields like doctors, lawyers, cops, firefighters, teachers, contractors, and bankers than there are Italian American mobsters. But the majority of Italian American imagery on TV is that mobsters. This is an unrealistic portrayal compared to the percentage or ratio in the real world. This imagery gives a negative representation to not Italians of what it is to be Italian American.

> My personal suggestion is for the Italian American youth to inform themselves on what Italian culture REALLY is so we can stop giving ourselves a negative and false image to show the world.

2 *Enhance knowledge through education; combat a rigid and static vision; promote art, Italian, and Italian American culture (including food).*

> Particularly important is the observation that introduces the paragraph, where it is highlighted that—in order to make the cultural transition effective—it must satisfy those who are involved, both in terms of the relevance attributed to this culture, but also for the satisfaction that it brings from an emotional point of view:

> It needs to be both relevant and emotionally satisfying for those involved in order for it to be both taught and continued.

> Offer more opportunities for the youth—classes, trips, jobs. Education is key.

3 *Uphold and teach values and traditions (festivals, events...):*

> Know one's own family history and cultural heritage; embrace and preserve the oral history of immigrants who are still alive; practice the traditions actively, not just knowing them (keeping tradition alive); affirm the importance of understanding and knowing where we come from.

Gather the oral history of those immigrants still alive in the country from Italy and make sure they're stored somewhere prominent and accessible. The value, as with most things, is in the story.

We must never lose sight of why we are passing on tradition and information—it is important to know one's heritage. It gives insight into how we think, do, feel and act.

4 *Recreate and strengthen the generational pact*:

The "elders" must transmit culture and traditions to young people, especially to children; the elderly must accept and embrace the changing times and means of communication used by young people; moreover, there must be a change of perspective that "targets the youth."

Older folks need to make it a point to keep traditions and cultural in the lives of children from a young age.

The older generation needs to realize that the world is rapidly changing and that the younger generation is their hope for combining on the heritage. They need to stay away from older ideas and embrace more modern ideas. Example—get involved with social media, not email lists. Encourage online courses for Italian language, not school-based courses. Promote authentic Italian cuisine, not Olive Garden–esque cuisine. Teach Italian history using tactile learning techniques, not verbal or auditory.

5 *Instill Italian and Italian American culture and traditions, especially in young children; create a sense of community among the children*:

Teaching our children traditions we hold important to us and encourage them to take Italian in school to learn not only the language, but to learn more about Italy and its history alongside all of the contributions Italians have made.

Kids should learn more about their culture when they are growing up, not just when they start high school and take a language course. If kids grow up without learning about their culture they just assimilate into the American culture and have no connection to their roots.

Education for the youth is imperative to keep alive the Italian American culture. I think children should be taught the language of their ancestors and the history. Travel programs should be encouraged where the entire family can participate. I believe that elementary schools especially in neighborhoods with a high percentage of Italian Americans should be teaching the children Italian, not Spanish or French. Children will be more motivated to learn their heritage language and this will also boost their self-esteem and self-worth when their Nonna or Nonno can help them with their homework or when they can take a family trip to Italy and communicate with their Italian relatives.

Create schools for bigger awareness of Italian American culture for young children. Encourage learning Italian and visiting Italy as a young child, so that Americans can actually be exposed to Italy, rather than the idea of Italy they know from other Italian Americans.

6 *Parental and family responsibility is important in transmitting culture to young people (parents and grandparents)*:

It all starts with the family. We need to reach out to parents and give them tools to teach their kids about Italian and Italian American history and culture.

It has to be done in the home, first, then in centers and communities.

For families to continue to interact for many occasions, holidays, family dinners, going to church together and continuing to keep an open and feeling of togetherness going throughout the time they spend together. And also to keep the food and recipes from past generations and keep them going too.

It is very important to keep the traditions at home. Parents need to keep the history alive at home so the children have a connection and interest with the culture. Taking children to Italian events and cultural centers will continue what they start at home.

I think that nuclear and extended families preserving authentic Italian traditions, customs, and ideals and passing them on in the home to their children is the best way to keep alive the Italian American culture.

I think the key to keeping Italian American culture alive is the family. Community organizations and clubs may be helpful, but I believe teaching Italian traditions to children and being part of it while growing up ingrain the traditions in them and makes them a normal part of life.

7 *It is important to have a vision/contact with modern Italy; it is important to study its art, literature, history; moreover, it is essential to travel to Italy, as well as to use social networks*:

As often as possible, expose your children to real Italian culture (make sure they hear you speaking in Italian or listening to an Italian song, put on Italian TV or Radio Stations or Movies, etc.). Have more young people visit Italy, if possible for an educational purpose (not just vacation). Make sure Italian Americans know who their Italian relatives are, if there are any, and establish contacts with them. Make sure Italian American parents teach their Italian American children where they came from and why they should be proud.

Bring people to Italy. There is no place better to learn about Italian culture and customs then Italy itself. There is enough exposure of American culture in America, so bring people somewhere where they are exposed to Italian culture and they can decide what aspects of Italian culture should be preserved in America.

8 *Learn/teach the Italian language*:

There needs to be a renewed effort on the part of parents need to teach their children the Italian language. Language can create an undeniable bond between Italian Americans. Without language, or travel back to the country, many Italian Americans are uninterested in attending the wonderful events put on the by some of the Italian American associations, because they simply can't identify fully or feel like they belong. This is one of the biggest discrepancies I find between Italian Americans and other ethnic groups. They stay more tightly knit because of a common language.

More practical applications and incentives for Americans (even those without Italian ancestry) to learn Italian. I really believe that language is the key to culture, and the unfortunate reality is that Americans today don't care about foreign language and culture because they don't have to.

9 *The role of organizations and the action of politicians is important: cultural promotion, reform of associations in the direction of their greater relevance for young people, passage of the "torch" to young people:*[2]

Politicians willing to promote Italian causes, Italian organizations remaining active and concerned, reaching out to youth.

More Italian organizations that cater to the youth, teaching them the language and culture in a FUN way that will interest them; Italian American groups must learn to work together.

Reformed organizations—Italian culture is great, but what steers me away from it is the extreme traditionalism, religion and sexism. America seems more liberal than Italy and that type of liberal thinking should be more integrated in these Italian American organizations.

Centers for Italian American studies and other organizations, agencies, etc. need to find a way to connect with today's Italian American youth and resurrect pride in Italian American heritage.

Current organizations have lost any relevance with youth.

10 *Promote associations among young Italian Americans; associations between working categories, as well as the creation of youth organizations;*

It is also important to encourage a sense of community among young people, create community cohesion (keep in touch and get together), and involve young people in the community.

Focus on the youth!! Make youth groups easy to find online and have them sponsored by larger Italian American foundations. They are as important, if not more important, than groups focused on the middle-aged Italian Americans. There are so many young professionals that will shape the future of the United States. Getting these people engaged in their community now, while they are young, is the only way to have them stay engaged later in life after their immigrant parents and grandparents pass away.

Create and promote social organizations for young Italian Americans, so that they join and have more contact with others of Italian descent.

Encourage young Italian Americans to get involved with more cultural organizations. A lot of educated young people like myself want to identify more with being a yuppie and less with being a particular ethnicity. Finding a way to marry the two might get more young folks involved.

There should also be more Italian American communities. Our "Little Italy" in New York City is really dwindling; we need to establish a community in more places for Italian Americans, and others who are interested, to unite.

Social media amplifies the voice of the individual, so it is an incredibly helpful tool in presenting both the shared experience, but also the diversity within the Italian American community. I think it's a huge opportunity to educate the public on Italian culture and Italian American culture.

Read one another's writing, visit one another's art exhibits, and continue learning about the foods and traditions of Italy. Reach out to other Italian Americans and create communities that celebrate past traditions but continue to make new ones.

I see in my community that the Chinese, Korean, and Greek people have after school learning centers that encourage the learning of their culture. They sing the songs that come from their backgrounds and learn their native languages. They form youth sports groups and religious learning. My husband is Greek and they have their own schools that teach the kids the language traditions and fundamentals of their culture. Also, when I do attend church with my husband the church is packed and afterward everyone gets together in the church cafeteria or sitting area for coffee and authentic Greek dishes. They are close knit and they all know their language. I wish that I could find a place like that for me as an American Italian!

Reach out to working professionals who are of that population and have a desire to know more of Italy and foster relationship building via various events.

Young people need to feel a sense of camaraderie rather than competition. Italian American kids should get to know each other while growing up, in situations outside of the church. We can't rely on that as increasingly people are paying less and less attention to those organizations. If there is a feeling that people are in a network of friends who want to help each other, everyone will feel more positively toward the community as a whole rather than just our own families. Members of organizations need to actively recruit and embrace people who are not part of the organization. These things tend to be very cliquey so without direct invitations most people who are not already involved won't want to be. The older folk should be looking for creative and dynamic young people who can carry on and keep things fresh and relevant.

Go deep into the Italian American communities and talk to the laborers and the lower middle class that are not the professionals at the front of the Italian American community and organizations. It is possible they just do not have the access to all this information.

11 *Understand the differences between young Italian Americans and new Italian youth immigrants; encourage meetings and contact between Italian Americans and Italians:*

Embrace change. Understand young Italian Americans and new Italian immigrants have different ideas, needs, and interests than Italian Americans of thirty, forty, fifty-plus years ago. Start to understand and promote new traditions and vision of Italy. Focus on more sophisticated and culturally relevant things like such as art (in all forms).

Encourage friendship and exchange between Italian Americans and Italians.

12 *Create events that involve both Italian American and other Americans, since it is important to participate in the events of other Americans with different backgrounds:*

Getting the word out there more and have more thing people can participate in.

Make it relevant and make sure people who are not one hundred percent Italian can still feel like they can be part of it and grow. De Blasio basically did that when he changed his name to his mother's maiden name from Warren Wilhelm. Make it relevant and make the appearance of legitimate success.

Subsequently, the frequency distributions of the emergent interpretative categories were calculated. The final picture is summarized in Table 9.4. More than 20% believe that values and traditions should be taught to future generations. In the second place on the list, the importance of learning Italian language, as well as parental and family responsibility in the transmission of cultural background, is highlighted. What emerges from the responses provided by the youth highlights, as in other parts of the study, the importance of transmitting values and traditions to future generations. The most significant transmitters of this information are parents and the family in general. This passage of information begins within the family and then continues through secondary socialization, not only instilling knowledge, but also producing love for one's origins and history.

Table 9.4 Suggestions for keeping Italian American culture alive (percentage values)

	%
Teaching values and traditions	20.6
Learning the Italian language	13.7
Parental and familial responsibility	13.4
Increasing knowledge through education	12.3
Promoting associations among young Italian Americans, building community	11.2
Spreading the authentic culture, promoting a positive image	9.7
Visiting and contact with Italy	8.7
Instilling the culture in children	6.1
Roles of the organizations	4.0
Promoting contacts between Italian Americans and Italians	3.2
Strengthen the generational pact	3.2
Promoting contacts between Italian Americans and other Americans with different backgrounds	2.9

10

Knowledge of and Attachment to the Italian and Italian American Cultures

In order to reach an explanatory summary that enables the construction of different identification models regarding Italian cultural heritage, two interpretative categories have been taken into consideration: first, the level of knowledge of the Italian and Italian American cultures and second, the attachment, the connection, and the emotional bond to these cultures. To obtain synthetic scores that would provide a measurement of the position of the respondents on the two continuums along which the two dimensions unfold, two factorial analyses were carried out. The first analysis established variables related to knowledge and cultural interest toward Italy, Italians, and Italian Americans; the second examined variables related to the perception, opinions, feelings, and attitudes related to the representation of Italians and of Italian Americans from an emotional and relational point of view.

THE LEVEL OF KNOWLEDGE OF ITALIAN AND ITALIAN AMERICAN CULTURE

To analyze the level of knowledge of Italian and Italian American culture, the answers obtained to the questions in the following areas were submitted to factorial analysis: (1) on knowledge of Italian and Italian American culture, (2) on the use and knowledge of Italian language and dialects, (3) on interest in Italian politics, culture, and economics, (4) on the news obtained on contemporary Italy, and (5) on the direct knowledge that the respondents have of Italy from having visited it. The result of the analysis to which the answers to the twenty-five questions summarized above were subjected made it possible to derive six factors, independent of each other, which synthetically represent the set of relations between the opinions expressed.

The first factor, which is also the most important in describing the level of knowledge of Italian and Italian American culture, can be called "knowledge of traditional popular culture" and collects the homogeneous opinions expressed regarding the knowledge of Italian and Italian American religious traditions, traditional festivals, songs, prayers, and ways of saying; the knowledge of Italian and Italian American traditions and customs is also present, albeit less clearly and homogeneously.

The second factor can be denoted as "historical, literary, artistic knowledge" and collects homogeneous answers to questions concerning the level of knowledge of Italian and Italian American history, literature, and artistic production.

The third factor—designated as "knowledge of contemporary Italy"—includes the items that refer to the use and knowledge of the Italian language and its dialects, visits to Italy, obtaining news about it, and interest in Italian culture in general.

The fourth factor, which can be referred to as "knowledge of folk tales and music," collects homogeneous answers to the items related to the knowledge of Italian and Italian American musicians, singers, and the folk tales of the two cultures.

The fifth factor, defined as "political-economic interest," collects the homogeneous answers to questions relating to interest in Italian politics and economics.

The sixth factor, finally, can be called "culinary knowledge": it contains the answers to the questions related to the knowledge of both Italian American and Italian recipes.

Once the factors described above were identified, the score on each of the factors was calculated for each interviewee. For the first factor, more than 86% of respondents recorded a score between 0.50 and 1. This indicates a very high level of "knowledge of traditional popular culture," considering that the scale respondents used to evaluate their own level of knowledge was between a lot (= 1) and nothing (= 0). It is primarily the males who attained the high scores, while the intermediate scores predominantly represent women. This indicates that a high level of knowledge of traditional popular culture especially characterizes males. The immigration generation also correlates significantly to scores (sig. = .000). The highest scores are mainly the second generation's prerogative, while scores from 0.67 and below are predominantly respondents of the fourth generation. Knowledge of traditional and popular culture is, therefore, higher among second generation youth. Social class also acts as a discriminator for the points (sig. = .026). There is a prevalent placement of middle-class youth on the score of 1, while the score 0.83 represents above all the young upper middle and upper class.

More than 90% of respondents generate scores between 0.50 and 1 on the second factor, which summarizes the level of "historical, literary and artistic knowledge." These data lead us to observe that there is an elevated level of historical, literary, and artistic knowledge among the vast majority of the interviewees. As in the previous factor, gender is a significant variant in the scores (sig. = .004). Once again, the males are distributed primarily over the scores between 0.83 and 1, while the intermediate scores—between 0.33 and 0.67—are primarily representative of women. As for the relationship with the generation of immigration, we observe that the score 1 (high degree of knowledge) especially represents the second generation, while those who are positioned on 0.67 and 0.83 fall mainly in the third generation.

The third factor represents the dimension linked to the level of "knowledge of contemporary Italy." Observing the trend of frequency distribution, it emerges that the sample of respondents is quite uneven regarding the level of knowledge of contemporary Italy. In summary, 37% of respondents receive the score of 0.25; 25.2% are positioned between 0.38 and 0.5; 26% are between 0.63 and 0.75; while the group of those who acquire scores between 0.88 and 1 is almost equal to 12 %. The immigration generation correlates significantly with the scores (sig. = .000). The lowest scores (from 0 to 0.25) are chiefly achieved by those belonging to the fourth generation, while the intermediate ones (from 0.38 to 0.5) are predominantly distributed to the young people belonging to the third generation and, finally, on high scores (from 0.63 to 1) there is the prevalence of those belonging to the second generation. Social class membership is also a discriminator for the points values. The higher points values are the prerogative especially of the upper middle class.

The fourth factor represents the level of "musical and folktale knowledge." Of those interviewed, 65% achieved scores of 0.66 and 1 on this factor, indicating high levels of knowledge of Italian and Italian American music and musicians.

On the fifth factor, which expresses "the political-economic interest toward Italy," more than half of the respondents reach a score between 0.50 and 1 which indicates a high interest in both the Italian economy and Italian politics. Conversely, the other half of the sample, instead, exhibit little or no interest in these issues. The intersection of the scores with gender shows that it is above all the males to place themselves on the score 1 (high degree of interest) down to the score 0.33, while the lowest scores—between 0 and 0.17—are mainly a feminine prerogative. Regarding membership in a social class, young people belonging to the upper middle class mostly have scores between 0.50 and 1, thus demonstrating a high interest for the economy and the Italian political scene.

"Culinary knowledge" tied to ethnic heritage appears quite high. Over 90% of respondents reach scores between 0.67 and 1 which express a high level of knowledge as well as the use of traditional Italian and Italian American recipes.

ATTACHMENT AND EMOTIONAL CONNECTION TO THE ITALIAN AND ITALIAN AMERICAN CULTURES

For a more in-depth understanding of the themes that make up the attachment and emotional connection with the ethnic background and cultural heritage of both cultures by the young people interviewed, thirty-two questions have been subjected to factorial analysis that considers their various aspects. The questions cover: (1) contacts with relatives and friends in Italy, (2) media used to stay in touch with the Italian American community, (3) attachment to regions and significant places, (4) chain of continuity regarding the sense of emotional attachment to Italy and the United States, (5) meaning and importance attributed to the ethnic background, (6) meanings and the sense of belonging connected to feeling Italian American, (7) sentiments connected to feeling Italian American, (8) contacts with the "new" Italian immigrants, (9) feelings and perceptions toward Italy. From the factorial analysis, nine synthetic factors emerged, independent of each other, which allow us to interpret the dimensions associated with the sense of attachment to the Italian and Italian American cultures and its components.

The first factor represents "attachment to family origins" and collects the homogeneous answers to the questions regarding contacts with relatives in Italy, visits to the family's places of origin, how one feels in various situations, European and Italian.

The second factor expresses "attachment to Italy." It includes the answers to the questions regarding the importance of ethnic background, to the feeling of attachment to Italy and to the Italian region/s from which their ancestors hail, to the intensity of the emotional bond with Italy over the course of time, and to feeling Italian American in different situations.

The third factor denotes "connection with Italian American culture." This factor collects the homogeneous answers to the questions regarding the sense of belonging to the Italian American community in the United States, feelings of belonging to the Italian American culture, and to the sense of connectedness with one's own Italian origins.

The fourth factor reveals the dimension tied to the "emotional value of belonging to the Italian American community." Responses here are related to the questions concerning the feeling of shame at being Italian American that can emerge in some circumstances, to that of pride linked to this belonging, and the conflict that can arise from one's ethnic background.

The fifth factor focuses on "interpersonal relations with Italians and Italian Americans." It collects the answers to the questions that refer to contacts with young Italians of recent immigration in the New York area, to those with Italian friends who live in Italy, to the use of social media for staying connected in the Italian American community, to the sense of belonging to a wide network of people who share Italian culture, its values, and its interests.

The sixth factor represents the feeling of "admiration toward Italy." Answers collected here express feelings of contempt and disappointment toward Italy as well as those of admiration and identification with it.

The seventh factor brings out the dimension of "attachment to the United States." These are the responses referring to feeling particularly American in some situations, to the emotional bond with the United States over time, and to the importance attributed to the different ethnic backgrounds of people's origin.

The eighth factor highlights "the importance of ethnic heritage." The answers that converge here refer to the two items where an opinion was asked regarding the fact that, over time, ethnic groups arriving in the United States are no longer significantly dissimilar from each other and to the fact of feeling "ethnic" or not in most cases.

Finally, the ninth and last factor, called the "value of ethnic heritage," collects homogeneous answers to questions regarding the special loyalty that people in America are able to nurture for their ethnic groups, the attribution of excessive relevance by some people to ethnic background, and the possible feeling of indifference toward Italian society, or toward what represents one's own personal ethnic background.

Once the factors were identified, the scores were calculated for each of them. Among the dimensions constituting the young Italian Americans' attachment and the emotional bond with their Italian ethnic heritage, "attachment to family origins" has turned out to be the first and thus also the most relevant factor. The calculation of the scores highlights the fact that more than 42% show a low attachment (from 0 to 0.2 points), 35% (from 0.3 to 0.6 points) an average attachment, and 23% of the interviewees show a strongly felt link (from 0.7 to 1 points) with Italian family origins. Analyzing this relationship with the other variables, we find that the immigration generation shows a significant differentiation of the scores (sig. = .000). Basically, it can be stated that the lowest scores are attained by those belonging to the fourth and fifth generation, while the highest scores (from 0.6 to 1) especially characterize the second generation of the sample.

The second factor expresses the dimension of "attachment to Italy" and increasing scores indicate a higher strength of the link. The lowest score—0—was not reached by any of the respondents. Overall, the attachment to Italy appears strongly felt. In fact, in this factor, over 48% obtain a point value between 0.83 and 1. Twelve percent of the interviewees, conversely, express a low attachment to Italy (from 0.17 to 0.33 points), while the strength of the connection expressed by the intermediate points values (from 0.50 to 0.67) characterizes 39% of the interviewees. The relationship with immigration generation (sig. = .000) shows that primarily those belonging to the second generation attain the higher points values in this case.

"Connection with Italian American culture" is felt in a strong way by more than 56% of the interviewees, who achieve values between 0.83 and 1 for this factor. Just over 14% express a feeling of low attachment to it (0 and 0.33) and 29% of the interviewees are on intermediate scores (0.50 and 0.67). Age is a significant discriminator of the points value in this factor (sig. = .014). The score 0.33 mainly designates young people aged between twenty-four and twenty-nine, while the score of 0.67 is reached above all by the thirty-year-olds. For the score 1, which expresses the maximum degree of attachment to the Italian American culture, we notice a decreasing trend from the youngest to age thirty.

The "emotional value of belonging to the Italian American community" appears to be very strong for more than half of the interviewees. This is another factor that included no instances of a score of 0. Eleven percent express a low level of attachment (from 0.17 to 0.33) and 27% an average degree (from 0.50 to 0.67) on this dimension. The relationship with the immigration generation is significant (sig. = .012) and shows that it is predominantly young people belonging to the second generation who obtain low scores on this factor, while the scores between 0.67 and 0.83 chiefly connote young people of the fourth generation. The score 1—which expresses the maximum degree of emotional attachment to the Italian American community—especially characterizes the young people of the third generation.

If we analyze the expression of "interpersonal relationships between young Italian Americans and Italians" through the scores on the factor that represents them, it emerges that this area is not a "strong" dimension for more than half of the interviewees, who achieve scores between 0 and 0.25. Thirty percent reach intermediate scores—from 0.38 to 0.63—and only 10% demonstrate an active, participatory relationship with young Italian and Italian American peers (scores between 0.75 and 1). Generation of immigration serves as a discriminator in this points value. The highest scores—from 0.75 to 1—are occupied primarily by second-generation youths, while the remaining generations are positioned on other scores.

The dimension of "admiration toward Italy" shows that over 82% of the interviewees reach a score of 1 in this factor, expressing strong feelings of admiration and identification toward Italy.

The factor that expresses the "connection of the interviewees with the United States" indicates a very strong link for more than 50% of the respondents who achieve high scores, between 0.75 and 1. Only 8% are positioned on a points value equal to 0.25 or to 0. Gender represents a variable that discriminates the scores in the factor significantly (sig. = .055): it is primarily girls who feel the bond toward the United States less strongly compared to the males.

Regarding the factor that indicates "the importance of ethnic heritage" for young people, it is noted that over 67% of those interviewed attribute great importance in this case. Those who do not consider ethnic heritage as important—obtaining scores of 0.25 and 0—are represented by over 31% of the sample. Gender serves as a discriminator in the points' value (sig. = .030). Males prevail among those who consider ethnic heritage to be very important.

The last factor that emerges from the factorial analysis represent the "value of ethnic heritage." The high scores express the idea that this attachment still counts a lot in America while, conversely, the lower ones express a position of detachment from the value of this heritage. From the frequency distribution of the scores it is observed that the respondents favor the intermediate scores with a frequency equal to over 62% (between 0.38 and 0.63). Just over 31% are placed on the highest scores, expressing the highest value attributed to ethnic heritage. This factor does not display significant relationships with other variables.

From the analysis of the data it emerges, in short, how the passing of time makes people slowly forget the origins from which they come. Furthermore, there seems to be a tendency for girls to acquire the culture of the host nation more quickly than boys.

PART II

IDENTITY PROFILES

11

The Italian American
Identity in Generational Flux

PREMISE

Italian American identity has faced conflicts, ambivalences, as well as losses, and Italians in America have constantly renegotiated the relationship between local cultures and their own origins. Each of the generations has rebuilt and reinvented this identity and has been marked by breakages and divergences[1] as changes over time have affected values, myths, and metaphorical interpretations that formed the basis for the first immigrant's entry into American society (Gardaphé, 2004).

Gambino (1974) observes that ethnic groups, in their journey toward a new identity, go through three phases: in the first one, access to the wider society is not available to the group; this was the case for Italian immigrants as well as other European ethnic groups. In the second stage, the group self-reproaches and feels guilt regarding its difference; it avoids contact and places itself in a subordinate position with respect to society. This period especially characterized the second generation of European ethnic groups and particularly the Italian Americans. In the third phase, the group is faced with two possibilities. Its members can let the old values die and become "American jellyfish, transparent souls in search of the superficial" (p. 357), or they can revitalize their traditions and contribute in new ways to enrich American culture.

From the mid-nineteenth century to the second half of the twentieth century, America had transformed from a predominantly agricultural society to an industrial one and, later, into a society where white-collar workers represented a major occupation. The significance of the general process of structural mobility was accentuated by the parallel change of the system of education which, at the high school level, went from selective to mass (Alba, 1985). The impact of emigration for the Italians of America had profound repercussions at both the working and the family level.

In terms of work, the most significant change was the shift from predominantly agricultural occupations in Italy to jobs that revolved around the urban and industrialized economies of large cities and surrounding areas where Italian immigrants settled mainly in the United States (Lopreato, 1970). Changes in the family system, in the case of Italian immigrants, did not translate—as highlighted by considerable sociological and historical literature—into a break in the family balance with consequent failures, separations, and disruptions; instead, it resulted in the consolidation of the extended family (Kessner, 1977). The connections within the family were activated by immigration and became crucial links as part of the migration chain (Alba, 1985).

CONSTRUCTION OF THE ITALIAN AMERICAN IDENTITY

The complex Italian American culture has long resisted assimilation, and the English spelling of *Italian American* expresses that cultural history in a single term with five possible ways to represent it, ways that correspond to different phases of the assimilation of Italian immigrants in the United States (Muscio, 2007a): Italo Americans (1870–1929), Italian-Americans (1930–1941), Americans (1942–1959), Italian Americans (1960–1990), and now American Italians. The two terms, detached at the beginning, reflected the condition of six million Italians who emigrated to North America; their terminological separation reflected the social distance between Italians and Americans. During the first years of settlement in American society, the Italian community locked itself up within Little Italies: if this produced isolation and marginalization on the one hand, on the other it favored the preservation of the immigrants' particular identities. Parochialism and regionalism were two criteria that guided subdivision by origin in the neighborhoods of the Little Italies, where the Italian immigrants kept their regional dialects and their local traditions alive, to not least of the gastronomic ones that have always been at the center of the Italian identity, both in Italy and abroad (Vecoli, 2002). Most central was the family, a fundamental institution of the community in America (Barzini, 1964).

The second phase, "with the hyphens," was established in the 1930s. This was the product of the change of perspective and openness to ethnic diversity brought on, on the one hand, by the New Deal and on the other, by the fascist regime in Italy, which displayed a certain political interest in "Italians abroad." The introduction of the hyphen meant that *Italo* became a qualifying adjective of *American*, thus expressing the awareness "Italo-Americans" possessed regarding their diversity: they were primarily American, but with a different cultural origin. Moreover, the hyphen served as an indication of the integration and understanding of the two identities (Muscio, 2007a). In reality, the "hyphen" did not express—according to what Aaron (1964) highlights and Tamburri (1991) recalls—a sense of closeness between the two cultures. On the contrary, it initially represented the reluctance of the dominant group to accept the new arrivals, the tendency to keep them at "a hyphen's length from the established community" (Tamburri, 1991, p. 43). Thus, the hyphen is not a connective component, and it is even "more of a disjunctive element when it is used in a dyad indicating national origin, ethnicity, race, or gender. It is... a 'colonializing sign' that hides its own ideological and subjugating force by trying to play it off as grammatical accuracy" (ibid., p. 44).

During the 1930s, Italian Americans developed their own modern culture, which emerged clearly in literature, film, and even in politics, where the figure of Fiorello La Guardia became well known. Furthermore, the international prestige that Italy achieved with the establishment of Mussolini's dictatorship stimulated the ethnic pride of Italian Americans and their identification with Italy, even if there were many opponents of fascism among them (Luconi, 2007).

This beginning phase of a virtuous cycle was interrupted by the war, during which the Italian became an enemy of the acquired homeland; immigrants thus abandoned their mother tongue and tried to hide all the signs of their original culture, and even, in extreme cases, Americanized their surnames. The generation spanning from the World War II to the sixties suppressed *italianità* in favor of an almost total assimilation. They had become Americans, and the assimilation they had once refused was now willfully and forcibly sought. It was a generation in the balance between inborn *italianità* and acquired "American-ness" (divided loyalties), a generation that pursued the process of Americanization despite a perceived diversity between itself and the Americans (Casella, 1998).

Ethnic identity along national lines, which surfaced first in the decades before the outbreak of the war, was consolidated and, during the years of World War II, a new racial identity emerged for Italian Americans: "Faced with the growing polarization of US society divided by color, Italian Americans definitively abandoned the intermediate racial connotation that had characterized them at the end of the previous century and began to see their place among the whites" (Luconi, 2007, p. 41). At the end of the war, during the fifties, Italian Americans became increasingly involved in American society, achieving good results in the field of scholastic education and in the labor market where they established themselves in increasingly prestigious positions. Those years also witnessed a new wave of immigration composed of Italians who decided to join their relatives established in America, due to social and economic problems at home after the end of the war. American-ness thus became a fundamental and voluntarily sought component by Italian Americans. The 1960s marked an important phase for the Italian American community which, at that time, had successfully established itself in the U.S. landscape, particularly in the field of cinematography through names like Francis Ford Coppola and Martin Scorsese. The civil rights movement took place in those years, in a context of aspiring to multicultural tolerance.

The two components of identity amalgamated and merged into the term that then identified them as Italian Americans. This signaled a process of integration that saw Italian Americans as protagonists in a growing number of evidentiary instances including employment and education in their rise into the middle class. Those years saw the birth of various associations for the protection of the Italian American community, which, through reinforcement from the mass media, were continually associated with organized crime, offering this negative and stereotyped collective representation to the general public.

Since the eighties, there has been a revival of the image of Italians in America, and *italianità* was associated—in a phase marked by materialism and consumerism in the United States (as Sorokin and Veblen observed)—to good taste and to refinement, especially in the food and fashion industries. From a study carried out in those same years among Italian immigrants in Toronto by Demaria Harney (1998) and quoted by Krase (2004) it emerged that there was, at the beginning of that decade, a transformation in the way in which *italianità* and the Italian community were imagined.

> The image of the Italians and of *italianità* was remodeled. People who were once considered to be rural simpletons became entrepreneurs of simple projects, testimony to an ancient wisdom, or innovators in the field of fashion and industrial design. The representation of Italians as organized criminals was thus transformed into that of Italian businessmen—hardworking and rich in intuition and insight. The result of all this was that the children of Italian immigrants had to grapple with new meanings through which to build their

italianità: the meanings of work, education, and gender changed with the generational transition, leading to the creation of misunderstandings. (Harney, 1998, quoted by Krase, 2004, pp. 172–73)

Many Italian Americans rediscovered their ties with Italy through travel, study of the language, and recognition of the greatness of Italian artistic and cultural heritage.

In more recent times, a new Italian American definition has been affirmed, summarized in the term *American Italian*, though it is rarely used in common language, where *Italian American* is still preferred (Muscio & Spagnoletti, 2007). Between Italian Americans and American Italians there are different nuances of meaning: in the first case we refer to the prevalence of the American component, as revealed by saying "of Italian origin." Instead, American Italians emphasizes the Italian component, as is the case when saying "Italians born in America." Then there is Tamburri's proposal (1991), which considers it more appropriate to replace the hyphen with the slash (Italian/American), thus obtaining the effect of overcoming the physical space between the two terms, placing them close to each other and thus also facilitating the reduction of ideological distance.

Italian American integration at every level in American society is now a fact; at the beginning of the second millennium the Italian American community has reached an excellent degree of social legitimization and does not need to confirm an established Americanism, "but it can claim the Italian origins, no longer a reason for shame, on the contrary, pride and glamorous identity" (Muscio, 2007a, p. 17).

Today, Italianness is associated with positive images, such as good food, style in dress and design, family unity, culture, all characteristics that have contributed to enhancing the sense of pride linked to this cultural and historical heritage with the certainty that the contribution of Italians has led to a positive change in American society. As Camaiti Hostert (2007) observed,

> Being Italian is no longer associated with the lack of something (in the specific case of physical and behavioral characteristics regarding the WASP canons), but instead to something more, consisting of the presence of articulated manifestations of feeling. What once condemned them to be second-class citizens not only makes them richer today, but has also contributed to making the society around them richer, through the ability to express emotions and passions.... They are also capable, after having compared one with another, of achieving an inner balance that helps to improve relationships among their

own group and also shows the ability to review their roles not only within the family, but also in the society where they live, presenting at first glance an ethnic background freed from those stereotypes to which they had condemned themselves. (p. 139).

THE FIRST GENERATION OF IMMIGRANTS AND ITS IMPACT ON AMERICAN SOCIETY

For the first generation of Italian immigrants, America was perceived in strong contrast to Italy, creating identity conflict. For them, it represented, above all, a metaphor of separation, and one of the first battles that the immigrants had to confront was identification with America (Gardaphé, 2004, p. 14). From the first moment they arrived, they immediately realized their difference, their non-Americanness, and this produced a primitive confrontation between "me," the Italian, and "the other," the American. This created in them a kind of confusion of what was and was not American, and this confusion extended to the next generation: "It was not a problem of knowing what being American was; rather, the problem came in trying to avoid everything that common knowledge said being American was not" (p. 16).

The mindset of Italian immigrants at the time of the great migration had formed in the traditional country culture of rural Southern Italy, and the transplant to America was not able to change this identity structure. This strong rooting of immigrants in Southern Italian society profoundly influenced the Italian American group in the sense that it was shaped by the culture and characteristics of this society, which also influenced the American perception of Italian Americans (Alba, 1985). J. Guglielmo (2003) observes, in fact, that "Southern Italy was more than a geographical space with flexible borders... it was a metaphor for anarchy, rebellion, poverty, and the lack of 'civilization'" (p. 9).

First-generation immigrants did not speak English, dreamed of returning home, and therefore did not want to send their children to school. They feared losing control over them and that they would forget the link with their community of origin: it "is not an abstract 'distant homeland', but a village with a name—perhaps distorted—whose faded postcard is preserved with religious affection" (Muscio, 2007b). In the cities, Italians would gravitate toward areas that contained other Italians, in ethnic colonies or enclaves, the Little Italies.[2] Even within them, residents maintained their regional origins; immigrants from the same provinces or cities settled next to each other, forming "Little Sicilies" or

"Little Calabrias": "The Old World parochialism was brought into the new one, and city or provincial identifications remained important" (Alba, 1985, p. 49). Thus, the Italian immigrants' first impact on American society produced a double sense of separation within them: from the "other," the American, but also from their own compatriots (Gabaccia, 1984).

Even later, the first generation had a hard time integrating. As Alba (1985) notes, the extent to which an immigrant generation can undergo a cultural transformation and become acculturated is limited. Despite the exceptions, most immigrants from different countries remained distinguishable from other Americans, even after a prolonged period of residence. In fact, many of them came as adults, after growing up and spending their early years in another society; upon arrival, their personalities were mostly established and it is not possible to expect a radical change from the impact with the new context. They remained distinguishable both externally (accent, clothing, poses) but also inwardly (cultural values) (Alba, 1985).

THE SECOND GENERATION

The conflicts and antagonisms that the immigrant generation encountered had strong repercussions on the second generation, creating the conditions for a dual sense of belonging to two parallel worlds: the small and selective world of the family of origin, neighborhood, and Little Italies and the great world of America that exerted its strong attractive power. This double belonging inevitably "produced a cultural clash and a generational conflict: parents asked their children to respect the mentality of the homeland versus the children who wanted to be Americans above all" (Vecoli, 1985, p. 94). This dissension resulted in the search for identification with all that America represented: for the second generation, this identification meant being what the "others" were, those who received the attention of the media. Satisfying the strong desire to be the "others" meant disobeying and challenging parents, grandparents, and all those who remembered the non-American ancestors; it implied turning their backs on the past, on their cultural heritage.

The second generation was therefore subjected to great pressure and suffered a strong identity conflict when faced with the dilemma of choosing between being Italian or American: it suffered marginality, incomplete belonging to both worlds, and the constant feeling of being torn apart by two opposing lifestyles. Members of this generation learned that being Italian meant being inferior, to be ashamed of their parents for broken English and for expressive behaviors, resulting in a self-aversion from having internalized the negative stereotypes of the antagonists (Vecoli, 1985). *Italianità* became an obstacle for entry into the mainstream of American culture and the process of Americanization was accomplished by abandoning all the traits of one's ethnic heritage to embrace an American identity that was reflected—as far as the media communicated—in a "wealthy, fashionable, materialistic and future-oriented" America (ibid.).

Alba (1985) defines the second generation as a "transitional generation," because it simultaneously experienced the profound influence of their parents' culture while also having to adapt to the needs of a new way of life. Born and raised on American soil, the children of Italian immigrants attended schools and were exposed to American culture through films and popular music. Their loyalty to the culture of Southern Italy faded in contrast to the seductive force exerted by some features of American culture, such as greater tolerance and individualism within the family and in the sphere of sexuality.

The first generation placed a low emphasis on the value of education, and children were ushered into the world of work as soon as possible. This resistance to the achievement of scholastic goals entailed a restriction of work mobility and precluded part of the second generation from access to jobs that required high educational credentials. In any case, occupational mobility characterized this generation and being Italian American meant automatically belonging to the working class (Vecoli, 1985, p. 95).[3]

With regard to U.S. society, the second generation had to face a challenge that was more difficult to overcome than what the first generation had gone through. In fact, the members of this group were not able to maintain the same degree of isolation that had characterized the first generation and had to learn to relate to American institutions (Gambino, 1972). Gambino points out that "what was a winning social strategy for their parents created a conflictive crisis for them. These circumstances split their personalities into two oppositional halves" (p. 432).[4]

Looking more closely at the relationship between the first and second generations, one observes a certain ambiguity: on the one hand, generational conflict arose, but on the other hand the pact between generations was kept alive and created continuity (Covello, 1967). "The second generation represents," as Alba notes, "an important step towards acculturation, but its components still strongly feel the influence and desirability of the family ethos of southern Italy" (Alba,

1985, p. 58). Lopreato (1970) also pointed out that "saying the generations were in conflict is not the same as saying that the children of immigrants invariably struck out on their own. The Italian family was too solid and too venerated by the average individual to permit unbridgeable emotional differences between its members" (p. 68). Therefore, despite the occurrence of such tensions, there was great continuity of values between the first and second generations: immigrant families passed the morality of peasant Italy on to their children and the second generation maintained close ties with their parents (Vecoli, 1985).

The psychological strategies adopted to overcome the dilemma of choice in identification as either Italian or American were summarized by Child (1943, cited in Alba, 1985) according to three possibilities:

1. the "in-group" response emphasized identifying with the Italian group, and those who adopted this solution tried to keep the lifestyle of the motherland as much as possible in the various social contexts;
2. the "rebel" reaction was adopted by those who identified as Americans and rejected Italian culture and traditions as unfit for American society;
3. the third strategy was an attempt to avoid the dilemma of choice; Child defined this reaction as "indifferent" and implied the rejection of the conflict. Those who adopted this tactic tried to disregard the fact that the distinction between nationalities was important and even denied the existence of prejudice and discrimination against those who had Italian origins.

Following interviews conducted during his field study,[5] Child concluded that the prevailing reaction in the analyzed sample was the "indifferent" one, which translated to these subjects remaining within the Italian group only because of their own passivity.

THIRD GENERATION

The rise of the third generation, which among the ethnic groups began to reach adulthood on a large scale during the 1950s, involved the revival of ethnic consciousness, which increased considerably during the 1960s. No longer in a defensive position with regard to ancestral origins, since they were now an established presence in the scholastic and occupational systems, this generation was able to assert its ethnic identity with strength and trust. It was thus demonstrated that the immigrants' grandchildren had leapt forward on the socioeconomic scale, in education, employment, and income.

The 1960s represented the starting point of what has been called the ethnic revival. At that time, the "strong" American identity was questioned for being a fragile facade, and its origins turned out to be much more complex. The homogeneity of the middle class was shattered in the midst of racial, ethnic, and class conflict, as well as in the liberation movements from traditional morality (Greeley, 1971). In those years, third-generation Italian Americans were facing the crumbling of the concept of a monolithic and compact American identity, subject to attacks by particularistic movements and groups of the population who were fighting to obtain recognition of their civil rights. Once the original American ideal was lost, the Italians needed to replace it with another model. It was then that the concept of "the old country"—*la bella Italia*[6]—came into being and this Italy became the metaphor for the post-immigrant generations. But, in the meantime, Italy had changed and the metaphors of the past could not be found in the reality of the present (Gardaphé, 2004). Thus, Italian America was born from the tension between the metaphor of Italy and that of America.

It can be said then that the rediscovery and strengthening of Italian American identity derived from the concomitance of a process of Americanization that took place in the third generation—following a rapid increase in economical, occupational, and educational mobility—with, at the same time, the reawakening of interest for ethnic and cultural roots. Despite this push toward the affirmation of ethnic identity, the third generation suffered a strong identity crisis. In fact, this generation was the one that was most affected by the ambivalence of *italianità*. The parents, namely, the second generation, despite being subjected to criticism and rebellion by their children, managed to instill in them the values of the peasant society: a belief in hard work, respect for authority, and loyalty to the family. At the same time, they inculcated in their children American values: ambition, success, and individualism (Gardaphé, 2004, p. 102). The third generation received conflicting messages, and the contradictory signals sent by the parents to the children created confused references that resulted in an identity crisis, accentuated by the rapid upward mobility in which they were involved.

So it was that the third generation started looking for something that had been lost; this led to the realization of the well-known law formulated by Hansen (1938) of the "return of the third generation." He predicted that ethnicity would resurface: the grandchildren of immigrants, confident in their Americanism and free from their parents' inferiority complex, would seek to pursue their curiosity toward their roots in the Old World.

YOUTH AND THE CHOSEN IDENTITY

Since the eighties, the idea has become increasingly clear that ethnic identification is defined through a process of individualization, composed of conscious and unconscious elements, wherein subjectivity assumes great importance; this process leads to greater emphasis on individual decision-making aspects. For the fourth and subsequent Italian American generations the identity recognition of their ethnic components becomes, in large part, a choice and a personal interpretation of identity, according to a process of individualization and fragmentation.

The individual decision-making element appears to be decisive in Alba's (1985) interpretation of ethnicity in those years, which sustained that—in any way the Italian American being was expressed—it was the individual who made this choice and the decision taken by one person would not have been identical to that of another. The ethnicity that survived in the melting pot would have been private and voluntary: "Symbolic ethnicity is very different from the ethnicity of the past, which was an assumed part of daily life, collective and at the same time imposed on the individual by the fact of being born within the group" (p. 173). The ethnicity of American whites had thus passed from the status of irrevocable fact to birth as constituting an ingredient in a lifestyle.

THE NEW SECOND GENERATION

The annual *Current Population Survey* (*CPS*) of 2005 highlighted that the more than thirty million second-generation individuals living in the United States accounted for a total of 11% of U.S. citizens. The majority of the current second generation is composed of nonwhites; in fact, they are mostly Asian immigrants, blacks coming from Africa and West India, and Latin Americans. For those who represent the "new second generation," the adaptation process is relatively easy (Portes & Rumbaut, 1996).[7]

Contemporary immigration is heterogeneous in terms of human capital and modes of inclusion, and it presents two main patterns: on the one hand, immigrant professionals and entrepreneurs, and migrant workers on the other. Political refugees are in addition to these types. The receiving social context, combined with the human capital that the migrants bring with them from their society of origin, determines the various means of inclusion as well as the occupational and economic mobility trajectories they follow.

The second generation of today is faced with a pluralist and fragmented environment that simultaneously offers a wealth of opportunities but also serious threats to a successful adaptation process (Waters, 1994). Therefore, in the present historical context the central question is not whether the second generation will be assimilated into American society, but which segment of society it will be assimilated into (Portes & Rumbaut, 1996). Portes and Rumbaut (1996) also point out that when second-generation children follow a process of acculturation without abandoning their parents' language and the key elements of their culture, it is easier for parents to offer guidance and support to their children's search for success and achievement (selective acculturation).[8]

The model is therefore associated with a strong parental-social capital in the form of stable families, cohesive communities, and commonly—but not always—with a fluid bilingualism (English plus the language of the parents). The role of selective acculturation during adolescence has been demonstrated to promote positive adaptation. The opposite model is called dissonant acculturation, where learning English and the American way of life is accompanied by the abandonment of one's parents' language and culture. Using only the foreign language (English in this case) marks the breaking of intrafamily communication and the loss of parental control over their children. Dissonant acculturation does not necessarily lead to downward assimilation, but it places the children at risk due to the absence or weakness of family support against the aforementioned barriers and threats. It is also demonstrated empirically that among the second generation of young people, those who speak two languages fluently achieve superior results in terms of psychological adaptation and scholastic achievement during adolescence compared to young people who speak only English and have therefore lost the use of the parental language.

CHARACTERISTICS OF THE INTERVIEWEES ACCORDING TO THEIR GENERATION OF IMMIGRATION

Moving from theoretical reflections to the empirical results of the study, the course of analysis reveals how there were generational characterizations that the interviewed subjects have in common. This consideration has led to examining the connections between the immigration generation and some significant explanatory variables in order to build generational identity patterns. The results are presented according to the three generational typologies found in the sample.

Considering the small number of those belonging to the fifth generation, the variable of immigration generation has been recoded by reaggregating the fourth generation with the subsequent ones (see Table 11.1).

Table 11.1 Recoded Generation

	NO.	%
Second generation	108	39.0
Third generation	110	39.7
Fourth and later generations	57	20.6
TOTAL	275	99.3
N/A	2	0.7
TOTAL	277	100.0

SECOND GENERATION

Structural Data

From the sample, 39% of young Italian Americans living in the Greater New York area claimed membership in the second generation. Intersecting the generation with the period of arrival in the United States by their Italian parent/s conveys that this generation is composed mainly of children of Italians who arrived in America from World War II onward. In age, the second generation consists mainly of respondents who are in the younger age group of the sample. With respect to gender, this group is predominantly women, and their marital status is primarily married. As for their level of education, we find that most subjects possess secondary school diplomas, but some also have doctorates. Regarding employment, the second generation is formed primarily of students, employees, and teachers. Class self-placement shows a prevalence of the upper class.

Analyzing their relationship with media, we note that, in television enjoyment, these young people are especially positioned among those who watch it from two to six hours per day, while they devote mainly from zero to two hours daily to reading the newspapers. Group members are busy reading books generally for up to two hours, or two to six hours a day. The majority are connoted as heavy users of the internet (more than six hours a day).

Socialization and Values

From the perspective of values, second-generation youths mostly believe theirs share some similarity with paternal values, while little continuity is detected with those of their mothers. More generally, the values held by the family achieve predominantly the score of 4 in the scale of importance between 1 and 5, while culture is accorded mainly values of 5 and 3. Among the factors produced by the factorial analysis of values, young people belonging to the second generation mainly emphasize individualism, emotional support, materialism, and religiosity. There is an observable mix of elements connected to American-style pragmatism united with those that connote an attitude of compassion supported also by religious motivations. Analyzing the context of friendships, the research has established the cognitive objective of understanding—as already seen—whether the interviewed young people grew up in ethnically mixed or segregated environments.

In the case of second-generation young people, the prevalence of two groups is observed with reference to friendships during primary school: the first group consists of those who have mostly interacted with only Italian Americans, while the second group includes those who have cultivated friendships in ethnically mixed environments in which Italian Americans were not present. The trend in the choice of friendships during secondary school sees the accentuation of a closure toward mixed environments and the preference for exclusively Italian American friendships. With regard to the present, most show a tendency toward friendships from different ethnic backgrounds, demonstrating in this sense an openness, but in these amicable contexts, Italian Americans are not present.

In the course of childhood, some interviewees were friends with only Italian American children: this attendance most likely refers to other second-generation Italian American children, or children of Italians as themselves. When some interviewees said that today they attend mixed environments where Italian Americans are not present, this might indicate the fact that second-generation young people tend to distance themselves from those who belong to previous generations of Italian Americans with whom they have little in common and from which they feel very distant.

Ethnic Self-identification

Moving to an analysis of ethnic self-identification, it is observed that among the second-generation young people there are no marked indications for feeling white, American, Italian, or Italian American. These identifications probably assume a less distinguishable relevance in this group, considering also that there are no mentions that specifically characterize the ethnic nature of the partner. Ethnic connotation of the mother and father was especially indicated as Italian. Further indications come from the intersection with two indexes that have been used to construct the typology of identification as "Italian American."

What is observed for the second generation is that the score 1, which indicates the highest degree of connection and proximity to Italy in identification as Italian American, is above average, which indicates that identification predominantly acknowledges Italy. At the same time, however, they obtain above-average scores compared to the value 1 also on the index indicating the proximity to Italian American culture in America. In this case, identification benefits from both reference components. The position of proximity both to America and to Italy in their self-identification as Italian American within the typology constructed from the two previous indexes is what characterizes the majority of second-generation young people.[9]

Continuing the analysis of self-identification as Italian American, in terms of emotional bonds and associated feelings, it emerges that these young people feel above all and most often proud of being Italian American. At the same time, the majority of them also admitted to experiencing a feeling of shame in some circumstances connected to this identification. Their ethnic background is a source, for most of these young people, of inner conflict.

As time passes, the emotional connections with significant places can change. In the case of second-generation young people, the relationship with the place where they live and with the United States has remained mostly stable, while that with Italy has experienced a crescendo of intensity.

With respect to eating habits, there is a prevalence of interviewees who eat Italian and Italian American dishes every day.

The Image of Italian Americans

Interviewees consider most of the characteristics that have differentiated Italian Americans from other groups in the United States to be in danger of extinction; there are also those among the second-generation young people who believe that these characteristics will not completely disappear but will be less and less evident.

Concerning the opinion whether there are people who, despite being Italian American, do not admit they are, these young people predominantly think there are very few or almost none. There are comparatively few individuals who, despite coming from other ethnic backgrounds, identify with the Italian American lifestyle. Generally, the interviewees feel little sense of belonging to the Italian American community. In fact, the prevalent subset represents those who claim the Italian Americans do not give signs of being part of the community.

Again in reference to the collective identity aspects of belonging, the opinions are largely divided in two: on the one hand there are those who believe that Italian Americans have their associations and are well organized as a united community, on the other (although very few in absolute value) there are those who think it is a community in name only and nobody or almost no one believes they are a part of it.

The comparison between Italian Americans and other groups living in the United States leads to the observation, in their opinion, that they are, in general, fairly well esteemed. As for the general sense of power that the Italian American group holds, the majority of those who are a part of the second-generation respondents believe they have little. The relationships that characterize the comprehensive vision of the group are mainly founded on a sense of relaxation, based on their agreement that Italian Americans get along fairly well with each other.

The summary elements that emerge from the responses linked to the image of Italian Americans highlight how reactions to the stereotypes attributed to the group and to the media's portrayal of Italian Americans prevails for the composition of this generation's vision. Young people of this group demonstrate the greatest degree of disappointment on these two aspects with respect to the other generations studied.

Image of Italy and Italians

Among the second-generation youth, there is a prevalence of those who have visited Italy many times. The majority, moreover, confirm that they have relatives in the nation of origin. Even the relational fabric at the friend level seems tightly woven. In fact, most of these interviewees declared that they have some or many friends living in Italy with whom they are in contact.

This trend is also confirmed when analyzing this group's friendships with new Italian immigrants around the same age: in fact, they have mostly integrated them into their friend groups, even if there are some who, despite having had contact with these new immigrants, do not count them among their friends. These interviewees predominantly get news about Italy daily or weekly. They use social media to stay connected with the Italian American community. The better part of them understand and speak Italian occasionally or frequently. The same goes for dialects and, in this case, with respect to the modalities of knowledge of the Italian language, add also the option of those who do not speak them but understand them well enough.

This group's perception of Italy and Italians is connected to a high level of personal involvement with Italy and with Italians, accompanied by the evaluation of the public/private defects that negatively characterize the nation. This last aspect justifies the feeling of disillusionment and disappointment toward Italy that very often accompanies its image. The Italian representation is also based on the sense of admiration and identification with the homeland and with the recognition of the taste and refinement of Italian culture.

Stereotypes, Prejudices, and Discrimination
The greater part of the interviewees claimed to have come into contact with stereotypes connected to the image of the Italian Americans. They also believe that these stereotypes mainly do not correspond to reality and that the current representation of Italian Americans proposed by the media is not at all realistic nowadays. A prevailing opinion among these young people is that the majority of Italian Americans, when confronted by the stereotypes that represent them through the media, react by feeling offended. The majority of the interviewees claim to have been the object of discriminatory acts or behaviors resulting from their ethnic background.

Affiliations and Memberships
The education that interviewees received was for most of them very or somewhat marked by religious faith. Most claim to be Catholic and attribute a very high importance to faith and spirituality. Moreover, the majority of them are part of churches or local religious communities. Participation in religious rites constitutes a varied framework; some, in fact, take part weekly, some monthly, some a few times a year, and finally, some only attend for the most important religious holidays.

In the context of political participation, these young people have mostly claimed that they do not identify with any political party. Interviewees for the most part are dedicated in terms of participation and activism within organizations and associations, while the vision they have of relations between Italian American associations and organizations appears to be marked mainly by competition or pure informational exchange.

The Future

There are two opposing tendencies that prevail among the young people's visions of the future of Italian American culture: on the one hand there are those who believe that it will disappear, will be lost and assimilated into the American mainstream; on the other there are those who believe that it will renew and evolve as it continues to grow and transform. By separating the emotional/affective aspect of their attachment to Italian and Italian American culture from their knowledge of the elements that compose it, attachment to family origins and to Italy appears to be the primary reference for the first aspect, that of the emotional connection, for the second-generation youths. Furthermore, their link is also characterized by a strong relational component, since among them we find above-average values in the dimension of interpersonal relations with Italians and Italian Americans.

Italian and Italian American cultural knowledge is based on both popular and traditional culture as well as "high" culture (historical, artistic, and literary). Furthermore, knowledge of contemporary Italy and an interest in its political and economic aspects complete the overall vision of this generation.

THIRD GENERATION

Structural Data

For the third generation, their grandparents' arrival years were mainly during the "great migration" and also between the two world wars. It should be noted, however, that in this generation there is a prevalence of young people who do not know their Italian ancestors' years of arrival.

The largest group in this generation of the sample are intermediate age males. The majority that responded are single or cohabit with a partner. Most of those interwees have a master's degree or a PhD. The main occupations of third-generation young people are merchants and artisans, while the social class in which they are most frequently recognized is the middle class. As for the use of the internet, there is a tendency to rather massive use; most of them are connected to the net for more than six hours a day, while they mainly dedicate between two and six hours daily to reading books.

Socialization and Values

Sharing the values of the father is very or somewhat high and there is a great similarity to their mothers' values. In the scale of values both family and culture occupy positions of great importance. In fact, on a scale between 1 and 5, the family especially gets a score of 4, while the culture mostly achieves scores of 4 and 5.

During primary school these young people grew up in contact with friends from different backgrounds, including Italian Americans. Growing up and during the years of secondary school they have friends of mostly different ethnic backgrounds, but the perspective has changed because there were no longer Italian Americans among them. For some this latter tendency has been confirmed in the present and, even today, they spend time in mixed environments where Italian Americans are not present. At the opposite extreme, other young people have only chosen friends among Italian Americans.

Ethnic Self-identification
Regarding their declared ethnicity, this group primarily feels white, American, Italian. With reference to the ethnicity of their partners, they predominantly mentioned the connotation as Italian and Italian American. As for the ethnic qualification of their parents, both were primarily indicated as white, American, and Italian American.

Using the constructed indices to measure the degree of closeness to Italy or Italian American culture in the United States as references for identification as Italian Americans and crossing them with the generation variable, the third generation achieves above-average values on the score that indicates the greatest distance from Italy in identification. With respect to the typology that summarizes the position of respondents regarding their proximity to Italy and America as references for identifying as Italian Americans, the young people of the third generation present above-average values both for those who feel close to Italy and not to America, and, vice versa, among those who feel close to America and not to Italy.

Chiefly, emotional attachment both to the United States and their locale there has tended to grow over time, while the connection with Italy has remained stable. As for their pride in being Italian American, the majority of third-generation respondents always feel it and never feel ashamed of this identification. Furthermore, the majority do not indicate any interior conflict resulting from this recognition.

Eating habits predominantly include Italian and Italian American dishes consumed two or three times per week.

Image of Italian Americans
The characterization of Italian Americans throughout the country compared to other ethnic groups is generally seen as constant over time. The number of

people who, despite being Italian American, do not openly admit it appears, in the opinion of these young people, rather small. Not so numerically relevant, according to the prevailing opinion, there are those who identify with the manners and poses of Italian Americans, even if they are not.

There is the conviction among the young people of the third generation that Italian Americans feel a great sense of belonging to the community. From the community organization point of view, the majority opinion holds that there are Italian American organizations and associations that operate in a disorganized fashion and lack community vision.

According to that prevailing opinion held by third-generation respondents, the esteem enjoyed by Italian Americans compared to other ethnic groups is very high. The resonant image under the profile of the power that Italian Americans hold places them at very or fairly high levels. The relations among the members of the group seen as a whole are also marked by ease: most of the respondents believe that they get along very well.

The summary dimensions of the image highlight that it is composed above all by positive connotations, that is, from the culture and values that distinguish them, from their physical and personality traits, from their sense of belonging to the community, from the prestige and power that they hold compared to other groups present in the United States and, finally, from the "sharing of the stereotypes" that revolve around this image and with which there is a high identification.

Image of Italy and Italians

The majority of these interviewees have never visited Italy or have been only a couple of times. There is also a prevalence of those who claim to have no relatives in Italy that they know of and those who have few friends in Italy or no one with whom they are in contact. The majority of them also allege to have only occasionally met new Italian immigrants within the same age range. They receive news about Italy monthly or annually. They mostly use social media to stay connected within the Italian American community.

The Italian language is not part of the wealth of knowledge for the larger part of these young people; in fact, most declared that either they do not understand it or speak it or they understand it a little but never speak it. As for dialects, the majority understands them a little but never speaks them, while others have pointed out that they do not understand and do not speak them.

The summary image of Italy and Italians rests principally on the evaluation of the system of values attributed to Italians, namely, on a series of positive distinguishing features such as honor, respect, solidarity, but also on the poor sense of accepting rules and obligations. Also within the image there is the perception of distance from Italian society.

Stereotypes, Prejudices, and Discrimination
There is a prevalent opinion among these young people that some of the media stereotypes representing Italian Americans are real. This opinion confirms the point of view that this image is currently realistic in some respects. Faced with this media-based stereotyping, the prevalent reaction that Italian Americans manifest is indifference. Still, respondents of this generation largely indicated that they were subject to discrimination because of their ethnic background.

Affiliations and Memberships
The majority of the third-generation interviewees received an education that was only slightly or not at all religious. Currently, most claim to be Catholics or declare they have a personal creed. The majority belong to local churches or religious communities. For most, the importance attributed to religious faith and spirituality is quite high. This does not necessarily imply a diligent practice. In fact, the attendance of religious rites is generally monthly, annually, or during important religious holidays.

Political affiliation sees them divided into those who identify either as Republicans or Democrats. Their vision of relations between Italian American associations and organizations appears to be prevalently based on the cooperation the two.

The Future
The predominant vision among these young people regarding the future of Italian American culture foresees stability and therefore continuity and persistence. The emotional and affective attachment to Italian and Italian American culture is based primarily on two dimensions: on the one hand, the emotional connection with the Italian American community and, on the other, to the United States. Regarding the knowledge of Italian and Italian American culture, what stands out is the knowledge of traditional and popular culture and of Italian and Italian American food.

THE FOURTH AND FIFTH GENERATIONS

Structural Data
For the fourth and fifth generations, their ancestors' years of arrival were for the most part during the "great migration." Among them there is a prevalence

of young people who do not know precisely when their Italian ancestors arrived in America. The ages of the interviewees from these generations are primarily between twenty-four and twenty-nine years. In terms of gender, this group is mostly comprised of men and most of them do not have children.

With respect to education level, the better part of them possess an associate's or a bachelor's degree. They are occupied mostly as traders and artisans, as employees in public and private services, and as technicians. Regarding self-determination of class, the lower class predominates within this group.

For the most part, they spend two to six hours reading newspapers and some of them use the internet for up to two hours a day, while others use it for two to six hours. The majority of these young people spend a maximum of two hours reading books on a daily basis.

Socialization and Values

In terms of similarly held values, the interviewees largely maintain that there is a great affinity with the values of both parents. In general, the aspects that emerge with the greatest emphasis within this group in terms of values are individualism, materialism, and cultural and social sharing.

Among these interviewees, the choice of friendships during primary school saw a marked presence of peers from different ethnic backgrounds, including Italian Americans. Even during secondary school, they continued to make friends with the same characteristics on an ethnic level, and the same tendency is observed in their current friendships. The emergent constant indicates an opening up to different ethnic backgrounds without limitations of any kind.

Ethnic Self-identification

Ethnicity is represented for the most part through feeling white, American, and Italian American. Among the young people who fall into these generations there is a majority who do not have a husband/wife or a partner. As for the ethnicity of the partner, the interviewees stated mainly that he/she is white, American, Italian American. With regard to parental ethnicity, the respondents indicated both maternal and paternal mainly as white, American, and Italian American.

There is an observably marked tendency toward ethnic homogeneity in the generational transition between parents and children. Analyzing their identification as Italian Americans through a position of proximity or distance from Italy, it emerges that the young people of fourth and subsequent generations perceive a very notable distance from the homeland of their ancestors. Specifically, within the typology built to measure whether the Italian American identification relies more on the Italian side in Italy or on the Italian one in America, the young people of fourth and fifth generation are placed mainly in two categories: either they do not feel close to either one, or they only feel close to America.

Regarding the link that unites them to the place where they live, most of them said that this has decreased, even if there are subjects who have indicated that it has grown. Although the total number of respondents is quite low, there is a notable tendency toward diminution in the link with both Italy and the United States, thus indicating a reduction in attachment on all three sides (Italy, United States, place of residence).

Analyzing the feelings connected to identification, the observation reveals they feel especially proud—most of the time—of being Italian American. For most of them this identification is also a basis for inner conflict. The Italian and Italian American culinary tradition affects the eating habits of these young people who have largely indicated that they prefer these kinds of dishes twice or three times a week.

Image of Italian Americans
The characteristics that have differentiated Italian Americans from other groups over the course of time tend not to completely disappear, but they do become less and less evident. According to the young people from these generations, the number of those who do not admit bearing Italian American ancestry are very small. Instead, with respect to the opinion concerning the people who, although not Italian American, identify with the ways and mannerism of Italian Americans, these interviewees primarily think that there are many or, at least some of them.

As for the sense of belonging to the community of Italian Americans, it is the predominant opinion among these interviewees that it is felt to some degree. Their prevailing vision is shared with the third-generation group's vision of a deficient community organization under the profile of unity, even if there are social associations of Italian Americans within it. The regard and esteem that Italian Americans experience in comparison with the other groups in the United States are considered very low. Even the power that they possess would seem to be, in the prevailing opinion of these respondents, very reduced.

The relational aspect among the members of the group as a whole is characterized by easygoing relationships; they believe, in fact, that the members of the Italian American community mostly get along very well with each other.

The image of Italian Americans according to the components of these generations is constructed via dimensions that are aggregated around physical and personality traits and "sharing stereotypes," with which there is a significant level of identification.

Image of Italy and Italians
The young people of fourth and fifth generation, as well as those of the previous generation, are mostly characterized by not ever visiting Italy or having gone only a couple of times. There is a majority percentage among them who affirm they do not have relatives in Italy to the best of their knowledge. The Italian network of friendly relations is poor; most have indicated that they have no Italian friend with whom they are in contact. Even in the United States, the members of this group seem to have no relationship with the new Italian immigrants of more or less their age; in fact, those who have indicated "no contact" with them stood out. Most respondents who fall into these generations receive news weekly about Italy. They tend not to have contact with the Italian American community via social media.

The Italian language is, in most cases, lost: some do not understand it and do not speak it, others understand it a bit, but never speak it. The situation regarding dialects is even worse: most have indicated that they do not understand them and that they do not speak them. Their synthetic image of Italians is based around two main dimensions: the distance that is perceived by Italian society as well as the lack of affinity between Italian and American society. Furthermore, the vision of Italy and Italians marked by localism and familism prevails in this group; this way of representing Italy is more evident in this generation than in the others.

Stereotypes, Prejudices, and Discrimination
The majority of respondents of the fourth and subsequent generations believe that the media's representation of Italian Americans is realistic in some respects. The opinion of the members of the group regarding the reaction to the media's stereotypical vision of Italian Americans focuses on three aspects: there are those who believe this to be entertaining, those who internalize and emphasize these stereotypes, and, lastly (even if the absolute value is very low), those who think the stereotypes are not real.

As for discriminatory actions suffered on a personal or family level, the majority of young people of this group indicated that they were not subjected to them.

Affiliations and Memberships
This group has received, in most cases, an education that is not faith-based. The majority of those interviewed said that they do not currently have a religious

preference, but they do have a personal creed. For their part there is an attribution of varying importance to the aspect of interior and personal life; the majority considers it to be of no importance, but there are also those who attribute some importance to it. Chiefly, they do not belong to any local church or religious community and never participate in religious services.

From the political point of view, independents predominate. The group tends not to partake in associations and organizations and they mostly consider the relationships between Italian American associations to be nonexistent.

The Future

For some of these young people, the future of Italian American culture does not seem very positive, in the sense that they believe that it will decline, decrease in importance, and dissolve into the American mainstream. Others, however, believe it will continue to exist. The two dimensions that represent their attachment to Italian and Italian American culture include the importance attributed to their ethnic heritage and its value, without any further connotations that might provide a broader picture of the meaning they attribute to it. This group expresses their knowledge of Italian and Italian American culture through the sole dimension of musical knowledge (echoes in the subtext, the lyric, and the voice of Caruso...).

IN SUMMARY

The generational analysis conducted shows how moving away from their ancestors' time of arrival in the United States affects the characteristics and modalities of the relationship that binds young people to their original culture: as time moves away from landing in America, the more these links tend to weaken, fade, hybridize, and sometimes disappear completely.[10]

Considering the structural characteristics of the four generations examined, it is noted that second-generation young people tend to be on the younger side of the sample, they are mostly women, married, employed in the service sector and students, with high educational qualifications, who self-identify as upper class. The third-generation sample includes mostly male subjects, in the intermediate age group, single, with a very high level of education, mainly employed in commerce and crafts, and belonging to the middle class. Those who are part of the fourth and subsequent generations are located mainly in the age group of twenty-four to twenty-seven years, mostly male, and without offspring. Employed for the most part in the service sector, in commerce, and in crafts, these interviewees have a medium-high level of education and claim they belong chiefly to the lower class.

An interesting piece of primary data concerns the memory that young people have of the year when their predecessors arrived in America. For the second generation this date is easy to remember, considering that the parents of most of them came to the United States from the second postwar period onward. The situation is different for third and subsequent generations. Their Italian ancestors arrived especially during the "great migration" period and in the years between the two world wars. The majority of young people no longer have a precise memory of the date of their arrival.

Analyzing ethnic self-identification, some significant differences emerge that characterize the generational flux. Second-generation youths have not markedly indicated any characterization as whites, Americans, Italians, or Italian Americans; they also did not do so when they were asked to express their partners' ethnicities. As for the ethnic connotation of parents, these have been defined mainly as Italians. As the evidence will show, this identification appears more nuanced and less defined in this group than it is among the components of succeeding generations. Unlike them, the third-generation youths have specified they feel mostly white, American, and Italian, while their parents are ethnically connoted as whites, Americans, and Italian Americans. In terms of the fourth and subsequent generations, it is noted that their ethnic self-identification above all emphasizes feeling white, American, and Italian American and coincides with the prevalent ethnic connotation attributed to their parents, bringing out, in this case, an ethnic homogeneity in the generational transition.

Among the characterizations chosen by the interviewees, feeling Italian American is favored by generations of the oldest settlement, while those who have a more recent past on American soil define themselves above all as Italians, thus demonstrating their proximity to Italy as much as to the United States. For the second generation, being white is not a noted characteristic in their ethnic identification, since they are likely to take this for granted: for them, this connotation does not have the meaning of a "historical conquest," nor is it valued as a recognition that the Italians have acquired after a long and troubled journey and that, as such, they would tend to emphasize explicitly through this designation.

What has been observed up to now is confirmed by the examination of the indexes that express the positions of the interviewees in their identification as Italian Americans through their proximity to Italy or the United States. The second generation has—generally—an equidistant position from both Italian and American society and shows a propensity to benefit from each culture. Young people belonging to the third generation do not show a homogeneous identification with respect to these two territorial references; some, in fact, feel closer to Italy than to America, while others, on the contrary, favor America more than Italy. It should be noted, however, that compared to the other generations studied there is the greater propensity for the third to deviate from Italy in identifying as Italian Americans. A more accentuated tendency to distance oneself from Italy as part of this identity reference is expressed by the fourth and subsequent generations: these interviewees are divided between those who do not feel close to Italy or America and those who look only to America as a reference in identification.

The link with the place where the greatest number of second-generation young people live has remained stable over time, as well as that with the United States, while the connection with Italy has been growing over the years. For third-generation components, the attachment to the place where they live and the one toward the United States have increased over the years, while the one with Italy has remained stable. The fourth and subsequent generations have a tendency to express a decrease in attachment to all three places mentioned. The analysis of these trends also highlights a situation of emotional loosening over the generations toward the places of greatest impact on their ethnic identification.

The emotional aspects of this identification present generational differentiations. First of all, it should be noted that all generations show pride for being/feeling Italian American. The majority of second-generation components have admitted, however, a feeling of shame in some circumstances connected to this identification, which is also a reason, again for the majority, of internal conflict. Most third-generation respondents never feel ashamed of being/feeling Italian American and also do not experience internal conflict due to ethnic background. Among the young people of the fourth and subsequent generations the inner conflict linked to this identity recognition reemerges, which was also expressed by the second generation.

Analyzing the second-generation youths' preeminent self-perceived image of Italian Americans, it is observed that the characteristics that have differentiated them over time from other groups in the United States will tend to disappear or, at most, will be less and less evident in the future. For the third-generation components these distinctive traits will tend to remain constant over time, while for the fourth and fifth generation young people they will fade and, even if they do not totally disappear, will become less and less evident.

The second-generation respondents believe that the sense of belonging to the Italian American community is weakly felt and that few Italian Americans perceive it. Contrary to this, young people of the third generation are convinced that Italian Americans feel strongly about community membership, while the young people of the fourth and fifth generation believe that Italian Americans recognize themselves somewhat in this affiliation.

The self-perceived image of the community appears in the eyes of second-generation young people mainly as well organized and united, while, conversely, the vision of third-generation respondents is that of a context rich in organizations and associations, although disorganized and disunited. The same opinion is shared by the members of the fourth and fifth generations, who reaffirm the presence of a rather complex associative and organizational fabric which lacks unity.

The comparison of Italian Americans with other groups living in the United States leads the majority of second-generation young people to believe that they are somewhat well esteemed, have little power, and get along well with each other. An extremely positive vision of the group of Italian Americans is common to the majority of third-generation members, who express the belief that the groups enjoys very high prestige as well as rather vast power. The relations within the Italian American community are also characterized positively, marked by an easygoing nature and a very broad level of agreement among its components. Of the diametrically opposed opinion are the young people of the fourth and fifth generation, who believe that the consideration and esteem enjoyed by Italian Americans in comparison with other groups existing in the United States are low, while the power they possess would seem to be reduced. As for the relational aspect, their position coincides with that expressed previously by the components of the other generations: they too are of the opinion that Italian Americans get along well with each other.

The self-perceived image of Italian Americans focuses on characteristics that differentiate the visions of the various generations. For those belonging to the second generation, the composition of the image is mainly based on the reaction to the stereotypes attributed to the group and on the media's representations of Italian Americans. This highlights a reactive position toward an externally constructed image of Italian Americans. The third-generation young people see the creation of this representation based on positive connotations, namely culture and values, physical and personality traits, the sense of belonging to the community, the prestige and power they hold and, finally, "sharing the stereotypes" that are imposed on them, with which this generation identifies highly. For the young people of fourth and subsequent generations as well, the dimensions which most define the image of Italian Americans include the "sharing of stereotypes"—toward which there is a significant level of identification—and by physical and personality traits.

The images of Italy and Italians for second-generation young people are linked to a high level of personal involvement that is expressed by direct contact with Italy visits, through the frequency of news obtained from the media, spending time with friends and relatives in Italy, as well as among Italians who recently settled in New York. Moreover, most of them speak Italian and know dialects. Their perception of Italy is twofold: on the one hand positive aspects prevail, such as the taste and refinement of Italian culture, but it also characterized by the connotation of public and private defects. This elicits not only a feeling of admiration and identification, but also disillusion and disappointment regarding Italy.

Most of the young people of third and subsequent generations, unlike the second, have never visited Italy, have no relatives or friends with whom contacts are maintained, and do not spend time with recently immigrated young Italians in New York. The Italian language and dialects are also not part of their wealth of knowledge.

The dimensions of the image of Italy serve to differentiate the third from the fourth and from the fifth generation. The former definitely have a positive vision, characterized by the evaluation of the value system attributed to the Italians, where favorable features including respect, honor, and solidarity stand out, though the lack of acceptance of rules and obligations are also highlighted. There is also a perceived sense of distance from Italian society. The young people of the fourth and fifth generations see Italy as characterized above all by localism and familism and feel a sense of great distance from the country accompanied by the recognition of a lack of resemblance between Italian and American society.

The majority of second-generation respondents pointed out that the stereotypes linked to the image of Italian Americans do not correspond to reality, and the representation of Italian Americans proposed by the media is not realistic either. In addition, they believe that most Italian Americans feel offended by this media representation. Young people also pointed out that the discrimination perpetuated toward them or members of their family related to ethnic background has tainted their personal history.

The third-generation young people, as opposed to the earlier ones, believe that the stereotypes associated with the image of Italian Americans through the media are real, and that Italian Americans react with indifference when confronted with them. They also claim that they are not subject to personal and family discrimination due to ethnic background.

Very similar to that of the majority of third-generation respondents is the perception of young people of the fourth and subsequent generations regarding the media representation of Italian Americans, which they consider to be realistic, in some respects. Moreover, they express discordant opinions pertaining to the reactions of Italian Americans when confronted with this stereotypical depiction performed by the media: some react with amusement, others internalize these stereotypes and emphasize them, while others think they are not real. On a family and personal level, the majority claim that they have not been discriminated against because of their Italian descent.

The vision of the future of Italian American culture that characterizes young people of the second generation takes two divergent paths: some believe that it will disappear and be assimilated into the American mainstream, others instead imagine that it will evolve and renew itself, continuing to transform and grow. The emotional bonds and attachments to Italian and Italian American culture are marked by affection for family origins and Italy as well as by a strong relational component that involves personal ties with Italians and Italian Americans. The knowledge of the two cultures is well rounded and is based both on the popular and traditional culture and on the historical, literary, and artistic one. Even aspects related to the knowledge of contemporary Italy from an economic and political point of view are counted in their background information.

Third-generation young people have a vision of the future of Italian American culture that confirms its stability, continuity, and persistence. The emotional and affective attachment to Italian and Italian American culture is based on their linkage with both the Italian American community and the United States. The knowledge of the two cultures relies especially on competence in the field of popular and traditional culture, as well as Italian and Italian American food.

On the future of Italian American culture, young people of the fourth and fifth generation present a inhomogeneous vision in the sense that some believe it will tend to decline and decrease in importance, while for others it will continue to exist. Attachment to the two cultures rests on the importance and value attributed to ethnic heritage, while knowledge of both hinges exclusively on their competence in the realm of music.

In conclusion, the study shows that the second generation possesses a recent history of settlement in America and, benefiting from this short historical distance that links it to Italy, expresses a lively and heartfelt bond with Italian heritage, corroborated by a direct knowledge—linked fundamentally through the knowledge of language and dialects—that was able to bridge the gap which has been long established between the two sides of the ocean.

The third generation appears to be characterized by a self-reflective vision that tends to focus mainly on the positive aspects of the Italian heritage, though this vision is more idealized than real. In fact, personal involvement with modern Italy is lacking in this group; so these young people feel Italian, but as "Italians of America."

The fourth and fifth generation suffer the most from the unraveling of the connection with their Italian past; nevertheless, they proudly continue to maintain an emotional connection with a homeland that they do not know directly, yet this does not mean they have forgotten about it, even if they perceive it as a distant and profoundly different place from the American society in which they live.

12

Profiles of Young Italian Americans: Sketches in Chiaroscuro

FOUR WAYS TO INTERPRET THE ITALIAN ETHNIC LEGACY

The analysis conducted so far has enabled the perception of some tendencies regarding the ways young Italian Americans represent their ethnic background. These tendencies formed a basis for reflection that was further developed to construct some ideal-typical profiles, which might briefly describe the different modalities of how young people relate to their ethnic heritage.

Theoretically, I started from two spheres considered relevant to define the young people's connection to Italian heritage: their level of knowledge and the degree of their attachment to Italian and Italian American culture. By dichotomizing these two spheres of interest on extreme positions, that is, "high/low level of knowledge" and "high/low level of attachment," a conceptual space was created composed of four positions with four ways of interpreting how Italian and Italian American heritage and culture are placed. The scheme being referred to is as follows:

	HIGH LEVEL OF KNOWLEDGE	LOW LEVEL OF KNOWLEDGE
HIGH LEVEL OF ATTACHMENT	Accepted/integrated *italianità*	Emotional *italianità*
LOW LEVEL OF ATTACHMENT	Rejected *italianità*	Abandoned *italianità*

As a consequence, "accepted/integrated *italianità*" is defined by a high level of knowledge of Italian and Italian American culture together with a strong attachment to both, while "emotional *italianità*" is characterized by a low level of knowledge and a strong attachment to both Italian and Italian American culture. "Rejected *italianità*" refers to a high level of knowledge and a low level of attachment to both cultures, and, lastly, "abandoned *italianità*" is characterized by a low level of attachment, accompanied by a low level of knowledge about both components.

Moving from the theoretical model to the implementation of concepts, some variables produced by the two factorial analyses regarding dimensions of the level of "knowledge" and of "attachment and bond" with the Italian and Italian American[1] culture described above seemed relevant. From the various dimensions composing the two areas of analysis, three variables have been selected related to the sphere of knowledge and six to the emotional sphere. Having undergone a "k-means cluster analysis," four groups were created to describe their characterization with respect to these dimensions.

The aspects of knowledge are based on three main dimensions: (1) knowledge of Italian and Italian American popular culture (traditions, festivals, religiosity, prayers, proverbs, common sayings, etc.), (2) knowledge of Italian and Italian American history, literature, and art, and (3) knowledge of contemporary Italy.

The emotional and attachment aspects were examined from six perspectives: (1) attachment to family origins, (2) relationship with Italy, (3) link with Italian American culture, (4) emotional value of belonging to the Italian American community, (5) interpersonal relationships with Italian Americans and Italians, and (6) attachment to the United States.

The result of the analysis led to the creation of four groups that trace the interviewees' profiles according the way they relate to their ethnic heritage. The groups will be examined in relation to their value, cultural, and behavioral dimensions in order to delineate the appearance of each one. Given the small number of the cases in the sample, however, the analysis is obviously only exploratory and therefore the results should be read as developing trends.

The characteristics of the four groups can be summarized according to that reported in table 12.1.

Table 12.1 highlights the relationship between the identified groups and the methods and dimensions used to express their Italian and Italian American ethnic heritage. By examining these characterizations, it was possible to construct

Table 12.1 Characteristics of the Four Groups of Young Italian Americans

	THEY KNOW	THEY DON'T KNOW	THEY ARE CONNECTED	THEY ARE NOT CONNECTED
First group	– Italian and Italian American popular culture (traditions, religion, prayers, festivals, common sayings) – Italian and Italian American history, art, and literature – contemporary Italy	——	– to the origins of the family – to Italy	– to Italian American culture – to the Italian American community – to the United States
Second group	– Italian and Italian American popular culture – Italian and Italian American history, art, and literature – contemporary Italy	——	– to the origins of the family – to Italy – to Italian American culture – to the Italian American community – in relationships with Italians and Italian Americans of the same age	– to the United States
Third group	——	– Italian and Italian American popular culture – Italian and Italian American history, art, and literature – contemporary Italy	– to the United States	– to the origins of the family – to Italy – to Italian American culture – to the Italian American community – in any relationships with Italians and Italian Americans of the same age
Fourth group	– Italian and Italian American popular culture	– contemporary Italy	– to Italian American culture – to the Italian American community – to the United States	– to the origins of the family – to Italy – in few relationships with Italians and Italian Americans of the same age

a typology that summarizes and interprets how young Italian Americans experience their relationship with their ethnic background, ultimately building a classification according to four groups so labeled:

1. The "contemporaries"
2. The "integrated"
3. The "disinherited"
4. The "traditionals"[2]

From a first reading of the emergent characteristics resulting from the aggregation produced by cluster analysis, some distinctive traits that describe the four profiles are observable:

> the "contemporaries" (19.3%, equal to 37 subjects) demonstrate that they have a well-developed cultural knowledge of their ethnic heritage and, in particular, of contemporary Italy, which seems to guide their identification with Italy more than the United States. The dimensions of their *italianità*, however, seem to be encapsulated in a private rather than a collective sphere. Affectively attached to Italy, they demonstrate a lesser affinity for the United States and the Italian American culture and community. Negative stereotypes that surround the Italian American community may account for poor recognition of the collective component by this group. These young people may want to create distance and not see themselves as belonging to the group, due to the fact that they are primarily "educated" people in relation to their ethnic background and "aware" of their *italianità*.

> The "integrated" (25.5%, or 49 respondents) show a positive above-average trend in all the dimensions studied, except for attachment to the United States, where the value is negative (below average). In this group, knowledge profile refers to the whole cultural framework that makes up *italianità*, including the current status of Italy. Their level of emotional attachment diffuses into the most personal aspect of this belonging, as well as the community aspect.

> The "disinherited" (19.3%, equal to 37 individuals) represent the opposite ideal-type to the previous one, that is, they achieve negative values on all dimensions, with the exception of the one referring to their link with the United States. *Italianità* has been abandoned, and the irrelevance of the adjective defines them as the group who has not received the "legacy of the fathers."

> The "traditionals" (35.9%, equal to 69 subjects). This is the most populous group in the typology. In fact, their knowledge is restricted to Italian and

Italian American popular and traditional culture, and they have no knowledge of contemporary Italy. They seem more connected to the American side of their relationship to Italian heritage, rather than to Italy and to any familial or personal bonds there. The lack or scarcity of relationships with Italians and Italian Americans, combined with their limited knowledge of contemporary Italy and lack of attachment to it, seem to position the members of this group in a temporal dimension that exists more in the past than the present.

SKETCH OF THE FOUR GROUPS

Preliminary analysis of the four groups reveals connotations that outline the different profiles and distinguish the young people in relation to their ethnic background. Tables 12.2 and 12.3 summarize how the structural variables and some of the responses related to ethnicity are distributed in the four groups.

THE CONTEMPORARIES

Sociographic Data
In this group we find mainly second-generation respondents, females, and the youngest of the sample, ranging from eighteen to twenty-three years. In terms of their occupations, they are primarily students. The greater number of them are married or have a partner. Self-identification of class shows the young people of this group predominantly identify as upper class. In their free time, they watch a moderate amount of TV and use the internet between two and six hours daily.

Socialization and Values
In terms of values, this group is distinguished by the prevalence of people concerned about the environment. During their years of primary and secondary school they spent time, in most cases, with friends coming from mixed ethnic backgrounds, including Italian Americans.

Ethnic Self-identification
Regarding their interest in their ethnic background, it emerges that this group find it very important. They define themselves mostly as American and Italian. The majority of them did not indicate being white. The predominant ethnicity of their partners is white and American. Their mothers' ethnicity is described by the adjectives white and Italian American and the fathers' as Italian. Most said they often felt proud of being Italian American, but the majority of them

Table 12.2 The Principal Structural Variables According to the Four Groups

	THE CONTEMPORARIES	THE INTEGRATED	THE DISINHERITED	THE TRADITIONALS	ABSOLUTE VALUES
Males	12.0	34.0	10.0	44.0	50
Females	21.8	22.5	22.5	33.1	142
AGE					
18 to 23 years	21.2	28.8	16.7	33.3	66
24 to 29 years	19.4	23.6	18.1	38.9	72
30 to 34 years	16.7	24.1	24.1	35.2	54
GENERATION OF IMMIGRATION					
second	30.1	39.7	12.3	17.8	73
third	8.2	23.3	17.8	50.7	73
fourth and beyond	20.5	4.5	34.1	40.9	44
MARITAL STATUS					
single	20.3	24.5	19.6	35.7	143
married	21.9	21.9	18.8	37.5	32
divorced	0.0	33.3	33.3	33.3	3
cohabiting	7.70	38.5	15.4	38.5	13
EDUCATION LEVEL					
secondary school	100.0	0.0	0.0	0.0	1
high school	13.0	17.4	21.7	47.8	23
university diploma	9.1	18.2	18.2	54.5	11
bachelor's degree	17.8	30.1	20.5	31.5	73
master's degree	19.6	21.6	19.6	39.2	51
professional certification	0.0	33.3	66.7	0.0	3
doctorate (PhD, EdD)	18.2	27.3	18.2	36.4	11
other educational titles	41.2	29.4	5.9	23.5	17
SOCIAL CLASS					
lower class	22.2	20.0	24.4	33.3	45
middle class	14.0	25.8	19.4	40.9	93
upper class	26.9	28.8	15.4	28.8	52
OCCUPATION					
teacher, employee	19.2	34.6	17.3	28.8	52
manager, entrepreneur, freelance, professional	20.3	23.7	20.3	35.6	59
artisan, merchant	7.7	30.8	23.1	38.5	13
technician, public/private service sector	13.3	16.7	20.0	50.0	30
student	29.0	16.1	19.4	35.5	31
other occupations	0.0	50.0	25.0	25.0	4

Table 12.3 Some Variables Related to Ethnicity According to the Four Groups

	THE CONTEMPORARIES	THE INTEGRATED	THE DISINHERITED	THE TRADITIONALS	ABSOLUTE VALUES
I FEEL					
close to Italy / close to America	19.5	51.2	3.7	25.6	82
not close to Italy/ not close to America	8.7	0.0	54.3	37.0	46
close to Italy/ not close to America	47.1	14.7	14.7	23.5	34
not close to Italy/ close to America	3.3	6.7	13.3	76.7	30
ETHNICITY					
White	16.4	22.4	22.4	38.8	134
American	20.3	22.0	20.3	37.3	118
Italian	21.1	26.8	17.9	34.1	123
Italian American	19.8	28.6	15.9	35.7	126
Black	0.0	0.0	100	0.0	1
Native American	0.0	100	0.0	0.0	1
Irish	5.0	15.0	30.0	50.0	20
German	21.4	7.1	28.6	42.9	14
Jewish	0.0	25.0	50.0	25.0	4
Asian	0.0	0.0	0.0	0.0	0
Hispanic	25.0	0.0	50.0	25.0	4
Other ethnicity	42.9	14.3	14.3	28.6	14
HOW IMPORTANT IS YOUR ETHNIC BACKGROUND?					
very important	20.1	31.5	10.1	38.3	149
somewhat important	16.3	4.7	51.2	27.9	43
DO YOU FEEL PROUD TO BE ITALIAN AMERICAN?					
always	8.6	31.4	14.3	45.7	140
most of the time	53.3	11.1	26.7	8.9	45
sometimes	14.3	0.0	71.4	14.3	7
ARE THERE CIRCUMSTANCES IN WHICH YOU ARE ASHAMED TO BE ITALIAN AMERICAN?					
yes	55.3	10.6	31.9	2.1	47
no	7.6	30.3	15.2	46.9	145
DO YOU FEEL AN INTERIOR CONFLICT TIED TO YOUR ETHNIC BACKGROUND?					
yes	46.3	12	30	12.0	50
no	9.9	30.3	15.5	44.4	142
DURING YOUR CHILDHOOD, WERE YOUR FRIENDS...					
only Italian American	7.1	46.4	3.6	42.9	28
from diverse backgrounds including Italian Americans	20.9	23.6	20.9	34.5	148
from diverse backgrounds excluding Italian Americans	25.0	6.3	31.3	37.5	16

cont'd on page 286

Table 12.3 (cont'd)

DURING YOUR ADOLESCENCE, WERE YOUR FRIENDS...					
only Italian American	0	46.2	15.4	38.5	13
from diverse backgrounds including Italian Americans	19.5	24.5	18.9	37.1	159
from diverse backgrounds excluding Italian Americans	26.3	21.1	26.3	26.3	19
CURRENTLY YOUR FRIENDS ARE...					
only Italian American	18.2	45.5	0	36.4	11
from diverse backgrounds including Italian Americans	18.1	24.4	19.4	38.1	160
from diverse backgrounds excluding Italian Americans	25.0	25.0	30.0	20.0	20

also said that in some circumstances they felt ashamed of being so. Furthermore, their own ethnic background could be a source of inner conflict, as the majority of the respondents in this group pointed out.

Previous observations with regard to their identification as Italian Americans who "refer" to Italy is confirmed by the intersection with the "typology of identification of feeling Italian American": in this respect, the members of the group show a marked propensity to feel closer to Italy than to America. In particular, the attachment of the members of this group to the towns, cities, or neighborhoods where they live has remained stable over time, while their attachment to Italy has grown. For the majority of young people in this group, the link to the United States has been decreasing over time, while those who maintain that it has remained stable are a minority.

Image of Italy and Italians

Those subjects who understand the Italian language and speak it, either occasionally or habitually, predominate among the members of the group. With regard to the use of dialects, those who understand them prevail among "contemporaries," even if some speak them and others do not. The application of the technique of semantic differential demonstrates accentuation of the perceived Italian characteristics of adaptivity, thrift, altruism, and self-determination in the self-perceived image of both the Italian Americans and the Italians.

As previously mentioned, for an in-depth analysis of the dimensions that constitute the interviewees' images of Italian Americans, Italy, and Italians, two factorial analyses were conducted, producing nine dimensions with respect to their visions of Italy and Italians, and eight dimensions that represent their image of Italian Americans. The intersection of the average scores in the factors with the responses to questions about a relationship with Italy and Italians highlights the extent to which the "contemporaries" are personally involved with that nation—of which they regularly receive news and information—and with the Italians with whom they maintain friendships.

The young people of this group have a perception of Italian society compared to American that tends to be marked by the differences that characterize them. They are apt to express a more critical assessment toward Italy; its image appears, in their eyes, blurred by negative connotations in response to suspicions of corruption and organized crime and other unfavorable characteristics they associate with the profile of Italians in general, which link it to superficiality, cunning, and sloppiness. In addition, some feel a sense of disappointment and disillusionment toward Italy. At the same time, this group also displays, more than the other three, a sense of identification and admiration toward Italy, as well as recognizing the refinement and taste of Italian culture.

Their shared image of Italy appears to be twofold: on the one hand, it seems inspired by an unveiled vision of the nation, based on reports of the reality of the problems afflicting it, which produces feelings of disappointment and disillusionment; on the other hand, it generates strong feelings of admiration and identification that bring out the attachment they feel toward Italy.

These young people's direct relationship with Italy is realized through the fact that—in the majority of cases—they have visited the country many times. They have relatives and friends there (some or a few) with whom they are in contact. They also receive information about what is happening in Italy, mostly weekly and in some cases at least monthly. In the New York area, where they live, they are in contact with new Italian immigrants who are more or less the same age as they; in most cases, the meeting is occasional, but some consider them part of the group of friends.

Even food links them strongly to Italy: most claim that they eat Italian dishes every day.

Image of Italian Americans
Just as the image of Italy and the Italians was examined, there was also an attempt to deepen the perception of the image of Italian Americans. The intersection of the averages obtained on the dimensions that emerged from the factorial analysis,

crossed with the responses to the questions related to the stereotypes concerning the Italian Americans, highlights the deeply offended feelings that the members of the group of "contemporaries" experience when Italian Americans are grouped together within the stereotypes that surround them (specifically, the *Guido* subculture). This feeling is accompanied by awareness that these stereotypes have a high impact on the generally held image of Italian Americans.

Stereotypes, Prejudices, and Discrimination
Responses to the question that inquired how the majority of Italian Americans react to the stereotypes that commonly connote them were mostly in favor of embracing and emphasizing them, but also, although less markedly, that the respondents were offended. A widespread stereotype, as noted, connects young Italian Americans to the *Guido* subculture. The prevalent reaction of the interviewees when the stereotype is mentioned by Italian Americans is to feel offended in some way, but if the reference is made by other Americans, the youths primarily react with indifference. They also believe there is still some discrimination against Italian Americans today.

This confirms this group's lack of identification with the Italian American community, as an expression of reactive behavior and of distance from the negative stereotypes that affect the image of Italian Americans in general; the members of this group prefer—on the other hand—to express their ethnicity as a personal and "private" experience. Consistent with this observation, most pointed out that they do not connect to the Italian American community through social media.

Affiliations and Memberships
The majority of those who make up this group profess to hold the Catholic faith, although religious creed has a rather limited importance in their lives. For most young people, education, in this respect, has been rather mild, totally nonreligious for some, although, for others, very religious. The frequency of their attendance at religious rites—despite their rather limited number—discloses that members of the group participate on a weekly or monthly basis. People who are not members of spiritual communities or local churches prevail in this group.

Listing of political preference reveals a greater concentration of subjects claiming affiliation with the Democratic Party, and the presence of fewer respondents who do not identify with any political party. With respect to associations, "contemporaries" are active; most of them belong to a group or an association.

The Future

As for the future of Italian American culture, the prevalent vision among these respondents is that it will disappear, will be lost, and will be assimilated by the American mainstream.

THE INTEGRATED

Sociographic Data

In this group, as in the previous one, second-generation young people stand out and, in terms of gender, males. The age group is very young (between eighteen and twenty-three years). As for the level of education, we find mostly bachelor's degree holders, or subjects with a professional certificate. For employment, the group consists mainly of teachers, employees, artisans, and merchants. The majority of them do not have partners. They tend to self-identify as upper class. As for television viewing, they usually spend between two and six hours a day, and less than two hours, respectively, to reading newspapers and books and using the internet.

Socialization and Values

The group includes those who are in greater number connoted by the dimensions, in the value sense, of materialism, of religiosity and for the importance attributed to what has been defined as the dimension of cultural and social sharing, which collects the answers related to friendship, culture, and stable work. Throughout primary and secondary school they mostly spent time with only Italian American friends. The same tendency is also confirmed in their current choices of friends.

Ethnic Self-identification

Members of the group display high interest in ethnic background. Their identification as Italian and Italian American is accentuated, while being white and American receive less mention. The ethnicity of their partners is characterized above all as Italian and Italian American, while being white and American are largely unmentioned. Maternal and paternal ethnicity are most often defined as Italian. Most respondents did not use the adjectives white, American, or Italian American in this category.

Most of the members of the group pointed out that they always feel proud of being Italian American in any circumstance. Some say they have not had the chance to be ashamed, and others claim that ethnic background is not a reason for inner conflict.

Among these young people, ethnic identification is predominantly expressed through the feeling of being close to both Italy and America. As with the young people of the previous group, Italian food is preferred to others; in this case, Italian dishes are consumed daily. Over the years, the link to the places where the respondents from this group live has remained mostly stable, while the connection with Italy has been growing and the one with the United States has suffered a decline.

Image of Italy and Italians

The representation of Italians and Italian Americans is most characterized in this group by their persistence in pursuit of their goals, which they see as attributable to both ethnic groups. The image of Italy and of the Italians held by the members of this group is inspired by the positive values that they attribute to the Italians, such as honor, respect, honesty, solidarity, kindness, generosity, courage, morality, and the search for the common good, accompanied by a low acceptance of rules and obligations. Like the previous group, they are personally and directly involved with Italy and with Italians, both in terms of staying updated and personal relationships.

Like the image held by the "contemporaries," there is a vision of Italy among the "integrated" that recalls a negative image, linked to the "public/private defects" of Italians, but they also admit to a sense of admiration and identification with the Italians' cultural refinement. In this case, as in the previous one, we are dealing with a mixed, twofold image, although the positive vision that accompanies the recognition of its values is highlighted in a marked way. The vision of these young people lacks the aspect of disappointment and disillusionment that emerges in the profile of the previous group. Therefore, this absence leads to a more markedly positive vision of Italy.

The members of this group, as well as those categorized in the previous profile, have visited Italy many times, where they have relatives and friends (many or some) with whom they are in contact. Most of these young people receive daily information about what happens in Italy. They are also connected with young Italian immigrants who have recently arrived in the United States: they meet them occasionally or only at work, but in some cases they are part of their group of friends. Regarding their knowledge of the Italian language, most subjects in the group understand and speak it. Use of the language by some is occasional, while by others it is habitual. The members of this group are also connoted for their understanding of dialects, which some use commonly, others occasionally, while others—even if they understand them—never speak them.

The group is in the habit of using social media to stay in contact within the Italian American community. Their familiarity with these platforms likely stems from the fact that these respondents are young and thus more accustomed to the new technologies.

Image of Italian Americans
The self-image of Italian Americans held by the "integrated" group is characterized by a cultural and value-based aspect as well as through physical and personality-based traits, and also by the sense of belonging to the Italian American community. What emerges, overall, is a composite image, which, as observed for the "contemporaries," takes offense at the negative stereotypes (in particular the *Guido* subculture) associated with Italian Americans. This strong reaction to the labeling of the group through stereotypes is embodied in disagreement over the question of whether the media express a realistic image of who Italians Americans are today.

Stereotypes, Prejudices, and Discrimination
The members of this group claim that the majority of Italian Americans react to stereotypes with either indifference, amusement, or the tendency to embrace and emphasize them. As for the *Guido* subculture, whether in the case of Italian Americans or other Americans making reference to it, the prevalent reaction of the young people in this group is to feel offended in some way when the subculture is mentioned. They maintain that there is currently much or some discrimination toward Italian Americans.

Affiliations and Memberships
In terms of their religious faith, Catholics are prevalent among the "integrated." They attribute a somewhat high importance to religion in their lives. The majority received an education somewhat qualified by religious faith, while for others it was very marked. This group's participation in religious rites conveys a variety of habits, composed of those who go to church weekly, those who go monthly or annually, or those who attend only on religious holidays. The "integrated" are mostly members of religious and spiritual communities or local churches and, more generally, they participate in groups and associations. Political leanings especially favor the Republican and Independent parties.

The Future

For the majority of the young people in the group, their vision of the future with respect to the Italian American culture encompasses evolution, that is, growth and change.

THE DISINHERITED

Sociographic Data

Most of the respondents in this group belong to the fourth or succeeding generations and are female. These comprise the highest age group of the sample (between thirty and thirty-four years). With respect to schooling, most possess a bachelor's degree and, under the occupational profile, artisans and merchants are prevalent. The majority of these young people denote their social status as lower class. Most dedicate between two and six hours a day to using the Internet and less than two hours daily to reading books.

Socialization and Values

The most notable value dimension within this group is individualism. It consists, as we know, of an original principle that represents the ineradicable root of America and its culture, which, as embodied by the "disinherited," might represent an indicator of greater assimilation. Regarding friendship, during primary school, they had number of friends from mixed backgrounds, including Italian Americans.

Ethnic Self-identification

For the most part, the members of this group consider themselves mildly interested in their ethnic background. Most of them feel that they are white and American; the Italian and Italian American options were chosen by a minority. Their partners' ethnicity was expressed above all through the adjectives white, Italian, and Italian American. Maternal ethnicity is described as white, American, and Italian American, while the adjectives identifying paternal ethnicity are white and American.

Those who fall into this group have also claimed to be proud of feeling/being Italian American only sometimes, that is, on certain occasions. A majority of the subjects highlighted the fact that there are circumstances when they are ashamed of being Italian American and that ethnic background can cause internal conflict. Their ethnic identification, however, suffers a certain detachment both from Italy and from America, though they seem very close to the latter.

The majority noted that they ate Italian dishes two to three times per week. This is the group that, compared to the other three, displays a low frequency of including Italian dishes in their diet. As for their links with significant places, more of them feel that over time the attachment to the place they live has been decreasing and attachment to Italy has undergone a decline as well, while attachment to the United States has grown.

Image of Italy and Italians
Analyzing the images of Italian Americans and Italians as perceived by the members of this group, we note that three characteristics stand out: submission as a characteristic of the image of Italian Americans and superficiality and openness characterizing, instead, both Italian Americans and Italian. Regarding their perception of Italy, the emerging peculiarities are especially their distancing from Italian society and, at the same time, their understanding of the differences between Italian and American society. Moreover, the group is characterized in a more marked way, compared to the other three, by a vision of Italy linked to an acute localism and familism, which they would say characterizes the Italian societal fabric.

The majority have never visited Italy; some have gone there a few times. Most of them have no known relatives in Italy, nor do they have any friends there with whom they keep in contact. Regarding recently immigrated young Italian people, the prevailing position is of no contact. Information concerning Italy is not of interest to them, considering that most people do not pay attention to it at all, and others pay attention only once a year.

The use and comprehension of the Italian language are completely lost in the majority of cases. Some have a limited understanding of the language, but they never speak it. Dialects have totally disappeared from the linguistic repertoire of the group. In general, there is a clear separation from Italian heritage, characterized both by the absence of relationships and by the non-use of the language.

Image of Italian Americans
Observing the characteristics related to their image of Italian Americans, it emerges that the "disinherited" group members' perception is connected above all to the prestige and power that Italian Americans have in the United States. They attribute a very high importance to those dimensions. It is also noted that within this group the majority are convinced that stereotypes heavily influence this image and that representation through the media sends a distorted image

of today's Italian Americans. The majority of this group has no contact with the Italian American community through social media.

Stereotypes, Prejudices, and Discrimination
As for the idea that they have about the reaction that most Italian Americans display regarding the stereotypes that represent them, the tendency is either not to consider them as real or to be amused. When the *Guido* subculture is referenced by Italian Americans, the members of this group react with amusement or consider it an accurate image. With regard to discrimination against Italian Americans nowadays, some believe there is still some form of it, while others argue that it is no longer present. The latter position is more prevalent.

Affiliations and Memberships
From a religious point of view, the group favors personal interpretations of faith rather than adherence to any of the great currents of belief: among them there are those who claim to have their own spiritual creeds, as well as unbelievers. The majority in the group attributes little or no importance to this sphere. The education received by this group was, for most, not built on faith, thus presenting another characteristic that differentiates this group from Italian Catholic culture. Attending services has no importance for them; most declared that they never went to church, others that they only went on the religious holidays. In the majority of cases, the members of the group are not affiliated with religious communities and churches. Mostly, they do not participate in associations and organizations. The larger portion of this group claims a preference for the Democratic Party.

The Future
In this group, as in the previous one, their picture of the future of Italian American culture is linked to two contrasting visions: those who believe that the culture will evolve and change and those who, on the contrary, believe that it will decline and decrease in importance.

THE TRADITIONALS

Sociographic Data
Young people of the third, fourth, and fifth generations of immigration are conspicuous among the "traditionals." They are mainly males and tend to occupy the intermediate age group of the sample. In terms of their education level, most possess a high school diploma, bachelor's degree, and a master's degree. By occupation, the group is mostly composed of those employed in both public and

private services and as technicians, and they are primarily place themselves in the middle class. Most of them do not have a partner.

The majority watch television from two to six hours daily, while this group ranks highest as heavy users of the internet, for more than six hours a day. As a group, they tend spend two to six hours a day reading books.

Socialization and Values
Their value projection appears more varied than the other groups'. Values that appear to prevail are individualism, emotional support, and religiosity. During primary school, these young people chiefly made Italian American friends, while during secondary school they opened up to developing friendships from different ethnic backgrounds, including Italian Americans. The latter tendency also appears predominant for current friendships.

Ethnic Self-identification
In this group a majority of subjects declared themselves very interested in their ethnic background. They do, however, feel white and American above all. The "Italian" and "Italian American" modalities were not often selected. Their partners' ethnicity was most often expressed using the adjectives white and American. As for their parents, they were primarily identified as white, American, and Italian American.

Their pride in being Italian American is expressed very strongly, especially by those—the majority—who claim to feel this way in every circumstance, all the time. This group comprises those who never feel ashamed of being Italian American, which underlines that their ethnic background is no reason for internal conflict. The ethnic identification of the "traditionals" is influenced by equal attachment to the United States and Italy.

Their appreciation for Italian cuisine is somewhat felt, considering that most of them prefer Italian dishes two to three times a week. Their attachment to the place where they live has grown over time, while the one with Italy has remained stable, and the link with the United States has been increasing.

Image of Italy and Italians
Comparing the images of Italian Americans and Italians in the perception of the interviewees, the members of this group especially emphasize the aspect of determination and commitment that characterizes both groups, as well as modesty in the case of Italians. Analyzing the image that the "traditionals" have of Italy, it is observed that they refer to the positive values and image of Italians,

denoting the virtues of honesty, honor, respect, kindness, and solidarity. Nevertheless, they feel very distant from Italian society. The major portion of this group includes those who have never visited Italy or who have been there only sometimes. Most also claim not to have knowledge of relatives in Italy, nor do they have any friends with whom they are in contact. There is also no contact with young Italian immigrants who recently arrived in the United States.

Little or no interest is given to news concerning Italy; most have declared they get news of the country annually or not at all. Comprehension and use of the Italian language present a multifaceted situation within the profile. The largest group consists of those who understand a little Italian but never speak it. At the same time there are subjects who have a rather good understanding of the language but never speak it, and finally, there is a group which neither understands nor speaks it at all. In summary, the people who make up this group are united by their non-use of the Italian language, whether or not they understand it. Regarding dialects, the majority understand them a little but never speak them; others have no knowledge of them at all.

Image of Italian Americans
For the "traditionals," the representation of Italian Americans is modeled through value elements and cultural traits, physical and personality characteristics, and the sense of belonging to the Italian American community. The prestige and power that Italian Americans have in the United States are very important for shaping the image. Another strongly felt connotation of the image is recognition of group membership. In any case, the majority of the group does not use social media to connect with the Italian American community.

Stereotypes, Prejudices, and Discrimination
As for the possible reaction of the majority of Italian Americans to the stereotypes that represent them, the "traditionals" mostly claim to be offended. Faced with mention of *Guidos* and *Guidettes*, either by Italian Americans themselves or by other Americans, the young people of the group react above all with good humor or indifference. Most maintain that there is no longer discrimination toward Italian Americans.

Affiliations and Memberships
Religious belief classifies members of the group primarily as Catholic, although a very few are Protestant. The majority attribute a high level of importance to spirituality. Religious education has been mildly imparted throughout this group.

In addition, the majority of the group participate in local churches or religious communities, most of them weekly.

Most of these young people do not participate in associations or organizations. In terms of their political affiliation, the subjects principally declare themselves to be Independents or Republicans. Some among them define themselves as Libertarian.

The Future
The future of the Italian American culture is viewed by the "traditionals" as a reaffirmation and continuation of the existence of this culture.

CHARACTERISTICS OF THE FOUR PROFILES

Following the analysis of the four typologies, a summary of some emergent indications is possible. The "contemporaries" and the "integrated" divide the second generation in half regarding the ways they represent and interpret *italianità*. While both groups are deeply connected to their ethnic heritage, they possess opposing views of *italianità* from a relational point of view: for the former, it is predominantly "private," while for the latter it has a collective value as well.

The first—especially female—students and respondents clustered at the younger end of the sample, possess a "cultured," "intellectual" image of their Italian background: they know popular and high culture, language, and dialects. Moreover, they tend to identify as upper class. Definitions under the ethnic profile highlight that the majority feel "American" and "Italian." They do not indicate being white as part of their identification. The absence of this trait might betray a double meaning: on the one hand, the lack of knowledge of the history of Italians in America and of the path that led them be acknowledged as whites; on the other hand, their lack of direct experience, as being white is now generally attributed to Italians and therefore taken for granted. Also, their responses have been shaped by openness, as they have, in fact, grown up in ethnically heterogeneous environments.

The characteristics that qualify this identity profile appear to be based on a defensive position, detached in some way from the negative aspects of Italian and Italian American reality. Although they feel very close both to Italy and to America, they express a critical position toward contemporary Italy and regarding the Italian American community.

Their involvement in modern Italy is direct and personal and has both cognitive and relational bases: they have visited many times, frequently receive news, have friends and relatives in Italy with whom they are in contact, as well as relationships with new Italian immigrants in New York, and they eat Italian food almost every day. Precisely because of the significance and knowledge of Italy in their life, they have a disenchanted and critical vision, which is, simultaneously, emotional: they feel a sense of disappointment and disillusionment about the known dysfunctions that characterize the country, but also admire and identify with the aspects of value and taste that accompany the country's artistic and cultural heritage.

Their identification of themselves as Italian American involves conflicting feelings: most of the time they feel proud, but they also feel shame in some cases, and this duality can create inner conflict. The aspect that stands out as a reason to distance themselves from the Italian American identity is connected to the stereotypes. For those young interviewees there are feelings of offense and awareness linked to the impact stereotypes have on the image of Italian Americans. This is why they perceive themselves as different and feel distant from the Italian American community, whose reaction in the face of negative stereotypes is, in their opinion, generally to embrace and emphasize them and only rarely to feel offended. In addition, they believe there is still some discrimination against Italian Americans today.

Although they do not conspicuously acknowledge themselves as belonging within the Italian American community, they are generally active in associations. Furthermore, even though they are mainly Catholics, they have only a mild connection with religion, both because their education has been marked by minimal faith values and because religion does not occupy a relevant position in their existence. Politically, they tend to relate to the Democrats, but some do not align themselves with any political party. Regarding the future of Italian American culture, the prevalent position is that it will fade away, it will be lost, and it will assimilate into the American mainstream.

The other face of the second-generation identification is represented by the "integrated" group. As with the "contemporaries," they are younger and attribute great importance to their ethnic background. What differentiates them is they are primarily males and working people, mainly in the fields of education, commerce, and handicraft, and in the clerical sector.

Regarding the connection with *italianità*, the overall reading of the characteristics that converge in this model tends to disclose a double cultural belonging and double ethnicity. This group also expresses the bidirectional neo-assimilation model, in which they play the role of "mediators or connectors," a liaison between the past, the present, and the future of this composite community. Very connected and close both to Italy and to the United States, they define themselves ethnically as both Italians and Italian Americans. They also self-identify in the upper social class. With respect to their ethnic heritage, they claim to always feel proud of being Italian American and never ashamed of this designation, which does not provoke any internal conflict in them.

Their experience with Italian society and with Italians is direct and personal; it encompasses both the informational and the relational fields. They too, like the "contemporaries," have traveled to Italy many times, speak Italian and use dialects, eat Italian food almost daily, have contacts with Italian relatives and friends, receive news and information daily, and meet new Italian immigrants in New York. While their image of Italy is more positive than that of the "contemporaries," it is twofold even for them: on the one hand, they have a negative perception linked to Italian vices and distortions; on the other hand, the image is positively represented and elicits admiration and identification from the group members.

Raised in environments where their friends were predominantly Italian Americans, they place membership to the community among the characteristics that make up the image of Italian Americans—in addition to culture, values, and physical and personality traits. It is in this regard that the group sharply contrasts from the preceding one. Their expressions of ethnicity are articulated not only in the private sphere, but are also communal: they stay connected to the community through social media.

Negative stereotypes also affect these young people, who as a group are offended by them. They do not recognize themselves in the media-proposed images of Italian Americans, and they do not consider those images realistic. Moreover, they believe that the reactions of the Italian American community to the stereotypes linked to the *Guido* subculture can be described through feelings of indifference, amusement, but also as a tendency to embrace and emphasize them. By their account, there is still very much or some discrimination toward Italian Americans within American society today.

Like their peers in the previous category, they actively participate in associations. Predominantly Catholics, they have received a very or somewhat religious education. The value of religion reverberates in their lives, and is of considerable importance to them. Politically they are primarily conservatives and independents. They perceive the future of Italian American culture as consisting of evolution and change, but they also imagine that its importance may fade and diminish.

This group stands out above all for the wealth of the relationships that support its placement in the Italian American community. For this group, the elements of the past coexist in connection with a modernized perspective resulting from their personal relationships with Italy and its culture. Because of these connotations, members of this group could be the ones who will pass on many more of the values they view as characteristically Italian American to their children.

The two following profiles—the "disinherited" and the "traditionals"—comprise a marked convergence of young people from the third, fourth, and successive generations of immigration. Their relationship with Italian heritage seems to have faded and lost vitality. It is known that as the distance from their arrival on American soil grows, the generations' links with their original ethnicity tends to weaken. These two profiles confirm that trend, although in very different ways. The "disinherited" express a sense of detachment from both American and Italian society, and is the group that attributes a lower degree of importance to their ethnic background than the other three. Composed primarily of girls belonging to the fourth and fifth generations of immigration, they are among the "oldest" respondents in the sample and place themselves in the lower social class. From an ethnic point of view, they define themselves as white and American and show some feelings of attachment to the United States.

This group presents evidence of the fact that the living ties with Italy have been severed. There is a prevailing sense of detachment, abandonment, and renunciation of their Italian background, despite their self-identification as Italian Americans. This identification, however, probably occurs only on an emotional level and is not substantiated by a conscious choice: they are "orphans" and to them the legacy has not been transmitted. They are the disinherited, as it were. In this regard, it should be clarified what it means to inherit; as Recalcati (2013) argues, in this context, the central issue consists of transmitting desire. He affirms that inheritance implies a specific movement between identification and disidentification, but it is neither one nor the other:

> In order to possess authentically what you have inherited you must reconquer it.... If the first legacy is that of blood and enjoyment, the second is the human and symbolic of desire.... In fact, inheritance is not a genetic patrimony that is acquired by descent, because it involves above all the singular

act of wanting to inherit, to consent to the inheritance, to regain the inheritance (Recalcati, 2011, p. 19).

The word *desire*[3] does not define "unlimited enjoyment, without law, erratic, devoid of responsibility, fiercely compulsive and unruly, but rather the capacity for work, enterprise, project, momentum, creativity, invention, love, exchange, openness, creation" (Recalcati, 2012, p. 16).

Referring again to Recalcati's words, we add the definition of the concept of symbolic filiation, seen as a link between generations: "Heredity is the foundational principle of every symbolic filiation. . . . Filiation, implying the movement of inheritance, supposes that there is a transmission of desire from one generation to the next" (2013, p. 137). And again: "Inheritance is never a legacy of blood, it is not a consolidation of a solid identity: what is inherited is always a testimony" (ibid., p. 146).

Thus, inheritance is not a passive, static concept, taken for granted; and it does not lead to the constitution of a prefabricated identity and a repetition of the past:

> Inheritance is never by nature, by destiny or by historical necessity. It is not an obligation, although it implies a bond, a symbolic debt. . . the authentic inheritance is not a fact of blood or biology. . . . The inheritance is not the appropriation of an income, but it is a reconquest always in progress. Inheriting then coincides with existence itself, with the creation of the subject, never completed once and for all, throughout our existence. We are nothing more than the stratified whole of all traces, impressions, words, meanings that came from the Other constituting us. (Recalcati, 2013, pp. 122–23)

This does not mean that the past should no longer exist and that memory should be erased. On the contrary, in this way, as in the case of the interpretative model under examination, the inheritance fails: "There is another way of failing the inheritance. . . . It is about severing the link with the past, the refusal of memory, the cancellation of the symbolic debt that accompanies our origin from the Other. Inheritance. . . does not end with the activation of memory, yet without memory there can be no inheritance" (ibid., p. 130). Therefore, to inherit it is necessary to preserve the memory: "Inheritance cannot then be the cancellation of this word and of this memory of the Other—of the symbolic debt that binds us to it—nor can it be a passive repetition (ibid., p. 124). For members of the "disinherited" group, identification as Italian Americans is sometimes a matter both of pride and also of shame, which leads to emotional conflict.

The interviewees' image of Italy and Italians is affected by the lack of direct experience and knowledge: most have never visited Italy, are not interested in information about Italian society, and do not speak the language or dialects. They do not have contact with friends or relatives in the country of origin or with the new Italian immigrants in New York. Their vision of Italy is based on localism and familism, and they see Italians as submissive and superficial. On the whole, they feel distant from Italian society, and their attachment to this country has been decreasing over time. There is only one element that reconnects them to their homeland: food. In fact, they eat Italian dishes two or three times a week.

Media representations of Italian Americans are considered false and not in correspondence with current reality. Negative stereotypes weigh on this image even for this group. What distinguishes Italian Americans in America is the position of prestige and power they have achieved, and that they now experience no—or at least very little—discrimination as a group. Like the "contemporaries," they are not "communitarian": they do not maintain contacts with the Italian American community nor are they active with respect to associations. The stereotypes surrounding the *Guido* subculture are not seen as real and can therefore arouse amusement in Italian Americans.

Mostly they are not believers or spiritually inclined, as they have not received a religious education and attribute little or no importance to faith for their own existence. Politically they identify especially as Democrats. As for the future of Italian American culture, they express two opposing views: there are those who maintain that it will evolve and change, while others say that it will tend to decline. In short, the data confirm a clear separation from the Italian heritage, connoted by the absence of relationships and the lack of use of the language. Widening the interpretation, the "disinherited" might be seen as the tip of the emerging iceberg representing the group who do not feel or do not know they are "Italian American."

The fourth and last group, the "traditionals," is predominantly comprised of young males, who are in the intermediate age group of the sample, belonging to the third, fourth, and subsequent generations, service industry workers, and middle-class people. They and the "disinherited" share the value placed on individualism, even if in their case it is accompanied by an emphasis placed on emotional support and religiosity.

From an ethnic point of view, they define themselves as white and American and express a high interest in ethnicity. They feel closer to the United States than to Italy; toward the former they experience a strong attachment that has been increasing over time. In contrast, their connection with Italy has remained stable over the years. They claim to always feel proud of being Italian American and never to feel ashamed of this identification, which, likewise, never causes them any internal identity conflict. This facilitates their expression of security and pride in being Italian American, as a group that has a stable place within American society, which is also accompanied by the idea that there is no longer any discrimination against Italian Americans. Except for this last aspect, their emotional configuration is shared with the "integrated," and follows the same pattern.

In the course of their lives, friendships have included the Italian Americans, accompanied during adolescence and up to the present age by friends of all ethnic backgrounds. Cultural knowledge is linked primarily to aspects of tradition.

Theirs is a positive image of Italy, where the virtues of honesty, respect, honor, and solidarity prevail. It is an image read about or recounted by others—for instance, in the stories of grandparents or parents—since most of the group is culturally detached from Italy and they have never visited in person, as also occurs with the "disinherited." In fact, young people in this group have no Italian contacts whatsoever: they do not have relatives or friends with whom they have relationships, they are not interested in the news concerning this country, and do not even have relations with young Italian new immigrants in New York. For them, the Italian language is more understood than it is spoken, or is neither understood nor spoken at all. Even dialects, though understood a bit, are not spoken.

Another aspect that unites them to the "integrated" is their sense of community and their recognition that they belong to the group: in fact, they feel part of the Italian American community even if this identification only exists at a perceptive level and translates neither into associative activism nor the search for communication methods through social media. They interpret the image of Italian Americans through cultural and value characteristics as well as by the physical and personality traits, and also by the prestige and power Italian Americans have earned in American society. For "traditionals" the negative stereotypes linked to their representation arouse reactions of either offense or indifference.

The emphasis placed on religion among the values deemed important is reinforced by the equally high relevance they confer on faith in their lives. Despite having received minimal religious education, primarily Catholic or Protestant, they express their beliefs by participating in rites and attending local churches. From a political point of view, they recognize themselves especially within the Republican creed or as independents. Italian American culture is projected, in their opinion, toward the future and they imagine that it will continue to exist.

These Italian Americans seem to have retained more of the "stereotypical" image of Italian culture, the one transmitted by the media rather than through relationships (now lost) with the country of their families' origins. The "passive transmission of the inheritance" describes the overall picture that emerges from this typology, a static and crystallized preservation of ethnic heritage and especially of tradition that does not provide for a personal and active reelaboration. Their identification is not confirmed by active participation in the community, but by the past.

In this case as well, the words of Recalcati (2013) clarify the concept of passive transmission of inheritance:

> To inherit cannot be reduced to a simple repetition of the past, a passive movement of absorbing what has already been. Inheritance is not the reproduction of what has already happened. Rather, the repetition of the past, the excess of identification, of gluing, of alienation, its passive absorption or its veneration, are ways in which the act of inheritance fails... inheritance is above all a decision of the subject, a progressive "reconquest." This movement is the opposite of a nostalgic withdrawal. The "reconquest" of inheritance means subverting the passive replication of the previous state. Inheriting is never cloning, it is never the passive reproduction of an ideal model drawn from the past.... the heir does not only look backwards.... Inheritance is the effect of a reconquest of what has existed; it is the product of choice, of a subjective assumption of our entire history which is, above all, the history of the Other. (pp. 124–125)

But what is inherited, then? "Inheritance does not imply the discovery of a pre-made identity, of timeless roots, because it is a movement that goes beyond the familiar. One does not inherit a certification of identity, because there is no genetic inheritance. Filiation, being symbolic, disrupts the descent of the lineage. The potential for desire is what's inherited. Desire is at stake in every authentic heritage" (ibid., pp. 137–138). If we interpret inheritance as an "open risk" and not as a "consolidation of an already acquired belonging," we can see that "roots do not seal the identity; it must be reclaimed each time by a movement of wandering.... Inheritance as a reconquest is never an uncritical fidelity to the past; it is not archival memory or rent" (ibid., p. 130).

In reality, the "traditionals" are individualists, but their cases lack the sense of isolation, which instead characterizes the situation of the "disinherited": they feel they are within American society and also belong to the Italian American community, of which, moreover, they are an expression, an active presence. These young people seem to express a culture that they have received passively from their families, almost like the passage of a "torch" that they continue to bear forward, bringing memories back to life; they also receive these memories from a community that often continues to repeat itself in the name of the past. They seem to express, in other words, a not evolving hibernate culture and are convinced that they are Italians due to the elements of tradition they carry inside. This fact sometimes makes them feel "more Italian than Italians," yet Italy's current state is of little interest to them.

Even the ties of language have been cut, which for them has inhibited the evolution of the Italian language and dialects. There appears to be a legacy of words as a subtext that emerges from the past and sometimes returns to the mind, words that are perhaps still used in conversations with their grandfathers and grandmothers. The syntagms of the past reemerge from memory, called up by the strength of the remembrance; but they are "commemorative" words, not a language. In reality, the position of the "traditionals" regarding *italianità* expresses the complex and very often contradictory return to the traditions that is perceivable in many aspects of contemporary life and that frequently connect it to other notions such as identity, memory, and especially roots (Bettini, 2011).

In fact, the association between identity and tradition is a recurrent factor in cultural debate, and often the identity of a group is conceived as deriving directly and solely from tradition: we often hear that "identity is founded on tradition" (Bettini, 2011, p. 11). By doing so, the past is delegated the power to tell us "who we are" in the present. A cause and effect relationship is established between tradition and identity, where identity is produced by tradition and a group's cultural tradition is often associated with the image of the roots. As Bettini (2011) maintains, "Roots occupy a dominant position in contemporary metaphorology related to identity" (p. 19). But metaphors—as noted—are cognitive tools and the ones specific to roots have "the ability to strongly influence any discourse on identity and tradition... the roots-based image allows the direct replacement of argument with a vision" (ibid., p. 20). Furthermore, through the image of the roots, and therefore the corresponding tree, "tradition is transformed into something biologically primordial, which is immersed in the earth, something that sustains and nourishes—who? Clearly *us*, our own identity" (p. 25).

Thus, the relationship of perception between identity and tradition is laden with a force that springs from nature: "If a tree is such a tree because it has grown from those roots, we are who we are because we have grown from the roots of our cultural tradition" (Bettini, 2011, p. 26). Besides, the position that the roots occupy is also significant: the roots are at the bottom, compared to the trunk and leaves, and this illuminates the semantic field of what is fundamental. Bettini notes that this metaphor aims to construct what he calls "a device of authority," which, "by virtue of the image, is nourished by strong semantic nuclei including life, nature, biological necessity, position hierarchy and so on" (p. 28).

When cultural identity comes into play, the ramifications of this authority device convey a significant meaning onto the life of individuals; this cultural identity so founded is extended to an entire group, and the individuals, rooted in a specific tradition, are unable to independently choose their own cultural identity: "We can only recognize ourselves in what others have built for us" (ibid., p. 29).

It is clear that in each of us there are ways of seeing and thinking that have been inherited from the past and that the tradition into which we are inserted (the language we learn as children, the food habits received in the family, the ways of thinking, to react and even to gesticulate, etc.) contribute markedly to solidifying the personality of an individual, as well as the collective personality of the group of which he/she is part and the feeling of belonging to the group itself. However, all of this should not lead to an oppositional choice where the passive bearers of a traditional identity are opposed to individuals who refuse any link with the community that shares their language and culture.

One should, therefore, appeal to different definitions and images to indicate the tradition, not linking it to "a biological fatality" or to an "inevitable descent" but to something more open and free: a definition not in "vertical" terms, but in "horizontal" terms (Bettini, 2013, p. 39). Bettini suggests a river and its tributaries as an alternative image to that of the tree, in reference to their intrinsic fluidity. This horizontal vision of tradition would present the possibility of integration with other aspects of life, a sense of belonging to tradition without feeling imprisoned by it.

By changing the defining connotations of tradition and seeing it as a set of lifestyles, it becomes something that is constructed and learned. In fact, Bettini observes that "without a continuous learning process, any tradition is snuffed out before long" (p. 47). Like any other type of knowledge, it is the result of specific choices of acculturation and learning. Thus, "the strength of a tradition does not derive from the fact that it comes from the past, as we normally believe or are told, but from the fact that we continue to teach its contents in the present. Or even from the fact that one *begins* to teach or spread these elements in the present as happens in the case of invented traditions.... A tradition is increasingly solid the more the framework that sustains it exists in the present, that is, the more we continue to repeat and *teach* that the tradition is strong and ancient" (p. 50). Furthermore, since tradition is studied and learned, it is inextricably linked to the existence of writing.

Tradition, therefore, refers to a past, though such an affirmation should be accepted with caution, as some traditions that appear to be or are claimed to be old may often have a recent origin and are sometimes completely invented (Hobsbawm, 1987). Hobsbawm defines the invented traditions as "a set of practices, generally regulated by openly or tacitly accepted norms, and endowed with a ritual and symbolic nature, which aim to instill certain repetitive values and norms of behavior in which continuity with the past is automatically implied. In fact, where possible, these generally try to affirm their continuity with an appropriately selected historical past" (pp. 3–4). It is not necessary for the historical past on which the new tradition is founded to be out of reach or lost in the mists of time; the historical past to which the invented tradition refers enables the affirmation of its continuity over time, even if this aspect appears wholly fictitious. Constructing this past allows for an almost obligatory repetitiveness.

The interest that surrounds the invented traditions derives precisely from the emergent contrast: steadiness and immutability versus the modern world in continuous and incessant change. After all, the very purpose and characteristic of all traditions, including those invented, is immutability; the past to which they refer, real or invented, imposes fixed and usually formalized practices, including such repetition.

The collective or group memory is another fundamental element that enters this debate. This memory refers to various frameworks regarding social nature that influence its contents. If these social frameworks change, the memories of the past also change. The social group acknowledges its past and its tradition by adapting it to the social frameworks of the present, and simultaneously projecting its own future. Bettini highlights that there are groups that "remember more, or do so for longer, and others that remember less" (Bettini, 2013, p. 59). Some groups suffer from what has been called "structural amnesia" or "social amnesia" (Burke, 2000).

In the case of Italian Americans, Vecoli (2000) points out that the transmission of cultural heritage within the family and in institutions is carried out poorly or incompletely. This has led to what he calls a "generation of lost souls" (p. 83). And, provided that ethnicity is a form of memory, it is observable that many Italian Americans suffer from amnesia. Recalling Freud, he points out that "forgetting is a way to evade the pain of remembering" and that numerous aspects of the Italian American experience have been painful. But precisely for this reason, he is convinced that the work to be done is not passing these painful memories into silence, but bringing the memory of conflicts, sectarianism, and repression to the surface. Also, it should be noted that "you remember because you want to remember, and remember what, for various reasons, you decide to remember" (Bettini, 2011, p. 59).

Viewing traditions as horizontal and not vertical, considering them as coming not from the earth but from the continuous learning and reconstruction of the collective memory entails a complex change in perspective. And choosing one model of tradition rather than another is a sensitive decision because it will determine the processes of collective reconstruction of memory. This choice can have profound impact on school programs and training curricula as well as repercussions on the cultural memory of future generations. As Bettini notes, this implies making "decisions related to the awareness of contemporaneity and also to the collective memory of future generations" (2013, p. 81).

Finally, in the composite panorama that represents young Italian Americans, one wonders who among them will be responsible for passing down Italian cultural heritage, delivering it to the future. There are echoes of a previously noted separation, found in the discussion on "visible" and "invisible" Italian American writers.[4]

Even in the profiles analyzed up to this point, such a connotation appears explanatory with respect to the Italian legacy, in the sense that the "disinherited" and the "contemporaries," whose existing link with *italianità* is detached from the collective dimension, appear "invisible" in the attestation and transmission of this background.

Unlike them, the Italian identification of both the "integrated" and the "traditionals" is established within a community dimension and, as such, it appears "visible." The latter two models, though coexistent, express two alternative ways of interpreting this heritage and also reflect two different ways of imagining the future of Italian culture and tradition. They are likely to be more active in the collective sphere than the two preceding groups—the "contemporaries" and the "disinherited"—in continuing to perpetuate this bond, but each will do so in a unique way: the "traditionals" are more fixated on the past, as preservers of tradition and, therefore, are more at risk of falling, of forgetfulness, and of abandonment in the face of a reality that is evolving faster all the time; the "integrated" build bridges that connect the past to the future and engage in a more dynamic and current perspective.

The four profiles drawn all represent ideal types from within the Italian American community. Naturally, modeling reality allows some elements of a situation to be represented in a simplified way, and it is obvious that these four ways of imagining the relationship with *italianità* coexist and express themselves in hybridized forms; as such, they indicate trends in progress. There is much to invent, create, and process by mixing elements of a reality that continuously evolves and changes.

CONCLUDING REFLECTIONS

Very often, during the period when I was doing my research work, I received phone calls from people who were asking for explanations about the survey I was conducting. After the objectives and goals were explained to them, they usually showed a willingness to help me spread the news and to recruit relatives, friends, and acquaintances, or to take part directly. Before proceeding, I had to ask them three routine questions that preceded completing the questionnaire. Occasionally, when I arrived at my third question, the age of the potential participant, the subject had to be excluded for being outside the established age bracket. Someone of a mature age asked me: "But why study young people? What do they know about what it means to be Italian American? We know about it, not them." I could already form some considerations just from this statement: on the one hand there was a sense of distrust that young people could be repositories of knowledge on this experience; on the other hand rests the admission of having failed in the "transfer of desire," as Recalcati would say, but also of not being able to instill a love of this wealth of knowledge to be passed on to young people as a "generational gift." At that point, I had to explain that hearing the opinion of young people signified an examination of the present, but especially, and at the same time, of the future. Yet this inquiry remained: "But what do the young people know about being Italian American?"

I have attempted to answer this question with my work. I did it through a privileged observatory, namely an "expert pool," so to speak, composed of people who filled out the questionnaire and thus decided to convey, to express their way of being/feeling Italian American, as they interpret it, what expectations they have for the future, and how they see or do not see personal involvement in the project of delivering this heritage to the next generations.

Some of these young people have actively inherited this background, in the sense that they have contributed in a personal way and have chosen to make it their own, others have received it passively, almost as if passing the torch and taking it for granted, and still others have not inherited it or that legacy has been "lost" through the generations.

In August 2013, at a presentation in Pittsburgh of the research I was conducting, a young person asked me: "But what am I supposed to identify with? I haven't inherited anything from my family. I have no memories or recollections." In response, I said the following: "The fact that one happens to be an orphan doesn't signify the lack of ability to retrace the imprints left on the ground by our parents', grandparents', and great-grandparents' footsteps. You need only to look for them and they will be found. And you show real signs of such an interest. One of them is simply attending this conference on such a sultry August day."

To generate young people's interest in my work, I participated in many events, meetings, festivals; I held conferences; I entered the classrooms at the end of the lesson, I talked about it in the corridors and on the campus gardens; I socialized and spent free time with them (I even went to a soccer tournament organized by young Italians and Italian Americans!). I took a trip to places where I could meet them: I saw numerous young Italian Americans and spoke with many of them regarding their own experiences and my work.

At the end of the field research, before starting to analyze the data, it almost felt as though I knew each one of these young people, even if that was not the case, hidden as they were by the anonymity of the online questionnaire; yet there were many I did meet in person with whom I exchanged ideas.

At this point I sought to analytically exhibit the results of this project, which has deeply enriched me and taught me very much.

The final conclusions, for those with the patience to read the many preceding pages, could already be discerned, as "the assassin has already been revealed in the course of the story." So, I only want to indicate "points of emphasis," which may have already been observed, but are now reinforced by the results of my study.

VARIOUS WAYS OF BEING ITALIAN AMERICAN

There are various ways of being Italian American. Those who identify with this heritage perceive themselves within a virtual community of people, ideas, and different ways of interpreting *italianità* through a multiplicity of identities and belonging. It is an *italianità* without a state, recognized via a history and a common past that constitute some, but not all, of its founding elements. It is a culture made of diverse components, some of which are transmitted while others are let go. In this identification and this representation there is a coexistence of ascribed and acquired characteristics, elements chosen and not chosen, some consciously and others unconsciously.

This stateless ethnicity is not based on spatial proximity, but on networks of relationships that follow shifting trails because the territory, the social space where they have been left behind, changes. Thus, it is necessary to have the tools to recognize them. New means of communication (social media, for example) transmit cultural capital and create lines of continuity among the people who are the nodes of these networks.

The complex Italian American identity must be studied, therefore, through the changes that have affected race, gender, class, religion, and lifestyle.

The young people interviewed represent a group of subjects who have self-identified as Italian American. Therefore, the study conducted is, by definition, within the Italian American community.

The sample is composed of interviewees who exhibit an elevated critical awareness and a good sense of self-reflection. These are people with a high level of education, who occupy high-profile positions in the U.S. labor market, mostly from the middle and upper middle classes, from families who also have a high level of education and an elevated status within American social strata. They are not forced to struggle to attain an approved position in the social structure, and are completely assimilated into a society that provides space for their ethnic heritage.

The main purpose of the study was to create the least possible approximate picture of the opinions, attitudes, behaviors, and perceptions of young people regarding the lineage that connects them to their family past as well as to a culture that is still fighting to be recognized by the dominant one (Cappelli, 2015a). The underlying research question addressed changes in the way that young people either identify or feel uninvolved and distant, including all the intermediate nuances thereof, with their background and Italian cultural heritage. Although the study has been exploratory, the emergent indications of trends give a broad interpretive framework that quite adequately manages to describe and represent current reality, in its complexity.

There are two further questions that arise before the final commentary on the data: "What do we know about those who do not self-identify as Italian Americans, despite possessing this lineage?" "How do we classify that blurry yet numerous cohort of young people who do not identify with this label?" That world of young people outside these defining borders represents another side of the coin. This study has provided us with an inverted mirror through which to glimpse and imagine that other side. The young interviewees indirectly described this other side through their critical observations and the representations they provided for the articulated and complex reality of today's Italian Americans.

To many young Italian Americans, the sense of this identification is completely out of reach; for others, being/feeling Italian American only coincides with a label to which it is difficult to attribute profound meanings, even if more often than not—and despite everything—it is associated with a fierce sense of pride.

The observations highlighted by interviewees during the research described and represented this inheritance that unites them, revealing both problematic issues and strengths; they expressed worries, criticisms, and desires, with the intent to improve, to meet, to find each other, and to reconnect. Although they represent only a part of the population of Italian Americans in this age group, they can be, together with others who care about the Italian heritage, the catalysts of change and reconnection, both inside and outside the Italian American community.

Some reflections highlight a "distancing" from negative aspects, such as the stereotypes connected to Italian origin, which are not recognized as aptly descriptive by many young people. More generally, the notes and main points that have emerged help us to reflect on what paths might be followed to visualize the future of this culture, to revitalize it and reinvigorate it, so that it can evolve and prosper, with the help and involvement of the younger generations.

I will now try to summarize and highlight the most pertinent features that have emerged, the critical nodes, and the trends that lie ahead.

THE ITALIAN AMERICAN IDENTITY: ATTRIBUTIONS OF MEANING

The fundamental question in the debate on ethnicity is whether this attribute is predominantly connected to descendancy or if it is largely a personal choice. Being of Italian descent does not presuppose having internalized this lineage as a part of one's identity. The ways of understanding and interpreting one's Italian American-ness vary from subject to subject; and the path that leads to self-identification fluctuates from individual to individual. In fact, for some who have no connection with Italian heritage by birth, being Italian American can coincide with a chosen lifestyle, with a model to follow.

The results of the study highlight both the need to free oneself from essentialist visions of identity as well as the need to accept a variegated, interpretive range of *italianità*. This is not all. This identity coexists simultaneously with many other identities, with other memberships and identifications. As noted by Bassetti (Bassetti & d'Aquino, 2010),

> A plurality of memberships is inevitable. Now we live in a world where each of us is the bearer of a plurality of identities, each person belonging to more than one aggregating dimension, not only in ethnic terms, but of nationality and religion and also in terms of tastes, culture, passions, interests... in the emergent new world system, the Italics may have an advantage. Because this new set of multiple memberships with which we will all have to contend integrates and "fits together" more easily with the new system of spontaneous and self-generated loyalties rather than with the current system of loyalties built or imposed from on high. The globalized world, or rather the glocalized world, will be a set of communities, no longer aggregated according to the old territorial criterion of borders established by the nation-state, but on connections that will not depend on geographical limits (p. 107).

In parallel, there is the metaphorical image of a multicultural man with an identity based not on belonging but on the ability to place himself with awareness above all belonging: an individual who lives on the borders, fluid and mobile, able to address the differences and similarities between human beings. This person constructs his or her identity at the edges of two or more cultures, where none of these are considered central, since the individual is placed on a metalevel situated above or beyond individual belongings.

Regarding the identity question, the sample has clearly conveyed the relevance of the ethnic background in almost every case. Such heritage is quite strong and heartfelt. The reasons for this importance present the coexistence of elements that are sometimes in conflict, deeply rooted in the framing of one's identity structure (parts of identity, source of psychological security, resemblance and sense of belonging, difference from the other "whites," continuity and connection), associated with feelings and emotions, connected to relational aspects, linked to the need for knowledge (knowledge of one's personal history, knowledge of the history of the group), anchored to the values transmitted during childhood and adolescence and interpreted in a diachronic dimension that links the past, present, and future (parts of daily life, connection with today's Italy, desire to pass ethnic heritage to their children).

DIFFERENT IDENTITY MODELS

It is intriguing to examine the different identity models that describe the relationship between the Italian background and being American which have emerged from the research. Interviews with the young people reveal how the definition of identity is inclusive, to a variety of extents, regarding *italianità*.

Tracing the meeting of these two identity components, the balancing of them assumes different points of equilibrium, which give rise to differentiated and multiple identifications. In the majority of analyzed cases the two cultures are mixed in an integrated form that takes on a different shade of significance for each subject. The first model is *dual ethnicity*, through which young people express their own understanding of their condition as an integrated identity composed of the two ethnicities: a double cultural belonging that is a dynamic union of two worlds, the Italian and the American, which exist simultaneously; this connection is perceived as an advantage, an "added value" in their life experience.

For others, however, this double belonging is not experienced in the best terms: feeling part of two cultures can create inner conflict and an ambivalence that may generate identity confusion. This situation can also produce feelings of marginality, exclusion, diversity understood as inferiority, a "double non-belonging" that causes the individual to perceive himself as living in a sort of "middle ground." There are still other cases where Italian heritage and culture have been rejected or are in the background and young people have embraced only or predominantly American culture. What the research has shown is that these conditions where identity is recognized or rejected in part are not stable over time nor conclusively defined. The recognition of one's own Italian character changes in the different periods of a person's life and, even if it is acknowledged, becomes accentuated or dimmed in certain circumstances.

For another group, the uniqueness of individual identity conflicts with the plural image of the group, in which the person finds no possibility of expression, and feels suffocated and massified. Here is what one interviewee said in this regard:

> Many times, Italian Americans, especially Southern Italians, are depicted in popular culture in ways that are unfavorable. Beyond the stereotypes, it seems that sometimes within Italian and Italian American cultures there isn't an understanding of the diversity. It is good to feel that there is a shared experience, but very often, you don't see a lot of room for individuality within that collective identity. In the collective identity of the group there is no space for

the expression of a personal identity. Sometimes, the identity of the group is permeated by nostalgia of the past. It is this child like nostalgia of the past, that renders this identity stagnant and above all at odds with my world view.

Enlarging the reflection from the field of Italian American studies to the interpretation of the globalization process according to the perspective offered by Maalouf (1998), it appears that this process can lead to reinforcing a civilization's dominance or the hegemony of a power. Further analysis of his reflections reveal the inherent possibility of two risks: "The first, seeing the slow, deliberate disappearance of languages, traditions, and cultures; the second, seeing those promoting the threatened culture adopt ever more radical and more suicidal behaviors" (p. 107). The risks of this hegemony are real and there is no doubt that Western civilization has acquired and maintained, for centuries now, a privileged position with respect to all others, establishing the absolute preeminence of its political and economic system. Therefore, one wonders about

> what will become of the various cultures?... What will the climate be where globalization is developed in the future, if it appears ever more destructive to cultures, languages, rites, traditions, and as a destroyer of identities? If we are all compelled to renounce our own selves to gain access to modernity as it defines itself and as it will define, won't the traditionalist reaction be generalized, along with violence? (ibid., p. 108)

Globalization poses a serious threat to cultural diversity, languages, and ways of life. Yet the threatened cultures have—as Maalouf claims—"the means to defend themselves... to fight for their very survival" (1998, p. 117). Among these, he specifies the great opportunity offered by new means of communication for fostering a shared culture.

The final vision that emerges from this scenario, translated to the scope of identity, enables the perception of one's identity as the sum of different memberships; where there are people "whose original culture does not coincide with one of the societies in which they live, who must be able to assume a double belonging and maintain their adherence to the culture of origin without too many lacerations" (ibid., p. 147). This statement is not only valid for immigrants, but also for people—Maalouf specifies—who, despite having always lived in the same society, maintain an emotional bond with their culture of origin. This aptly describes the Italian Americans, a group with such a double belonging.

But this is not a process that concerns only the individual. In fact, if on the one hand every individual should have an awareness of the multiple memberships that comprise his/ her identity, the same process belongs to societies that "should also accept the multiple memberships that have shaped their identity throughout history... they should make the effort to show, through visible symbols, that they embrace their diversity... so that each individual can identify with what surrounds him/her, and with the image of the country in which he/she lives... instead of seeking refuge in an idealized past" (Maalouf, 1998, pp. 148–151).

THE VALUES

The value connotation is the determining characterization of being Italian American for many interviewees. Family and food are the two components most often associated with the perception of one's *italianità*. Major emphasis is placed on the family, a value that is reinforced, very often, by feelings connected to ethnic belonging. The family is a characteristic of the Italian American community distinguished for its solidity: it is understood as a foundational value, as a unifying and cohesive element of the household, as an indissoluble bond with one's relatives. Although the Italian family has undergone profound changes during the last century, it remains strongly significant in the mental image of young Italian Americans, despite the changes in its structure and form.

In the ranking of values expressed by young people, the family occupies the first place, followed by love and health, while power and the possession of material goods are generally considered to be of little importance. What emerges from the survey highlights a substantial ethical continuity between parents and children, which extends also to gestures, behavior, and external physical appearance. Greater discontinuity is observed in the translation of value references regarding disposition toward action, that is, in the ways of thinking, of facing life, and in verbal modalities.

THE MISREPRESENTATION OF THE IMAGE OF ITALIAN AMERICANS

The misrepresentation of the image of Italian Americans through the media and the negative stereotypes associated with it represent a crucial point. Of the quintessential stereotypes connected to the Italian Americans, there are essentially two that remain: the mafioso and the *Guido*. Being Italian American, for some interviewees, is connected to the unfavorable connotation in reference to these negative stereotypes, often reinforced by the media. Some television programs focus on a portion of Italian American culture that exalts materialism and aggression, and very often Italian Americans are represented by the media in a miserable way. Many young people, therefore, distance themselves from these negative connotations connected to Italian origin, with which they do not identify.

The relevant fact is that there are clear differences between reality and the presented image of the Italian Americans; it has been amply demonstrated that the stereotypes attributed to Italian Americans do not correspond to the reality and to the experience of the majority of group members. Undoubtedly, however, media is a strong influencer in supporting and conveying such representations: often they are internalized to such an extent that the boundary between reality and fiction fades. This clarifies the admission of many respondents that these mental constructions are grounded in factual reality. Therefore, it appears there is a need to overturn the cultural representation regarding the image and the identity of Italian Americans today. The link between the Mafia and Italoamerica is, in fact, still pervasive today in the American collective consciousness, and Italian Americans have a deep desire to rid themselves of this stereotype (Cappelli, 2015a; De Stefano, 2006).

There is a misstep in the intended target of the Italian American organizations that have mobilized anti-defamation campaigns to combat Mafia representation, namely, the real damage that the Mafia phenomenon has caused to the status of the group in the American society is not being denounced. In fact, such actions address only one aspect of the phenomenon, that is to say the artistic representations, considered defamatory for the whole community; actions are directed, therefore, to fight a supposed damaged reputation caused by such interpretations of the phenomenon. The connection between the Mafia and Italoamerica is continually revived through artistic expressions that perpetuate stereotypical images and Italian American clichés. Not to be overlooked is that often these representations are drawn from within the Italian community itself and embraced by its audience (Cappelli, 2015a).

Undoubtedly, the media have a strong influence as agents of socialization and, to comprehend this influence, their role in this process needs to be more thoroughly analyzed. Some authors have targeted television as serving in this role (especially various types of fiction), seen as one of the principal image makers and sources of mental representations in social reality. This medium cultivates images of reality, produces acculturation and cements belief systems, mental representations, attitudes. And more than that. It also produces the emotional behaviors that correspond to the belief systems (Wolf, 1992).

Other than television, different socializing agencies are encountered and interact in the perception and knowledge of social reality; it is therefore equally important to analyze the relationships and interrelations between them. To reduce and shatter the media's power of socialization we must also study the variables that structure its use and its understanding: it's a matter of a continuous process of negotiating between other agents of socialization, when they come into play. Understanding the relationship between media and socialization must therefore follow two paths of reflection: on the one hand, identify the media's specific contribution to the general process of socialization, on the other observe the complexity that arises from the links between the complementary and conflicting actions of the various socialization agencies.

Another focal point recalls the role that media play as a constructor of social reality. Such a study implies the necessity of having to closely analyze the impact that the symbolic representations of the media have on subjective perceptions of social reality. Other than the various contents of the media and the systems of individual representation, one also needs to account for the "process through which the symbolic representations of the media are used as resources to develop the knowledge systems of its beneficiaries" (Wolf, 1992).

The media are able to construct reality in different contexts: they may institutionalize the representations of reality; conversely it might build social definitions for broader contexts of meaning that frame the sphere of daily life experiences. This is a process during which they do not act in isolation, since the formation of reality is a complex procedure.

But how can the representations developed and disseminated by the media become cognitive and social resources for subjects' interactions? The power of the media to construct social reality is a power that travels through human minds and conforms to the strategies that subjects use to continuously cross the boundaries that separate the different spheres of social reality. "It is a power that is recognized in the actions of subjects, not in the characteristics of the media representations" (ibid., p. 118). In the interaction that brings about the creation of social reality by the media, the knowledge of the recipients and their ability to process information are especially relevant; thus, the users and their daily reality play a fundamental role. The media would have less potential for influence as the individuals' level of competence grows, both in the elaboration and interpretation of information in texts, and in interaction with the television screen. In addition, the attitudes toward the most powerful of these media forms—television—count. A critical spectator is likely to possess a process of developing images of reality very differently from the spectator who engages in passive reception.

Beyond that, the dynamics that characterize the moment of use take on a strategic role in the process of constructing social reality. The sources of experience and connections that form the entirety of the user's social relationships are also relevant. It should be added that the media affect the process of the formation of culture. The media construct social reality through a process that, at first glance, appears invisible to the user; it is therefore very important to make it visible, since the characteristic of "invisibility" is the condition of its efficiency and effectiveness.

The representations of social reality diffused by the media enter social interaction contexts where subjects use them as resources to orient, to understand, to align themselves in their daily actions. Moreover, the representations disseminated by the media can be taken as "objects of mutual knowledge, a common basis, a resource whose knowledge can be taken for granted" (Wolf, 1992, p. 118). In other words, these images of reality constitute a common frame of reference and an institutionalized resource, until proven otherwise. The media outlets, therefore, simultaneously represent a resource and a constraint: in their use they produce and reproduce their own existence as a structurally stable, institutionalized, and shareable resource; and this has repercussions on the features that characterize their use.

The relationship between the media and the process of socialization has been analyzed in different contexts, including the sphere of racial and ethnic identities; in regard to the observation that the media, and in particular television, provide stereotyped, distorted, and incomplete images of these areas of social action, the research has demonstrated that the unavoidable presence of stereotypes is much more articulated and segmented than it appears at first glance (Wolf, 1992).

From the study of the effects of the mass media on prejudice, some scholars have elaborated the hypothesis of parasocial contact, according to which parasocial interactions, connected to the use of the media, can produce the same effects as real interactions.[1] In fact, these interactions involve the same processes, including the acquisition of information and the creation of affective and emotional ties. According to the authors of the study, viewers consider the characters of movies and TV shows as real acquaintances. The media-generated representations can be the products of dominant stereotypes, but they can also reinforce them. Furthermore, prejudices regarding ethnic identity can be internalized.

It is known that in an era of globalization, stereotypes can be conveyed with extraordinary effectiveness by the communications media of late modernity. These constructs are incorporated into the habitus of social actors as part of a real system of schemes, perceptions, thoughts, and actions (Bourdieu, 1991). It is important to understand and examine the ambiguous connection between the stereotype and the media. Is it a sort of media fashion? Is it a consumerist model? We are very often exposed to media marketing.

Applying these reflections to the context of research, it appears that the stereotypes embedded in the media's image of Italian Americans have become consumer products on a par with others, products that improve ratings. Thus, it matters little if the Italian American community is negatively affected by those images. Many Italian Americans watch these shows and see themselves in certain aspects of those representations; others, on the contrary, fight to remove them. The effect of this action, paradoxically, is to raise even more interest in the issues that the media have already illuminated. While appreciating the views of characters in television series such as *The Sopranos*, *Happy Days*, or *Everybody Loves Raymond*, which are in heavy rotation on American channels, many young people adopt a necessary sense of detachment to look "beyond what they see" and to affirm through real interaction what they consider to be Italian American particularities; for others, unfortunately, in the absence of referents to be emulated during their process of forming the adult identity, they acknowledge and even flatten their own identities in deference to these stereotypical images produced by others.

The media are responsible for the dissemination of these stereotypes, although in some cases they are based on real and concrete facts. The desirable solution is a greater understanding, on the part of media users, of the differences between objective and visual reality, through knowledge of the Italian American community as an integrated element in American society. It is important to counterbalance and contrast these negative stereotypical images by proposing positive models, that is, by more strongly emphasizing aspects of merit and value related to Italian and Italian American culture in general. The key words are *information* and *knowledge*.

THE RECOGNITION AND SENSE OF BELONGING
TO THE ITALIAN AMERICAN COMMUNITY

Young people refer to the community in their consideration of the collective image of the group. Here as well, interpretations are disparate, based on an individual's perception and on personal experience regarding their own identification with the Italian American community as a whole, which presents problematic aspects. This creates an environment in which discontinuity and disconnection are expressed and may lead to intergenerational contrast.

For some young people, the community exists as a space for recognition and cohesion, while for others—although existing—it is fragmented and divided. Others have stated that they do not feel as if they belong to it and that they also feel lost and disoriented. Still others feel that the identification with the community aspect induces feelings of pride.

Even the perception they have, more generally, of the Italian American's sense of belonging to the community divides them: a large portion of young people believe that Italian Americans do not recognize it at all, while half of them believe that they feel quite a part of it. The joint vision they hold regarding associations and the sense of community once again highlights the perception of a scarcity of community cohesion that is shared by most young people, albeit accompanied by a fair level of Italian American associationism. Specifically, almost half of the respondents believe that Italian Americans have their associations, but they are not organized as a cohesive community.

Another critical point is represented by relationships, or rather, the lack thereof, between young Italian Americans and new Italian immigrants who are in the same age range as the interviewees. More than half of the respondents point out that they don't have any contact with them and only one-tenth indicated interacting with them to the extent that they would be considered part of their group of friends. Even the manner in which the Italian Americans see themselves compared to the Italians is a point of divergence. While the young Italian Americans claim to feel a great resemblance to the Italians, as emerged from the comparison of the two ideal type images, the two worlds do not communicate, which has created a void that has not yet been filled. Of course, this vision expressed by the Italian Americans should be counterbalanced by information about how Italians see them in turn, but this issue is not the object of interest in this study. In general, the image that emerges from these reflections portrays an Italian American community composed of distinct groups, more communities, one might say, that do not necessarily want to communicate or that, if they try to do so, display mutual distrustful behavior.

There is the old immigration group: the Italian Americans of second, third, and successive generations. There are the new Italian immigrants, those who have been settled in New York for some years now and often have both American and Italian passports. And finally, there is a group of Italians who have only been in the United States a short time or have just arrived. Each group possesses entirely different characteristics.

The division of the Italian American community is one of its characteristics with a long history. Already in the days of the great migration, when the abandonment of Italy was dictated by necessity connected to the lack of structural conditions conducive to survival, the migration was regional: it was not a migration of Italians. Instead, it was a migration of Sicilians or people of Campania, who maintained those territorial divisions even after they had settled in America. Here as well, there was no cohesion; rather, it was a divided community.

Later, then, there were tensions between the Italians who arrived after World War II and their "countrymen born in America." This resentment, from the second group regarding the first, was dictated by the fact that the newcomers had achieved rapid socioeconomic success, in opposition to the battle that the first generations had to fight in order to establish themselves; moreover, a large number who immigrated around the nineteen-seventies were better educated than their predecessors and worked in professional capacities, although a perception persisted that painted these immigrants as poor and needy (Kessner & Caroli, 1982, cited in Ruberto & Sciorra, 2016). For their part, the new immigrants, despite having been helped directly or indirectly by the Italian American communities previously established in the United States, "to some extent, felt superior to their cousins born in America, who were seen as culturally different from them: many Italian Americans did not speak standard Italian or they spoke it badly; they had a poor understanding of the political, economic and cultural scene of contemporary Italy; they often seemed to favor the economic mobility achieved through occupations by the working class rather than through university education" (idem., quoted in Ruberto & Sciorra, 2016, p. 12).

Beginning in the seventies, while there was a continuation of working-class immigrants arriving in the United States, an ever-increasing group of men and women who were often transnationals in their daily lives began to arrive as well, either in possession of a university degree or as students, with career aspirations in both cases (Ruberto & Sciorra, 2016). This was initially an emigration of the elites that, over time, became what was termed "new mobility"; the latter included young graduates who were not able to find work in Italy (Tirabassi & del Pra', 2014, cited in Ruberto & Sciorra, 2016). Ruberto and Sciorra (2016) point out how the distance between the first generations of emigrant Italians and the elite migrations represents a constant that influenced relationship of these groups over time. There is practically no contact between these groups.

Today the "new Italian immigrants," those that were previously defined as "migrant elites" live in New York and other places in the United States; they are young adults, born in Italy, with a high level of education, who have emigrated by choice, of their own will. This group shares little with the old generations of Italian immigrants, not even with the fourth and fifth generations of their descendants, who are more or less the same age. They feel like ambassadors of a different Italy—a more modern Italy—to be proud of, not an Italy they were forced to leave due to lack of employment. Coming to America, these Italians felt they were representatives of a strong Italy and did not want to be reminded, or did not like to see, the Italy of the earlier immigration. There is a strong contrast between how the first immigrants and the new Italian immigrants were welcomed: the first, when they arrived, were ostracized and discriminated against. Yet it is thanks to the work and the achievements of this group that the road for the new immigrants has been smoothed, allowing them to be accepted in a very different way. The difference between the two groups is, however, quite profound. The new Italian immigrants no longer perceive the parochial divisions that marked the context of interactions among the first immigrants. Today these Italian regional divisions are not conducive to divisions in America and the group, in this sense, appears more unified.

There has also been a more recent Italian immigration, the latest of all, those who have just arrived in the United States, ambassadors of yet another Italy. Although the cultural and scholastic level is very high among group members, they are the representatives of an immigration that is often marked by necessity, the lack of jobs. Between the new Italian immigrants and these, which we could call "very new" immigrants, contacts are more frequent and similarly there are many commonalities, linked to a vision of Italy as a highly developed country, which does not elicit feelings of inferiority. These two groups within the community thus enter more easily into contact with each other, while those descended from the first immigrants—those born on American soil and as a group, as we have seen, subject to internal divisions, exist as a separate, self-contained group. Thus, there is a great deal of separation between the immigration generations: the community's perceived image of itself is divided; nevertheless, a dense, crosshatched network of relationships exists that connects the various nodes, or at least those who feel they belong to this community.

What emerges from the research appears to project a situation in which we continue to reproduce the perceived inequalities and divisions that, as noted, have marked the history of the Italian Americans from its beginnings and continue to be transmitted to the younger generations.

PARTICIPATION IN ASSOCIATIONS

Another central point is the extent of participation by young people in Italian American associations, which appears to demonstrate a tendency to shrink and decline. This aspect has already been observed in the panorama of the Italian American communities; the same effect is occuring in Europe. As we have seen, this decrease in participation started a long time ago and the trend continues today. Although a large number of respondents participate in groups, associations, and organizations, many young people express a sense of exclusion from the associations that sometimes seem to focus on the "rhetoric of immigration," which does not give space to new ideas and does not offer openings for new generations. On the other hand, there seems to be an emerging sense of passive behavior among the youth, who do not take on the responsibility or the initiative to introduce changes.

There appears to be an existence of two parallel worlds that, beyond their wealth, differ in the languages spoken in each world, and have difficulty communicating with one another. The age of the people who participate in the associative life of Italian American organizations tends to be consistently increasing and, in general, participation shows a tendency toward decline; there is, therefore a need for generational change in the associations. Among the suggestions that young people have indicated for achieving this change and renewal is to introduce initiatives closer to youth interests, their requests, and their needs. Many young people expect greater support, both from associations and from the entire Italian American community in general, encouraging the development of youthful forms of expression and creativity.

CONNECTION/RECONNECTION WITH ITALY

Finally, the dimension linked to the connection/reconnection with Italy appears crucial.

The image of Italy is composite: in some cases it is real, in others it is only imagined; for others, the representation is reinvented, mythologized, and idealized. It is the idyllic place, *la dolce vita*, the mythic dream, the Italy of the past and of nostalgia. Italy lives not only in the symbolic imagination of these young people, but for many it also represents a concrete reality, experienced in their own personal histories through repeat visits.

In every instance, this perception holds a great importance in the search for the Italian American identity in general. It has often occurred that young people, going to Italy, understood the difference between being Italian and Italian American through the comparison and understanding of how much is shared and what is different between the two nations. There are various ways to establish this awareness: one of these is to take a trip to Italy, which allows the individuals to figure out that they are not "Italians," as they might have been encouraged to believe through the transmission of the past collective imaginations of generation after generation, but Italian Americans. In interpreting the meaning of the trip, Birindelli (2011) emphasizes its dual value, both as a stimulating experience and as a pleasure in itself. Moreover, precisely because of this dual aspect, the trip is a "potent means for discovering and constructing one's identity" (p. 120).

The traveler who goes far away from his protected environment (family, friends, habits) encounters the unknown, and the experience of diversity generates the capacity in him to compare and differentiate. In this sense, the journey can be considered one of the primary means of accessing profound experiences. Taken out of his ordinary environment, the young person is forced to undergo a direct experience that leads him to become aware of "who is having this experience." This concerns identity characteristics that would not be revealed in the traveler's well-trodden, familiar world. "The journey is a paradigmatic experience, the model of a genuine and direct experience that transforms the person who is taking it" (Leed, 1991, p. 5). In the case of the young person, a heuristic reason for traveling abroad—says Leed (1991)—is to take him out of his "comfort zone." Furthermore, it is interesting to note that the changes in character that occur as a result of the journey do not constitute the introduction of some new personality trait in the traveler, but the revelation of something that was already present: "In the difficult and dangerous journey, the traveler's self is impoverished and reduced to its fundamental elements, allowing the person to see what these essential aspects are" (ibid., p. 8). Separated from the "comfort zone" that affirms the identity, the self is no longer a "located self" (Birindelli, 2011).

IN CONCLUSION: THE MOVEMENT TOWARD CHANGE HAS ALREADY BEGUN

The journey made by Italian Americans in search of their deepest roots in Italy brings them full circle, connected to the journey that their ancestors took in the opposite direction. It is the search for a reconnection with something bigger than what is behind personal and family stories; it is a connection with Italian culture, with its richness and its history. At the same time, painful memories surface that many Italian Americans have tried to erase, that keep them from their children and grandchildren. However, these are memories that must be revisited through historicization, to be understood and become shared heritage.

Nonetheless, it is also a matter of taking this story beyond the Italian American community, involving other Americans, so that the contributions that Italian Americans have made to America over the years can be visible to all. The wider the scope of this knowledge, which ought to permeate every level of society, the more the negative stereotypes that still weigh on the image of Italian Americans, associating them with caricatured aspects and a popular culture viewed more like a consumer product than a legacy of historic traditions, will fall into the background.

Even as my journey through the world of young Italian Americans is ending, I am led to acknowledge the importance of making "reconciliations," "reconnections," and active changes that involve the community, families, institutions, and young people. There will certainly be concerted efforts, combined and widespread, that will bind families and institutions together in a joint project, to bring back connections and links with the past, revitalizing its memory. At the same time, we must look to the present and future, to modern Italy, and allow for the personal reinterpretation of this inheritance in everyday life. Every young Italian American has their own formula, their own way of doing it.

From an educational standpoint, spreading programs of Italian American studies in universities within the American studies curriculum represents one channel, while learning the Italian language is another. Few of the young people involved in the study mentioned the role that educational institutions can play in promoting their sense of ethnic identity. As opposed to other groups of ethnic Americans who have not only taught their children but all young Americans about their cultural past and present, the Italian Americans interviewed did not seem to expect public institutions to play this role. This is a point that merits reflection.

The young people must be able to find support and engage in meetings where bidirectional exchanges with previous generations occur. These young people, in their transition to adulthood, are looking for identifications with meaningful "others"; the elder generations should not remove themselves and shirk this passage but instead help the younger ones find reasons to feel connected to this inheritance, yet also provide a space to exchange ideas, involving the youth and making them responsible for finding their own "way" of interpreting and loving this culture through knowledge and their own personal contribution.

NOTES

CHAPTER ONE

1. Within the current study, specific reference is made to the real second generation. Recently, Rumbaut (2004) proposed a classification that established four different generations among the children of immigrants, based on birthplace and age at the time of arrival in the new country: the "2," the "1.75," the "1.5," and the "1.25." The "2" is the real second generation, composed of individuals born within the receiving society; the "1.75" is comprised of the children of immigrants arriving in the new country by age five. Generation "1.5" is composed of immigrant children when they were 6 to 12 years of age, and the "1.25" is made up of those children coming into the new society as adolescents, between 13 and 17 years of age.
2. For more information on the generations in America, see Strauss, Howe (1991); Taylor (2014); Twenge (2006); Twenge, Campbell (2009).
3. The information published regarding the study outlined its cognitive goals and overall purpose and also requested that the applicants take part in a voluntary survey. The call for volunteers was featured in *Italian Tribune*, IACN (*Italian American Community News*), *i-Italy*, *America Oggi*, *ComUNICO* (*The Voice of Unico National*), *L'Italo Americano*, *We the Italians*, *NYSOSIA News* (*Order Sons of Italy in America—Grand Lodge of New York*), GIA (*Giornale Italo Americano*), and *Arba Sicula*.
4. For detailed references to the associations, organizations, and foundations involved in the research, see the introduction to this volume.
5. The adjectives refer to personality characteristics, not to physical features, and were selected based on in-depth interviews and the pretest. Furthermore, in constructing the semantic differential, the descriptive adjectives regarding personality structure were chosen based on a six factors subdivision (Lee, Ashton, 2012) seeking to cover all of the observed dimensions. The six dimensions analyzed in the lexical studies on personality structure include honesty-humility, emotion, extroversion, agreeableness, conscientiousness, and openness to experience (HEXACO). These represent six groups of characteristics, and every person is scored within each group in order to synthesize his or her personality.

CHAPTER TWO

1. There are three approaches to the empirical study of values that can be regarded as exemplary: the Rokeach approach (1973) is based on an integrated theory of values, viewing these as a collection of firm beliefs, bearing an emotional orientation and with a weak connection among them; the findings of Schwartz (1992) are based on a strong theory of values that postulates the existence of an integrated system of ten kinds of universal values with an equal significance in every culture; lastly, the Inglehart approach (1990) has as a fundamental presupposition that the configuration of societal values is primarily dependent on that society's level of economic development. For further reference, see M. Roccato's essay (2008). See also L. Sciolla, 1998, 2004, 2008.
2. These are two international research observatories focused on the world of human values, utilizing sample surveys from a great number of interviewed cases involving many countries. Further information can be found at the following webpages: http://www.europeanvaluesstudy.eu; http://www.worldvaluessurvey.org/wvs.jsp.
3. The sixth 2007 Iard report examining the state of the youth in Italy claims that health—first included in the 2004 survey—occupies the first position within the hierarchy of "important aspects of life." Prior to this, family had always occupied the highest position. From 2000 to 2004, these developing trends were confirmed, as increasing emphasis was attributed to the areas of narrow social relationships (family, love, friendship), the role of work on the scale of priorities diminished, and expression of low interest in political activity, and, more generally, there is little interest toward social activism and community life (Iard Report, 2007).
4. In the United States, the reaction to Banfield's work occurred a decade after the publication of the volume. At the end of the sixties, many American academics produced numerous critical works within which they distanced themselves from this author and what he represented. The strongest criticisms came from Anglo-American anthropologists, joined also by sociologists. If we analyze the criticisms of the text, we notice a consensus regarding the fact that Banfield had produced a mostly correct ethnographic work and, at the same time, a mostly incorrect theoretical interpretation (for further information, refer to Kertzer, 2007).
5. The analyzed sample included individuals of over 25 years of age living in Roseto, Bangor, and Nazareth, with a total of 3,116 subjects.

CHAPTER THREE

1. A mass emigration from Italy began after 1880 (Vecoli, 1995). Before the twentieth century, emigrants were primarily northerners, but some also came from Campania. From the beginning of the twentieth century up to the beginning of World War I, the migratory flows came primarily from South Italy. In 1917, the U.S. Congress launched the Literacy Act, a law that intended to prevent access

to the United States for people who were under sixteen years old and those who didn't know how to read and write in their language of origin. The law did not achieve the desired results, so in 1921 and in 1924 Congress approved two laws that introduced a quota system for the group from each nationality, which drastically reduced immigration. Italy was permitted just four thousand entrances annually (Pretelli, 2011).

2 The law was established by the Democratic administration of President Lyndon B. Johnson and it was the fruit of a renewed liberal-progressive climate. This law ended the national quotas, establishing a maximum ceiling of 120,000 visas for the Western Hemisphere and 170,000 for the rest of the world. For every non-American country, including Italy, the annual number of visas could not exceed a total of 20,000 units (Pretelli, 2011). The law was approved by virtue of the lobbying efforts of the American Committee on Italian Migration (Cavaioli, 1979).

3 Chirico (2014) notes that the conviction is present, representing a widely held though erroneous opinion, that racial and cultural insensitivity are conducive to a low sense of self-esteem. On the other hand, the opposing theory is also known, namely that a strong sense of identity, which includes ethnic identification, brings success over a wide number of areas.

4 Reference here is made to the research conducted by Aileen Riotto Sirey, Anthony Patti, and Lisa Mann; the results of which are collected in the pamphlet *Ethnotherapy: An Exploration of Italian-American Identity* (National Institute for the Psychotherapies, 1985), The results of the research project confirmed that the experience of ethnotherapy significantly enhanced self-esteem and the sense of ethnic group belonging in the participants.

5 Ethnotherapy is described by the authors as "a short period of group experience, which permits the participants to explore issues tied to ethnic identity and self-esteem. Designed primarily as a therapeutic experience for the participants, this type of group experience becomes a potent means of facilitating the beginning of a process of self-awareness and helps for the individuals to better understand the interaction between their own subculture and the majority culture" (Riotto Sirey et al.,1985).

CHAPTER FOUR

1 This situation reflects the condition of marginality understood as a conflict experienced by those people who live in two different cultural contexts. The two cultures are usually in a hierarchical position: one holds power and prestige and is usually defined as a dominant culture, while the other is a secondary culture and is assessed as being inferior to the first (for further information on the concept of "marginal man," see Johnston, 1965). Moreover, it should be remembered that Stonequist (1937) was the first to introduce the term *marginality* and, in his attempt to trace its origins, he observed: "Any time there are transitions and cultural conflicts, marginal personalities are created" (p. 3).

2   The emotional value of the connections to places can be both positive and negative. Some studies have highlighted the negative effects on the psychophysical level of the eradication due to involuntary causes with the creation of various gradations of the nostalgia effect (for further information on the theme of attachment as well as on that of social and territorial belonging, see Pollini, 2000, 2003; Cattarinussi, 2000).

CHAPTER FIVE

1   See Mignone, 2008.

CHAPTER SIX

1   Barthes (1974) notes that mythology is only a fragment of the vast science of signs known as semiology. Semiology is a science of forms that studies certain significations independently of their content; it postulates a relationship between two terms, a signifier and a signified. Unlike common language, wherein the signifier expresses the meaning, "in every semiological system I am not concerned with two but with three different terms; because what I perceive is not merely one term after another, but the correlation that unites them: there is therefore the signifier, the signified and the sign, this last being the associative total of the first two terms" (p. 195). This tridimensional model is found in myth. Moreover, semiology teaches that "the myth is tasked with establishing a historical intention as a nature, a contingency as eternity" (p. 222).
2   Among these he cites: "Italy is not just a *country*, it is a civilization, an admired *culture*, imitated and envied by the whole world," "The Italian language was invented by the Italian national poet, Dante Alighieri," "The Italian family is eternal," "Italy is destined to govern Africa." These constitute a genre of propaganda that was instilled in the Italians who were living in the colonies and lasted until 1941, the year Benito Mussolini declared war on the United States.
3   Haller (1993) intends the term *Italianisms* in reference to the linguistic phenomena of Italian origin inherited by the English and Anglo-American languages and consecrated through spoken and/or written use.
4   For more information on the theme of nostalgia see Jankélévitch, 1974; Prete, 1992; Serra, 2018.
5   For further information on the use of Italian language and dialects in migratory contexts, see the two essays by Serra, 2017a and 2017b.
6   This observation is based on previously mentioned study conducted between 1994 and 2005 on forty Italian immigrants.
7   See chapter 9 regarding the future prospects of Italian American and Italian culture in the US.
8   Lazzari (2000) points out that language and culture are closely linked to the family and collective memory of the mobility experience. He argues that the removal

from or rupture with one's origins, both socially and geographically, reaches the point of replacing the memory of one's roots with a new cultural memory acquired in the dramatic and urgent situation of separation from one's homeland. For further information, see F. Lazzari (2000), *L'attore sociale fra appartenenza e mobilità. Analisi comparate e proposte socio-educative* (Padova: Cedam).

9   Many Italian American organizations—including the National Italian American Foundation (NIAF), Order Sons of Italy in America (OSIA), the Columbus Citizens Foundation, UNICO National, the National Organization of Italian American Women (NOIAW), as well as many others—make a significant contribution to the effort to keep the connection with Italy alive. They organize cultural and study visits in Italy, and also offer scholarships to students and teachers.

CHAPTER SEVEN

1   This is the well-known "Thomas theorem" developed by William Isaac Thomas through the concept of the "self-fulfilling prophecy." According to Thomas, a situation defined by the actors as real becomes real through its consequences.
2   As Boileau notes (1981), following Marden and Meyer (1968), the dominant group is the one "whose distinctive culture and / or physiognomy is defined as superior in the society, and which treats other groups that have other cultures and/or physiognomies differently and unequally in that same society" (p. 23).
3   As noted by Bryson (2014), probably the most complete book on the story of Sacco and Vanzetti was written in 1991 by the historian Paul Avrich, titled *Sacco and Vanzetti: The Anarchist Background*.
4   See the study by E. C. Banfield (1958), *The Moral Basis of a Backward Society* Glencoe, IL: Free Press.
5   In a note to the text, the author states that in reality the Italians did not have a particular tendency to illegality and, in 1910, constituted 11% of the immigrant population, but only 7% of foreigners in prison. Recalling Kobler (1972), he points out that, in terms of incarceration rates, out of a population of one hundred thousand individuals, Italians as a nationality were twelfth out of seventeen.
6   A color line means a social and legal system in which people of different races are separated and do not have the same rights and opportunities.
7   "Jim Crow Laws" were state and local laws that enforced racial segregation in the Southern states of the United States.

CHAPTER EIGHT

1   Quinnipiac University Survey, June 4–9, 2003; Gallup Poll, February 17–19, 2003, cit. in S. Huntington (2004).
2   Putnam and Campbell have conducted diverse and extensive surveys among Americans covering religious and faith-based topics. In 2006, the first survey

was carried out on a random sample of 3,108 Americans, which was followed by another survey in the subsequent year that included 1,909 subjects belonging to the same sample from the previous year. The surveys are known as Faith Matters Surveys and, together, they constitute one of the most detailed studies on the themes of American religion and their civic life.

3   The functions of deviance indicated by Durkheim include maintaining integration and social cohesion. By collectively reacting to deviance and deviants, the members of society that respect the laws reaffirm their norms and values, thereby acquiring an awareness of group solidarity. Therefore, if the deviance is contained within reasonable limits, it performs an integrative and cohesive function.

4   This observation, reported by Sciorra, is taken from Susan Brenna, "Raising Their Literary Voices," *New York Newsday*, April 3, 1995, sec. B, pp. 4–5.

5   The author conducted forty-five in-depth interviews with men and women belonging to three distinct groups: the first group was composed of recent Southern Italian immigrants residing in the New York Metropolitan area (15); the second group was made up of fifteen first, second, and third generation respondents, and, finally, the third group—considered a control group—consisted of fifteen WASPs.

6   By political alienation, he intended "the individual's rejection of the dominant political rules, values, and institutions of a society based on the real or imagined exclusion of the individual from the political processes of society operated by other individuals or groups" (Gallo, 1974, p. 17).

7   Comparing these data to information relating to young Italians, the Iard Institute's investigations conducted until 2006 on the young people's world show a prevalent separation of youth from the political dimension. In particular, the sixth Iard report of 2006 shows that, among the age group between fifteen and twenty-four years old, those who consider themselves incompetent or who are disgusted by politics represent the majority of young people. Looking at the fifteen-to-thirty-four-years group, on the other hand, they are almost symmetrically divided between interested (engaged or not) and distant (due to lack of competence or disgust). While the youth appear to be divided in their attitude toward politics, they are much less disunited with respect to concrete participation. On the whole, political participation is very widespread among the youth (only 23% never participate), and the most frequent forms are talking about politics and attending a political debate, even on television. The less widespread methods of participation are, especially, those connected to relations with the political parties. Mainly, concrete participation is a way of relating to politics that goes beyond the party system and works through often innovative methods (for further information, see Buzzi et al., cur., 2007). The research carried out by the Toniolo Institute and the Cariplo Foundation in 2013 also confirms young people's disaffection and lack of confidence in political institutions, primarily

toward the parties, but it also highlights a growing excitement and a renewed desire for participation (Istituto Toniolo, 2013).

8   Strictly speaking, "McDonaldizing" means creating cheap restaurants designed as chains, easy to export to other locations through the sale of usage rights or royalties. McDonaldization is considered part of a larger process, called Americanization and defined by Ritzer (1997, 2005) as the propagation of American ideas, customs, social models, industry, and capital in the world.

9   The United States entered the war on April 6, 1917. In the years prior, many Americans had expressed, even officially, the desire to stay out of the war that was ravaging Europe. Moreover, in the wake of the great immigration from Europe, the "new" Americans were reluctant to enter a conflict that might have required them to fight against their own homeland. Since the outbreak of the war in Europe, until the beginning of 1917, the Wilson administration had proclaimed American neutrality. Opposing pressure from wealthy American businessmen as well as some pro-war intellectuals affected the president's decision—six months after his reelection—to take part in the conflict. For more information on the political, social, and cultural climate in America at the time of the Great War, see Serra, 2015.

10 UNICO is an acronym that stands for Unity, Neighborliness, Integrity, Charity, and Opportunity.

11 The cultivation theory studies the effects of television viewing on the population. It was formulated by Gerbner between the sixties and seventies. It is a theory of cumulative effects according to which the massive use of the television medium has no immediate effect on thought, but produces a "cultivation" effect over the long term, causing a change in the perception of reality, wherein the viewer comes to live in a world modeled on what is broadcast on television (TV-World).

CHAPTER NINE

1   For further insights and information on the life of these Italian American associations and organizations, as well as the results of the research referring to the association among interviewed young people, see chapter 8.

2   As many authors have noted (Grossberg, 1992; Lesko, 2000; Whyn & White, 1997), young people have lower social status and are in a less powerful position than adults. In particular, Grossberg noted that the categorization of people as youths serves adults more than the young people themselves. To understand the reasons that lead to the verification of this differential in terms of power, one can refer to the model linked to the social construction of adolescence, seen as a period of transition between childhood and adulthood (Whyn & White, 1997). Through this representation, the words of young people are considered as representative of themselves during an incomplete stage of life, which can undermine

the abilities of young people to describe themselves with any authority (Knopp Biklen, 2007).

CHAPTER ELEVEN

1. As noted by Taylor (2014), generational gaps are certainly not new. Alexis de Tocqueville—almost two centuries ago—was amazed that in America "each generation is a new people."
2. Krase (1983, 2003) observes that Italian American culture has a particularly strong territorial orientation. Specifically, like all real and imagined ethnic neighborhoods, Little Italies are a product and a source of social and cultural capital. Idealized urban ethnic spaces are "representations of spaces" as well as "spaces of representation." Krase (1997) defined them as oblivion, ruin, ethnic thematic parks, immigration museums, and anthropological gardens.
3. The children of immigrants in Europe over the last decades face quite a different situation and their integration does not happen as easily as it could happen a century ago at the time of the great American migrations, where the second generation experienced rapid upward social mobility. Particularly in Europe, the second generations are facing difficulties integrating into the social structure and the fabric of society—for example, regarding Great Britain and France—to the point that scholastic failures these individuals often face and their lack of success in entering the qualified labor market can lead to phenomena of social exclusion, deviance, and opposition to the receiving society and its institutions (Ambrosini, 2004). Moreover, what has been defined as the "paradox of integration" is verified: while the parents often remained invisible, engaged in occupations in which few national workers participated, the children are exposed to a much wider range of opportunities, also sought by the natives, thus creating situations in which they are more likely to encounter racism and discrimination (Ambrosini, 2005).
4. The concept of "double consciousness" is expressed by Du Bois in the 1903 book *The Souls of Black Folk* as "the feeling of looking at one's own self through the eyes of others," as a double awareness of African Americans confronted by American racism and at the same time being American and black citizens. These two identities represent two simultaneous selves—the American and the African. Through this metaphor Du Bois expresses the dignity of the battle to successfully create an integrated synthesis of oneself, the result of these two conflicting identities (Schaefer, 2008). The concept of the identity divided between two worlds linked to the experience of Italian immigrants in America finds poetic expression through the testimony of Joseph Tusiani (1982), defined as the poet of the two lands.
5. The study, conducted between 1937 and 1938, analyzed the behavior of some male inhabitants of the Little Italy in New Haven (Connecticut). To this end,

four research methods were used: participant observation, life stories, informal interviews, and standardized interviews. Although the sample was considered to be very small, Child's three types of reactions, which described strategies implemented by the second generation to respond to the identity conflict created by their dual membership in Italian and American culture, were very illuminating.

6   This term, based on climate, environment, and culture, was provided by Giacomo Castelvetro, from Modena, exiled to England for religious reasons at the beginning of the seventeenth century. Feeling nostalgia for his homeland, he wrote a treatise on Italian food culture: "Brief account of all the roots, of all the herbs and all the fruits, which are eaten—raw or cooked—in Italy," referring to the traditional cuisine based on a wide range of plant products. Cited in M. Montanari (2010), *L'identità italiana in cucina* (Rome-Bari: Laterza).

7   The observations proposed by Portes and Rumbaut are based mainly on the study known as "The Children of Immigrants Longitudinal Study (CILS)," a panel that involved the second generation of young immigrants and lasted ten years. The research was conducted in South Florida (in the Miami metropolitan area) and in Southern California (in the San Diego metropolitan area). In total, 5,262 students took part in the first survey—conducted between 1992 and 1993—with an average age of fourteen, representing seventy-seven different nationalities. The first follow-up was carried out three years later, between 1995–96, with a sample consisting of 4, 288 respondents, equal to 81.5% of the original sample.

8   For more information on selective acculturation, see Portes & Rumbaut, 1996; Portes, 2004; Ambrosini, 2008.

9   The second generation's relationship with *italianità* tends toward dual cultural belonging and double ethnicity. It also expresses the model of bidirectional neo-assimilation (for further details on this model, see Alba & Nee, 1997, 2003; Nee & Alba, 2004). Within the composite Italian American community, members of this generation often play the role of "mediators or connectors," a link between the past, the present, and the future.

10 The generational decrease of Italian cultural and ethnic identity is also revealed by a study conducted in Chicago between 2009 and 2012 on 135 Italian Americans belonging to the second and later generations. For further information see A. Balodimas-Bartolomei, 2015.

CHAPTER TWELVE

1   As noted, knowledge and emotion are two closely related dimensions. Knowledge, in fact, starts from something that is situated in the emotional dimension, and the emotion marks a point from which something in the human subject is set in motion. This is the groundwork on which the directions and strategies of thought are modeled and defined (Fidanza, 1990). Furthermore, new research trends focusing on the "subject matter" have highlighted the emo-

tional roots of human behavior. Emotions, passions, feelings, and affections represent the deep origins of the whole culture, or as Cattarinussi claims (2000), "the first bricks on which it is formed" (p. 13). Emotions, therefore, are central to the understanding of human behavior, for the individual and his private history as well as society and its collective values. Although they differ from one another, the spheres of affectivity and of knowledge interact (for further information on the themes of emotions and feelings, see Cattarinussi, 2000).

2   This context recalls the well-known typology proposed by Thomas and Znaniecki's *The Polish Peasant in Europe and America*—published between 1918 and 1920, where the two authors, analyzing the adaptation of immigrants to the new culture, identified three types of personality: the philistine, the bohemian, and the creative. Thomas continued to research immigrants in the United States, and reworked the previously outlined typology of immigrants, classifying the different types according to their "definition of the situation," that is, to the way they perceived reality and formulated a subjective answer to the demands and changes of social life. The types proposed are six: stable settler, temporary settler, political idealist (with subtype of the propagandist), the "everything is alright" type, the boor, and the intellectual. For more information on the types referred to here, see J. Madge (1966), R. Scramaglia & R. Lavarini (2007), B. Cattarinussi (2010).

3   Recalcati (2012) notes that the word *desire* is capable of fully encompassing the experience of psychoanalysis, and it remains the selected word. Both Lacan and Freud relentlessly return to this word, since there is no experience of the unconscious that is not an experience of desire. It contains multiple meanings and there are numerous portraits of desire. Recalcati clarifies this concept in a book where he traverses a gallery of portraits of desire, which illustrate the main ways in which Jacques Lacan defined them.

4   See Gardaphé (1992), op. cit.

CONCLUDING REFLECTIONS

1   This specific type of interaction between individuals was analyzed by Horton and Wohl in the 1950s, following the emergence of electronic media. The advent of television entailed a profound change in the scope of social interactions, since it created the illusion that it was possible to have a face-to-face interaction and a relationship of intimacy with the protagonists on the screen. This new relationship was defined by the two authors as "para-social interaction." From a psychological point of view, although it is mediated, it resembles face-to-face interaction and viewers think they know the TV characters as friends (for further information, see Horton & Wohl, 1956).

BIBLIOGRAPHY

Aaron, D. (1964). The hyphenate writer and American letters. *Smith Alumnae Quarterly* 55, 4.

Accolla, P., & d'Aquino, N. (2008). *Italici. An encounter with Piero Bassetti*. New York, NY: Bordighera Press.

Alba, R. D. (1985). *Italian Americans. Into the twilight of ethnicity*. Englewood Cliffs, NJ: Prentice-Hall.

———. (1990). *Ethnic identity: The transformation of white America*. New Haven, CT: Yale University Press.

Alba, R. D., & Nee V. (1997). Rethinking assimilation theory for a new era of immigration. *International Migration Review*, 31, 4.

———. (2003). *Remaking the American mainstream: Assimilation and contemporary immigration*. Cambridge, MA: Harvard University Press.

Alba, R. D. et al. (Eds.) (2008). *Immigration and religion in America: Comparative and historical perspectives*. New York, NY: New York University Press.

Allport, G. W. (1954). *The nature of prejudice*. New York, NY: Addison-Wesley.

Ambrosini, M. (2004). Il futuro in mezzo a noi. Le seconde generazioni scaturite dall'immigrazione nella società italiana dei prossimi anni. In M. Ambrosini & S. Molina (Cur.), *Seconde generazioni. Un'introduzione al futuro dell'immigrazione in Italia*. Torino: Fondazione Giovanni Agnelli.

———. (2005). *Sociologia delle migrazioni*. Bologna: il Mulino.

———. (2008). *Un'altra globalizzazione. La sfida delle migrazioni transnazionali*. Bologna: il Mulino.

Andreozzi, J. (2000). Organizations. In S. J. LaGumina et al. (Eds.), *The Italian American experience: An encyclopedia*. New York, NY: Garland.

Ashmore, R. D., Deaux, K., & McLaughlin-Volpe, T. (2004). An organizing framework of collective identity: Articulation and significance of multidimensionality. *Psychological Bulletin*, 130.

Avrich, P. (1991). *Sacco and Vanzetti: The Anarchist background*. Princeton, NJ: Princeton University Press.

Balodimas-Bartolomei, A. (2015). Italianità Americana: A study of ethnic identity among second- third- and third-plus-generation Italian Americans. In G. Guida (Eds.), *What is Italian America?* New York, NY: Bordighera Press.

Banfield, E. C. (1958). *The moral basis of a backward society*. Glencoe, IL: Free Press.
Barolini, H. (1988). *Festa: Recipes and recollections of Italian holidays*. New York, NY: Harcourt Brace.
Barth, F. (1969). Introduction. In F. Barth (Ed.), *Ethnic group and boundaries. The social organization of culture difference*. London: Allen & Unwin.
Barthes, R. (1974). *Miti d'oggi*. Torino: Einaudi.
Barzini, L. (1964). *The Italians*. New York, NY: Atheneum.
Bassetti, P., & d'Aquino, N. (2010). *Italic lessons. An on-going Dialog*. New York, NY: Bordighera Press.
Belasco, W. J., & Scranton, P. (Eds.) (2002). *Food nations: Selling taste in consumer societies*. New York, NY: Routledge.
Belliotti, R. A. (1995). *Seeking identity. Individualism versus community in an ethnic context*. Lawrence, KS: University Press of Kansas.
Bertellini, G. (1999). Epica spettacolare e splendori del vero. L'influenza del cinema storico italiano in America. In G. P. Brunetta (Ed.), *Storia del cinema mondiale*. Torino: Einaudi.
Bettini, M. (2011). *Contro le radici. Tradizione, identità, memoria*. Bologna: il Mulino.
Birindelli, P. (2011). Playing as reality: Youngsters experience in late modernity. In M. Ferrari Occhionero & M. Nocenzi (Cur.), *I giovani e le sfide del future*. Roma: Aracne.
Boileau, A. M. (1981). Gruppi etnici e interazione sociale. In A. M. Boileau & E. Sussi, *Dominanza e minoranze. Immagini e rapporti interetnici al confine nordorientale*. Udine: Grillo.
———. (1987a). Pregiudizio. In F. Demarchi, A. Ellena, & B. Cattarinussi (Cur.), *Nuovo Dizionario di Sociologia*. Milano: San Paolo.
———. (1987b). Stereotipo. In F. Demarchi, A. Ellena, & B. Cattarinussi (Cur.), *Nuovo Dizionario di Sociologia*. Milano: San Paolo.
Boileau, A. M., & Sussi, E. (1981). *Dominanza e minoranze. Immagini e rapporti interetnici al confine nordorientale*. Udine: Grillo.
Bona, M. J. (2000). *Claiming a tradition: Italian American women writers*. Carbondale, IL: Southern Illinois University Press.
———. (2015). Rivendicare una tradizione. Le scrittrici italoamericane. In O. Capelli (Ed.), *Cultura e politica nell'America italiana*. Firenze: Franco Cesati.
Bourdieu, P. (1991). *Language and symbolic power*. Cambridge, MA: Harvard University Press.
Bruhn, J. G. & Wolf, S. (1979). *The Roseto story. An anatomy of health*. Norman, OK: University of Oklahoma Press.
Bryson, B. (2014). *L'estate in cui accadde tutto*. Milano: Guanda.
Bugiardini, S. (2002). L'associazionismo negli USA. In P. Bevilacqua, A. De Clementi, & E. Franzina (Cur.), *Storia dell'emigrazione italiana. Arrivi*. Roma: Donzelli.
———. (2006). L'accesso in politica. L'esperienza degli italo-americani di New York. *NEOS—Rivista di Storia dell'Emigrazione Siciliana*, I, 1.

Burke, P. (2000). *Sogni, gesti, beffe. Saggi di storia culturale*. Bologna: il Mulino.
Buzzi, C. et al. (Cur.) (2007). *Rapporto giovani. Sesta indagine dell'Istituto IARD sulla condizione giovanile in Italia*. Bologna: il Mulino.
Calvino, I. (1990). Introduzione. In C. Pavese, *La letteratura americana e altri saggi*. Torino: Einaudi.
Camaiti Hostert, A. (2007). Identità di genere nel cinema italoamericano: Nancy Savoca e Marylou Tibaldo Buongiorno. In G. Muscio & G. Spagnoletti (Cur.), *Quei bravi ragazzi*. Venezia: Marsilio.
Canadé Sautman, F. (2011). Creolizing the lack: Interpreting race and racism in Italian America. In J. Krase (Ed.), *The status of interpretation in Italian American studies. Proceedings of the first Forum in Italian American Criticism (FIAC)*. Stony Brook, NY: Forum Italicum Publishing.
Cappelli, O. (2011). The name of the *Guido*. A case study in Italian/American identity politics. In L. Airos & O. Cappelli (Eds.), *Guido. Italian/American Youth and identity Politics*. New York, NY: Bordighera Press.
———. (Ed.) (2012). *Italian signs, American politics. Current affairs. Historical perspectives. Empirical analyses*. New York, NY: John D. Calandra Italian American Institute.
———. (2012a). Introduction. In O. Cappelli (Ed.), *Italian signs, American politics. Current affairs. Historical perspectives. Empirical analyses*. New York, NY: John D. Calandra Italian American Institute.
———. (Ed.) (2015). *Cultura e politica nell'America italiana*. Firenze: Franco Cesati.
———. (2015a). Introduzione. Tracce politiche nella letteratura italoamericana. In O. Cappelli (Ed.), *Italian signs, American politics. Current affairs. Historical perspectives. Empirical analyses*. New York, NY: John D. Calandra Italian American Institute.
Casella, P. (1998). *Hollywood Italian*. Milano: Delai Editore.
Cattarinussi, B. (Cur.) (2000). *Emozioni e sentimenti nella vita sociale*. Milano: FrancoAngeli.
———. (Cur.) (2010). *La sociologia attraverso le tipologie*. Milano, FrancoAngeli.
Cavaioli, F. J. (1979). Italian-Americans slay the immigration dragon. The national-origins quota system. *Italian Americana*, 1.
Chatterton, P., & Hollands, R. (2003). *Urban nightscapes: Youth cultures, pleasure spaces, and corporate power*. New York, NY: Routledge.
Child, I. L. (1943). *Italian or American? The second generation in conflict*. New Haven, CT: Yale University Press.
Chirico, D. (2011a). Guido: A generation rebellion. In L. Airos & O. Cappelli (Eds.), *Guido. Italian/American youth and identity politics*. New York: Bordighera Press.
———. (2011b). The dog catches his tail: A critical reflection on the value of an Italian American identity in personal development. In J. Krase (Ed.), *The status of interpretation in Italian American studies. Proceedings of the first Forum in Italian American Criticism (FIAC)*. Stony Brook, NY: Forum Italicum Publishing.
———. (2014). Italian identity in the third millennium: How to claim an Italian

American identity. In A. J. Tamburri (Ed.), *Meditations on Identity. Meditazioni su identità*. New York, NY: Bordighera Press.

Cinotto, S. (2001). *Una famiglia che mangia insieme: cibo ed etnicità nella comunità italoamericana di New York, 1920–1940*. Torino: Otto.

——. (2009). La cucina diasporica: il cibo come segno di identità culturale. In P. Corti & M. Sanfilippo (Cur.), *Storia d'Italia. Annali, 24: Migrazioni*. Torino: Einaudi.

Cipolla, C. (Cur.) (1978). *Tocqueville: il teorico della partecipazione*. Bologna: Cappelli.

Colasanti, G. (1994). *Il pregiudizio*. Milano: FrancoAngeli.

Cook, I., & Crang, P. (1996). The world on the plate: Culinary culture, displacement, and geographical knowledge. *Journal of Material Culture*, 1.

Covello, L. (1967). *The social background of the Italo-American school child*. Leiden: E. J. Brill.

Crispino, A. J. (1980). *The assimilation of ethnic groups: The Italian case*. Staten Island, NY: Center for Migration Studies.

D'Alfonso, A. (2004). Il futuro della cultura italiana. In N. Ceramella & G. Massara (Cur.), *Merica. Forme della cultura italoamericana*. Isernia: Iannone.

Demaria Harney, N. (1998). *Eh, paesan! Being Italian in Toronto*. Toronto: University of Toronto Press.

De Stefano, G. (2006). *An offer we can't refuse. The Mafia in the mind of America*. New York, NY: Faber and Faber.

Dolci, R. (2013). Study abroad in Italy. In R. Dolci & A. J. Tamburri (Eds.), *Why study Italian. Diverse perspectives on a theme*. New York, NY: Calandra Institute Transactions.

Du Bois, W. E. B. (1903). *The souls of black folk*. Chicago: A. C. McClurg.

Ehrlich, H. J. (1973). *The social psychology of prejudice. A systematic theoretical review and propositional inventory of the American social psychological study of prejudice*. New York, NY: Wiley.

Epstein, A. L. (1978). *L'identità etnica. Tre studi sull'etnicità*. Torino: Loescher.

Erikson, E. H. (1963). *Childhood and society*. New York, NY: Norton.

——. (1968). *Identity, youth, and crisis*. New York, NY: Norton.

Fellin, L. (2014). The Italian new wave: Identity work and socialization practices in a community of new Italian immigrants in America. *Forum Italicum*, 48, 2.

Ferraro, T. J. (2005). *Feeling Italian. The art of ethnicity in America*. New York, NY: New York University Press.

Fidanza, P. (1990). Legame emotivo e conoscenza. *Atque*, 2.

Fischer, M. J. (1986). Ethnicity and the post-modern arts of memory. In J. Clifford & G. E. Marcus (Eds.), *Writing culture. The poetics and politics of ethnography*. Berkeley, CA: University of California Press.

Flügel, J. (1948). *The psychoanalytic study of the family*. London: Hogarth Press.

Foerster R. F. (1969). *The Italian emigration of our times*. New York: Arno Press and New York Times.

Franzina, E. (2007). Il pregiudizio degli italiani sugli italoamericani. In G. Muscio & G. Spagnoletti (Cur.), *Quei bravi ragazzi*. Venezia: Marsilio.

Fried, M. (1967). Functions of the working-class community in modern urban society: Implications for forced relocation. *Journal of the American Institute of Planners*, 33.
Gabaccia, D. R. (1984). *From Sicily to Elizabeth Street: Housing and social change among Italian immigrants, 1880–1930*. Albany, NY: State University of New York Press.
———. (1998). Food, recipes, cookbooks, and Italian-American life. *Italian Americana*, XVI, 1.
———. (1997–98). Ethnicity in the business world. Italians in American food industries. *Italian American Review*, 2.
———. (2000). *Italy's many diasporas*. London: UCL Press.
———. (2003). Race, nation, hyphen. Italian-Americans and American multiculturalism in comparative perspective. In J. Guglielmo & S. Salerno (Eds.), *Are Italians white? How race is made in America*. New York, NY: Routledge.
Galasso, G. (1982). *L'altra Europa. Per un'antropologia storica del Mezzogiorno d'Italia*, Milano: Mondadori.
Galland, O., & Lemel, Y. (2006). Sociologie des valeurs: theories et mesures appliquées au cas européen. *Revue Française de Sociologie*, 47.
Gallo, P. J. (1974). *Ethnic alienation. The Italian-Americans*. Cranbury, NJ: Fairleigh Dickinson University Press.
Gambino, R. (1972). The Italian-Americans. *Chicago Tribune*, May 7.
———. (1974). *Blood of my blood. The dilemma of the Italian-American*. Garden City, NY: Anchor Press.
Gans, H. J. (1962). *The urban villagers: Group and class in the life of Italian Americans*. New York, NY: Free Press of Glencoe.
———. (1979). Symbolic ethnicity: The future of ethnic groups and cultures in America. In H. J. Gans et al. (Eds.), *On the making of Americans: Essays in honor of David Riesman*. Philadelphia, PA: University of Pennsylvania Press.
Gardaphé, F. L. (1992). Visibility or invisibility: The postmodern prerogative in the Italian/American narrative. *Almanacco*, II, 1.
———. (1996a). *Dagoes read. Tradition and the Italian/American writer*. Buffalo, NY: Guernica.
———. (1996b). *Italian signs, American streets: The evolution of Italian American narrative*. Durham, NC: Duke University Press.
———. (2004). *Leaving Little Italy. Essaying Italian American culture*. Albany, NY: State University of New York Press.
———. (2008). Beyond the immigrant paradigm: Identities and the future of Italian American studies. Paper at the conference "Italians in the Americas," John D. Calandra Italian American Institute—Queens College (CUNY, New York, NY, April 24–26 2008, typescript).
———. (2010). Invisible people. Shadows and light in Italian American culture. In W J. Connell & F. L. Gardaphé (Eds.), *Anti-Italianism. Essay on a prejudice*. New York, NY: Palgrave Macmillan.
———. (2012). *Segni Italiani, strade americane: l'evoluzione della letteratura italiana americana*. Firenze: Franco Cesati.

——. (2015). Segni italiani, strade americane: l'evoluzione della letteratura italiana americana. In O. Cappelli (Cur.), *Cultura e politica nell'America italiana*. Firenze: Franco Cesati.

Gerbner, G. (1998). Cultivation analysis: An overview. *Mass Communication and Society*, 3/4.

——. et al. (1986). *Living with television: The dynamics of the cultivation process*. New York, NY: Praeger.

Gillon, S. (2004). *Boomer nation*. New York, NY: Free Press.

Giunta, E., & Patti, S. (Eds.) (1998). *A tavola: Food, tradition and community among Italian Americans*, Selected Essays of the 29th Annual Conference of the American Italian Historical Association, Staten Island, NY, AIHA.

Gordon, M. M. (1964). *Assimilation in American life: The role of race, religion, and national origins*. New York, NY: Oxford University Press.

Grant, M. (1916). *The passing of the great race*. New York, NY: Scribner's Son.

Greeley, A. M. (1971). *Why can't they be like us: America's white ethnic groups*. New York, NY: Dutton.

Grossberg, L. (1992). *We gotta get out of this place*. New York, NY: Routledge.

Gubert, R. (2000). Territorial belonging. In E. F. Borgatta & R. J. V. Montgomery (Eds.), *Encyclopedia of sociology*. New York, NY: Macmillan.

Guglielmo, J. (2003). White lies, dark truths. In J. Guglielmo & S. Salerno (Eds.), *Are Italians white? How race is made in America*. New York, NY: Routledge.

Guglielmo, T. A. (2003). "No color barrier." Italians, race, and power in the United States. In J. Guglielmo & S. Salerno (Eds.), *Are Italians white? How race is made in America*. New York, NY: Routledge.

Haller, H. W. (1993). *Una lingua perduta e ritrovata. L'italiano degli italo-americani*. Firenze: La Nuova Italia.

Hansen, M. L. (1938). *The problem of the third generation immigrant*. Rock Island, IL: Augustana Historical Society.

Hobsbawm, E. J. (1987). Introduzione: come si inventa una tradizione. In E. J. Hobsbawm & T. Ranger (Cur.), *L'invenzione della tradizione*. Torino: Einaudi.

Horton, D., & Wohl, R. R. (1956). Mass communication and para-social interaction: Observations on intimacy at a distance. *Psychiatry*, 19.

Huntington, S. P. (2004). *La nuova America. Le sfide della società multiculturale*. Milano: Garzanti.

Inglehart, R. (1990). *Culture shift in advanced industrial societies*. Princeton, NJ: Princeton University Press.

Istituto Giuseppe Toniolo (2013). *La condizione giovanile in Italia. Rapporto Giovani 2013*. Bologna: il Mulino.

Jacobson, M. F. (1998). *Whiteness of a different color: European immigrants and the alchemy of race*. Cambridge, MA: Harvard University Press.

Jankélévitch, V. (1974). *L'irréversible et la nostalgie*. Paris: Flammarion.

Johnson, C. L. (1985). *Growing up and growing old in Italian-American families*. New Brunswick, NJ: Rutgers University Press.

Johnston, R. (1965). The concept of the "marginal man." A new approach. *International Migration*, 3, 1–2.

Kertzer, D. I. (2007). Banfield, i suoi critici e la cultura. *Contemporanea*, 10, 4.

Kessner, T. (1977). *The golden door. Italian and Jewish immigrant mobility in New York City 1880–1915*. New York, NY: Oxford University Press.

Kessner, T., & Caroli, B. B. (1982). *Today's immigrants: Their stories*. New York, NY: Oxford University Press.

Klein, J. (1980). *Jewish identity and self-esteem: Healing wounds through ethnotherapy*. New York, NY: Institute on Pluralism and Group Identity of the American Jewish Committee.

Knopp Biklen, S. (2007). Trouble on memory lane. Adults and self-retrospection in researching youth. In A. L. Best (Ed.), *Representing youth. methodological issues in critical youth studies*. New York, NY: New York University Press.

Kobler, J. (1972). *The life and world of Al Capone*. London: Michael Joseph.

Krase, J. (1983). The Italian-American community: An essay on multiple social realities. In R. N. Juliani (Ed.), *The family and community life of Italian Americans*. Staten Island, NY: The Italian American Historical Association.

———. (1987). America's Little Italies: Past, present, and future. In D. Candeloro, F. L. Gardaphé, & P. A. Giordano (Eds.), *Italian ethnics: Their languages, literature, and lives*. Proceedings of the 20th Annual Conference of the American Italian Historical Association, Chicago, IL.

———. (1996). Little Italies in New York City: A semiotic approach. *The Italian American Review*, 5, 1.

———. (1997). The spatial semiotics of Little Italies and Italian Americans. In M. Aste et al. (Eds.), *Industry, technology, labor and the Italian American communities*. Staten Island, NY: American Italian Historical Association.

———. (2003). Italian American urban landscapes: Images of social and cultural capital. *Italian Americana*, XXII, 1.

———. (2004). Little Italy, identità e semiotica spaziale. In N. Ceramella & G. Massara (Cur.), *Merica. Forme della cultura italoamericana*. Isernia: Cosmo Iannone Editore.

———. (2007). Seeing ethnic succession in Little and Big Italy. In J. Krase, F. B. Pesci, & F. Alduino (Eds.), *Italian Americans before mass migration: We've always been here*. New York, NY: American Italian Historical Association, John D. Calandra Italian American Institute.

Lazzari, F. (2000). *L'attore sociale fra appartenenza e mobilità. Analisi comparate e proposte socio-educative*. Padova: Cedam.

Lee, K., & Ashton, M. C. (2012). *The H factor of personality. Why some people are manipulative, self-entitled, materialistic, and exploitive—and why it matters for everyone*. Waterloo, Ont: Wifrid Laurier University Press.

Leed, E. J. (1991). *The mind of the traveller. From Gilgamesh to global tourism*. New York, NY: Basic.

Lesko, N. (2000). *Act your age*. New York, NY: Routledge.

Lichter, R., & Lichter, L. (1982). *Italian-American characters in television entertainment* (Prepared for the Commission for Social Justice, New York, NY).

Lieberson, S. (1985). Unhyphenated whites in the United States. *Ethnic and Racial Studies*, 8.

Lopreato, J. (1970). *Italian Americans*. Routledge, New York, NY: Routledge.

Luconi, S. (2000). Anticommunism, Americanization, and ethnic identity. Italian Americans and the 1948 parliamentary elections in Italy. *Historians*, 2.

——. (2002). La partecipazione politica in America del Nord. In P. Bevilacqua et al. (Cur.), *Storia dell'emigrazione italiana. Arrivi*, vol. II. Roma: Donzelli.

——. (2004). Food and ethnic identity in Italian-American identity. *Prospero*, 11.

——. (2006). Il comportamento politico. *Altreitalie*, 32.

——. (2007). Il pregiudizio anti-italiano negli Stati Uniti tra identità etnica e questione razziale. In G. Muscio & G. Spagnoletti (Cur.), *Quei bravi ragazzi*. Venezia: Marsilio.

——. (2009). From William C. Celentano to Barack Obama. Ethnic and racial identity in Italian-American postwar political experience, 1945–2008. *Altreitalie*, 38–39.

——. (2010). La rappresentazione degli italiani nell'immaginario statunitense. *Diacronie. Studi di Storia Contemporanea*, RL; http://www.studistorici.com/2011/01/29/luconi_numero_5.

Maalouf, A. (1998). *L'identità*. Milano: Bompiani.

Madge, J. (1966). *Lo sviluppo dei metodi della ricerca empirica in sociologia*. Bologna: il Mulino.

Maglione Chiacchio, C. A. (1985). Current patterns of socialization and adaptation in an Italian American community. In J. Krase & W. Egelman (Eds.), *The melting pot and beyond. Italian Americans in the year 2000*, Proceedings of the XVIII Annual Conference of the American Italian Historical Association, Providence, RI, 7–9 November 1985.

Mancini, T. (2006). *Psicologia dell'identità etnica. Sé e appartenenze culturali*. Roma: Carocci.

Marden, C. F., & Meyer, G. (1968). *Minorities in American society*. New York, NY: American Book Company.

Mazzara, B. M. (1996). *Appartenenza e pregiudizio. Psicologia sociale delle relazioni etniche*. Roma: Carocci.

——. (1997). *Stereotipi e pregiudizi*. Bologna: il Mulino.

Merton, R. K. (1966). *Teoria e struttura sociale*. Bologna: il Mulino.

Mignone, M. B. (2006). Politics and ethnic identity within the Italian American experience. *NEOS. Rivista di storia dell'emigrazione siciliana*, anno I, 1.

——. (2008). *Italy today: Facing the challenges of the new millennium* New York, NY: Peter Lang.

Mitrano, J. R. (1999). The garbage can model of ethnic identity formation: A case study of Generation X Italian Americans. *The Italian American Review*, VII, 1.

Montanari, M. (2010). *L'identità italiana in cucina*. Roma-Bari: Laterza.

Muscio, G. (2007a). Introduzione. In G. Muscio & S. Spagnoletti (Cur.), *Quei bravi ragazzi*, Venezia: Marsilio.

——. (2007b). Italian American doc. In G. Muscio & S. Spagnoletti (Cur.), *Quei bravi ragazzi*. Venezia: Marsilio.

Muscio, G., & Spagnoletti, G. (Cur.) (2007). *Quei bravi ragazzi*. Venezia: Marsilio.

Myrdal, G. et al. (1944). *An American dilemma: The negro problems and modern democracy*. New York, NY: Harper & Brothers.

Nee, V., & Alba, R. D. (2004). Toward a new definition. In T. Jacoby (Ed.), *Reinventing the melting pot. The new immigrants and what it means to be American*. New York, NY: Basic.

Orsi, R. A. (1992). The religious boundaries of an inbetween people: Street *feste* and the problem of the dark-skinned other in Italian Harlem, 1920–1990. *American Quarterly*, 44, 3.

Ortoleva, P. (1992). La tradizione e l'abbondanza. Riflessioni sulla cucina degli italiani d'America. *Altreitalie*, 7.

Pasqualini, C. (2012). Dalla banca dati sui giovani. Il punto sui giovani. Anno 2012— Un confronto europeo. *Politiche sociali e servizi*, XIV.

Phinney, J. S. (1996). Understanding ethnic diversity: The role of ethnic identity. *American Behavioral Scientist*, 40, 2.

Pollini, G. (2000). Social Belonging. In E. F. Borgatta & R. J. V. Montgomery (Eds.), *Encyclopedia of Sociology*. New York, NY: Macmillan.

——. (2003). L'appartenenza sociale e comunitaria. In F. Lazzari & A. Merler (Cur.), *La sociologia della solidarietà*. Milano: FrancoAngeli.

Portes, A. (2004). For the second generation, one step at a time. In T. Jacoby (Ed.), *Reinventing the melting pot. The new immigrants and what it means to be American*. New York, NY: Basic.

Portes, A., & Rumbaut, R. G. (1996). *Immigrant America: A portrait*. Berkeley, CA: University of California Press.

Prencipe, L. (1976). L'associazionismo italiano all'estero: una continua storia di "relazioni." Il contributo al processo di unificazione. https://www.google.it/?gws_rd=ssl#q=associazionismo+italo+americano; accesso del 30 novembre 2015.

Prete, A. (Cur.) (1992). *Nostalgia. Storia di un sentimento*. Milano: Raffaello Cortina Editore.

Pretelli, M. (2011). *L'emigrazione italiana negli Stati Uniti*. Bologna: il Mulino.

Putnam, R. D., & Campbell, D. E. (2010). *American grace. How religion divides and unites us*. New York, NY: Simon and Schuster.

Recalcati, M. (2011). *Cosa resta del padre? La paternità nell'epoca ipermoderna*. Milano: Raffaello Cortina.

——. (2012). *Ritratti del desiderio*. Milano: Raffaello Cortina.

——. (2013). *Il complesso di Telemaco. Genitori e figli dopo il tramonto del padre*. Milano: Feltrinelli.

Richards, D. A. J. (2004). *Italiani d'America. Razza e identità etnica*. Milano: Giuffrè.
Riotto Sirey, A., Patti, A., & Mann, L. (1985). *Ethnotherapy. An exploration of Italian-American identity*, National Institute for the Psychotherapies, (pamphlet).
Ritzer, G. (1997). *Il mondo alla McDonald*. Bologna: il Mulino.
———. (2005). *La globalizzazione del nulla*. Bra (CN): Slow Food Editore.
Roccato, M. (2008). La rilevazione empirica dei valori. *Rassegna Italiana di Sociologia*, XLIX, 1.
Rokeach, M. (1973). *The nature of the human values*. New York, NY: Free Press.
Ruberto, L. E., & Sciorra, J. (2016). Introduction: Real Italians, new immigrants. In L. E. Ruberto & J. Sciorra (Eds.), *New Italian migrations to the United States, vol. 1: Politics and history since 1945*. Urbana, IL: University of Illinois Press.
Rumbaut, R. G. (2004). Ages, life stages, and generational cohorts: Decomposing the immigrant first and second generations in the United States. *International Migration Review*, 38, 3.
Sassatelli, R. (2004). Presentazione. L'alimentazione: gusti, pratiche e politiche. *Rassegna Italiana di Sociologia*, 4.
Schaefer, R. T. (Ed.) (2008). *Encyclopedia of race, ethnicity, and society*, vol. 1. Los Angeles, CA: Sage.
Schepis, M. F. (2006). L'identità dell'italo-americano di terza generazione. *NEOS. Rivista di Storia dell'emigrazione siciliana*, I, 1.
Schwartz, S. H. (1992). Universals in the content and structure of values: Theoretical advances and empirical tests in 20 countries. In M. P. Zanna (Ed.), *Advances in experimental social psychology*. San Diego, CA: Academic Press.
Sciolla, L. (1998). Valori. In *Enciclopedia delle Scienze Sociali Treccani*. Roma.
———. (2004). *La sfida dei valori*. Bologna: il Mulino.
———. (2008). La forza dei valori. *Rassegna Italiana di Sociologia*, XLIX, 1.
Sciorra, J. (2003). Italians against racism. The murder of Yusuf Hawkins (R.I.P.) and my march on Bensonhurst. In J. Guglielmo & S. Salerno (Eds.), *Are Italians white? How race is made in America*. New York, NY: Routledge.
Scramaglia, R., & Lavarini, R. (2007). *Il grande mosaico della società. Persone, beni, sentimenti*. Milano: Hoepli.
Serra, R. (2015). Le reazioni americane alla Grande Guerra—Il contributo di George Herbert Mead nell'ambito accademico e culturale. In C. Cipolla & A. Ardissone (Cur.), *La grande Sociologia di fronte alla Grande Guerra*. Milano: FrancoAngeli.
———. (2017). *Il senso delle origini. Indagine sui giovani italoamericani di New York*. Milano: FrancoAngeli.
———. (2017a). Intrecci linguistici. Lingue e dialetti italiani tra i giovani italoamericani nella grande area di New York. *Forum Italicum*, Sage, 50, 3.
———. (2017b). Italian language and Italian dialects: Tendecies and perspectives among the young Italian Americans in the greater New York City area. In V. Bavaro et al. (Eds.), *Harbors, flows, and migrations. The USA in/and the world*. Newcastle upon Tyne: Cambridge Scholars.

———. (2017c). Contemporary Italian American identities. In W. J. Connell & S. G. Pugliese (Eds.), *The Routledge history of Italian Americans*. New York, NY: Routledge.

———. (2018). Ritorni immaginari. I significati della nostalgia. In R. Serra & M. Pascoli (Cur.), *Nuovi sentieri sociologici. Riflessioni sugli studi in un ricercatore sociale*. Milano: FrancoAngeli.

Shibutani, T., & Kwan, K. M. (1965). *Ethnic stratification: A comparative approach*. New York: Macmillan.

Smith, J. (1977). The immigrant family and cultural change: Two generations of Italians and Jews in Providence, Rhode Island. (Paper presented at the Joint Conference of Italian American Historical Association and the American Jewish Historical Society, Waltham, MA).

Smith, T. W. (1992). *A profile of Italian Americans: 1972–1991*. Washington, DC: National Italian American Foundation.

Sowell, T. (1996). *Migrations and cultures: A world view*. New York, NY: Basic.

Stendhal, K. (1968). *The school of St. Mathew and its use of the Old Testament*. Philadelphia, PA: Fortress Press.

Stonequist, E. (1937). *The marginal man*. New York, NY: Scribner's.

Strauss, W., & Howe, N. (1991). *The history of America's future, 1584 to 2069*. New York, NY: Morrow.

Suttles, G. D. (1968). *The social order of the slum. Ethnicity and territory in the inner city*. Chicago, IL: University of Chicago Press.

Tajfel, H. et al. (1971). Social categorization and intergroup behavior. *European Journal of Social Psychology*, 1.

Tamburri, A. J. (1991). *To hyphenate or not to hyphenate. The Italian/American writer: An other American*. Montreal: Guernica.

———. (2010). *Una semiotica dell'etnicità. Nuove segnalature per la scrittura italiano/americana*. Firenze: Franco Cesati.

———. (Ed.) (2014). *Meditations on Identity. Meditazioni su identità*. New York, NY: Bordighera Press.

———. (2015a). Meditazioni notturne sugli americani italiani e l'alterità. In O. Cappelli (Ed.), *Italian signs, American politics. Current affairs. Historical perspectives. Empirical analyses*. New York, NY: John D. Calandra Italian American Institute.

———. (2015b). Oltre la "pizza" e la "nonna." Nuove direttive per gli studi culturali italiano/americani. In O. Cappelli (Ed.), *Italian signs, American politics. Current affairs. Historical perspectives. Empirical analyses*. New York, NY: John D. Calandra Italian American Institute.

Tamburri, A. J. et al. (Eds.) (1991). *From the margin: Writings in Italian Americana*. West Lafayette, IN: Purdue University Press.

Taylor, P. (2014). *The next America. Boomers, millennials, and the looming generational showdown*. New York, NY: PublicAffairs.

Teti, V. (2013). *Maledetto Sud*. Torino, Einaudi.

Thomas, W. I., & Znaniecki, F. (1968). *Il contadino polacco*. Milano: Edizioni di Comunità.
Tirabassi, M., & del Pra', A. (2014). *La meglio Italia. Le mobilità italiane nel XXI secolo*. Torino: Accademia University Press.
Topp, M. M. (2003). "It is providential that there are foreigners here": Whiteness and masculinity in the making of Italian syndacalist identity. In J. Guglielmo & S. Salerno (Eds.), *Are Italians white? How race is made in America*. New York, NY: Routledge.
Torrioni, P. M., & Albano, R. (2008). Come si apprendono i valori in famiglia. *Rassegna Italiana di Sociologia*, XLIX, 1.
Tortora, C. (2014). Heritage, nation vs. heritage language: Towards a more nuanced rhetoric of "heritage" in Italian language pedagogy. *Forum Italicum*, 48, 2.
Tricarico, D. (2007). Youth culture, ethnic choice, and the identity politics of *Guido*. *Voices in Italian Americana*, 18, 1.
———. (2010). Narrating *Guido*. Contested meanings of an Italian American youth subculture. In W. J. Connell & F. L. Gardaphé (Eds.), *Anti-Italianism. Essay on a prejudice*. New York, NY: Palgrave Macmillan.
———. (2011). *Guidos* on MTV: Tangled up in the feedback loop. In L. Airos & O. Cappelli (Eds.), *Guido. Italian/American youth and identity politics*. New York, NY: Bordighera Press.
Tusiani, J. (1982). *Gente mia e altre poesie*. San Marco in Lamis: Gruppo Cittadella Est.
Twenge, J. M. (2006). *Generation Me. Why today's young Americans are more confident, assertive, entitled—and more miserable than ever before*. New York, NY: Free Press.
———. & Campbell, K. W. (2009). *The narcissism epidemic. Living in the age of entitlement*. New York: Atria Paperback.
U.S. Census Bureau, Census 2000. http://www.census.gov/prod/2004pubs/c2kbr-35.pdf.
———. (2008–10). *American community survey*. 3-Year Estimates.
———. (2010). *American community survey*. 1-Year Estimates; http://factfinder2.census.gov.
Vecoli, R. J. (1974). The Italian Americans. *The Center Magazine*, 7, 41.
———. (1983). The Italian Immigrants in the United States labor movement from 1880 to 1929. In B. Bezza (Cur.), *Gli italiani fuori d'Italia. Gli emigranti italiani nei movimenti operai dei paesi d'adozione 1880–1940*. Milano: FrancoAngeli.
———. (1985). The search for an Italian-American identity. Continuity and change. In L. F. Tomasi (Ed.), *Italian Americans. New perspectives in Italian immigration and ethnicity*. New York, NY: Center for Migration Studies.
———. (1995). The Italian diaspora. 1876–1976. In R. Cohen (Ed.), *The Cambridge survey of world migration*. Cambridge: Cambridge University Press.
———. (1996). The significance of immigration in the formation of an American identity. *The History Teacher*, 30, 1.
———. (2000). Are Italian Americans just white folks? In F. M. Sorrentino & J. Krase (Eds.), *The Review of Italian American Studies*. New York, NY: Lexington Books.

——. (2002). Negli Stati Uniti. In P. Bevilacqua, A. De Clementi, & F. Franzina (Cur.), *Storia dell'emigrazione italiana. Arrivi*. Roma: Donzelli.
Viscusi, R. (1990). Breaking the silence: Strategic imperatives for Italian American culture. *Voices in Italian Americana*, 1, l.
——. (1996). Making Italy little. In F. Loriggio (Ed.), *Social pluralism and literary history. The literature of the Italian emigration*. Toronto: Guernica.
——. (2006). *Buried Caesar and other secrets of Italian American writing*. Albany, NY: State University of New York Press.
——. (2015a). I Cesari sepolti ed altri segreti dell'America italiana. In O. Cappelli (Ed.), *Italian signs, American politics. Current affairs. Historical perspectives. Empirical analyses*. New York, NY: John D. Calandra Italian American Institute.
——. (2015b). Rompere il silenzio. Imperativi strategici per la cultura italiana/americana. In O. Cappelli (Ed.), *Italian signs, American politics. Current affairs. Historical perspectives. Empirical analyses*. New York, NY: John D. Calandra Italian American Institute.
Voci, A., & Pagotto, L. (2010). *Il pregiudizio. Che cos'è, come si riduce*. Roma-Bari: Laterza.
Waters, M. (1990). *Ethnic options. Choosing identities in America*. Los Angeles, CE: University of California Press.
——. (1994). Ethnic and racial identities of second-generation black immigrants in New York City. *International Migration Review*, 28, 4.
Whyn, J., & White, R. (1997). *Rethinking youth*. Sydney: Allen and Unwin.
Whyte, W. F. (1943). *Street corner society. The social structure of an Italian slum*. Chicago, IL: The University of Chicago Press.
Wolf, M. (1992). *Gli effetti sociali dei media*. Milano: Bompiani.
Yans-McLaughlin, V. (1982). *Family and community. Italian immigrants in Buffalo, 1880–1930*. Champaign: University of Illinois Press.
Zanfrini, L. (2004). *Sociologia della convivenza interetnica*. Roma-Bari: Laterza.

INDEX

Aaron, D., 249
acculturation, 78–81, 164–65, 229;
   of second-generation immigrants,
   254–55, 257–64, 271–77, 284–86t;
   of third-generation immigrants,
   255–56, 264–67, 271–77, 284–86t;
   of fourth-generation immigrants,
   267–77, 284–86t; dissonant, 118, 258;
   social integration and, 120–21
African Americans, 11, 188, 338n4; civil rights movement and, 168, 192, 250, 256; enfranchisement of, 173–74; Italian Americans and, 192–93; Myrdal on, 156; Richards on, 171–72; Topp on, 171–73
age categories, 19t, 27, 28, 284t, 337n2
Alba, R. D., 166; on ethnic organizations, 206; on ethnicity, 43, 78–79, 88–89, 253, 257; on familism, 254–55
Allport, G. W., 153
Ambrosini, M., 338n3
American Community Survey (ACS), 12, 13
American Italian Historical Association, 206, 223
"American Italians," 52t, 53, 64–65, 202, 233, 248, 251. See also Italian Americans
"American-ness," 249
Anagrafe degli italiani residenti all'estero (AIRE), 12

anti-Semitism, 165, 174
anticommunism, 191
Argentina, Italian immigrants of, 11
Ashmore, R. D., 66
atheism, 187–88
Avrich, Paul, 335n3

Balodimas-Bartolomei, A., 339n10
Banfield, E. C., 28–29, 332n4
Barolini, Helen, 131, 197
Barthes, Roland, 125, 126, 334n1
Bassetti, P., 83, 206, 224, 315
Belliotti, R. A., 29, 193
Berlusconi, Silvio, 130
Bertellini, G., 128
Bettini, M., 305–6, 308
bilingualism, 53, 106–7, 258. See also Italian language
Birindelli, P., 327
Bloch, Marc, 221
blood feud, 162
Boileau, A. M., 152, 159, 335n2
Bona, M. J., 81–82
Bourdieu, Pierre, 322
Brazil, Italian immigrants of, 11
Bridgeport, Conn., 79–80
brigandage myths, 162
Brooklyn College, 15; Center for Italian American Studies at, 223; Italian American students at, ix–x
Bryson, B., 166–67, 335n3

355

Bugiardini, S., 202–4
Bush, George W., 195

Calandra Institute of Italian American Studies (Queens College), x, 2, 207t, 208, 210, 223
Calvino, Italo, 128
Campbell, D. E., 187, 335n2
Cappelli, O., 195, 218
Cariplo Institute, 336n7
Casa Italiana Zerilli-Marimó, 223
Casandrino, Italy, 33
Castelvetro, Giacomo, 339n6
Cattarinussi, B., 340n1
Center for Italian American Studies, 223
Child, I. L., 255, 338n5
Children of Immigrants Longitudinal Study (CILS), 339n7
Chirico, D., 84, 333n3; on cultural transmission, 219; on "Guido" subculture, 183; on immigrants, 127; on self-hatred, 118
Cinotto, S., 28, 34, 91–92
civil rights movement, 168, 192, 250, 256
class. *See* socioeconomic status
Clinton, Bill, 195
Coccia Institute for the Italian Experience in America, 223
colonialism, 128–29, 161, 218, 249, 334n2
color versus race, 169–70. *See also* racism
Columbus Citizens Foundation, 207t, 223, 335n9
Columbus Day festivities, 75–76, 218
communities. *See* Italian American communities
consumerism, 100, 183–85, 250, 322, 328. *See also* materialism
"contemporaries" group, 282–89, 297–309
Coppola, Francis Ford, 250
cosmopolitanism, 224, 233

Covello, L., 30
creolization, 198, 218–19. *See also* hybridization
criminality. *See* organized crime
Crispino, A. James, 79–80
cuisine, 70, 79, 90–92, 197–99; American traditions of, 130–31, 228; Castelvetro on, 339n6; Italianisms used in, 127; knowledge of, 240; Mediterranean diet and, 199; stereotypes of, 177–78
cultivation theory, 214–15, 337n11
cultural knowledge, 51, 87, 92, 95–97, 103; contacts for, 56; ethnic identity and, 3, 16–17; levels of, 131–32, 132t, 237–40, 279–83
"cultural philanthropy," 223
cultural sharing factor, 26, 28
Cuomo, Andrew, 191
Cuomo, Mario, 191
Current Population Survey (CPS), 257

D'Alfonso, A., 83
Dante Alighieri, 334n2
Dante Alighieri Society, 204
d'Aquino, N., 83, 218, 224, 315
Darwin, Charles, 173–74
De Blasio, Bill, 168, 234–35
DeLillo, Don, 88
descendants, 54t, 85–86, 92–94
dialects, Italian, 136–44, 138, 140t, 141t. *See also* Italian language
Dinkins, David, 192
"discursive power," 217
"disinherited" group, 282, 292–94, 297–309
diversity, 84–85, 130, 218, 220
domestic abuse, 180
"double consciousness," 253, 254, 338n4
dual citizenship, 12, 104, 106
Durkheim, Emile, 336n3

education level, 20, 259, 284t; of Italian American fathers, 36; of Italian American mothers, 35
Ehrlich, H. J., 151
emotional connections to Italian culture, 5, 16–17, 33, 66–67, 199–202, 240–44
emotional support factor, 27
Enlightenment philosophy, 160
environmentalist dimension, 26–28
Epstein, A. L., 55, 60, 66, 88
ethnic categories, 88, 174. *See also* self-identification
ethnic identity, 17, 43–76; during 1960s, 78–79; during 1970s, 77–79; during 1980s, 78–81, 257; after-school programs and, 233; choice of, 87–88; double life of, 33; emotional connections to, 66–67; in generational flux, 243, 247–48, 271–77, 284–86t; importance of, 57–58, 57–66, 65, 241–42; internal conflict from, 68–76, 76t; Maalouf on, 221–22; marginalization of, 63–64; of partners, 46t; pathways of, 47–49; percentage of, 45t; physical characteristics of, 65–66; socioeconomic status and, 80; transmission of, 55–57, 56t, 97–98, 219–24, 228–31; unconscious elements of, 88–89; visibility of, 88–89; young people's choice of, 257. *See also* Italian American identity
ethnic memory, 80, 87
ethnic pride, 59–60, 249, 269, 273
ethnicity, 44, 285t; Alba on, 43, 78–79, 88–89, 257; of children's friends, 40t; "elusive," 78–79; Gambino on, 77; interpretations of, 47–49, 47t; of partners, 46; reinvented, 80; symbolic, 257; "symbolic," 79–81; "twilight" of, 78, 88–89. *See also* white ethnicity
"ethnotherapy," 67, 333nn4–5

"European Americans," 81
European Values Study (EVS), 23, 332n2
Everybody Loves Raymond (TV show), 182t, 322
"evil eye" (*malocchio*), 93–94

Faith Matters Surveys, 188
familism, 90–92, 148, 254–55; "amoral," 28–29; Cinotto on, 28, 34; gender inequality in, 29–30; importance attributed to, 24t, 26t; "laws" of, 29. *See also* Italian American families
fathers, 38t; ethnicity of, 36; Italian spoken with, 141t; religiosity of, 189
"feeling Italian," 16, 45t, 52–53, 84, 86, 284t
Fellin, L., 53–54, 138
Ferlinghetti, Lawrence, 87, 129
Ferraro, Geraldine, 191
Ferraro, T. J., 84
Fischer, M. J., 80
Flügel, J., 55
folklore, 93–94, 131–32, 132t, 239; nostalgia for, 127, 129
Freud, Sigmund, 308, 340n3
Fuccillo, Vincent J., x

Gabaccia, D. R., 173–74, 197
Gallo, Patrick J., 193, 194, 336n6
Gambino, R., 247; on cuisine, 197; on double consciousness, 254; on ethnicity, 77; on Sicilian relationships, 29
Gans, H. J., 30–31, 79, 80
Gardaphé, F. L., 12; on American dream, 125–26; on cultural transmission, 219–20, 222–24; on Italian American literature, 88–89; on racism, 170–71; on stereotypes, 167–69
gender: demographics of, 13, 19, 284t; emotional support factor and, 27; materialism factor and, 28; religiosity and, 188; values and, 27–28

Generation X, 14, 337n2
Gerbner, G., 214–15, 337n11
German Americans, 11, 46, 99
Giuliani, Rudolph, 168, 191
"glocalism," 224
Godfather movies, 73, 95, 100, 219
Gordon, Milton, 79
Grant, Madison, 167
Grossberg, L., 337n2
group membership, 100–102; indicators of, 117–24, 117t, 120t; recognition of, 122–23
Guglielmo, Thomas A., 161, 169–70, 252
"Guido" subculture, 7, 71, 99–100, 122; "Guidettes" and, 122, 182, 185; interview questions on, 185–86, 185t; stereotypes of, 179–80, 182–85; Tricarico on, 183–85. *See also* stereotypes

Haller, H. W., 127, 334n3
Handlin, Oscar, ix
Hansen, M. L., 256
Harney, Demaria, 250–51
Hart-Celler Act (1965), 51
Hawkins, Yusuf, 192–93
Hewittown, N.J., 33
Hispanics, 35, 36, 44, 46, 166, 285t
Hobsbawm, E. J., 307
Horton, D., 340n1
hybridization, 136, 198, 218–19, 271, 309

Iacocca, Lee, 168
Iard Report, 332n3, 336n7
immigration, ix, 124, 219–21, 223–24; first-generation, 252–55; second-generation, 253–55, 257–64, 271–77, 284–86t; third-generation, 255–56, 264–67, 271–77, 284–86t; fourth-generation, 267–77, 284t; American dream and, 92–93, 125–26; cardiovascular disease and, 31; demographics of, 11–12; Handlin's study of, ix; highest period of, 7, 51, 94, 110–11, 272; Italian regions affected by, 50t, 332n1; legal restrictions on, 332nn1–2; memories of, 17, 49–51, 49t; racial discrimination and, 169–74; reactions against, 164–65; regional breakdown of, 50t; typology of, 340n2
Impellitteri, Vincent, 168, 191
individualism, 27, 148, 260, 268
Inglehart, R., 23, 332n1
"integrated" group, 120–21, 282, 289–92, 297–309, 338n3
internet use, 214–16, 215t, 216t, 259, 264. *See also* social media
"intersectional cultural veto," 164–65
Irish Americans, 11, 203, 218
"Italian/American," 105, 126–29, 221, 223, 251. *See also* "American Italians"
Italian American Civic League, 207t
Italian American Civil Rights League, 168
Italian American communities, 100–101; cardiovascular disease in, 31; cultural transmission by, 219–22, 225t; familism and, 29; future of, 19, 97, 119t; identity formation in, 219–20; perceived structure of, 117–21, 117t; as "urban villages," 30–32
Italian American families, 248; adaptations of, 30; composition of, 21; cultural transmission by, 219–22, 225t, 228–31; emotional atmosphere of, 33; fathers of, 36, 38t; godparents of, 29; importance of, 24–25, 24t; Italian spoken within, 141t; Jewish families and, 32–33; mothers of, 35, 38t; scholarship on, 28–34; socialization by, 37–39; stereotypes of, 178. *See also* familism
Italian American identity, 51–55, 53t, 109, 110t; in 1960s, 78–79; in 1970s, 77–79; in 1980s, 79–81; of

first-generation immigrants, 252–55; of second-generation immigrants, 253–55, 257–64, 271–77, 284–86t; of third-generation immigrants, 255–56, 264–67, 271–77, 284–86t; of fourth-generation immigrants, 267–76, 284–86t; construction of, 248–52; cultural transmission of, 55–57, 56t, 97–98, 219–24, 225t; future of, 224–35, 225–27t, 264, 267, 271, 277; in generational flux, 243, 247–77; hybridization of, 219; meanings of, 314–15; models of, 315–18; plurality of, 84–85, 96–97, 102–7. *See also* ethnic identity

Italian American Institute to Foster Higher Education, 67

Italian American literature, 88–89, 128

Italian American organizations, 7, 119–20, 120t, 202–14, 207t, 210t, 212, 214; second-generation immigrants' view of, 263; third-generation immigrants' view of, 266, 267; fourth-generation immigrants' view of, 270–71; activities of, 212–14, 214t; cultural transmission by, 222–24; future of, 226–27, 226t, 232–33; participation in, 208–9, 298, 326; satisfaction with, 209–12, 212t. *See also specific organizations*

Italian American Studies Association, 206, 223

Italian Americans, 85–102; African Americans and, 192–93; demographics of, 11–14, 19–20; descendants of, 54t, 85–86, 92–94; differences with other ethnic groups, 119t; historical terms for, 248–49; Italians versus, 94–95, 104–7, 109–16, 127–31; legacy of, 279–83, 281t, 284–86t; origin myths of, 125–27; religiosity of, 188–89; self-hatred among, 118; stereotypes of, 149–86; visibility of, 88–89. *See also* "American Italians"

Italian Chambers of Commerce, 204

Italian language, 136–42; Americans' knowledge of, 72, 89–90, 92, 101, 140t; assimilation and, 171; bilingualism and, 53, 106–7, 258; dialects of, 136–37, 219; English words adopted from, 127, 334n3; future considerations with, 142–44; Italian Americans' use of, *138*, 140t, 141t, 225t, 226; learning opportunities for, 230–32; US census question about, 137; US periodicals in, 331n3

"Italian-ness," x, 53, 81, 198, 205

Italianisms, 127, 334n3

italianità ("Italic-ness"), 81–83, 249–51, 316, 339n9; attachment to, 279–83, 298–99, 323–26; expressions of, 177; re-imagining of, 250–51; second-generation immigrants and, 254; third-generation immigrants and, 256

Italians: Americans' relationships with, 243; Americans' views about, 18, 94–95, 104–7; origin myths about, 125–27; prejudice against, 159–63; "real," 94–95

italicità, 83–84, 224

italico, 83–84

Italoamerica, 116, 217–18; as criminal underworld, 126–27, 179, 319; as US colony, 116

Italoamericanità, 84

Italy, 238; Americans' images of, 126–31, 131t, 145–46, 256, 262–63, 266–67, 270; Americans' political awareness of, 195, 196t, 240; Americans' trips to, 134, 139, 201, 230, 231; emigration regions of, 50t, 332n1; emotional attachments to, 132–34, 144–48, 199–202; information sources about, 135–36, 136t;

Italy (cont'd)
  North-South conflicts in, 130, 160–67, 174, 252; organized crime in, 133, 145, 147, 162, 287; personal relationship with, 134–36; reconnection with, 327–28

Jacobson, M. F., 169
Jersey Shore (TV show), 73, 95, 99–101, 177, 180; popularity of, 182t; Tricarico on, 183
Jews, 32–33, 35, 36, 44, 46, 285t; NYC politics and, 190; prejudice against, 165, 174; of Rhode Island, 32–33
Jim Crow Laws, 166, 174, 335n7. *See also* racism
Johnson, C. L., 31–33
Johnson, Lyndon B., 192, 333n2

k-means cluster analysis, 280
Kennedy, John F., 191–92
Kobler, J., 335n5
Krase, Jerome, viii–xi; on Italian American identity, 84–85; on "Italianness," x, 81; on Little Italies, 83, 338n2

la bella Italia, 126–31, 131t, 145–46, 256
la dolce vita, 127, 128, 130, 327
La Guardia, Fiorello, 168, 190, 249
Lacan, Jacques, 340n3
Latinos, 35, 36, 44, 46, 166, 285t
Lazzari, F., 334n8
Leed, E. J., 327–28
Lippmann, Walter, 149–50
Literacy Act (1917), 332n1
Little Italies, 30–31, 220, 233, 252–53; history of, 248; Krase on, 83, 338n2; St. Gennaro festival in, 75
Little Sicilies, 252–53
Lopreato, J., 255
Luconi, S., 166, 190, 197

Maalouf, A., 136, 221–22, 317
Mafia. *See* organized crime
Maglione Chiacchio, C. A., 33–34
marginalization, 104, 316, 333n1; of ethnic identity, 63–65, 248, 253–54; *ordine della famiglia* and, 29; political, 190
materialism, 25–28, 69, 73, 250, 254; socialization and, 260, 268, 289. *See also* consumerism
Mazzara, B. M., 153; on self-fulfilling prophecy, 156–57; on stereotypes, 149, 150, 155–56, 160
McCarthyism, 191
McDonaldization, 197, 337n8
media portrayals, 73, 122, 178, 277, 302; broadening of, 228; consumerism and, 219; stereotyping in, 181–85
media use. *See* internet use
Mediterranean diet, 199. *See also* cuisine
methodological notes, 14–16
Mignone, M. B., 195
Millennial generation, 14, 337n2
Mitrano, J. R., 16; on family cooking, 92; on Italian American identity, 81–83
Mob Wives (TV show), 73, 182t
mothers, 38t; ethnicity of, 35; Italian spoken with, 141t; religiosity of, 189; stereotypes of, 178
Muscio, G., 164, 165, 252
Mussolini, Benito, 167, 249, 334n2
Myrdal, Gunnar, 156
myth, 162; Barthes on, 125, 126, 334n1

National Italian American Civic League, 205–6
National Italian American Foundation (NIAF), 12, 206, 207t, 208, 223, 335n9
National Opinion Research Center, 193

National Organization of Italian American Women (NOIAW), 206, 207t, 208, 335n9
Nazism, 99
Nixon, Richard M., 192
nostalgia, 221–22, 334n2; Ferlinghetti on, 129; Viscusi on, 127–29

Obama, Barack, 195
occupation, 20, 284t; of fathers, 36; of mothers, 35; rural/urban, 248
Occupy movement, 196
"one-drop rule," 172. *See also* race
Order Sons of Italy in America (OSIA), 99, 191, 205, 207t, 208, 223, 335n9. *See also* Italian American organizations
ordine della famiglia, 29
organized crime, 167–68; anti-defamation campaigns and, 319; in Italy, 133, 145, 147, 162, 287; myth of, 126–27, 218; positive identification with, 179; stereotypes of, 71, 73, 100, 165, 180, 250. *See also* stereotypes
origin myths, 125–27, 218
oriundo ("native"), 69–70
Orsi, R. A., 171
Ortoleva, P., 197
Osgood's semantic differential technique, 18, 109, 110t

padrone system, 203
Pagotto, L., 154, 155
Pasqualini, C., 4
Pastore, John, 191
"patriotism through heritage," 93
peer group socialization, 39–41, 40t
Pelosi, Nancy, 191
personality traits, 16, 121, 122; of Italian Americans versus Italians, 109–15, 110t, 111t, 112; marginalized, 333n1;

native language and, 136; six dimensions of, 331n5
Phinney, J. S., 102
physical traits, 82, 101, 121; ethnic identification with, 65, 65–66, 110t, 122; of Italians, 116t; of parents, 38t
Polish Americans, 340n2
political involvement, 190–96, 196t, 232
Pope, Generoso, 191
Portes, A., 258
positivism, 161–62, 165, 173
prejudice, 153–57; Boileau on, 335n2, 335n2; definitions of, 153–54; ethnic, 110–12, 158–59; interview questions on, 174–80; against Italian Americans, 163–69; against Italians, 159–63; against Jews, 165, 174; propaganda and, 334n2; psychology of, 155; self-fulfilling prophecy and, 156–57; stereotype versus, 149, 151, 153, 154, 158–59
Pretelli, M., 190, 195, 197, 199
Providence, R.I., 32–33
psychological dimension of identity, 17
Putnam, R. D., 187, 335n2

Queens College (CUNY), 2, 15

race, 164; color and, 169–70; Gabaccia on, 173–74; Guglielmo on, 169–70; "one-drop rule" of, 172; Orsi on, 171; Richards on, 171–72; Topp on, 172–73
racism, 92, 169–74, 192–93; "double consciousness" in, 338n4; eugenics and, 167; Gardaphé on, 170–71; Jim Crow Laws and, 166, 174, 335n7; social Darwinism and, 173–74; stereotypes and, 165; white privilege and, 169–74
Recalcati, M., 301, 304, 340n3
religiosity, 25–28, 35–36, 187–89
Renaissance, Italian, 96, 160, 167

Richards, D. A. J., 165, 171–72
Rimanelli, Giose, 88
Riotto Sirey, Aileen, 67, 175, 333n4; on media stereotypes, 181; on sense of community, 119–20
Risorgimento, 160–61, 203
Ritzer, G., 337n8
Rokeach, M., 332n1
Roosevelt, Franklin D., 191, 249
Roseto, Penna., 31
Ruberto, L. E., 94
Rumbaut, R. G., 258, 331n1

Sacco, Nicola, 164, 335n3
San Gennaro festival, 75, 210
Sassatelli, R., 198
Saturday Night Fever (film), 183
Sautman, Canadé, 218–19
Scalia, Antonio, 168
Schepis, M. F., 128
Schwartz, S. H., 332n1
Sciorra, Joseph, 94, 192–93
Scorsese, Martin, 250
self-fulfilling prophecy, 156–57, 335n1
self-identification, 17, 52t, 53t, 272, 298; of second-generation immigrants, 260–61; of third-generation immigrants, 265; of fourth-generation immigrants, 268–69; materialism factor with, 27; with stereotypes, 98–100, 254
self-image, 3–5, 18; dimensions of, 121–24; "double consciousness" of, 253, 254, 338n4; of Italian Americans versus Italians, 109–15, 110t, 111t, *112*; others' images versus, 72–73
semantic differential technique, 18, 109, 110t
semiology, 334n1
September 11th attacks, 191
Smith, T. W., 188
social Darwinism, 173–74

social media, 207, 226t, 231, 233. *See also* internet use
socialization, 37–39, 38t, 97–98; of second-generation immigrants, 260; of third-generation immigrants, 264–65; of fourth-generation immigrants, 268; "reverse," 37; values and, 17
socioeconomic status, 20, 284t; cultural knowledge and, 239; ethnic identity and, 80; political awareness and, 240; prestige and, 121–23, 302
Sons of Italy. *See* Order Sons of Italy in America
Sopranos, The (TV series), 64, 73, 95, 182t, 219, 224
Sorokin, Pitirim, 250
Stendhal, K., 187
stereotypes, 18, 68, 92, 149–86, 276; second-generations' view of, 263; third-generations' view of, 267; fourth-generation's view of, 267; avoidance of, 228; Boileau on, 152, 159; definitions of, 149; Gardaphé on, 167–69; interview questions on, 174–80; Italian American organizations and, 208; of Italian Americans, 163–69; Krase on, xi; labeling of, 16, 74–76; Lippmann on, 149–50; Mazzara on, 149, 150, 155–56, 160; of "national characteristics," 159–60; of organized crime, 71, 73, 100, 165, 180, 250; overcoming of, 101–2; prejudice versus, 149, 151, 153, 154, 158–59; racism and, 165; reaction to, 122, 123; self-fulfilling prophecy and, 156–57; self-identification with, 98–100, 254; sharing of, 122, 123; "truth" of, 180; Viscusi on, 126–27
Stonequist, E., 333n1
Suttles, G. D., 33

Tamburri, A. J., 81, 218, 249; on cultural transmission, 221–23; on ethnic

cuisine, 131; on "Italian/American," 223, 251; on *italicità*, 84
territorial attachments, 7, 199–202, 199t, 200, 201
Teti, V., 49–50, 161, 162
Thomas, William Isaac, 335n1, 340n2
Tocqueville, Alexis de, 202, 338n1
Toniolo Institute, 336n7
Topp, M. M., 172–73
Torrioni, D., 37
Tortora, C., 137
"traditionals" group, 282–83, 294–97, 294–309
Tricarico, D., 183–85
Truman, Harry S., 191
Tusiani, Joseph, 338n4

UNICO (Unity, Neighborliness, Integrity, Charity, and Opportunity) clubs, 205–6, 207t, 223, 335n9, 337n10
"uniqueness," 16, 316–17
"urban villages," 30–31. *See also* Little Italies

values, 16, 23–28, 318; of second-generation immigrants, 260; of third-generation immigrants, 264–65; of fourth-generation immigrants, 268; approaches to, 332n1; cultural, 37, 121, 122; definition of, 23; health implications of, 31; imagined, 129; personal, 26t, 90–91; reference, 62–63; teaching of, 228–29
Vanzetti, Bartolomeo, 164, 335n3
Veblen, Thorstein, 250
Vecoli, Rudolph J., ix, 11; on family emotional atmosphere, 33; on Handlin, ix; on Italian American identity, 81, 253, 307
Vietnam War, 192
Viscusi, Robert, 104–5, 174; on American images of Italy, 127–29; on "discursive power," 217; on identifying with Italian culture, 110; on Italoamerica, 116, 126–27, 217–18; Sciorra on, 193; on "US imperial culture," 116
Voci, A., 154

WASPs (white Anglo-Saxon Protestants), 220; political involvement of, 194; social Darwinism and, 173–74; xenophobia of, 164–66
Waters, Mary, 44, 47–48, 80–81
white ethnicity, 35, 74; Alba on, 78–79, 206; Gabaccia on, 174; Gardaphé on, 171; privileges of, 169–74. *See also* ethnicity
Wilson, Woodrow, 337n9
Wohl, R. R., 340n1
Wolf, M., 321
World Values Study (WVS), 23, 25, 332n2

xenophobia, 164–65

Yans-McLaughlin, V., 29–30

Zanfrini, L., 152–53, 158
Znaniecki, F., 340n2

www.ingramcontent.com/pod-product-compliance
Lightning Source LLC
Chambersburg PA
CBHW030126240426
43672CB00005B/37